MEMORY
ORGANIZATION
AND STRUCTURE

MEMORY ORGANIZATION AND STRUCTURE

Edited by

C. RICHARD PUFF

Department of Psychology
Franklin and Marshall College
Lancaster, Pennsylvania

ACADEMIC PRESS

A Subsidiary of Harcourt Brace Jovanovich, Publishers

New York   London   Toronto   Sydney   San Francisco

ACADEMIC PRESS, INC.
111 Fifth Avenue, New York, New York 10003

United Kingdom Edition published by
ACADEMIC PRESS, INC. (LONDON) LTD.
24/28 Oval Road, London NW1 7DX

Library of Congress Cataloging in Publication Data

Main entry under title:

Memory organization and structure.

Includes bibliographies and index.
1. Memory. I. Puff, C. Richard.
BF371.M46   153.1'2   79−21039
ISBN 0−12−566750−7

PRINTED IN THE UNITED STATES OF AMERICA

79 80 81 82   9 8 7 6 5 4 3 2 1

Contents

PART **I**

INTRODUCTION

CHAPTER **1**

Memory Organization Research and Theory: The State of the Art   **3**

C. RICHARD PUFF

PART **II**

PERSPECTIVES ON THE MEASUREMENT OF ORGANIZATION

PART **III**

PERSPECTIVES ON THE STRUCTURE OF SEMANTIC MEMORY
AND SEMANTIC–EPISODIC RELATIONS

PART V
CONCLUSION

CHAPTER 12
Organization, Structure, and Memory: Three Perspectives

375

JAMES F. VOSS

List of Contributors

Numbers in parentheses indicate the pages on which the authors' contributions begin.

WILLIAM F. BATTIG* (321), Department of Psychology, University of Colorado, Boulder, Colorado 80309

FRANCIS S. BELLEZZA (321), Department of Psychology, Ohio University, Athens, Ohio 45701

KATHLEEN CORSALE (219), Learning Research and Development Center, University of Pittsburgh, Pittsburgh, Pennsylvania 15260

STÉPHANE EHRLICH (195), Laboratoire de Psychologie, Université de Poitiers, 86022 Poiters, France

MICHAEL FRIENDLY (85), Department of Psychology, York University, Downsview, Toronto H3J 1P3, Canada

ALBERT L. INGRAM (21), Department of Psychology, University of Pittsburgh, Pittsburgh, Pennsylvania 15261

JANET L. LACHMAN (133), Department of Psychology, University of Houston, Houston, Texas 77004

ROY LACHMAN (133), Department of Psychology, University of Houston, Houston, Texas 77004

JEAN M. MANDLER (259), Department of Psychology, University of California, San Diego, La Jolla, California 92093

*Deceased.

GEORGE MANDLER (303), Department of Psychology, University of California, San Diego, La Jolla, California 92093

MARTIN D. MURPHY (51), Department of Psychology, University of Akron, Akron, Ohio 44325

PETER A. ORNSTEIN (219), Department of Psychology, University of North Carolina, Chapel Hill, North Carolina 27514

JAMES W. PELLEGRINO† (21), Department of Psychology, University of Pittsburgh, Pittsburgh, Pennsylvania 15261

C. RICHARD PUFF (3), Department of Psychology, Franklin and Marshall College, Lancaster, Pennsylvania 17604

JAMES F. VOSS (375), Department of Psychology and Learning Research and Development Center, University of Pittsburgh, Pittsburgh, Pennsylvania 15260

MICHAEL J. WATKINS (347), Department of Psychology, Princeton University, Princeton, New Jersey 08540

†Present Address: Graduate School of Education, University of California, Santa Barbara, Santa Barbara, California 93106

Preface

This book portrays our current understanding of the ways in which human memory is organized, how it comes to be organized in these ways, and the role that this organization plays in remembering. As is true in any area of active scientific research, the field of memory organization is characterized by diversity and change. The contributions to this volume amply reflect the diversity in choice of methods used to probe the nature of memory organization and the kinds of theoretical conceptions used to make sense of the findings. In short, there is no single, monolithic viewpoint that encompasses the entire field, and the contributions are best regarded as a collection of perspectives on some of the major issues faced at this particular point in time. My introductory chapter explores some of the similarities and differences in focus among the chapters in more detail.

The first major section of the book, Part II, comprises three chapters that focus primarily on one of the traditional problems in the field, the measurement and inferential status of output organization in free recall. Pellegrino and Ingram discuss the importance and general shape of theory to coordinate alternative output organization measures and strategies. Murphy then describes the application of his relatively atheoretical simulation approach to the evaluation of clustering measures. Friendly's chapter bridges between this section and the next because he presents the case for proximity analysis and graphic representation as being a general approach to the specification of structure which is not limited to free recall data.

The four chapters in Part III represent perspectives on the structure of semantic memory and the importance of the relationship between stored semantic information and the present episodic context. Lachman and Lachman explore the potential fruitfulness of an evolutionary perspective on theories of semantic memory to complement the more traditional emphasis on the machine analogy. Ehrlich discusses "flexible" and "permanent" semantic structures, stages in structural development, and the important interaction between structures and episodic contexts. The chapter by Ornstein and Corsale reviews organizational factors in children's memory with emphasis on the importance of changes in the permanent knowledge base. Jean Mandler presents an analysis of the similarities and differences between categorical and schematic organization including the way they cut across the traditional semantic–episodic distinction. Her explication of the contemporary view of schematic organization makes a particularly appropriate transition into the next section.

Part IV focuses on the scope of organizational concepts. The three chapters in this section illustrate some of the ways in which the boundaries of organizational theorizing are being extended by some of the most recent developments. George Mandler's chapter is an analysis of the range of organizational structures including the contemporary trend toward nonoperational conceptions. Battig and Bellezza present a rapprochement between organizational theory and the levels-of-processing framework by stressing the notion of organizational processing. In the final chapter in this section, Watkins elucidates a cueing approach to the structure of memory.

Part V is a single concluding chapter in which Voss highlights a number of the important issues in the past, the present, and the probable future of organizational research as he sees it. In doing so, he draws on his own work and the material presented in the earlier chapters.

Taken together, the perspectives collected here provide a comprehensive representation of the current state of the art of understanding memory organization and structure. The intended audience for the book includes those seeking an exposure to the range of things that contemporary investigators of memory organization are working on, as well as those interested in a detailed treatment of the specific topics. Readers already familiar with the area, but interested in gauging the recent progress, will find that process facilitated by comparing this presentation with the view of the field depicted in Tulving and Donaldson's 1972 volume. Some of the most notable developments since the earlier comprehensive review include the emergence of the adaptive perspective, the rapproachement with the levels-of-processing framework, the emphasis on semantic–episodic relations, and the increasingly cognitive orientation for much of the theorizing.

The impetus for this book was provided by a small conference on memory organization and structure held at Franklin and Marshall College in March of 1977. I am indebted to the College and the Andrew W. Mellon Foundation for supporting that activity. More new chapters have been added than resulted from the conference itself, but the core of original papers and the encouragement of the conference participants stimulated the efforts that have culminated in this volume.

Finally, it is with sadness that I must add a postscript noting the death of Bill Battig. The area of memory organization was a relatively recent interest for Bill, but with his characteristic intensity and celerity, he became one of its champions.

MEMORY
ORGANIZATION
AND STRUCTURE

PART **I**

INTRODUCTION

CHAPTER 1

C. RICHARD PUFF

Memory Organization Research and Theory: The State of the Art

It has been apparent for over 2000 years that human thought flows in organized sequences. The organization of memory is one manifestation of the organized way the mind works, and the objective of some of the present contributors is to use experiments on memory organization as a vehicle to probe the nature of human mental activity in general. Others of these organizational researchers are directly concerned with elucidating the structural characteristics of memory per se, whereas still others find that achieving a satisfactory understanding of a single organizational phenomenon is a sufficient challenge. Taken together, these are the goals that guide the kinds of empirical and theoretical activities represented in this book. The common bond uniting these various efforts is the belief in the organizational point of view. The essence of

MEMORY ORGANIZATION
AND STRUCTURE

this view is that organizational research and theorizing provide an especially fruitful kind of inferential leverage on the problem of understanding human mental activity.

I. THE CONCEPTS OF ORGANIZATION
AND STRUCTURE

The meanings of the terms "organization" and "structure" are not easily specified today. It was easier to provide a definition a few years ago when, following the pioneering work of W. A. Bousfield (1953), organization was virtually synonymous with the occurrence of clustering of categorically related items in free recall. The variety of uses of the terms has expanded rapidly over the years until there is now no single, generally accepted referent of either organization or structure. A partial list of the usages of these terms in this volume includes clustering, subjective organization, seriation, primary organization, secondary organization, categorical organization, schematic organization, hierarchical organization, structure of semantic memory, structure and organization of lexical memory, organizational processing, and so on.

The isolation of what these multiple usages have in common is a problem that seldom receives much attention. However, judging from what is explicit or implicit in the following chapters, there appears to be a basic commonality on the most general level of analysis. Using the wording most explicitly presented in Friendly's chapter, the common focus of most of the more specialized definitions and conceptions seems to be a concern with *patterned relations among elements* in a specified set.

The precise nature of the elements varies among representations of words (or names of words), concepts, events in a script or plan, and so on, as different investigators attempt to specify the organization found in different contexts. The specific nature of what are hypothesized to be the important relations varies among associations, labeled links, temporal relations, class inclusions, and probabilities in the specific views of the different theorists. Similarly, what are described as linear, hierarchical, pro-ordinate, multidimensional, vertical, and horizontal, and other patterns or configurations of relations are given emphasis in one or more chapters. Thus, regardless of the differences in vocabulary, emphasis, and tasks, there is, on the more general level, a common concern with the nature and influence of configured relations among elements.

The mixing of the terms "organization" and "structure" in almost every contemporary discussion raises the question of whether the two terms are consistently used to convey important conceptual differences. Some of the present authors do make, or imply, distinctions that they use with some consistency.

One general kind of distinction is that structure refers to the overall pattern, or configuration, of the representations of a set of elements (hierarchical, linear, etc.), whereas organization refers to the specific relations among the elements embodied in the configuration. For example, several subordinate elements are related to a single superordinate element, but not to each other, in a hierarchical structure; each element is related to a previous element and a subsequent element in a linear, or pro-ordinate, structure, and so on. George Mandler makes use of this kind of distinction, but he acknowledges that it is not generally followed in the field and even he does not employ it consistently.

Another kind of distinction, adopted by Friendly, is that structure is more theoretical, inferred, and explanatory, whereas organization is more observed, operational, and descriptive. This distinction, however, is not explicitly supported in any of the other chapters, and George Mandler denies this one clearly.

Structure has a ring of permanence to it, whereas organization can have more active or flexible connotations. Pellegrino and Ingram, for instance, view organization as a process (or set of processes) used in a strategic attempt to maximize memory performance. Battig and Bellezza also emphasize organization as a process that can determine the pattern of recall behavior without any corresponding structural representation of the items in memory, since the organizational process can operate at the time of retrieval of independently stored items. On the other hand, this kind of distinction is not found in other chapters. George Mandler uses process and structure concepts somewhat interchangeably and cautions that it may be premature to make strong distinctions between process and structure that we attempt to apply across the board. It seems reasonable that, at some level of analysis anyway, mental processes influence mental structures and mental structures influence mental processes. Thus, in Mandler's thinking, it may be preferable for the present to let each theory specify what is process and what is structure.

In short, while some authors find one or another distinction between the terms organization and structure to be useful, an analysis of the collected papers fails to reveal any consistent distinction. Most of the authors seem to use the terms in an essentially synonymous way. Jean Mandler explains that she, in fact, does so on the grounds that a cognitive structure is an organized set of concepts and procedures and that a cognitive organization is a structured set of concepts and procedures.

II. MAJOR THEMES

The categories used to divide the book into sections were derived inductively. They represent some of the major differences in focus that could be discerned when the contributors had written on topics essentially of their own choosing. Most of the chapters, however, speak to more than one important issue, and the book could be organized in multiple ways. The purpose of this section is to highlight some of the more general themes and conclusions that emerge from the collected chapters.

A. Status of Output Organization in Free Recall

Output organization, beginning with category clustering and subjective organization, was the major focus of organizational research for almost 20 years. More recently, however, there has been a sharp decline of interest in measured output organization. Several of the present chapters provide perspectives on this trend.

The chapters by Pellegrino and Ingram, Murphy, and Battig and Bellezza identify what they see as the important reasons for the decline in interest in measured output organization. One major class of factors is the number of such measures and their characteristics. The number of types of output organization being measured has expanded beyond clustering and subjective organization to include seriation, priority of recall of newly learned items, hierarchical clustering, primacy, recency, and so on. There has also been a proliferation of different specific measures of many of these types of organization along with a concomitant increase in the quantitative complexity involved in choosing a measure and applying it to data. Most of these measures are further criticized for being unidimensional and failing, therefore, to portray accurately the multidimensional nature of organization and the multiple underlying subprocesses that may be involved in its occurrence.

Despite the long history of considerable research activity, there is as yet no complete or coherent theory of output organization. Pellegrino and Ingram see the current controversy over the selection of an appropriate clustering measure as a direct result of this lack of theory. Murphy also sees current theories as too vague to provide an adequate criterion for selecting a measure. Moreover, Pellegrino and Ingram argue that an adequate theory would have the added benefit of integrating the various types of output organization that they see as the result of alternative strategies. In their view, this would require the incorporation of executive routines, or higher-order strategies, to coordinate the alternative strategies and select those most appropriate for a particular task. This contention is supported by their analysis of the strengths and weaknesses of Anderson's (1972) Free Recall by an Associative Net (FRAN) model, which they see as having been the most precisely spelled-out and influential model of organization in free recall.

Ornstein and Corsale extend the concern with measures of output organization to questions involving their interpretation. Some of their data suggest that the amount of young children's recall varies with the degree of structure (i.e., categorizing) imposed at input regardless of the amount of organization measured at output. Such findings lead them to question seriously whether output organization plays any causal role in mediating children's recall performance, or whether both recall and output organization might reflect the operation of other underlying mnemonic processes. In short, it seems possible that output organization may be, in at least some circumstances, only a by-product of memorial functioning.

Organization has also been ascribed little or no role in determining memory performance in the levels-of-processing approach as originally proposed by Craik and Lockhart (1972). Battig and Bellezza see the recent popularity of this theoretical view as one of the major factors contributing to the decline of interest in organization. They point out, moreover, that associated with the levels-of-processing position has been a concentration on research paradigms and techniques that, by stressing the processing of individual items, may well have minimized the possible involvement of organization and limited the usefulness of measures of the traditional types of output organization.

There is, on the other hand, some evidence here that tempers a totally pessimistic outlook concerning the future of measured output organization. Murphy addresses the problem of the choice among the many available clustering measures through the application of a simulation analysis. He argues, contrary to the most widely held view, that a theory does not have to precede the selection of a measure; rather, the application of the simulation approach may facilitate the process of developing an adequate theory. He contends, in addition, that the simulation approach lessens the danger of the circularity that exists in choosing a measure that has properties necessarily leading it to support the theory used as a criterion for selecting it. Friendly's chapter describes some of the newer measurement techniques that have the advantage of identifying the specific contents of the units of output organization. He argues in particular for the use of proximity analysis and graphic representation for portraying the multidimensional nature of organization. Friendly's outlook is further optimistic because his technique is not limited to a particular form of structural representation, nor is it limited to free-recall output data. Ornstein and Corsale support the usefulness of Friendly's technique through their applications of it in the study of the development of children's memory. Battig and Bellezza's major thesis, as examined more fully in a later section, is that the levels-of-processing theorists' lack of concern with organization has been a mistake, and that they must incorporate organizational processes directly in order to develop a satisfactory account of human memory. Any such reformulation does not, however, automatically imply a major role for output organization.

There are, then, grounds on which to counter many of the criticisms that have been involved in the decline of output organization in free recall. It remains to be seen whether the weight of the newer developments will be sufficient to reawaken substantial interest in output organization. It might be anticipated, however, that while output organization will continue to be of interest in its own right or as a helpful converging operation (Tulving & Bower, 1974), it may never again occupy a position of prominence in the field. The basic reason may be that it has served its larger purpose too well. As George Mandler points out, the organizational point of view is now widely accepted. Output organization was for many years a crucial part of the operational definition of organization and a robust demonstration of its "reality." Nonoperational views are now more common, and organizational processes are frequently assumed on a more a priori basis. The classical organizational phenomena are only some of the possible symptoms of the assumed organizational processes, and the trend, so well illustrated in the following chapters, seems to be toward pushing out the boundaries of the application of the organizational point of view.

B. Emphasis on Semantic–Episodic Interactions

It was in Tulving and Donaldson's forerunner to this volume that Tulving (1972) proposed the distinction between semantic and episodic memory. The fact that nearly every chapter here makes some descriptive use of these terms reflects how enormously useful these terms have been for categorizing various kinds of tasks and classes of evidence. The important question in the present context, however, concerns the two types of memory vis-à-vis organizational processes. The conclusions here speak to both the further usefulness of the semantic–episodic distinction and to the generality of any particular organizational principles.

At the time Tulving proposed the distinction there seemed to be little in common between those studying sequential dependencies in free-recall output and those beginning to theorize about the best way to capture the complex structure of semantic memory. Several of the present chapters still focus almost exclusively upon one of the two types of memory. Lachman and Lachman, for example, deal with semantic memory theories (spread of activation, feature comparison, etc.), variables (semantic distance, cognitive economy, etc.), and tasks (semantic verification, production, etc.) where the role of the present episodic context is presumably minimal. Murphy's chapter, on the other hand, deals strictly with the phenomenon of output organization in free recall. Similarly, Watkins' explication of the cueing approach to memory structure is restricted to Tulving's episodic realm, though he does offer a concluding comment that he sees no reason why it cannot be applied to memory in a more generic sense.

Several important perspectives on the semantic–episodic distinction are provided in other chapters. One such perspective is that there are common organizational and structural features that weaken the explanatory value of the distinction. Friendly makes this point strongly in advancing what he calls the single-structure hypothesis. This hypothesis posits that there is a single memory store that is drawn upon in all tasks. He places heavy emphasis on the influence of the structure and predicts on this basis that semantic and episodic retrieval should show similar patterns. He presents evidence of the existence of a basically invariant structure across free recall, free emission, and sorting tasks. Jean Mandler also finds significant common features. Her argument is that the two types of organization included in her analysis, categorical and schematic organization, cut across Tulving's semantic–episodic distinction in the sense that there is a generalized memory-representation of the important events in common episodes and that much of the knowledge thought to be stored in semantic memory is schematically (i.e., derived from episodes) as well as categorically (i.e., hierarchically) based. Accordingly, she suggests that Tulving's episodic memory be restricted to autobiographical information.

Another recurring view is that a complete account of memory performance must involve a consideration of the interaction of information from a number of sources. Ehrlich discusses the interaction of semantic structures and the effects of the present episodic context in some detail. His analysis considers three factors to be involved in determining which semantic structures will be used in any particular memory task. One is what he calls structural pre-determination based on extensive previous experience; the second is the selective and activating action of the present context; and the third is the subject's cognitive operations. Most tasks are seen as involving some combination of all of these, but, in general, context becomes more influential when relevant previous experience is weak or null, and vice versa.

In their analysis of what they call organizational processing of input items, Battig and Bellezza distinguish two dimensions along which it can occur. Horizontal organizational processing involves using or forming direct relations among the input items, whereas vertical processing involves incorporating the input items into other structures already existing in permanent memory. They thus draw together considerations of organization in free recall and the structure of semantic memory in order to account for the range of kinds of organizational processing.

The chapters by Jean Mandler and by Voss also stress how the processing of new material is determined by the nature of existing knowledge structures, or schemata. In these cases the emphasis is on memory for textual materials, sequences of events, and complex pictures. The structure of the output (e.g., the sequence of remembered events or the presence or absence of various kinds of information reflects the interaction of what was presented in the current context and the nature of the schema that was evoked.

Ornstein and Corsale's account of children's clustering in free recall draws upon information available in a permanent-memory knowledge base including knowledge of semantic categories, rules for operating on memory including the clustering strategy, and metamemory, or knowedge about the limitations and operation of memory. They argue further that since complex interactions between different kinds of stored information and the present context are becoming more clearly implicated, the distinction between semantic and episodic memory is probably not sufficiently precise to contribute appreciably to the explanation of children's free recall. Similarly, they feel that the existing models of semantic memory, which have developed with little consideration of interaction with episodic events, are of limited usefulness for describing the growing knowledge base of children. Such models present a rather static view with limited treatment of how structures are modified through experience and how new information is integrated into existing structures. Ehrlich's explication of his three-stage course of the development of semantic structures may thus represent an important advance along these lines.

Thus, contemporary organizational theorists seem to agree in stressing the importance of both the structure of a relatively permanent memory system and the information in the current episodic context in order to deal with an increasing range of memory phenomena. These interactive kinds of positions require a greater emphasis on the permanent (or relatively permanent) memory system than has been typical for output organization researchers and a greater consideration of modifiability and flexibility than has been characteristic of semantic memory researchers.

C. Emergence of an Adaptive Perspective

A new major conceptual orientation for thinking about organization and structure seems to be emerging to complement the machine perspective. The term "adaptive perspective" is adopted here to convey the essence of this view as involving the consideration of evolutionary, adaptive, ontogenetic or developmental, and cultural factors in understanding the nature and function of organization in human memory. None of the contributors present a completely worked-out statement of this position, but a number of the chapters stress topics consistent with the belief that new insights may be gained by exploring the implications of regarding the human subject as an evolving, adapting, developing, biological organism.

The case for the possible fruitfulness of applying an evolutionary perspective to semantic memory theory is presented in some detail by Lachman and Lachman. They propose three evolutionary generalizations that are followed by a set of seven postulates. They then show how these postulates bear upon some important issues in semantic memory theory and how they are useful in the interpretation of experimental data. The essential flavor of their analysis is well captured by one of their examples. Their Postulate 3, which states that the human representational system is not neutral with respect to content, implies a weak (partial) form of cognitive economy in terms of the storage of concepts and their properties. Thus, it might be expected that the property *has skin* may be directly stored with *buffalo,* but not with *hawk,* because the skin of a buffalo has been adaptively salient. This kind of partial cognitive economy contrasts with the strong (complete) form suggested by too heavy a reliance on the analogy with automata.

Ehrlich's analysis of the development of semantic memory structures also draws upon certain conceptual parallels (though some departures are also noted) with biological views of the phylogenetic evolution of the species and the ontogenetic development of the individual organism. He stresses the role of the changing nature of semantic structures in providing for the progressive acquisition of a potential for cognitive freedom and flexibility, along with the simultaneous development of other fixed (organized) structures providing for rapid and efficient behavior in frequently encountered situations. Consistent also with a general organismic position, and the Piagetian tradition, he proposes that the nature of the semantic structures at different stages of development is essentially qualitatively different. Semantic structures capable of serving a relational function (in addition to a referential function) do not, for example, emerge until the third of Ehrlich's proposed stages of the development of semantic memory structures.

George Mandler also touches on the adaptive nature of mental structures. His argument is that the nature of organizational structures is not solely determined by the spatiotemporal contiguities so obvious in the environment. Rather, while some structures may reflect such contiguities, other structures represent abstractions and classifications that transcend such contiguities. The possible use of alternative structures contributes to the adaptive flexibility of the human being.

The extension of this general viewpoint to include sociocultural influences is illustrated in the chapters by Jean Mandler and by the Lachmans. The Lachmans discuss the possible biological and cultural effects involved in the mapping of linguistic labels into categories. Salient categories appear to have one-to-one mapping and are well coded with high-frequency names. Biologically salient categories appear to be universally well coded whereas other instances of salience vary across cultures. Jean Mandler points out that formal schooling is involved in the effective use of categorical (hierarchical) organization, whereas schematic organization is more universally evident in the recall of storylike materials from a young age.

Voss's concluding chapter recapitulates and extends the adaptive perspective. Furthermore, he speculates that the tendency to view the individual in a broader biological-cultural context is one of the major directions in which memory theory will move in the future.

D. Extensions of the Organizational Point of View

The purpose of this section is to show some of the ways in which the organizational point of view has gone beyond output organization in free recall and the structure of semantic memory. Several of the chapters provide extensions of the organizational point of view into areas heretofore considered as illustrating the limitations, or marking the boundaries, of this view.

1. LEVELS-OF-PROCESSING

As previously mentioned, Battig and Bellezza identify the assurgency of the levels-of-processing view as a major factor in the recent decline of interest in output organization in free recall. According to their analysis, the proponents of the levels-of-processing view have found little need to consider organizational processes because they have focused upon a research paradigm that stresses the processing of individual items in relative isolation from others under incidental learning conditions where the deliberate deployment of mnemonic strategies is not obviously called for. These conditions would thus not be expected strongly to evoke traditional organizational strategies or to permit their measurement in the usual ways. Voss adds that the heavy reliance on lists of words rather than, for example, textual materials has led them to miss clear indications of the importance of the schematic type of organization. The authors express in both chapters the conviction that the levels-of-processing concept is not incompatible with organizational processes—that a rapprochement is necessary to provide a satisfactory account of a broader spectrum of human memory performance.

Battig and Bellezza show how a rapprochement can be achieved through focusing on what they call organizational processing. They explicate their view of organizational processing as involving the establishment of multiple-item relationships among the words to be remembered. This type of processing is thought to be best accomplished through instructions for the use of some type or organizational mnemonic technique that either establishes direct relationships between words (called horizontal processing) or relates them by incorporating them into some organizational structure already existing in memory (called vertical processing). They present a variety of evidence that optimal recall performance requires the use of the organizational type of semantic processing and that the locus of the facilitative effect is the improvement of retrieval efficiency primarily through the provision of an effective system of self-cueing. It might be noted that Battig and Bellezza's horizontal–vertical processing distinction, although sketched in only general terms at the present, does appear to differ somewhat from the horizontal–vertical association distinction made, for example, by Wickelgren (1979). The difference between the two views is perhaps made clearest by reference to the specific example of the case where the subjects are instructed to form an interactive image linking two successive list items. This would appear to be an instance of horizontal processing in Battig and Bellezza's analysis because it establishes a direct link between the items and does not involve incorporating them into a higher-order structure already available in memory as would be the case with vertical processing. It would, on the other hand, appear to be an instance of vertical association in Wickelgren's view because it involves the establishment of a chunk node that encodes part–whole relations and not just the order relation that would define it as horizontal association.

Voss also sketches a possible path to rapprochement by emphasizing organization in the sense of relating the event currently being processed to other aspects of the memory structure. This gives an organizational interpretation to the standard levels-of-processing notions of elaboration, differentiation, and storage–retrieval compatibility. The existing structure (perhaps in the form of a schema in his text-processing experiments) thus contributes elaboration to the input via the expectancies for potential next events, differentiation via the stored relational context for the input items, and greater storage–retrieval compatibility via the increased capacity to generate context at output if it is not provided by the experimenter.

Both chapters thus stress the need for levels-of-processing researchers to move from a concentration upon physical versus semantic processing to a greater consideration of different types of semantic processing. There is a common emphasis in both attempted rapprochements upon the importance of relating items currently being processed to organized structures already in permanent memory and the importance of retrieval processes involving, in particular, the proposition that organization provides for effective self-cueing.

2. INTRAITEM STRUCTURES

In George Mandler's view, if organization theory is more a point of view than an explicit operational theory, then there is nothing with which the organizational theorist should not attempt to deal. Nothing needs to be written off as beyond the scope of the organizational point of view. Accordingly, he proposes a class of structures, which he calls intraitem or integrative structures, in order to extend the structural view to a new set of issues.

Intraitem structures refer to organization *within individual* items or events independent of relations with other items or events. By virtue of attention and perceptual processing, structural nodes representing, for example, letters, phonological components, and spatial envelope become integrated (i.e., more compact, distinctive, and invariant) regardless of relations with other events and contexts. The postulation of this kind of structural development affords an organizational interpretation of the observation that increasing the processing time for an individual item, or repeating it, gives rise to increased familiarity and increased frequency-of-occurrence judgments. In this way, Mandler thus sketches how the organizational point of view might encompass even the most resistant of the so-called rote-learning effects.

3. RETRIEVAL CUEING AND ENCODING SPECIFICITY

It was previously noted that in the Battig and Bellezza chapter, as well as in that by Voss, self-generated recall cues were stressed as one of the important components of the extension of the organizational point of view to the levels-of-processing domain. Battig and Bellezza also note the apparent operation of the principle of encoding specificity in the self-cueing that occurs with organizational mnemonics. They propose that a subject-generated cue will be effective at recall only if it was present at the time of encoding.

The cueing function of organization and structure as well as the use of cued recall studies to probe the nature of organization and structure is also a major topic in other chapters. Jean Mandler attributes at least part of the retrieval superiority with schematic organization to the notion that the schema provides a more powerful set of retrieval cues (i.e., in the sense of their being nested and causally related) than is the case with categorical organization. Ehrlich's chapter includes a consideration of the interaction between contextual cue effectiveness and the permanence of the corresponding semantic memory structures, such that the selective action of the context is more important where the subject's prior experience has not led to the development of permanent structures. Ehrlich's analysis thus leads to an interpretation of the principle of encoding specificity as being relative; it operates strongly when the materials do not correspond to permanent structures and weakly or not at all when the materials do correspond to permanent structures.

The most extensive analysis of retrieval cueing is presented by Watkins, whose whole chapter is devoted to the topic. In his view, all recall is cued recall, and the understanding of memory depends upon the understanding of the principles of cued recall. Memory is specified by the probabilities of recall associated with different cues (i.e., by their effectiveness, or valences). A summary of cue valences and relations between them, called the cuegram, provides the relevant description of memory structure. Cue overload is the critical principle of forgetting, and subjective organization, for example, is interpreted as minimizing the load on the cues. The same kind of interpretation is also applied to a range of other paradigms and phenomena.

E. A General Cognitive Orientation

One notable feature of many of the views presented here is a general cognitive orientation. The chapters by George Mandler and by Voss include reviews of how organizational theory is important in moving away from classical associationism. Mandler stresses the weakness of contiguity as an explanation of organizational structures, whereas Voss conducts a detailed analysis of associative principles and their shortcomings. Despite his rather thorough rejection of associative principles, Voss does find some associative-like ideas still present in a modified form in contemporary models of the structure of semantic memory (e.g., the notion of labeled links and the building-block assumption reflected when individual representational nodes make up a larger semantic structure).

Having rejected the associationistic position, Voss points out the uneasiness generated by the lack of a general cognitive position to provide an overall orientation to the field. As Battig and Bellezza contend, it is probably premature to concentrate on developing a detailed and comprehensive theoretical formulation because organizational research is currently too unstable. However, the skeleton of the same rather general theoretical framework does seem to emerge repeatedly in the following chapters. Several of its features can be sketched.

The central feature of most of the more specific views is some notion of cognitive, mental, or psychological structure or structures. The existence of multiple structural configurations or the flexibility of the structures is typically stressed. The structures frequently have a nonoperational quality about them in the sense that they are not wholly tied to a limited set of independent and dependent variables. Rather, the influence of evolutionary history, ontogenetic development of the nervous system, and certain cultural experiences such as schooling are being related to the hypothesized nature of the structures in a still general way. Similarly, these structures are expected to be reflected in an increasingly wide variety of tasks and dependent measures that George Mandler refers to as symptoms of organization.

An important part of the cognitive orientation is revealed by the current inclination to refer to the collection of permanent memory structures as the individual's knowledge base—what the individual knows about conceptual, lexical, schematic, and other kinds of relations. Important kinds of knowledge also frequently include what the individual knows about the limitations of memory as well as a repertoire of potential strategies and skills (i.e., what Voss calls procedural knowledge) to overcome the limitations.

A further reflection of the cognitive flavor of many contemporary views is given by the increasing acknowledgement of the importance of the cognitive environment established in a particular task situation. The set and expectations created by the instructions or orienting activities are appealed to frequently, as are the goals and intentions of the subject. The chapter by Pellegrino and Ingram, as well as that by Voss, includes the speculation that one of the major directions for future cognitive theorizing in this area will be toward a problem-solving type of conceptualization. As they see it, this conception will emphasize the role that goal or purpose plays in determining which existing knowledge structures some new content will be mapped into or what new structures will have to be constructed to accommodate the new content.

Specific chapters may concentrate upon elucidating different aspects of this general framework, and slightly different vocabulary may be used to describe the same general notion. It would appear, however, that there is a general cognitive orientation beginning to emerge that encompasses much of the current theoretical effort.

III SUMMARY: TRENDS SINCE TULVING
AND DONALDSON

Perhaps the major impact of the Tulving and Donaldson (1972) volume was to greatly expand the domain of memory organization to include the structure of semantic memory in addition to the traditional concern with output organization in free recall. Tulving's own excellent chapter delineated how both of these realms of memory were of interest to the organizational theorist, though they embodied some differences in focus. Most of the themes described in the previous sections of this introduction represent developments or extensions since the earlier volume; therefore, relating them to the state of the field depicted by Tulving and Donaldson is provided largely as a summary.

The recent history of measured output organization has been tortuous. Some of the complaints about the measures (e.g., the limitation of subjective organization measures to units of only two items) that were expressed at the time of the earlier conference were countered shortly thereafter. Many of the currently important organizational measures were either developed or extensively modified after the March 1971 date of their conference (see, for example, Pellegrino, 1971; Roenker, Thompson, & Brown, 1971; and Sternberg & Tulving, 1977). Hierarchical clustering and the other new measurement techniques reviewed here by Friendly are also more recent advances. However, the very proliferation of such measures, the increasing quantitative complexity, and the domination of the levels-of-processing orientation seem recently to have precipitated a substantial decline in interest in measured output organization. The present volume, however, contains several perspectives on this issue that are once again more positive in outlook. Friendly's technique specifies the content of units and applies across tasks. Murphy's simulation technique helps to evaluate alternative clustering measures. Finally, Pellegrino and Ingram provide an orientation for thinking about types of output organization as output strategies ultimately amenable to integration via a theory embodying an executive routine.

Theories about the structure of semantic memory have flourished since Tulving and Donaldson's treatment. Several important new perspectives on the nature of such theories are presented here. The evolutionary perspective of Lachman and Lachman complements the machine analogy that has been dominant. Ehrlich's "free elements" view contrasts with earlier notions that the storehouse of memory is itself structured. In addition, the developmental perspectives provided by Ehrlich, as well as by Ornstein and Corsale, suggest that previous theories of semantic memory have been too static and too independent of interaction with episodic input to be significantly useful in describing the changing semantic structure of the child.

The more complete elaboration of the relationship, or interaction, between semantic and episodic memory, left as an unfinished task for future investigators by Tulving, has become a central concern in the area today. The original semantic–episodic distinction seems to have less explanatory power than it has descriptive value. The postulation of a common store (as in Friendly's chapter) and/or common "configurations" of organization (as in Jean Mandler's chapter) weaken the distinction, as does the necessity of contemplating complex interactions between the two systems (as in Ornstein and Corsale's chapter). There is thus an increasing tendency to talk about semantic and episodic information rather than memory systems.

Contemporary organizational theory has moved in still other notable directions since the Tulving and Donaldson era. Organizational views are now more frequently couched in more cognitive terms, stressing knowledge, strategies, expectations, set, goals, and intentions. The boundaries of the organizational point of view are seen here as having been pushed out to meet the challenge of the levels-of-processing position that had not yet come into vogue at the time of the earlier volume. Other extensions to be found here deal with cued recall, encoding specificity, and integrative structures underlying familiarity judgments. It is now hard to anticipate the eventual boundaries for this view, especially if the trend toward the acceptance of less strictly operational conceptions continues.

ACKNOWLEDGMENTS

I am grateful for the comments and suggestions on an earlier version of this paper provided by William F. Battig, Janet and Roy Lachman, Jean and George Mandler, Martin D. Murphy, Wendy C. Puff, Donald J. Tyrrell, and James Voss.

REFERENCES

Anderson, J. FRAN: A simulation model of free recall. In G. H. Bower (Ed.), *The psychology of learning and motivation* (Vol. 5). New York: Academic Press, 1972.

Bousfield, W. A. The occurrence of clustering in the recall of randomly arranged associates. *Journal of General Psychology*, 1953, *49*, 229–240.

Craik, F. I. M., & Lockhart, R. S. Levels of processing: A framework for memory research. *Journal of Verbal Learning and Verbal Behavior*, 1972, *11*, 671–684.

Pellegrino, J. W. A general measure of organization in free recall for variable unit size and internal sequential consistency. *Behavior Research Methods and Instrumentation*, 1971, *3*, 241–246.

Roenker, D. L., Thompson, C. P., & Brown, S. C. Comparison of measures for the estimation of clustering in free recall. *Psychological Bulletin*, 1971, *76*, 45–48.

Sternberg, R. J., & Tulving, E. The measurement of subjective organization in free recall. *Psychological Bulletin*, 1977, *84*, 539–556.

Tulving, E. Episodic and semantic memory. In E. Tulving & W. Donaldson (Eds.), *Organization of memory*. New York: Academic Press, 1972.

Tulving, E., & Bower, G. H. The logic of memory representations. In G. H. Bower (Ed.), *The psychology of learning and motivation* (Vol. 8). New York: Academic Press, 1974.

Tulving, E., & Donaldson, W. (Eds.), *Organization of memory*. New York: Academic Press, 1972.

Wickelgren, W. A. *Cognitive psychology*. Englewood Cliffs, N.J.: Prentice-Hall, 1979.

PART II

PERSPECTIVES ON THE
MEASUREMENT OF ORGANIZATION

CHAPTER **2**

JAMES W. PELLEGRINO
ALBERT L. INGRAM

Processes, Products, and Measures of Memory Organization

I. INTRODUCTION

During the past 20 years, the concept of organization has achieved a central status in most, if not all, theories of human learning and memory. There are numerous behavioral phenomena that have been attributed to organization, leaving little doubt as to its importance as a hypothetical and explanatory construct. Postman (1975) noted "that the ultimate sign of the success of a theoretical idea is that it comes to be taken for granted as part of the current body of knowledge in a discipline. This is what has happened to the concept of organization in recall, although some investigators still seem to find it useful to document it anew [p. 323]."

MEMORY ORGANIZATION
AND STRUCTURE

The purpose of this chapter is not to provide yet another demonstration of the phenomenon of memory organization, but to consider some of the issues associated with the lack of a precisely stated theory of organization. This theoretical deficit has led individuals such as Murdock (1974) to conclude that "organization theory is not so much a theory as a point of view. It is a belief, if you will, that there is more to human memory and learning than the simple associations studied under the aegis of behaviorism and interference theory [p. 215]."

Many researchers in the area of human memory would be inclined to agree that this assessment is still valid. An obvious question is why such a theory has not been forthcoming. In an attempt to answer this question, the first section of this chapter provides an overview of the concept of organization. Emphasis is on problems associated with the definition of organization, particularly the distinction between organization as process and the product of a process. A broad definition of organization is offered that is linked to a problem-solving view of list learning. The second section of this chapter is an attempt to provide an overview of the different types of organizational processes and strategies that fall within the domain of a theory of organization. Of special concern in this section are the problems that have arisen because single and multiple measures of organizational strategies have been derived in the absence of specific process theories. The final section of this chapter is an attempt to consider the strengths and weaknesses of the most precisely specified theory of organization, the Free Recall by Associative Net (FRAN) theory of Anderson (1972). Consideration is given to the role of such a theory in the development of a general theory of memory organization.

II. THE CONCEPT OF ORGANIZATION

The lack of a coherent and well-specified theory of organization may be partly attributed to the way in which organization has been defined and then studied. Many of the operational definitions that have been proposed are extremely circumscribed and paradigm specific. Furthermore, most definitions do not include the concept of an internal process, but rather focus on the characteristics of some external product (Voss, 1972). Examples of this problem can be seen in definitions offered by Mandler (1967) and Tulving (1968). Mandler has proposed that "A set of objects or events are said to be organized when a consistent relation among the members of the set can be specified and, specifically, when membership of the objects or subsets (groups, concepts, categories, chunks) is stable and identifiable [p. 330]." Such a definition is clearly applicable to the sorting paradigm that Mandler (1967; Mandler, Pearlstone, & Koopmans, 1969) has studied so extensively. The result of this definition is Mandler's specification of the measure of organization as the number of categories or groups used in achieving a stable sort. Thus, emphasis is placed upon the product of some internal process, with particular emphasis on the number of groups produced. Less emphasis is placed on the formation and content of those groups, two related areas of investigation that might provide some insight as to the nature of the process.

Tulving (1968) has provided definitions of organization that apply to the free-recall paradigm, and here too, emphasis is on characteristics of the product rather than on the process giving rise to the output structure. "Organization defined in the weak sense refers to consistent discrepancies between input and output orders that are independent of the subjects' prior familiarity with a set of input items [p. 15]." Organization defined in the strong sense is "when the output order of items is governed by semantic or phonetic relations among the items or by the subjects' prior, extra-experimental or intra-experimental acquaintance with the items constituting a list [p. 16]."

Tulving's definition of organization in the strong sense, or what he termed secondary organization, was meant to cover two basic free-recall phenomena, clustering and subjective organization. The emphasis upon organization as an empirical phenomenon that can be measured in the recall protocol has spawned a large amount of work on defining the "best" measures of organization. Thus organization has often been defined in terms of some single score or value that purportedly reflects the total amount of organization that a subject has demonstrated. As noted by Colle (1972), such an approach has not been directly tied to an explicit process theory of organization.

Despite the fact that most definitions of organization have been unduly restricted, it is important to note that researchers in this area have not ignored the distinction between organization as both a process or set of processes and the product or structure resulting from those processes (e.g., Tulving, 1962; Sternberg & Tulving, 1977). Clearly, the stable groups that result in a sorting task and the clustering and subjective organization that occur in free-recall protocols must result from some process(es) that acts upon the input in order to satisfy the goal of producing an internal representation that is stable, efficient, and readily retrievable. An adequate definition of organization must be capable of embracing such characteristics and also subsume the more restricted definitions offered in the past. Such a definition might take the following form—organization refers to the process(es) whereby the organism attempts systematically to store and retrieve the information presented so as to maximize performance. It must be recognized that this definition obviously does not satisfy the need for a theory of organization. Such a theory would have to specify in detail what the processes are and how they operate. However, the definition does satisfy a number of other minimal requirements that serve to establish some constraints on such a theory. First, it localizes organization within the organism (Voss, 1972). Second, it is not restricted to any particular paradigm or task (Bower, 1972). Third, it is not restricted to any particular form of internal representation, for example, hierarchical versus nonhierarchical. Fourth, it implies that stable memory structures are the end product. Fifth, it implies that the internally generated memory structure will be reflected in the outcome of the output or retrieval process, albeit less than perfectly given that a variety of output processes may operate. Finally, it implies intentionality on the part of the organism due to an awareness of inherent limitations on the amount of information that can be stored and/or retrieved at any point in time (Mandler, 1967; Miller, 1956).

The definition we have provided is intended to reflect a strong bias toward viewing learning–memory paradigms as problem-solving situations. It seems legitimate to conceive of list learning as problem solving because the individual is typically given a general goal, that is, try to learn all the words, sentences, etc., that I present to you so that you can recall (recognize) them for me at some later time. Some general rules are specified and the learner is then left to his or her own devices to attain the goal. Tulving (1964) and others have appropriately noted that in a task like free recall, individuals are not learning the items per se, since they already exist within the semantic knowledge system, but instead the individual must learn to discriminate the set of admissable items in the experimental context and to retrieve (reproduce) those items with minimal external support. In order to attain these specific goals learners have at their disposal a number of strategies, all of which can help overcome inherent limitations on the storage and retrieval of information. These strategies operate during the input and output phases of the task, and they are methods (means) to satisfy the overall goal of the task as well as specific subgoals. An example of a subgoal might be trying to remember those items that were not remembered on the preceding trial. To satisfy this particular subgoal, the individual may utilize a variety of coding (input) and retrieval (output) strategies, and these strategies, in turn, may consist of one or more elementary processes.

The distinction between strategy and process that we intend to use is the following: A strategy is a general tactic or method that may be applied in a variety of situations, and its value is a function of the task being attempted and of the existence and operation of alternative strategies. An example of a strategy that can be applied in list learning is attempting to form bizarre and interacting images to link the items in a paired associate list. The value of this strategy is a function of the concreteness of the list materials. To execute this strategy, one must employ more elementary processes such as encoding, search, comparison, discrimination, etc. Thus, for an interactive imagery strategy, one may need to utilize a variety of processes associated with the retrieval and generation of various codes within the permanent memory system.

It is reasonable to ask whether the definition of organization that we have offered and the emphasis on probelm solving can contribute to an understanding of the concept of organization and the development of a theory of organization. We are not going to propose a theory of organization at this point, but it should be clear that such a theory must be able to capture all the various levels of cognitive activity that serve to define organization. Thus, a theory of organization is not simply a theory of the elementary processes that serve to make up a particular strategy; it must also be a theory of the "executive" routines or higher order strategies that select among and coordinate various strategic activities. Such a theory must also specify the conditions that give rise to the use of a particular strategy.

One possible way to approach the development of a theory of organization is to develop a theory of organization in a task such as free recall, with particular emphasis given to elucidating the various strategies and processes governing free-recall performance. Of all the list-learning tasks, free recall seems to be the best candidate for the development of an organization theory that could have potential generalizability. Such an assumption is based on the fact that it is the least structured of all the list-learning tasks and therefore allows for more flexibility on the part of the individual learner (problem solver). This flexibility in solution seems to generate a variety of phenomena that demand a broad concept of organization. This emphasis on free recall is not intended to ignore the study of organization in other tasks. Bower (1970, 1972) provided excellent illustrations of apparent organizational phenomena in paired associate and serial recall tasks. The examples he provides of the use of mediation strategies in paired associate learning and grouping strategies in serial recall (see also Martin & Noreen, 1974) certainly fall within the scope of the definition of organization offered earlier. It is the case, however, that the free-recall paradigm has served as the major vehicle for studying organizational factors in memory, and it is within the large literature on performance in this task that many issues have been raised, some of which are in need of re-evaluation.

The next section of this chapter is a review and discussion of several organizational strategies that seem to govern free-recall performance. The presentation and discussion of these strategies serves two purposes. First, it permits a discussion of the availability of well-defined process explanations for each of the various organizational strategies that are elements of a theory of organization. The general lack of such process formulations led to some serious problems in the area of measurement, and this is discussed in detail. Second, any theory of organization in free recall must incorporate all of the various strategies that seem relevant to performance. This involves inclusion not only of the strategies within the theory, but also of the conditions surrounding the selection of a particular strategy. Thus, one of the issues to be considered is the interaction of various organizational strategies and the implications for theory and measurement of free-recall organization. The final section of this paper, contains a consideration of how well Anderson's detailed theory of free-recall learning (FRAN) handles these issues and whether a theory of free recall is simply a specific instance of a more general theory of memory organization.

III. ORGANIZATIONAL STRATEGIES IN FREE RECALL

A. Unitization—A General Strategy

One of the predominant strategies in virtually all list-learning and memory tasks is the unitization or chunking of individual items into larger units of information. For the purposes of the present discussion there is no attempt to separate out those aspects of unitization that may operate during the input or encoding–storage phase of list learning versus the output or retrieval phase of such tasks. In the past there has been controversy about whether organization was a storage and/or retrieval phenomenon (e.g., Allen, 1969; Slamecka, 1968, 1969). It would appear that there is a sufficiently large data base to indicate that retrieval cannot be independent of what occurs at input or storage (e.g., Pellegrino & Salzberg, 1975; Watkins & Tulving, 1975). Furthermore, studies of rehearsal patterns during input provide support for the correspondence between functional input order (e.g., Rundus, 1971) and actual output order or grouping.

Unitization as a strategy may involve several basic or elementary processes such as search, comparison, rehearsal, etc. A process theory capable of specifying all the elementary processing activities that operate in the context of a unitization strategy has not been specified, although fragments of such a process model can be found. The majority of research associated with studying unitization has focused on the two predominant manifestations of this strategy, namely, clustering and subjective organization. These two phenomena provide unequivocal support for the existence of this strategy, and the remainder of this discussion focuses on issues associated with the theory and measurement of these specific examples of the more general strategy.

1. CLUSTERING

The empirical phenomenon of clustering is most often mentioned in any argument for the existence of a strategy whereby individual items are grouped together into higher order units that serve as the functional basis for recall. The demonstration of clustering is based on the presentation and test of a list with certain predetermined relationships among the items. The relationships can be of a conceptual, associative, or acoustic nature (among others) with subsets of the items forming separate groups and each of the items within a particular subset sharing a certain characteristic. Clustering is said to have occurred if the ordering of items in the recall protocol reflects the experimenter-defined structure of the list. The nonrandomness of the recall protocol as contrasted with the typical random order of presentation presumably reflects the discovery and utilization of the structure implicit in the list. The earliest demonstrations of clustering were provided by Jenkins and Russell (1952) and Bousfield (1953).

The empirical phenomenon of recalling together items sharing a particular characteristic such as common category membership is only one basis for assuming that higher order units have been created. Certainly, if such units exist, then the members of those units should be produced in close spatial and temporal proximity. Considerable effort has gone into quantifying the degree of spatial proximity of conceptually related items in written recall with much less effort expended in studying the temporal characteristics of oral recall. However-er, the study of oral recall has provided strong evidence that retrieval is based upon higher order units. One example is a study by Gelfand (1971) on the oral recall of conceptually structured lists. The data of interest were interresponse times in the production of individual list members. When members of a particular category were recalled in sequence, short interresponse latencies were followed by long interresponse latencies, reflecting the point at which a transition between categories occurred. Such results are consistent with the assumption of at least two phases in the retrieval process: (a) accessing a particular memory unit, and (b) reading out the members of that unit. In cases where the memory units of interest cannot be specified preexperimentally, patterns of interresponse times have been suggested as a means of identifying these units (e.g., Chase & Simon, 1973; Reitman, 1976).

In addition to the temporal and spatial properties of recall protocols, there exist a variety of other data that support the concept of unitization. If the higher order unit serves as the basis for recall, then recall of the individual members of these units should be an all-or-none process. One way to demonstrate such an effect is to partition total recall into the number of categories represented in the recall protocol and the average number of instances recalled per category. These two measures, category recall (CR) and items per category (IPC), multiplicatively define total recall. If items are organized into units, then partitioning recall over successive trials or experimental conditions might be expected to indicate constancy in the value of IPC and changes in CR. Cohen (1966) showed such a result for the recall of conceptually structured lists. A more powerful demonstration of the same phenomenon has been provided in cueing studies. As an example, Tulving and Pearlstone (1966) compared the free and cued recall of conceptually structured lists varying in the number of categories and total list length. The difference between free and cued recall was restricted primarily to lists containing six or more categories. The benefits derived from presentation of category cues were attributable to increases in CR rather than to changes in IPC. Thus, Tulving and Pearlstone (1966) argued that more information was available than accessible and the loss of information was due to the failure to retrieve category units that were recallable in an all-or-none fashion. Studies by Tulving and Psotka (1971) and Strand (1971) on retroactive interference in categorized lists illustrated that there can be selective loss and reinstatement of the retrieval cues that provide access to the memory units and their contents.

There is little doubt about the existence of a unitization strategy in the acquisition and retention of conceptually structured lists. Debate does exist in the area of how to quantify or measure the extent to which such a strategy has been employed by an individual with respect to particular experimenter-defined units. The debate is a curious one since all participants agree on one of the basic components entering into the final measure, namely, the number of intraunit repetitions in the recall protocol. An intraunit repetition is the immediate sequential cooccurrence of two items from the same experimenter-defined unit. The observed number of repetitions can be related to a number of other statistical properties of the protocol being considered. These include the number of repetitions that could be expected by chance as well as the maximum and minimum number of possible repetitions. All of these statistical properties have been combined with the observed number of repetitions to derive some quantitative organizational score variously labeled RR, SCR, ARC, etc., and Murphy provides a detailed treatment of these indices. The proliferation of measures has led to several reviews and comparisons of these measures (e.g., Colle, 1972; Shuell, 1969, 1975), but with no apparent resolution of the issue as to which is the best measure. Most recently, Shuell (1975) raised the question of "best for what?" since the various measures differ in certain key assumptions.

Colle (1972) pointed out that the measurement problem is not simply an empirical question, but that the development and testing of measures must be intimately related to theoretical concerns. The current problems with respect to measuring the amount of unitization (clustering) stem from the lack of a precise theory of the process underlying the clustering phenomenon.

> One of the first problems which had to be solved was to demonstrate that category clustering did exist. Two approaches are possible. A theory describing the mechanism responsible for clustering could be constructed, and the measure of clustering derived from this theory (i.e., the clustering parameter) could be shown to be greater than zero. The simpler approach, which was taken, is to construct a theory which describes a recall mechanism that does not produce clustering, and to reject this theory . . . . The large number of repetitions (or the small number of runs) observed in the recall of categorized lists usually allows this theory to be rejected. Hence, the existence of a clustering effect can be established [Colle, 1972, p. 624].

Given that clustering does exist, one is still left with what Colle (1972) refers to as the scaling problem. Different assumptions have been made in attempting to develop measures that yield clustering values along a measurement scale. The debate that has ensued concerns which of these scaling solutions is most appropriate. There is no resolution of this debate because no tests have been provided of the theoretical adequacy of the assumptions involved in the various scaling methods.

Perhaps it is time to reconsider the motivation behind attempting to derive measures of clustering. Ultimately, such measures should contribute to answering empirical and theoretical questions. One such theoretical question is the relationship between level of recall and level of organization. Answers to these questions have been sought by using the various clustering indices that have been developed, and there is no agreement among the answers obtained. The lack of agreement may be attributable to differences in the theoretical assumptions and adequacy of the measurement procedures, as well as to statistical properties of the derived indices that render them inappropriate for answering certain questions. Thus, we agree with Colle (1972) when he asserts that "measures of clustering cannot be constructed without a theory which describes the mechanism producing clustering [p. 631]." The chapter by Murphy provides a basis for addressing some of the issues associated with the statistical adequacy of various measures. The detailed information that he provides about confoundings between measures and list–structure variables is extremely useful with respect to selecting measures that will allow tests of particular hypotheses about recall–organization relationships. There is an implicit theory in his simulation work, and this theory provides the basis for selecting an "unbiased" measure. Some might argue with such a theory, but efforts of this type are a first step toward specifying process models and sets of theoretical assumptions dealing with the storage and retrieval of list members.

Acceptance of the fact that there are problems in measuring clustering adequately does not imply that the phenomenon itself should be dismissed. One can reject the hypothesis that recall of conceptually structured lists is a random process. The nonrandomness of the recall order reflects interitem dependencies that typically correspond to the conceptual, associative, or acoustic structure that has been built into the list. Such interitem dependencies in recall order suggest a unitization strategy that is further supported by the selective loss and reinstatement of entire subsets of items from a list.

2. SUBJECTIVE ORGANIZATION

The operation of a unitization strategy has also been assumed for the learning of lists that do not have any immediately apparent structure, that is, lists of "unrelated" items. This assumption is based upon the fact that the recall order of the items comprising such a list is also nonrandom and shows increasing stereotypy over successive trials. The initial demonstration of this "subjective organization" phenomenon in unrelated lists was provided by Tulving (1962).

Sternberg and Tulving (1977) point out the different ways in which the term may be used.

> Subjective organization, like many other terms in psychology, refers to two different, albeit closely related, concepts. One is a psychological process; the other is a measure of the extent to which the process is revealed in observable behavior. . . . When the subject studies the list, he groups (organizes) more and more individual list items into higher order S units; when he recalls the list, he retrieves S units one at a time and produces the constituent words of each in succession . . . . To measure subjective organization usually means to measure the extent to which the output order of words is sequentially constrained over successive trials . . . . The degree of output consistency over trials can thus be used as an index of the extent to which a particular organization has occurred and is maintained from one trial to the next [p. 540].

A major issue in the study of subjective organization has concerned its measurement, and the problems have been somewhat more complex than in the case of clustering. When a conceptually structured list is the object of study, then it is possible to specify beforehand what higher order units are of interest. The utilization of those units can be measured in terms of simple sequential repetitions of any items from within that unit. The constraints on specific item ordering within that unit are of no concern. For example, it is of no consequence if an individual recalls *duck, chicken, goose, turkey* versus *duck, goose, chicken, turkey.* In both cases the number of category repetitions is three, and the variability of order within the category unit does not affect the measurement procedure and final score. However, when there is no prior basis for specifying what the units might be, then certain measurement procedures may be insensitive to detecting the existence of higher-order units in the recall protocol.

The initial attempts at measuring subjective organization in unrelated lists were based upon the number of intertrial repetition occurring between successive groups of trials (Bousfield & Bousfield, 1966; Bousfield, Puff, & Cowen, 1964; Tulving, 1962). The number of intertrial repetitions is assessed by examining successive sequential pairs of recalled items in a given trial and determining how many of these sequential adjacencies are reproduced on a subsequent trial. The early application of this technique and the derived measures, either SO (Tulving, 1962) or ITR (Bousfield & Bousfield, 1966), was limited to a unidirectional analysis of sequential constancies. Thus if items were sequentially recalled on one trial, but recalled in reverse sequential order on a subsequent trial, then the bidirectional repetition was not recorded. Subsequent work removed this particular restriction (e.g., Gorfein, Blair, & Rowland, 1968; Shuell, 1969).

Although most research has concentrated on deriving indices of spatial proximity, there have been efforts to ascertain whether the temporal properties of recall correspond to a strategy of unitization. An example of such research is a study by Puff (1972) that demonstrated a temporal organization phenomenon similar to that described earlier for categorized lists. When successive items were members of a pairwise unit, then interresponse times were lower than when successive items came from separate units. Thus the consistent spatial orderings observed in successive recalls can be related to functional units in the temporal production of a particular output sequence.

Although the spatial and temporal measurement techniques are obviously limited, they are sufficiently sensitive to allow rejection of the hypothesis that recall order is governed by random selection. Thus, as in the case of clustering, the initial problem of demonstrating that subjective organization exists was solved by being able to demonstrate that the value for intertrial repetitions was significantly above chance. Solution of this problem left yet another one, however. The Bousfield and Bousfield (1966) and Tulving (1962) procedures for measuring subjective organization and the subsequent modifications to handle bidirectionality were criticized for their inability to reflect adequately higher order units of organization, that is, units larger than size two (Mandler, 1967;, Postman, 1970, 1972). "For example, it is possible that a unit of four words will be recalled together on every trial, but if the words are recalled in a different order on successive trials, both measures will underestimate the organization present [Shuell, 1969, p. 361]." This particular problem can be readily illustrated by applying the subjective organization techniques to categorized lists. When this was done by Puff (1970), the value for subjective organization was very low and was not different from that obtained for an unrelated list of items. However, the value obtained for clustering was very high. Subjects were apparently recalling the items within categories in adjacent positions, but the recall orderings within categories were varying from trial to trial, thereby leading to low values of pairwise intertrial repetitions. Thus, despite the fact that pairwise intertrial repetitions allow rejection of a hypotheses of random recall, they may not provide a sufficient basis for measuring the degree of organization or unitization that has occurred.

Mandler, Worden, and Graesser (1974) offered other arguments for the inadequacy of a pairwise measurement approach. They attempted to disrupt learning by selectively removing list items and replacing them with new items for the next learning trial. In their first experiment, the selection procedure attempted to disrupt performance by eliminating the basis for pairwise organization as represented in the output order. Thus, every other item in the recall protocol was eliminated from the list, and this selective replacement condition was contrasted with nonselective replacement. All the replacement conditions disrupted learning, but there was no difference among them. Mandler et al. (1974) concluded that "The experiment did not provide evidence about acquisition in the absence of organization. Rather, it demonstrates the difficulty of disrupting subjective organization in any simple fashion. In particular, the results cast serious doubt on the assumption that the primary organizational structure of lists of unrelated items involves relations in pairs of items [p. 224]." A second experiment provided support for the assumption of higher order units with nodal elements. The elimination of these elements led to a serious disruption of acquisition performance.

In an attempt to resolve some of these potential measurement problems, Pellegrino (1971) developed procedures that permit the assessment of intertrial repetitions of any size unit under a variety of different sequential ordering constraints. Pellegrino and Battig (1974) pointed out that empirical justification for criticisms of the pairwise measurement techniques required a demonstration that higher order units were, in fact, formed and that such units had internal sequential variability across successive recalls. A systematic study of subjective organization, employing the measurement techniques developed by Pellegrino (1971), provided the necessary evidence for the existence of units larger than size two with internal sequential variability (Pellegrino & Battig, 1974). Of particular interest was the fact that the internal sequential variability of such units was greatest during the second half of learning and that typical random presentation of unrelated lists did not foster the development of such units until relatively late in learning.

Given that it is possible to demonstrate empirically that such higher order units exist, the question remains as to whether the measurement of such units makes a substantial difference in accounting for performance differences at the group or individual subject level. The values obtained for organization based upon higher order units were shown to be more consistent with recall differences among conditions, and multiple correlation analyses supported this conclusion at the group level. However, the assessment of higher order units did not significantly enhance the correlation between organization and recall for individual subjects in the typical unrelated random list condition. Thus, the utility of measuring higher order units is open to question. Resolution of this issue depends on whether the goal of applying the assessment techniques is to derive some quantitative value for the amount of subjective organization or to specify the structure of the higher order units that have been formed.

If the major concern is to measure the amount of subjective organization, then the same scaling issues apply as in the case of measuring clustering. Values for observed numbers of intertrial repetitions of unit sizes two, three, four, etc., can be obtained, along with other statistics such as the chance-expected values and maximum possible values (Pellegrino, 1971). These statistics can be combined in various ways to yield different scaling solutions for deriving a score for each unit size. Which scaling solution is most appropriate depends upon the assumptions and theoretical adequacy of each, just as in the case of clustering. Sternberg and Tulving (1977) attempted to determine which scaling solution is best and whether one needs to measure intertrial repetitions for units larger than size two. Their comparison among measurement procedures was not based upon the theoretical adequacy of the scaling solutions since current theory does not permit such an assessment. Instead, they employed psychometric criteria to evaluate the various measures. They justifiably point out that arguments for or against a particular measure have been based upon intuitive criteria that have been neither theoretically nor psychometrically verified. The psychometric criteria that they specified were (a) quantification, (b) reliability, (c) construct validity, and (d) empirical validity. The first two criteria are straightforward, but the latter two require some clarification. For construct validity they state:

> This criterion requires that there be some theory which relates the measure of subjective organization to the hypothesized organizing process. . . . The theory we propose to adopt is that described above as the theoretical basis for output adjacency measures (Tulving, 1962). This theory relates subjective organization as a psychological construct to subjective organization as a measured entity, and thus serves as a basis for the construct validation of the various measures. [The criterion of empirical validity] requires that there be a theory which relates measured subjective organization to some other measurement. We adopt the theory that increasing subjective organization underlies the improvement that occurs on successive trials of multitrial free recall [p. 547].

These criteria were applied to data derived from a multilist–multitrial free-recall study employing unrelated randomly presented lists. Sternberg and Tulving (1977) reported a variety of data concerned with the reliability and empirical validity criteria and conclude that the best measure of subjective organization is the modification of the original Bousfield and Bousfield (1966) intertrial repetition measure that expresses the deviation between the observed and chance-expected number of bidirectional pairwise repetitions. This conclusion may be appropriate given the limited set of conditions in which organization was assessed, and it is consistent with data reported by Pellegrino and Battig (1974) for similar conditions. As noted earlier, higher order units may not be formed until relatively late in learning, particularly in unrelated, randomly presented lists. Thus, the failure to find evidence supporting the existence, reliability, and utility of such units is not surprising. This does not, however, rule out their presence and value in understanding differences between a variety of list structures and presentation conditions that are known to affect recall. At best, Sternberg and Tulving's conclusion is of limited generality.

Issues of generalizability aside, it remains necessary to question the utility of this whole measurement and testing exercise. The separation of theory and measurement that Colle (1972) discussed in the case of clustering is still true for subjective organization. There is no evidence to support the theoretical adequacy of the measure designated as best, since the theory giving rise to the test of construct validity is general and does not specify the size or structure of the unit to be measured. The criterion of empirical validity that was employed limits the value of the whole measurement operation. Conceivably, the measure should permit the investigation of theoretical issues, one of which is the relationship between organization and recall. However, the measure that has been designated as best has the property of maximizing that relationship given that the correlation between organization and recall was one of the criteria for selection. Perhaps, the measure could be used as an individual difference variable as Sternberg and Tulving suggest, but the long-range gain of doing so has yet to be demonstrated. Even if a subjective organization score could be shown to be a reliable predictor of something meaningful, something other than level of recall, there would still be an interpretive problem arising from the loose theoretical underpinnings of the measure itself. Again, we are led to conclude that measurement apart from theory may be a somewhat empty exercise.

3. ORGANIZATIONAL STRUCTURE

Research emphasis has lately shifted toward identifying the structure of organization, that is, the higher order units that are formed, their constituent elements, and the relationships among these units and elements. Part of this shift in emphasis can be attributed to a recognition of the methodological and theoretical inadequacies of attempting to measure the amount of organization. Another contributing factor has been the emergence of theories concerned with the representation of knowledge in memory (e.g., Anderson & Bower,

1973; Kintsch, 1972, 1974; Norman & Rumelhart, 1975; Rumelhart, Lindsay, & Norman, 1972).

Various methods have been employed to assess organizational structure, and some involve departures from typical free-recall procedures. Examples of these include Mandler's (1967) sorting task, Seibel's (1965) study-sheet paradigm, and Buschke's (1977) two-dimensional recall task. Other methods are more concerned with data reduction techniques for typical multitrial free-recall protocols. Included among these are Friendly's (1977) proximity analysis techniques, Monk's (1973, 1976) hierarchical grouping analysis techniques, and hierarchical analysis techniques based upon multiple cued recalls (Reuter, 1976). Many of the more recently proposed methods are extensions of the basic techniques developed by Pellegrino (1971, 1972) for assessing different types of higher-order subjective organization units over successive recalls (e.g., Buschke, 1976; Monk, 1976; Reuter, 1976; Zangen, Ziegelbaum, & Buschke, 1976). A detailed treatment of these techniques can be found in Friendly's chapter in this volume.

There has been little systematic application of these techniques for assessing organizational structure, and it is to be expected that debate will ensue as to which technique is most appropriate. Evidence that this is happening can be found in Monk's (1976) and Reuter's (1976) criticism of the proximity analysis procedures developed by Friendly (1977). We hope that this debate will be tied to theoretical issues. Attempts to study the structure of organization, including the content, size, and development of higher-order units, may lead to the development of more precise and testable models of unitization with subsequent advancement in the quantification of organization, if the latter is deemed a desirable goal (see Buschke, 1976).

It is now 26 years since Bousfield's (1953) demonstration of clustering and 17 years since Tulving's (1962) demonstration of subjective organization. During that time considerable effort has gone into studying factors that affect free-recall learning and organization. Over that same period the study of free-recall learning and organization has become a major topic in the developmental literature (e.g., Jablonski, 1974) with assiduous application of the methods and procedures arising from the adult literature. It is not surprising that developmental research on free recall has generally emphasized quantitative rather than qualitative developmental changes (e.g., Brown, 1975).

Perhaps, attempts to study the structure of organization rather than simply the amount of organization, will provide the basis for new insight concerning both quantitative and qualitative developmental changes in the formation and utilization of higher-order memory units. This may be the case if the study of free recall is linked to emergent research on the nature and development of semantic memory. Evidence for such a shift in emphasis can be found in Ornstein and Corsale's chapter on organizational features in children's memories.

B. Situationally Determined Strategies

1. SERIATION

In typical free recall, emphasis is on the development of stable recall structures in the absence of any implicit or explicit structure at input. However, structure may be provided at input by presenting the items in a constant order, and it is well documented that when such constancy occurs there is superior recall performance (e.g., Jung & Skeebo, 1967; Mandler, 1969a, b; Postman, Burns, & Hasher, 1970; Wallace, 1970). This superiority in recall performance apparently results from the strong tendency of individuals to use the list order as the basis for ordering or organizing recall. Varying degrees of consistency in the order of item presentation lead to systematic increases in recall perform-ance that are related to the degree of input–output organization (e.g., Chapman, Pellegrino, & Battig, 1974). Mandler (1969a, b) has referred to this basis of organization as seriation and has demonstrated that it may be used almost as frequently as category clustering. The pervasiveness of seriation as an organiza-tional strategy under conditions where there is no constraint on the order of recall has led Mandler to argue that it is an important and sometimes preferred mode of organization in human thought.

Postman (1972) made some interesting observations on the relationship between seriation and semantic clustering as alternative strategies governing recall. He pointed out that these two bases of organization are often incompat-ible, but both may give rise to superior performance. The tendency to focus on measuring only one type of organization, for example, category clustering, obviously fails to represent the diversity of organizational modes that are possible. There is also a strong possibility that assessment of only one mode of organization could lead to some misleading conclusions about group and individual differences. Research on individual differences reported by Hunt, Frost, and Lunneborg (1973) shows how such a possibility could arise. One of the studies reported by Hunt et al. (1973) was a comparison between high and low verbal college students in single-trial free recall of categorized lists. There were two conditions of presentation with the members of common categories either contiguously blocked or randomly distributed. With the random presen-tation list, the high and low verbal subjects differed in terms of the amount of category clustering with the high verbals showing less semantic clustering at output, but higher recall than the low verbals. However, Hunt et al. (1973) reported that the high verbal subjects had a greater tendency to organize recall on the basis of the serial order of item presentation. If the emphasis had been on semantic clustering only, then one might have been led to conclude that semantic organization is inversely related to verbal ability. The assessment of seriation led to the somewhat different conclusion that high verbal individuals may be better able to maintain the sequential order of input.

This brief discussion of seriation was intended to emphasize two points.

First, adopting the serial order of item presentation as a basis for storage and retrieval may be an extremely efficient strategy when the conditions of list presentation allow for its use. This may be the case even when alternative bases of organization exist. Second, focusing on only one particular mode of recall organization to the exclusion of others may be extremely misleading. We will return to this latter point shortly after considering two further organizational strategies in free recall.

2. RECENCY

Like the term subjective organization, the term recency can be used to refer to two related phenomena. In its most typical usage recency refers to the enhanced recall of the items occurring at the end of a free-recall list. The term may also be used to refer to the strategy of recalling the terminal list items first. This strategy is what apparently underlies the superior recall performance on the terminal list items (e.g., Postman & Phillips, 1965). Recency may be viewed as an organizational strategy designed to maximize performance on a portion of the list: specifically, that portion of the list that is presumed to reside in the short-term store (e.g., Glanzer, 1972) and that is subject to loss from output interference occurring during the act of recall (Waugh & Norman, 1965).

Recency has generally been treated as an automatic retrieval strategy in recall from successive single-trial lists. However, recency seems to be a learned strategy that develops as a result of experience with multiple prior free-recall lists (Maskarinec & Brown, 1974). Recency is also not an automatic retrieval strategy in the recall of multitrial free-recall lists. Pellegrino and Battig (1974) showed that this strategy tends to appear on the second trial and that its maintenance depends on the type of list that is being learned.

Recency is a relatively low-level organizational strategy—what Tulving (1968) termed organization in the weak sense. Its importance for the present discussion of organization is that it represents yet another strategy that influences the amount, order, and structure of recall and can thus influence the values obtained for other organizational indices.

3. PRIORITY

There is one more organizational strategy that merits discussion because it also influences the order and structure of recall. Battig, Allen, and Jensen (1965) provided evidence that newly recalled items, that is those not recalled on prior trials, tend to occur early in the recall protocol, earlier than would be expected based upon random distribution. Battig et al. (1965) interpreted the priority effect as possibly indicating that subjects develop a strategy such that newly acquired items are given special attention in recall, possibly because they are more susceptible to forgetting. Questions arose concerning the possible artifactual nature of the priority effect (Baddeley, 1968; Postman & Keppel, 1968; Shuell & Keppel, 1968). The major contention was that previously incorrect items are more likely to occur in initial and terminal list positions during presentation, thus favoring their early recall due to the occurrence of primacy and recency effects. Also, when the recency effect was eliminated by having an interpolated task before recall, then there was no evidence for the occurrence of a priority effect. Thus, there appeared to be a complete inter-dependence of priority and recency effects. Subsequent research, however, has demonstrated that when conditions are created in which prior incorrect items never appear in the initial or terminal positions of the list, thus eliminating the possibility of contamination due to primacy and recency effects, there is still a substantial priority effect that increases over trials (Battig & Slaybaugh, 1969). Further evidence demonstrating the occurrence of a priority effect was provided by Brown and Thompson (1971) and Mandler and Griffith (1969).

The use of a new-item priority strategy for recall may result from processes occurring during list presentation and study. In a study of overt rehearsal processes during multitrial free recall, Einstein, Pellegrino, Mondani, and Battig (1974) showed that newly recalled items received a disproportionately large number of rehearsals on the study presentation prior to recall. The selective study and early recall of previously nonrecalled items is yet another way to maximize performance on certain items within a list. The possible interde-pendence between employment of the strategy and performance on new items is suggested by the fact that priority in the recall of newly learned items increases over trials as does the probability of recalling such items.

Part–whole transfer studies provide one further illustration of the use of a strategy that segregates old and new items and gives recall priority to new items. Petrich, Pellegrino, and Dhawan (1975) and Roberts (1969) showed that under typical part–whole free-recall transfer conditions there is evidence for recall priority of the new subset of items. This priority effect also increases over successive trials with the whole list. When the subject is informed about the structure of the whole list, recall priority for new items is further enhanced (Petrich et al., 1975) and the level of new-item recall priority is correlated with the level of recall of such items. Petrich et al. (1975) suggested that this new-item priority effect may explain why new-item recall remains superior to old-item recall even when the subject is informed about the list structure. The old items may suffer from output interference resulting from the adoption of this recall strategy.

C. Interrelationships among Organizational Strategies

Up to this point we have considered a variety of organizational strategies that a learner has at his disposal and that are manifested during free-recall learning. Each of these strategies can affect the level of recall, the particular items recalled, and the order in which they are recalled. Recognition of this fact poses some serious methodological and interpretive problems. The predominant tendency in measuring organization has been to focus on only one particular type of organization, typically either clustering or subjective organization, and to assume that this reflects the total amount of organization that has occurred. Such an approach obviously ignores the possibility that alternative modes of organization are possible or important and that recall may be determined by several strategies operating simultaneously. Even if the indices of clustering and subjective organization were sufficiently well specified and validated such that they adequately represented underlying processes, they could not adequately represent the level of organization shown by a particular subject. No single strategy index could be expected to account for the level and structure of a given recall attempt. Inconsistencies in the literature concerning the relationship between organization and recall may be attributed to this problem as well as to the more basic measurement problems discussed earlier.

Postman (1972) pointed out that

> As the evidence of multiple and divergent modes of organization accumulates, it will become increasingly important to specify their necessary and sufficient conditions and their relative weights in the performance of a given memory task. So far, the main thrust of experimental analysis has been directed toward the identification and measurement of the separate processes; the manner of their interaction now requires explicit attention .... The time appears to have come for a component analysis of organizational processes, and the analytic complexities are likely to be comparable [p. 34].

There have been relatively few attempts to undertake the type of analysis suggested by Postman. One such attempt was a study by Pellegrino and Battig (1974), which is reviewed in some detail. In this study four basic free-recall conditions were investigated, representing the crossing of categorized and unrelated lists with random and constant presentation orders. Several different indices of organization were obtained: These included recency, primacy, priority, subjective organization (including units larger than size two), and seriation. Each of these different organizational strategies was manifested in recall, often in reciprocal relationship to one another, and they differed as a function of the particular type of list condition. Evidence of this interactive effect across and within list conditions can be seen by examining the different indices shown in Figures 2.1 and 2.2. These figures show changes in various measures of organization as a function of trials and particular list manipulations. Figure 2.1 shows performance as a function of categorical versus unrelated lists. It can be seen that the level of subjective organization (output–output) was higher for categorized than unrelated lists. However, categorized lists showed less seriation (input–output), recency, and new-item priority than unrelated lists. A similar reciprocal pattern occurred in the comparison between constant and random presentation condidions, as shown in Figure 2.2

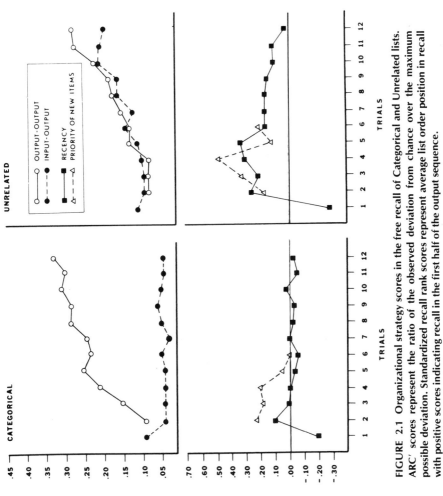

FIGURE 2.1 Organizational strategy scores in the free recall of Categorical and Unrelated lists. ARC' scores represent the ratio of the observed deviation from chance over the maximum possible deviation. Standardized recall rank scores represent average list order position in recall with positive scores indicating recall in the first half of the output sequence.

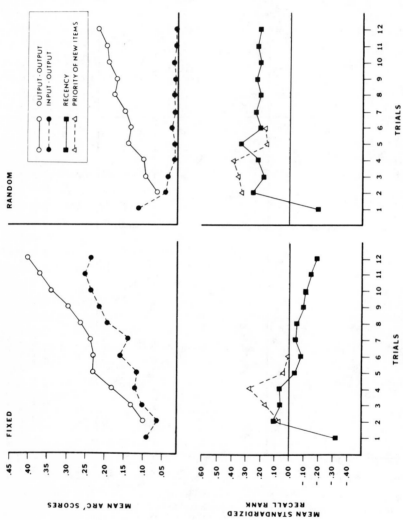

FIGURE 2.2 Organizational strategy scores in the free recall of Fixed and Random presentation conditions.

The extent to which a particular organizational strategy was manifested in recall also changed as a function of the level of practice as can be seen in both figures. A hierarchy of organizational strategies or series of stages was inferred such that subjects begin with a strong seriation strategy on the first trial followed by recency and priority strategies, finally culminating in higher order subjective organization strategies. The main difference between conditions appeared to be in the second and third stages of this organizational development. In those conditions where there are semantic categories, or fixed serial orders, or both, the development of priority and recency strategies is limited, and individuals appear to proceed more rapidly to an organizational stage involving the formation of higher order units. Only in the typical unrelated—random conditions do individuals maintain a recency strategy and show little development of higher order subjective organization units. It appears that higher order units per se are not sufficient to explain recall differences and that overall speed or ease of transition to this stage is equally important. Without semantic or sequential cues, individuals may be forced to operate with simpler organizational strategies.

This evidence for interactions among organizational strategies supports the contention that no single measure of organization, at least not the currently developed measures, can adequately account for the level and structure of recall. Intertrial shifts in organizational strategies need to be considered in any attempt to assess organizational structure. It is probably the case that stable organizational structures do not emerge until relatively late in learning. Thus, analytic procedures that attempt to assess the structure of organization and that are applied after learning is complete (Reuter, 1976) should not be seriously affected by the multiplicity of strategies that may exist during initial acquisition.

The interaction among strategies with potential reciprocal relationships may also explain why some studies attempting to influence one form of organization have not produced changes in the level of recall (e.g., Postman et al., 1970; Puff, 1970). These studies compared conditions where subjects were given typical free-recall instructions or were instructed to use consistent recall patterns across successive trials. The latter instructional manipulation increased the level of pairwise intertrial repetitions, but did not enhance the level of recall. This result may be due to a reduction in the utilization of other organizational strategies that may still operate in the standard instructional condition and thereby influence the level of recall. Unambiguous interpretation of the results of such studies is not possible since only one type of organization was assessed.

Finally, interactions among organizational strategies and changes in the utilization of these strategies over trials should be represented in any theory or model attempting to account for free-recall performance. The most comprehensive model for free recall is the FRAN model developed by Anderson (1972). The next section is a consideration of how it represents various organizational strategies and their interactive relationship.

IV. THEORIES OF ORGANIZATION

A. FRAN

A precise theory of free recall has been embodied in a computer program dubbed FRAN for Free Recall by an Associative Net (Anderson, 1972). This program was an attempt to simulate the performance of humans in free-recall tasks, and it is one of the few available efforts aimed at bringing together a variety of data into a coherent theory of processing and performance. The simulation specifically deals with the extent to which an associative theory of memory can account for extant free-recall data. One of its major contributions has been to locate the problems with such a theory. We will examine the processing assumptions of the model briefly and relate them to both the preceding discussion of organizational strategies in free recall and the wider concern of memory organization in general.

There are two major memory components in the FRAN simulation, a short-term and a long-term store. The long-term store consists of lexical items that are linked to one another by associative pathways in a netlike structure. There is at least one indirect association between any two items in this lexical network, but the primary associations for each entry were chosen on the basis of dictionary definitions and common free associations. In addition, there are one or two random associations for each entry, a feature that allows FRAN to simulate the idiosyncratic meanings that individuals often have for particular words.

When FRAN attempts to "learn" a list of words for subsequent recall she (he?) attaches a list tag to each of the words in the list. Tagging is a stochastic process and the probability of tagging an item varies with the length of time it spends in the short-term store. Duration in the short-term store is determined by its size, the length of the list to be learned, and the interitem associations that are processed during study. In the interval between item presentations, FRAN seeks out as many associative pathways as it can to link the current item to previously presented items. Associative pathways are tagged to guide the retrieval process. The final study operation selects items for a store called ENTRYSET. These items are the three list members that will be used to initiate the retrieval process, and the choice of these items is based upon the degree of interconnectedness to other list members.

At recall, FRAN first outputs all the items still in the short-term store and then randomly selects one word from those items or ENTRYSET to begin a search through the associative net for items that have list tags. The search is a depth-first procedure that follows each marked pathway to its end before going back to the nearest choice point and searching for another pathway. When all the pathways from the selected word have been examined, another word is selected to initiate the search process. To avoid repetition of the same item,

FRAN marks those items that it recalls. Finally, FRAN is capable of learning at output in much the same way that it learns the list during input. Each recalled word is entered into the short-term store where it is treated as a new item, and associative pathways to other list members are searched for and tagged. Thus, new retrieval pathways can be discovered during recall.

FRAN has proved competent at reproducing many aspects of human behavior in free-recall situations. In particular, the simulation shows a typical learning curve, a serial position function, and most importantly, organization phenomena. The organizational strategies incorporated in FRAN that result in the simulation of free-recall output phenomena include a recency strategy, as represented by the initial dumping of the contents of the short-term store, and a partial seriation strategy, as reflected by certain study biases. In addition, there is a unitization strategy implicit in the study processes and in the use of ENTRYSET to guide recall. The items in ENTRYSET are nodal items that serve as cues for recalling chunks or units of information in a more-or-less stereotyped manner across successive recalls.

One phenomenon that FRAN does not adequately simulate is category clustering. There are some clustering tendencies exhibited in the protocols, but not at a level approximating human performance. This deficiency seems to be due to the fact that FRAN does not use nonlist words in designating potential members for ENTRYSET. Thus, the failure to capture clustering is not due to the failure to have represented a unitization strategy, but to the particular constraints on the item selection processes as originally programmed. A modification of the processes and constraints on the strategy for ENTRYSET selection is easy to incorporate into the simulation, and it would certainly improve the match between the simulation and the real data for both clustering and subjective organization.

One of the most important properties of the FRAN theory is the fact that the theory and model provide an explicit link between the areas that Tulving (1972) designated as semantic and episodic memory. Strategies and phenomena of free-recall learning are associated with episodic memory, but it is clear that they are closely related to semantic memory as well. Without knowledge of the type represented in an associative network or general semantic memory system, the results of many free-recall experiments would be unintelligible. Expecting an individual to recall groups of words on the basis of common category membership is unrealistic in the absence of a sematic memory system in which knowledge about such categories is stored. While this may be taken for granted today, the semantic–episodic distinction is a relative newcomer and FRAN provided the first theoretical demonstration of the interaction between semantic and episodic memory functioning.

While the success of the model in simulating many basic free-recall phenomena is impressive, some of its failures result from the omission of certain strategies that have been discussed previously. Included among these are seriation and new-item priority. Before FRAN could simulate all the various organizational strategies and the shifts in the use of such strategies, some nontrivial changes would have to be made.

> The other important direction in which FRAN should be improved is to permit her to adopt a variety of strategies and to give her some heuristic principles by which to select a particular strategy for a particular free recall task. This is much more easily said than done. Essentially, a meta-program is needed that is capable of writing a set of different programs, each program reflecting a different strategy. The program that we have developed for execution of the associative strategy would be just one of the many strategy-implementing programs. . . . Although the task of programming such a meta-program is beyond our current capabilities and ideas, any fully adequate simulation program for human memory will have to take the form of such a meta-program [Anderson, 1972, p. 373].

B. Theoretical Transitions

Anderson's simulation work since proposing the FRAN theory illustrates both the form that more powerful theories and meta-programs can take and the directions that memory research has taken in general. This work also serves to demonstrate how verbal learning, and free recall in particular, have raised important theoretical questions that can only be answered by examining more complex phenomena; theories at one level can and must be incorporated into higher order theoretical systems. As Anderson noted, FRAN ultimately lacked the ability to assemble even those strategies needed to simulate human performance in free-recall tasks, and it was not designed to be extended beyond that circumscribed domain. Human Associative Memory (HAM) (Anderson & Bower, 1973) and ACT (Anderson, 1976) were successive attempts to develop systems with wider capabilities than FRAN that at the same time retained the capabilities of the original simulation.

The theory dubbed HAM is much more ambitious than FRAN, and it was designed to simulate both the structure of human knowledge and at least some of the processes that act on and use that structure. To achieve this greater power, it was necessary to change much of FRAN. Instead of the simple associations found in FRAN, HAM uses propositional networks that include both facts about the world and their contexts. If HAM were to learn a list of words in a free-recall experiment, it would replace the list tags of FRAN with a tree structure including propositions of the form "Word i occurred in the context of LIST [1973, p. 440]." Many other processing characteristics are similar in each system, and the two models would perform comparably. Most important here is the fact that HAM is capable of alleviating some of the deficiencies of FRAN not by presenting a new theory of free-recall learning, but by incorporating FRAN's abilities into a larger framework. FRAN's study and recall procedures could be expanded to take advantage of the more complex memory representation found in HAM and thus produce such phenomena as category clustering and subjective organization.

Just as HAM embodies and extends important aspects of FRAN, so can ACT be seen as a system which, although it goes beyond HAM, retains and encompasses some key features of the earlier theories. A large difference between FRAN and HAM lies in the nature of the memory representation—more complete and complex semantic processing required more than the simple associate scheme found in FRAN—and the HAM model focused almost entirely on the representational issue. Although there are also differences between HAM and ACT in their representation of knowledge, the crucial change has been toward a specification of the processes that act on the knowledge base, a change brought about by the addition of a production system and its attendant procedural knowledge. Anderson (1976) showed that ACT can also handle list-learning data, although an explicit extension of FRAN is not attempted.

There are two important progressions evident in Anderson's work. One is the movement away from a simple associative framework and the tasks associated with it to a wider view of the activities of memory. A consequence of this is the increasingly complex nature of the knowledge representations that Anderson proposes. The second progression is an increasing emphasis on the processes that act on and with memory structures. We mentioned previously Anderson's evaluation of the FRAN model in this connection; the other major instance of this shift can be seen in the difference between HAM and ACT. Where HAM was an attempt to study, as far as possible, just the structure of the data base, ACT represents no such claim. By including a production system as an integral part of ACT, Anderson acknowledges the importance of studying memory and processing together; strategies and other processes are, therefore, seen as inseparable from the memory base.

V. CONCLUDING COMMENTS

In this chapter we have attempted to deal with some of the issues that arise when one attempts to cope with organization as an important memory construct. The particular issue that was emphasized was the lack of an explicit theory of organization. In our attempt to deal with this problem we provided a definition of organization and then proceeded to explore some of its implications for the domain of a theory of organization. One important aspect of such a theory is the representation of the multiplicity of strategies that are associated with organization. Attempts to measure the extent to which individual organizational strategies have been involved in list learning, particularly free recall, without providing a theory or model of the processes have led down some blind alleys. Perhaps this is to be expected given the complexity of the overall problem. Even a well-developed theory of free recall fails to capture all the complexities of a theory of organization. Organization is a systems principle that deals with both the structure and operation of human memory. A theory of organization is a theory of how knowledge is represented as well as the executive routines, strategies, and processes that create, operate on, and utilize that knowledge base.

The study of organization in list learning has profoundly influenced our conceptions of human memory and the way it is currently being studied. Such studies have caused individuals to ask questions about a theory of organization, and this has led to a realization of the larger set of theoretical issues at stake. This is a large intellectual debt that is often overlooked.

ACKNOWLEDGEMENTS

Preparation of this chapter was supported by funds provided by the Learning Research and Development Center, University of Pittsburgh, which is funded in part by the National Institute of Education (NIE), U.S. Department of Health, Education, and Welfare.

The authors wish to express their appreciation for the helpful comments provided by Robert Glaser, Rob Kail, C. Richard Puff, and James Voss on an earlier version of this chapter.

REFERENCES

Allen, M. M. Cueing and retrieval in free recall. *Journal of Experimental Psychology*, 1969, *81*, 29-35.

Anderson, J. R. FRAN: A simulation model of free recall. In G. H. Bower (Ed.), *The psychology of learning and motivation* (Vol. 5). New York: Academic Press, 1972.

Anderson, J. R. *Language, memory, and thought*. Hillsdale, N.J.: Lawrence Erlbaum Associates, 1976.

Anderson, J. R., & Bower, G. H. *Human associative memory*. Washington, D.C.: Winston, 1973.

Baddeley, A. D. Prior recall of newly learned items and the recency effect in free recall. *Canadian Journal of Psychology*, 1968, *22*, 157–163.

Battig, W. F., Allen, M. M. & Jensen, A. R. Priority of free recall of newly learned items. *Journal of Verbal Learning and Verbal Behavior*, 1965, *4*, 175–179.

Battig, W. F., & Slaybaugh, G. D. Evidence that priority of free recall of newly learned items is not a recency artifact. *Journal of Verbal Learning and Verbal Behavior*, 1969, *8*, 556–558.

Bousfield, A. K., & Bousfield, W. A. Measurement of clustering and of sequential constancies in repeated free recall. *Psychological Reports*, 1966, *19*, 935–942.

Bousfield, W. A. The occurrence of clustering in the recall of randomly arranged associates. *Journal of General Psychology*, 1953, *49*, 229–240.

Bousfield, W. A., Puff, C. R., & Cowan, T. M. The development of constancies in sequential organization during free recall. *Journal of Verbal Learning and Verbal Behavior*, 1964, *3*, 489–495.

Bower, G. H. Organizational factors in memory. *Cognitive Psychology*, 1970, *1*, 18–46.

Bower, G. H. A selective review of organizational factors in memory. In E. Tulving, & W. Donaldson (Eds.), *Organization of memory*. New York: Academic Press, 1972.

Brown, A. L. The development of memory: Knowing, knowing about knowing, and knowing how to know. In H. W. Reese (Ed.), *Advances in child development and behavior* (Vol. 10). New York: Academic Press, 1975.

Brown, S. C. & Thompsom, C. P. The relationship between item strength and order of free recall. *Journal of Verbal Learning and Verbal Behavior*, 1971, *10*, 444–448.

Buschke, H. Learning is organized by chunking. *Journal of Verbal Learning and Verbal Behavior,* 1976, *15,* 313–324.

Buschke, H. Two dimensional recall: Immediate identification of clusters in episodic and semantic memory. *Journal of Verbal Learning and Verbal Behavior,* 1977, *16,* 201–216.

Chapman, C., Pellegrino, J. W., & Battig, W. F. Input sequence and grouping in free recall learning and organization. *American Journal of Psychology,* 1974, *87,* 565–577.

Chase, W. G., & Simon, H. A. Perception in chess. *Cognitive Psychology,* 1973, *4,* 55–81.

Cohen, B. H. Some-or-none characteristics of coding behavior. *Journal of Verbal Learning and Verbal Behavior,* 1966, *5,* 182–187.

Colle, H. A. The reification of clustering. *Journal of Verbal Learning and Verbal Behavior,* 1972, *11,* 624–633.

Einstein, G. O., Pellegrino, J. W., Mondani, M. S., & Battig, W. F. Free recall performance as a function of overt rehearsal frequency. *Journal of Experimental Psychology,* 1974, *103,* 440–449.

Friendly, M. C. In search of the M-Gram: The structure of organization in free recall. *Cognitive Psychology,* 1977, *9,* 188–249.

Gelfand, H. *Organization in free recall learning: Output contiguity and interresponse times as a function of presentation structure.* Unpublished doctoral dissertation, University of Michigan, 1971.

Glanzer, M. Storage mechanisms in recall. In G. H. Bower (Ed.), *The psychology of learning and motivation* (Vol. 5). New York: Academic Press, 1972.

Gorfein, D. S., Blair, C., & Rowland, C. The generality of free recall: I. Subjective organization as an ability factor. *Psychonomic Science,* 1968, *11,* 279–280.

Hunt, E., Frost, N. & Lunneborg, C. Individual differences in cognition: A new approach to intelligence. In G. H. Bower (Ed.), *The psychology of learning and motivation* (Vol. 7). New York: Academic Press, 1973.

Jablonski, E. M. Free recall in children. *Psychological Bulletin,* 1974, *81,* 522–539.

Jenkins, J. J. & Russell, W. A. Associative clustering during recall. *Journal of Abnormal and Social Psychology,* 1952, *47,* 818–821.

Jung, J. & Skeebo, S. Multitrial free recall as a function of constant versus varied input orders and list length. *Canadian Journal of Psychology,* 1967, *21,* 329–336.

Kintsch, W. Notes on the structure of semantic memory. In E. Tulving & W. Donaldson (Eds.), *Organization of memory.* New York: Academic Press, 1972.

Kintsch, W. *The representation of meaning in memory.* Hillsdale, N.J.: Lawrence Erlbaum Associates, 1974.

Mandler, G. Organization and memory. In K. W. Spence & J. T. Spence (Eds.), *The psychology of learning and motivation* (Vol. 1). New York: Academic Press, 1967.

Mandler, G. Input variables and output strategies in free recall of categorized words. *American Journal of Psychology,* 1969a, *82,* 531–539.

Mandler, G. Words, lists, and categories: An experimental view of organized memory. In J. L. Cowan (Ed.), *Studies in thought and language.* Tucson: University of Arizona Press, 1969b.

Mandler, G., & Griffith, N. Acquisition and organization of new items in the free recall of random lists. *Journal of Verbal Learning and Verbal Behavior,* 1969, *8,* 545–551.

Mandler, G., Pearlstone, Z., & Koopmans, H. S. Effects of organization and semantic similarity on recall and recognition. *Journal of Verbal Learning and Verbal Behavior,* 1969, *8,* 410–423.

Mandler, G., Worden, P. E., & Graesser, A. C. Subjective disorganization: Search for the locus of list organization. *Journal of Verbal Learning and Verbal Behavior,* 1974, *13,* 220–235.

Martin, E., & Noreen, D. L. Serial Learning: Identification of subjective subsequences. *Cognitive Psychology,* 1974, *6,* 421–435.

Maskarinec, A. S., & Brown, S. C. Positive and negative recency effects in free recall learning. *Journal of Verbal Learning and Verbal Behavior,* 1974, *13,* 328–334.

Miller, G. A. The magical number seven, plus or minus two: Some limits on our capacity for processing information. *Psychological Review,* 1956, *63,* 81–97.

Monk, A. F. *The structure of organization in free recall.* Unpublished doctoral dissertation, University of Bristol, 1973.

Monk, A. F. A new approach to the characterization of sequential structure in multi-trial free recall using hierarchical grouping analysis. *British Journal of Mathematical and Statistical Psychology,* 1976, *29*, 1–18.

Murdock, B. B. *Human memory: Theory and data.* Potomac, Md.: Lawrence Erlbaum Associates, 1974.

Norman, D. A., & Rumelhart, D. E. *Explorations in cognition.* San Francisco: W. H. Freeman, 1975.

Pellegrino, J. W. A general measure of organization in free recall for variable unit size and internal sequential consistency. *Behavior Research Methods & Instrumentation,* 1971, *3*, 241–246.

Pellegrino, J. W. A Fortran IV program for analyzing higher order subjective organization units in free recall learning. *Behavior Research Methods & Instrumentation,* 1972, *4*, 215–217.

Pellegrino, J. W., & Battig, W. F. Relationships among higher order organizational measures and free recall. *Journal of Experimental Psychology,* 1974, *102*, 463–472.

Pellegrino, J. W., & Salzberg, P. M. Encoding specificity in associative processing tasks. *Journal of Experimental Psychology: Human Learning and Memory,* 1975, *1*, 538–548.

Petrich, J., Pellegrino, J. W., & Dhawan, M. The role of list information in free recall transfer. *Journal of Experimental Psychology: Human Learning and Memory,* 1975, *1*, 326–336.

Postman, L. Effects of word frequency on acquisition and retention under conditions of free-recall learning. *Quarterly Journal of Experimental Psychology,* 1970, *22*, 185–195.

Postman, L. A pragmatic view of organization theory. In E. Tulving & W. Donaldson (Eds.), *Organization of memory.* New York: Academic Press, 1972.

Postman, L. Verbal learning and memory. *Annual review of psychology* (Vol. 26). Palo Alto: Annual Reviews, Inc., 1975.

Postman, L., Burns, S., & Hasher, L. Studies of learning to learn: X. Nonspecific transfer effects in free-recall learning. *Journal of Verbal Learning and Verbal Behavior,* 1970, *9*, 707–715.

Postman, L., & Keppel, G. Conditions determining the priority of new items in free recall. *Journal of Verbal Learning and Verbal Behavior,* 1968, *7*, 260–263.

Postman, L., & Phillips, L. W. Short-term temporal changes in free recall. *Quarterly Journal of Experimental Psychology,* 1965, *17*, 132–138.

Puff, C. R. Free recall with instructional manipulation of sequential ordering of output. *Journal of Experimental Psychology,* 1970, *84*, 540–542.

Puff, C. R. Temporal properties of organization in recall of unrelated words. *Journal of Experimental Psychology,* 1972, *92*, 225–231.

Reitman, J. S. Skilled perception in Go: Deducing memory structures from inter-response times. *Cognitive Psychology,* 1976, *8*, 336–356.

Reuter, H. *Hierarchical memory structures from systematic aspects of free recall output orders.* Unpublished manuscript, University of Michigan, 1976.

Roberts, W. A. The priority of recall of new items in transfer from part list learning to whole list learning. *Journal of Verbal Learning and Verbal Behavior,* 1969, *8*, 645–652.

Rumelhart, D. E., Lindsay, P. H., & Norman, D. A. A process model for long term memory. In E. Tulving & W. Donaldson (Eds.), *Organization of memory.* New York: Academic Press, 1972.

Rundus, D. Analysis of rehearsal processes in free recall. *Journal of Experimental Psychology,* 1971, *89*, 63–77.

Seibel, R. *Organization in human learning: The study sheet paradigm and experiments one and two.* Paper presented at the meeting of the Psychonomic Society, Chicago, October, 1965.

Shuell, T. J. Clustering and organization in free recall. *Psychological Bulletin,* 1969, *72*, 353–374.

Shuell, T. J. On sense and nonsense in measuring organization in free recall-oops, pardon me, my assumptions are showing. *Psychological Bulletin,* 1975, *82*, 720–724.

Shuell, T. J., & Keppel, G. Item priority in free recall. *Journal of Verbal Learning and Verbal Behavior,* 1968, *7*, 969–971.

Slamecka, N. J. An examination of trace storage in free recall. *Journal of Experimental Psychology,* 1968, *76*, 504–513.

Slamecka, N. J. Testing for associative storage in multitrial free recall. *Journal of Experimental Psychology,* 1969, *81*, 557–560.

Sternberg, R. J., & Tulving, E. The measurement of subjective organization in free recall. *Psychological Bulletin,* 1977, *84*, 539–556.

Strand, B. Z. Further investigation of retroactive inhibition in categorized free recall. *Journal of Experimental Psychology,* 1971, *87*, 198–201.

Tulving, E. Subjective organization in free recall of "unrelated words." *Psychological Review,* 1962, *69*, 344–354.

Tulving, E. Intratrial and intertrial retention: Notes toward a theory of free recall verbal learning. *Psychological Review,* 1964, *71*, 219–237.

Tulving, E. Theoretical issues in free recall. In T. R. Dixon & D. L. Horton (Eds.), *Verbal behavior and general behavior theory.* Englewood Cliffs, N.J.: Prentice-Hall, 1968.

Tulving, E. Episodic and semantic memory. In E. Tulving & W. Donaldson, (Eds.), *Organization of memory.* New York: Academic Press, 1972.

Tulving, E., & Pearlstone, Z. Availability versus accessibility of information in memory for words. *Journal of Verbal Learning and Verbal Behavior,* 1966, *5*, 381–391.

Tulving, E., & Psotka, J. Retroactive inhibition in free recall: Inaccessibility of information available in the memory store. *Journal of Experimental Psychology,* 1971, *87*, 1–8.

Voss, J. On the relationship of associative and organizational processes. In E. Tulving & W. Donaldson (Eds.), *Organization of memory.* New York: Academic Press, 1972.

Wallace, W. P. Consistency of emission order in free recall. *Journal of Verbal Learning and Verbal Behavior,* 1970, *9*, 58–68.

Watkins, M. J., & Tulving, E. Episodic memory: When recognition fails. *Journal of Experimental Psychology: General,* 1975, *1*, 5–29.

Waugh, N. C., & Norman, D. A. Primary memory. *Psychological Review,* 1965, *72*, 89–104.

Zangen, M., Ziegelbaum, P., & Buschke, H. CLUSTER: A program for identifying recurrent clusters. *Behavior Research Methods & Instrumentation,* 1976, *8*, 388.

CHAPTER **3**

Measurement of Category
Clustering in Free Recall

I. THE ISSUES

Bousfield (1953) asked subjects to recall words that were chosen from different conceptual categories and presented in random order. He found the items recalled to be grouped or clustered by category and hypothesized that

MEMORY ORGANIZATION
AND STRUCTURE

the clustering reflected some underlying organization on the part of the subject. Since the early Bousfield paper, a good deal of research effort has been devoted to developing measures to quantify clustering and to relate these measures to other important variables.

Organization theory has evolved to explain the role of clustering and organization in memory. With this theory, memory is seen as inherently limited in capacity. However, through the use of organization, units or chunks of information can be constructed that allow the capacity limits to be at least partially circumvented. A clear prediction with the theory is that measures of recall organization, such as clustering and subjective organization, ought to be related to the amount of recall because recall is to some degree dependent on organization. The degree of dependence is in part determined by the nature of the capacity limitation. Postman (1972) discussed a strong view of capacity limitation (i.e., the only way to circumvent the span of immediate memory is to organize) and a weak view (i.e., organization can reduce the degree of capacity limitation, but is not the only means to do so). With the strong view, organization and recall must be highly related once immediate memory span is exceeded; with the weak view, there should be a relation between organization and recall, but only under circumstances favoring the use of organization.

A good deal of research has been loosely based on organization theory, much of it dealing with the degree to which subjects use categories to structure their recall outputs. A number of clustering measures have been developed to reflect this tendency to organize by category. Recently, however, the usefulness of research on clustering has come under attack from several different directions.

A. Is Clustering of Any Contemporary Interest?

1. REASONS FOR PESSIMISM

First at a theoretical level, Friendly (Chapter 4), Pellegrino and Ingram (Chapter 2), and Tulving and Bower (1974) argue that organizational structure is inherently multidimensional. Clustering provides only a unidimensional reflection of organization and is therefore seen as fundamentally inadequate. It is further argued that the contents of the organizational units themselves are important. Both the proximity analysis approach of Friendly (Chapter 4) and Buschke's (1977) two-dimensional recall method allow the investigation of memory-unit contents, and both approaches have produced promising initial data.

A second difficulty arises when attempts are made to discover the underlying organizational process or strategy that leads to clustering. The problem arises because no unitary clustering strategy has been found or is likely to be discovered in the future. Instead, a number of different activities may be involved in the production of clustered output. A speculative, and probably oversimplified, account of these activities might go something like the following.

First, during study, individual items are encoded, and at some point the subject may become aware of the existence of categories of items in the list. Even though the free-recall task is episodic in Tulving's (1972) terms, these categories involve information in the semantic memory system. Thus, even free recall for categorized words clearly incorporates semantic as well as episodic processing. The amount of clustering might, in fact, be seen as reflecting the degree to which semantic factors are involved in this episodic task.

Upon noting the categories of items, the subject may then attempt to encode the items by category and rehearse same-category items together (Puff, 1974; Rundus, 1971) as new items are presented. The outcome of this organizational activity may be to unitize the items, to increase their likelihood of storage in long-term memory, or to increase the number or strength of the interconnections among the items and/or category labels, depending on one's theoretical model.

In any case, following study the subject may continue to rehearse same-category items together until the recall test. At recall the retrieval of both category names and exemplars probably occurs, often with a fairly constant proportion of items recalled from each category that is represented in the output (Cohen, 1963, 1966). Items vary in their availability for recall, depending on whether or not they were stored and on their accessibility (given that an item is stored, can it be retrieved with existing retrieval cues?). According to some models (e.g., Rundus, 1973), items are systematically recalled from a category until no new items from the category can be retrieved, at which time the subject switches to a new category. Eventually, when all categories are exhausted, retrieval may cease. Under some circumstances the subject may search some or all of the categories again, possibly generating items and then checking to see if they were in the input list and, if so, whether or not they were already recalled on the trial.

It is clear that the underlying organizational tendency, which is reflected by clustering measures, is really the product of a complex interaction of memory process, structure, and strategy. With this logic, the usefulness of a clustering measure, which provides only a single number to summarize this complex interaction, seems questionable. Instead separate measures of the important underlying processes are needed.

The third and final complication that has arisen involves the striking lack of agreement in the literature as to (a) the best clustering measure to be used and (b) the criteria appropriate for deciding which measure of clustering is best. For example, Frankel and Cole (1971) argue that the Z score measure is best because it gives higher scores to longer recall strings, since longer strings are more likely to be significantly different from random recall. Frender and Doubilet (1974) argue for Ratio of Repetition (RR) on the grounds that it is *not* correlated with the length of the recall string. Roenker, Thompson, and Brown (1971) argue that the Adjusted Ratio of Clustering (ARC) is the best measure since it has a fixed maximum value of 1.0 and a fixed chance value of zero.

This confusion of criteria is further compounded by the way the measures are often tested. As Colle (1972) points out, a common procedure is to stipulate the measure being proposed as the best reflection of organization and then to compare its scores with those of the other measures on a sample of data. If the measures are mathematically different, they will provide somewhat different scores than the measure stipulated to be optimal, and the other measures are therefore judged to be inferior. Clearly, the confusion that has arisen has not had a positive effect on the research area. In fact, Tulving and Bower (1974) predict a rather gloomy future for research on clustering, in part because "there is little agreement as to what are 'legitimate' measures [p. 282]."

The result of these criticisms appears to be a pessimism regarding the usefulness of research on clustering. Tulving and Bower (1974) suggest that the clustering method may be useful only "when used in conjunction with other methods, as one of several converging operations [p. 282]." Pellegrino (1975) concludes, "perhaps it is time for researchers in the area of organization to stop deriving new measures of clustering or verifying old ones and to concentrate instead on understanding the processes of organization. Reductions of recall protocols to quantitative values of clustering or subjective organization (e.g., Pellegrino, 1971) only allow for an assessment of above-chance organization and are convenient ways to ignore considering the process itself [p. 67]."

2. IN DEFENSE OF THE STUDY OF CLUSTERING

While the foregoing arguments have been persuasive, they should not lead to the abandonment of clustering research. The multidimensional aspect of organization can, and should be, investigated with the important methods of Buschke and Friendly, but clustering may be able to contribute, both as an overall summary statistic of category organization and as one of several measures of different aspects of recall output. With free-recall data we have, at present, measures of consistency of intertrial recall order or subjective organization (Tulving, 1962), priority of recall for newly remembered items (Battig, Allen, & Jensen, 1965), as well as effects of categories on recall or clustering. In this chapter, another measure is proposed. The new measure allows investigation of the effects of organization on the *items selected for recall* and complements clustering measures that deal with *order* of recall. The use of a number of different measures can provide a rich characterization of several aspects of free recall data (see, e.g., Pellegrino & Battig, 1974).

The focus on processes underlying clustering and recall advocated by Pellegrino (1975) and others certainly seems appropriate. However, the interest in process would seem to imply that we need more measures of as many different aspects of our data as possible, not that clustering ought to be disregarded. It seems that clustering can be a convenient measure of overall organization, and it ought to be useful in helping to validate measures that more directly reflect processes at a microlevel.

Finally, clustering can serve several other important functions. It, of course, provides a metric for assessing the reasonableness of organization theory. Clustering can also provide important data on one aspect of conceptual functioning across different subject populations or among individuals. Further, clustering can, along with other measures, reflect the effects of instructional and situational manipulations on conceptual organization.

However, for clustering to be useful in the preceding contexts, the issue of identifying the best measure must be resolved. At present, choice of measures for the researcher is difficult and often based on idiosyncratic criteria at best. The recommendations in the measurement literature have often been contradictory and have been of little help. Until we have a better handle on the measurement problem, further research on clustering will be difficult and even the interpretation of past work will be confused.

B. What Is the Best Measure?

One's choice of a best measure clearly hinges on the choice of criteria for evaluation. Unfortunately, in the clustering literature no single set of criteria has been agreed upon. In fact, direct contradictions are frequent in the literature. The evaluation problem has led to a proliferation of measures—each one best on some, possibly unique, set of criteria. In the absence of a means to choose among criteria, the literature has often degenerated into a priori statements that one approach is better than another, or alternatively, into statements that no measure is really better than any other and that the best measure depends on the purpose (preference?) of the researcher. What is needed, it seems, is evidence comparing the characteristics of the measures and showing under which conditions one measure is more appropriate than another.

Since the publication of Colle's (1972) paper, a key concern in evaluating the measures has been the role of theory. Measures are most useful when relevant to theory, and completely atheoretical measurement is probably impossible. However, the exact shape of the relation between measurement and theory has not always been agreed upon. In the next section of the paper, the issues surrounding evaluation of measures are discussed in more detail.

C. The Relationship between Clustering Measures and Theory

The question of the relation between measure and theory raises an important issue: Which is to come first, the theory or the measure? A traditional view is that atheoretical measures are constructed first and that they provide data upon which theory is built. A more recent notion is that measures really serve theory. It is pointed out that if they are to provide a fair test of a theory, measures must meet certain theoretical assumptions. Here, in some sense, the theory comes first and the measure is chosen to test the theory.

Both of the main approaches to solving the clustering measures problem have adopted the "theory first" view. However, it is argued here that while theory and measure must be matched to some degree so that data are relevant to the theory, it is possible to have too close a match between measure and theory. The problem is that a measure may be constructed so that it must support the theory rather than providing a test of it.

While the theory of most concern in this paper is organization theory, it should be noted that we are dealing with a general problem. For instance, clustering has been used to investigate theories of memory development (Murphy, Puff, & Campione, 1977) along with theories of individual differences in verbal ability (Hunt, Frost, & Lunneborg, 1973), intelligence level (Gerjouy & Spitz, 1966), and anxiety level (Mueller, Carlomusto, & Marler, 1977). A good measure of clustering must provide data that are relevant to each theory, but we argue that if the measure is to test the theory it cannot be biased in its favor. For example, if a measure of organization was confounded with level of recall so that it always gave higher scores to longer recall outputs, we would certainly find that organization increases with age, intelligence, and possibly verbal ability as well with that measure.

The logic for evaluating the measures and its relation to organization theory is discussed next since organization theory is most directly relevant to work on the clustering measures.

1. THE THEORETICAL APPROACH

The key notion with this view is that measures of organization cannot be evaluated without reference to a theory of organization. Colle (1972) discusses the baseline theory, that items are generated for recall randomly. He effectively points out that the degree of rejection of this random model (the statistical significance of our ability to reject the baseline theory) is not necessarily the best basis for measuring organization. Instead, what is needed is a good theory of nonrandom recall that can be tested using clustering and other measures.

Along with arguing for theory in evaluating the clustering measures, Colle argues that certain measures are more appropriate for testing some theories than others. According to Colle, a fault with current approaches to measuring clustering is that the "class of theories to which a measure applies has not been made clear [p. 626]." Again, Colle is correct in that it makes little sense to attempt to test a theory with a measure that is not relevant to it. Associated with this notion is an emphasis on considering the underlying assumptions of the various measures. Shuell (1969, 1975) not unreasonably suggests that the assumptions underlying a measure be considered in determining its appropriateness for a given theoretical test. Shuell argues that there is no such thing as a "best" measure independent of the theory being tested and the experimental problem under investigation.

While the arguments described under the theoretical approach have some merit, this by now "accepted" view has led to several problems. Although the ideal approach to developing a measure involves grounding it in an adequate theory, such a theory of organization and recall does not exist at this time. In fact, it is just such a theory that we are attempting to construct when we use the nontheoretically based measures. In effect, we are left in a bind such that a good measure cannot be chosen without an adequate theory, but the measure may be needed to allow the theory to be worked out. While this is a difficult situation, rather than abandoning work on the measures for lack of a theory, we might better try to work on both theory and measures at the same time using improvements in the measures to improve theory, and vice versa.

A second problem is that it appears doubtful that analyzing the assumptions of the various measures is likely to lead to much progress. There are several difficulties here. First, as will be shown later in the chapter, the stated assumptions for some measures bear little relation to their mathematical properties. The Item Clustering Index (ICI) (Robinson, 1966), which is purportedly based on assumptions that are consistent with organizational and developmental theory, may have mathematical properties that make it completely inappropriate to test such theories. Second, for any given measure there are an indefinite number of possible assumptions. For example, the Modified Ratio of Repetition (MRR) and the Clustering Index (C) are based on different assumptions. MRR is the ratio of repetitions to the maximum possible number of repetitions, while C is the ratio of repetitions to the maximum range in possible repetitions. Despite the difference in formulas and "assumptions," these measures are the same whenever the minimum number of repetitions is zero and are, for all practical purposes, *identical*.

A third problem with the theoretical view involves how the notion of theoretical appropriateness has been applied. Here we are dealing with the empirical approach to measure validation.

2. THE EMPIRICAL APPROACH

The rationale for this approach rests heavily on the tenets of the theoretical view. It is argued that since the measures problem cannot be solved in the absence of theory, a reasonable theory should be chosen and used to evaluate the adequacy of the various measures. The measure that provides results most consistent with the reasonable theory is then deemed to be best. Sternberg and Tulving (1977) adopted this approach in evaluating the measures of subjective organization by assuming a simple version of organization theory "that increasing subjective organization underlies the improvement that occurs on successive trials of multi-trial free recall [p. 547]." They found that the subjective organization equivalent to the Difference Score (DS) (Bousfield & Bousfield, 1966) clustering measure was most highly correlated with recall level and therefore more consistent with the theory than the subjective organization equivalent to ARC (Gerjuoy & Spitz, 1966). They concluded that the difference score provides a more theoretically meaningful measure of organization than does the adjusted ratio measure.

Moely and Jeffrey (1974) adopted a similar empirical approach in evaluating several clustering measures. They argued, again based on organization theory, that a good clustering measure should be highly correlated with recall and with the number of items recalled in each category, but not with the number of categories recalled. They found ICI to be the best measure.

While providing interesting data, the empirical approaches suffer from a glaring defect. Finding that a measure *supports* a theory is not the same as choosing a measure that is *relevant* to the theory (which is what Colle appears to be arguing for). With the empirical approach to validating measures we may be picking as best those measures that, because of their mathematical properties, are built so that they must support our theory. By our choice of measures we may be confirming the very theory that we want to test. It is not surprising that a measure that is chosen to support a theory then provides data that are more "theoretically meaningful" than data from other measures. In effect, we may be assuming the correctness of the theory by our choice of measures. Later in the chapter we argue that the measures that have been chosen as best on the empirical approach are, in fact, artifactually correlated with recall level so that they must (at least under nonrandom conditions) support organization theory.

3. THE SIMULATION APPROACH

So far we have argued that organization theory, while not well developed, is an important key in the search to understand memory and that the development of the theory has been seriously hindered by the difficulties found in attempts to solve the measures problem. The theoretical approach provides only vague criteria to use in evaluating measures, and the empirical approach suffers from a serious circularity problem. If we use a theory to validate measures, we may end up choosing as most appropriate those measures that support the theory.

The approach adopted in this chapter is similar to one advocated by Colle (1972) and to that used by Dalrymple-Alford (1971). We argue that, reduced to the simplest criteria, measures of organization must have two characteristics: They must measure what they purport to measure (organization), and they must not measure other aspects of the recall situation that are irrelevant to, but possibly confounded with, organization (Dalrymple-Alford, 1970; Frankel & Cole, 1971). Measures such as the number of repetitions (r) and number of categories (c) may reflect organization, but they are also heavily influenced by and highly correlated with the level of recall. When asking questions about the relationship between organization and recall, we must have separate measures of the two processes. If our measure of organization is also a measure of recall, we assume a high relation. Measures of recall and organization, then, must be separate and not artifactually correlated.

However, as pointed out by Dalrymple-Alford (1971), in real data we do not know the relation between organization and recall independent of the measures of organization. Since there may, in fact, be a genuine relation between organization and recall in subjects' data (there certainly is, if organization theory is correct), we cannot test for the independence of the measures of organization and recall with real data. Rather, what is needed are simulation data for which the relation between organization and recall is known. We can simulate recall strings of different lengths using the same organizational rule (e.g., random recall) and see if the measures stay constant over list length (as they should) or if they have a built-in correlation with the level of recall.

Another aspect of the recall situation that might confound the measures of organization is the category structure of the *input* list. With a 24-item list we might find different amounts of clustering if there are 12 as opposed to only 2 categories of items. Any differences found, however, might be due to the characteristics of the clustering measures rather than the subject's organizational processes. Just as we can vary the length of the recall list and observe any artifactual effects on the measures, we can also vary the number of categories (and at the same time, of course, the number of items per category) in the 24-item list to see the effects of these variables on the clustering measures.

The approach in the simulation analysis is, in a sense, one of exclusion. While it is difficult to know exactly what a clustering measure should measure (in the absence of a good theory), we know what a good clustering measure should *not* measure. Aspects of the recall situation such as the number of categories in the input list and number of items recalled are conceptually different from organization and are likely to be confounded with other variables of interest. A good measure, first and foremost, should not be confounded with these variables. It must be capable of showing a relation, such as that between organization and recall, if it exists in real data, but also must be capable of not showing the relation if none is present in the data. Since possible confoundings cannot be assessed in real data independent of the measures themselves, a simulation approach has been adopted in this research.

D. What the Clustering Measures Measure

1. SIMPLE RATIO MEASURES

Typically, the degree of clustering in a subject's recall is inferred from a measure based on the number of category repetitions (r) (the number of times two words from the same category appear together in the output list). Since r would be expected to increase with increasing levels of recall, even if recall is random, a clustering measure can be constructed by dividing r by some value related to the number of items recalled (n). This attempt to remove the effects of recall level on the measure of clustering has resulted in a number of different simple ratio measures: LR (Bousfield, 1953; Lambert, Ignatow, & Krauthamer, 1968), RR (Cohen, Sakoda, & Bousfield, 1954), MRR (Wallace & Underwood, 1964; Bower, Lesgold, & Tieman, 1969), ICI (Robinson, 1966), and PC. The formulas and characteristics, where available for these measures, are presented in Table 3.1. The chance values are all derived from the formula for the

Table 3.1
Formulas and Characteristics of the Clustering Measures

Measure	Formula	Maximum	Minimum	Chance	Undefined
LR	r/n	$\max/n$	$\min/n$	$[(E-1)(n-1)]/[n(N-1)]$	$n = 0$
RR	$r/(n-1)$	$\max/(n-1)$	$\min/(n-1)$	$(E-1)/(N-1)$	$n \leq 1$
MRR	$r/(n-c)$	1.0	$\min/\max$	$[(E-1)(n-1)]/[(n-c)(N-1)]$	$n = c$
ICI	$r/[c(E-1)]$	$\max/[c(E-1)]$	$\min/[c(E-1)]$	$(n-1)/[c(N-1)]$	$n = 0$
PC	j/n	1.0			$n = 0$
DS	$r - E(r)$	$\max - E(r)$	$\min - E(r)$	0	$n = 0$
Z	$DS/[\mathrm{Var}(r)]^{\frac{1}{2}}$	$[\max - E(r)]/[\mathrm{Var}(r)]^{\frac{1}{2}}$	$[\min - E(r)]/[\mathrm{Var}(r)]^{\frac{1}{2}}$	0	$c = 1,$ $c = n$
ARC	$DS/[\max - E(r)]$	1.0	$[\min - E(r)]/[\max - E(r)]$	0	$c = 1,$ $c = n$
C	$(r - \min)/(\max - \min)$	1.0	0	0	$c = 1,$ $c = n$
D	$DS/(\max - \min)$	$[\max - E(r)]/(\max - \min)$	$[\min - E(r)]/(\max - \min)$	0	$c = 1,$ $c = n$
ACAT	$[E(c) - c]/[E(c) - \min(c)]$	1.0	$[E(c) - \min(c)]/[\max(c) - E(c)]$	0	$n = 1,$ $n \geq N-E$
STR	See text.	1.0		0	$n = 1,$ $n \geq N-1$

Note. The formulas are for a to-be-remembered list of N items with E exemplars in each category. There are r category repetitions occuring in a recall list of n items from c different categories. The maximum number of repetitions in the recall list, max, is $n - c$; the minimum number of repetitions, min, is $2n^{*}_{i} - n - 1$, where n^{*}_{i} is the number of items in the category with the most items recalled.

expected number of repetitions, given that n items are randomly sampled without replacement from the input list (Cohen et al., 1954; Frender & Doubilet, 1974).

2. ORDER MEASURES

While the simple ratio measures have a number of advantages, including ease of computation, they have recently come under criticism (e.g., Bousfield & Bousfield, 1966; Dalrymple-Alford, 1970; Frankel & Cole, 1971) because they are in part dependent on the category composition of the items remembered. For example, if the recall output is aabbcc (where a is an item from one category, b another, and so on), the subject has recalled two items from each of three categories and obtained the maximum possible number of repetitions. The score on the LR measure is $3/6 = .50$. A second subject recalling aaabaa has recalled five items from one category and one from the second and has the minimum possible number of repetitions. However, the score for the second subject is also $3/6 = .50$. The solution advocated by a number of investigators (e.g., Dalrymple-Alford, 1970) has been to restrict the meaning of clustering to the *order* of the recall output, given the category structure of the items recalled. A number of such order measures have been developed: DS (Bousfield & Bousfield, 1966), Z (Frankel & Cole, 1971; Hudson & Dunn, 1969), ARC (Gerjuoy & Spitz, 1966; Roenker et al., 1971), and C and D (Dalrymple-Alford, 1970). The formulas and characteristics of these measures are also shown in Table 3.1. It should be noted (Pellegrino, 1975) that the expected number of repetitions for these measures is based on the Bousfield and Bousfield (1966) formula for the expected number of repetitions given that n_i items (where n_i is the number of items recalled in the i_{th} category) are recalled from each of M categories. These measures then, take as a given the category structure of the output list and reflect the degree of nonchance ordering of the output.

While we have attempted to differentiate clearly the simple ratio measures from the order measures, it should be noted that this is a simplification. For example, when the minimum number of repetitions is zero, as is usually the case, the formula for the order measure C reduces to that of the ratio measure MRR. Nevertheless, the distinction between the two types of measures will be retained as an organizational tool.

3. STRUCTURE MEASURES

The order of the items recalled is not the only aspect of the free-recall output that can reflect organization. The category structure of the items recalled (which is a given for the order measures) can also be seen as reflecting nonrandom or organized recall processes (Hubert & Levin, 1976; Puff, 1963). The information of interest here is related not to the order of recall, but to the items chosen by the subject to be recalled. Specifically, we can ask whether the items recalled are a random sample of the items in the input list or whether they are sampled nonrandomly because of the categories present in the list. The items chosen for recall may themselves reflect the use of organization independent of their order. Now we go back to the two subjects who recalled *aabbcc* and *aaabaa* and assume that the input list had 24 items, with four different categories and 6 items in each. The question of interest for a category structure measure of organization would be to what degree are the two recall outputs of 6 items (three categories with 2 items in each, and two categories with 5 items in one and one in another) nonrandom? What degree of organization is shown in the category structure of the items recalled?

The category structure of recall output, which to our knowledge has not yet been investigated empirically would seem to be, potentially at least, as important as the order of item recall. A good measure of category structure organization would provide information that is independent of that from the order measures. Also, it might provide a new perspective on free-recall data. In this section several different approaches are discussed in an effort to develop a measure of this aspect of organization.

While a number of researchers have mentioned the category structure aspect of organization, none, with the exception of Kaufman and Puff (Puff, 1963), have attempted to develop measures of it. In constructing a measure of this type of organization, we have the same problems as with the measures of order. We need a measure that is not influenced by the number of items recalled, and, for that purpose, we need to be able to compute expected values due to chance. The first and most obvious candidates for measuring category structure are two summary statistics, the number of categories recalled (c) and the average number of items recalled per category *(wpc)*. However, while these measures describe the category structure of the output list, they also describe the number of items recalled and are not independent of n. In fact, $c \times wpc = n$. The problem here is that if recall increases, one or both of our measures of category structure must increase as well; recall level is now, at least in part, redundant with our measures of category structure. A solution is to treat n as a given value and pick either c or wpc as our measure of category structure. It does not matter which variable is picked as the basis of the structure measure, since with the value of n set, they are redundant. However, if we pick c as our measure of structure, we encounter the same problems as in using r as a clustering measure, since c is related to recall level even when the items picked for recall are chosen randomly. This problem can be handled in a manner analogous to that of the order measures by subtracting an expected value of the number of categories recalled (based on the number of items recalled) from the number of categories actually recalled. Since a reasonable hypothesis is that high levels of organization might be reflected in *fewer* categories recalled than expected, the measure is actually constructed by subtracting the observed from the expected so that it will be positive with high levels of organization. We can then use this difference score to construct other measures of category structure. For instance,

ACAT, analogous to ARC, would be a ratio of the difference between observed and expected categories to the maximum difference between observed and expected. We now have measures of the two important aspects of recall output organization (the category structure of the items chosen for recall and the order of these items). With each type of measure we can see whether recall is random or organized.

Before evaluating the individual measures, we shall look at the nature of category structure in more detail. Conceptually, category structure reflects the composition of the items chosen for recall. To derive a measure of organization, we have simplified this notion to a measure based on the number of categories recalled. In a 24-item list with four categories, the expected number of categories recalled if 6 items are remembered is 3.45. Our first subject (aabbcc) recalled three categories, while the second (aaabaa) recalled only two; and as reflected by the category structure measure, the recall of the second subject (ACAT = .59) does seem to be less random than that of the first (ACAT = .18). However, there are several problems with using the number of categories as the basis for our structure measure. First, if recall is greater than the number of items in the list minus the number of exemplars in each category (18 in this case), all categories must be recalled and our category structure measure is undefined. Second, our measure does not reflect within category patterns of nonrandomness. For example, if one subject recalls 12 items from four categories (4as, 3bs, 3cs, and 2ds) and a second subject also recalls 12 items from four categories (5as, 5bs, 1c, and 1d), our measure of category structure is the same for both. However, the first subject's recall seems somehow more random than the second's. Puff (1963) has provided an approach to this issue by asking what is the probability of randomly picking exactly n_i items (where n_i is the number of items from the i_{th} category) from each of the M categories in the list. Assuming random item selection we can determine the exact probability of the observed recall output structure (which for the first subject is .399 and for the second is .003), and we can also compute the exact probabilities of all other combinations of 12 items (see Table 3.2).

We are now in a position to construct another measure of category structure, STR. It is based on the hypergeometric distribution and takes into account the nonrandomness of both the number of categories recalled and the distribution of items within categories. We can order the possible outcomes from least to most likely (as is done in Table 3.2) and then base our measure on the probability of obtaining a recall combination as probable or less probable than the one obtained. To put the STR measure on the same scale as ARC and ACAT, we can conceptually subtract an expected value from the cumulative probability and divide by the maximum possible range. The conceptual formula simplifies so that in actually computing the STR measure, the cumulative probabilities for the category structure of the recall output, and for the next less likely structure, are summed and subtracted from 1.0. This yields a measure with a chance value of 0 and a maximum value of 1.0.

Table 3.2
Possibilities Associated with All Possible Combinations of 12 Items
Recalled from a 24-Item List with Four Categories

Category				Exact	Cumulative	
a	b	c	d	probability	probability	STR
6	6	0	0	.000	.000	1.000
6	5	1	0	.000	.000	1.000
6	3	3	0	.002	.002	.998
6	4	2	0	.002	.004	.994
6	4	1	1	.002	.006	.989
5	5	2	0	.002	.009	.985
5	5	1	1	.003	.012	.979
4	4	4	0	.005	.017	.971
6	2	2	2	.005	.022	.961
6	3	2	1	.016	.038	.941
5	4	3	0	.016	.054	.909
3	3	3	3	.059	.113	.833
5	3	3	1	.064	.177	.710
5	4	2	1	.072	.249	.575
4	4	2	2	.112	.361	.390
5	3	2	2	.120	.481	.158
4	4	3	1	.120	.601	−.081
4	3	3	2	.399	1.000	−.601

We now have three sets of clustering measures: the older simple ratio measures, the measures of ordering, and the proposed measures of category structure. We now turn to an evaluation of these measures.

II. THE SIMULATIONS

A. Purpose

With the simulated data the properties of the various measures are compared under several different conditions. It is argued that a good measure should be sensitive to differences in organization, but should not be affected by variables other than organization. Organization was varied using a rule that generates nonrandom (clustered) recall at a level of organization determined by a clustering parameter.

Two extraneous variables that have been confounded with organization in the literature were investigated. The length of the recall list (number of items remembered) was systematically varied with organization held constant to see any possible effects of this variable on the measures. With a constant level of organization, a good measure should not be affected by changes in the length of the recall list.

Also investigated in the simulations was the number of categories in the input list. Again with organization held constant, changes on this variable should not affect a good measure. In conjunction with the simulations, an experiment varying number of categories was conducted with real subjects to provide comparison data for the simulation and to demonstrate the importance of one's choice of measures.

B. The Measures and List Length

That the measures of clustering should be independent of recall when it is random has been agreed·upon by most researchers, and many of the clustering measures have been shown to be independent. Cohen et al. (1954) and Frender and Doubilet (1974) showed the expected value of RR to be constant over list length. Measures that subtract an expected number of repetitions from the observed repetitions have a constant chance value of zero over list length.

However, while not generally acknowledged in the literature (e.g., Frankel & Cole, 1971), the independence of recall and clustering measures is at least as important for ordered as for random recall if a clustering measure is to be a parameter estimate of organization rather than providing only a significance test for nonrandomness (Colle, 1972). With ordered recall, as with random, given a constant amount of nonrandomness across list length, the value of the clustering measure should be constant as well. Recall level and measures of organization should be uncorrelated as long as the same organizational rule is used to generate the strings of different lengths. For this requirement to be met, we obviously need an organizational rule. Ideally, we should use the organizational rule that is used by the subjects in our experiments (Colle, 1972). To do this, though, requires a fairly complete and accurate theory of free recall, and such a theory is what we are trying to discover by using the measure. An alternative approach is to arbitrarily pick an organizational rule that is both relatively simple and that generates recall strings that appear to fit our idea of nonrandomness. We can then compare the performance of the various measures under the nonrandom recall condition with random recall. While it should be kept in mind that the organizational rule used in the simulations is not the one used by real subjects, it is hoped that effects due to organization (where they appear in the simulations) will be of sufficient magnitude to convince us that almost any rule for generating nonrandom output should give similar results.

1. METHOD

For the simulations, the rule chosen to generate the nonrandom strings has an organization parameter X and samples without replacement. The first item to be output is chosen randomly, with succeeding items chosen in one of two ways. With a probability of X, an item after the first is picked so as to be a category repetition if this is possible (that is, if there are any more items left in the relevant category). If the item is not chosen to be a repetition (with a probability of $1 - X$), a category is picked randomly and one item is recalled from that category. If all items from that category have been sampled, new categories are chosen until the list item is generated. The value of X then determines the likelihood of a repetition, with $X = 1.0$ yielding perfectly ordered output. The probability of a repetition, assuming that one is possible, is $X + (1 - X)/k$, where k is the number of nonexhausted categories remaining. For purposes of our nonrandom simulations, the value of X has been set at .5 yielding, for a 24-item list with four categories, output strings such as *aacdd* with 5 items recalled, *bbbadddcc* with 9 items recalled, and *baddddbbddcbccaaacc* with 19 items. It is important to note that the different length strings were all generated according to the same rule with the same clustering parameter value. Therefore, the degree of organization present is the same, on the average, for strings of different lengths. Other values of X from .25 to .75 have been simulated for some lists with the measures, and the pattern of results to be reported does not appear to be greatly affected by the level of the clustering parameter chosen.

The simulations were all done for input lists of 24 items. The basic strategy was to generate random and constrained $(X = .5)$ strings of items of lengths 3, 5, 7, . . ., 23. Fifty strings were generated at each odd-number list length for the random and constrained conditions. As it was generated, each string was scored for the number of repetitions, number of items in each category, etc., and the most common measures of organization were then computed for each separate string. This procedure yielded 50 scores for each of the measures under random and constrained conditions for each of the 11 list lengths, and a total of 1100 stat subjects. The simulation was carried out separately for input lists with three and eight categories.

There are a number of ways to analyze the data from these simulations. One possibility is to compute the mean value of each measure under each experimental condition and then correlate these means with organization and list length. A good measure should be highly correlated with organizational level, but not related to list length or the number of categories. A problem with this approach is that given sufficient power (enough stat subjects in each cell), any small relation between a measure and a possibly confounding variable is reflected in high correlations, even though that relation might be unimportant for practical purposes. This problem arises because correlations with the means do not reflect the amount of within-group variability present.

An alternative approach, which was adopted here, is to view the simulation as a giant experiment with two levels of organization, 11 different levels of list length, and 50 subjects per cell. The analysis of variance can then be used to see the effects of the independent variables on each measure. The same problem arises with this approach as in the case of the means correlations, however, since the magnitude of the F values and their significance will be determined in part by the number of stat subjects in each cell. A solution is to use as the measure of primary interest the proportion of variance accounted for (Hays, 1963) by the various factors. The important question then becomes how much of the measure's variance is due to differences in organization, as compared to differences in list length, or their interaction? A good measure of organization should have a high proportion of its variance controlled by organization and little due to any of the other factors. The advantage of the proportion-of-variance-accounted-for measure is that it provides an estimate of the relative importance of the experimental effects that is not dependent on the power of the statistical test.

2. RESULTS AND DISCUSSION

In the first analysis, we look at the effects of the number of items recalled (string length) on the various measures. In Table 3.3 are shown the means of the simple ratio, order, and structure measures for random and organized recall over a wide range of list lengths for a 24-item list with three categories. Looking first at random recall, it is clear that whereas r, c, and wpc increase with recall level, most of the other measures seem relatively constant. The expected value of RR is $(E - 1)/(N - 1)$, where E is the number of exemplars per category and N is the number of items in the input list. This expected value for the 24-item list with three categories is $7/23 = .304$, which is well approximated by our random recall. The means that are corrected by subtracting an expected value should have a chance value of zero, and this seems well approximated by the order measures DS, Z, ARC, and D, and the structure measures ACAT and STR. The only clustering measures that look as if they might be correlated with string length for random recall are MRR and C, which go from about .50 to .30 with recall of 5 and 23 items, and ICI, which increases with recall from .06 to .29.

With organized recall, the pattern of data changes dramatically. Here, along with r, c, and wpc, several other measures, notably ICI, DS, and Z and possibly MRR and ACAT, seem strongly related to recall level. With recall level varying from 3 to 23 items, ICI increases from .18 to .66, DS increases from .06 to 7.06, and Z from .13 to 3.28. The value of MRR decreases from .90 to .69. With organization constant, as determined by the organizational rule, these measures show clear and systematic changes with recall level. While none of the measures investigated appears completely independent of recall, some are definitely better than others.

Under some conditions (shown in Table 3.1) many of the measures are undefined. This difficulty was treated in the present simulations by assigning a value of zero when the measure could not be computed. Thus, some dependence of the measures on list length can be explained by our procedure. Examples are the low values of ARC at list length three with organized recall,

Table 3.3

Simulated Means for the Three Types of Measures over List Length for Random and Organized Recall on a 24-Item List with Three Categories

n	r	Ratio					Order					Structure			
		LR	RR	MRR	ICI	PC	DS	Z	ARC	C	D	c	wpc	ACAT	STR
							RANDOM								
3	.60	.20	.30	.50	.06	.37	.00	.00	.00	.40	.00	2.20	1.50	.00	.06
5	1.24	.25	.31	.51	.07	.44	−.02	−.02	−.02	.49	.00	2.60	2.00	−.02	.07
7	1.86	.27	.31	.46	.09	.47	.15	.15	.07	.45	.04	2.96	2.38	.07	−.16
9	2.44	.27	.31	.40	.12	.48	.05	.04	.01	.40	.01	2.96	3.06	.01	−.15
11	3.08	.28	.31	.39	.15	.51	.10	.07	.02	.39	.01	3.00	3.67	.02	−.03
13	3.50	.27	.29	.35	.17	.47	−.11	−.07	−.02	.35	−.01	3.00	4.33	−.02	−.05
15	4.18	.28	.30	.35	.20	.49	−.09	−.06	−.01	.35	−.01	3.00	5.00	.00	−.02
17	4.84	.28	.30	.35	.23	.50	−.04	−.02	.00	.35	.00	3.00	5.67	.00	−.08
19	5.30	.28	.29	.33	.25	.48	−.17	−.09	−.02	.33	−.01	3.00	6.33	.00	−.03
21	6.12	.29	.31	.34	.29	.52	.04	.02	.00	.34	.00	3.00	7.00	.00	.00
23	6.04	.26	.27	.30	.29	.46	−.66	−.30	−.05	.30	−.03	3.00	7.67	.00	.00
							ORGANIZED (X = .5)								
3	1.46	.49	.73	.90	.18	.79	.06	.13	.18	.34	.06	1.46	2.33	.61	.38
5	2.88	.58	.72	.91	.28	.83	.50	.69	.50	.59	.26	1.90	3.08	.47	.62
7	3.72	.53	.62	.81	.25	.78	.92	1.02	.51	.70	.29	2.46	3.10	.23	.57
9	5.26	.58	.66	.80	.33	.83	1.59	1.40	.55	.72	.33	2.42	3.87	.57	.66
11	6.52	.59	.65	.79	.36	.84	2.49	1.89	.58	.75	.36	2.72	4.18	.28	.65
13	7.74	.60	.65	.77	.39	.84	3.10	2.11	.57	.74	.34	2.90	4.55	.10	.75
15	9.00	.60	.64	.75	.43	.85	4.18	2.54	.58	.75	.35	3.00	5.00	.00	.60
17	9.94	.59	.62	.71	.47	.85	4.41	2.44	.52	.71	.32	3.00	5.67	.00	.75
19	11.96	.63	.66	.75	.57	.88	6.16	3.21	.60	.75	.39	3.00	6.33	.00	.71
21	13.34	.64	.67	.74	.64	.88	7.12	3.49	.60	.74	.40	3.00	7.00	.00	.47
23	13.76	.60	.63	.69	.66	.84	7.06	3.28	.53	.69	.35	3.00	7.67	.00	.00

the zero values of ACAT whenever recall is 15 or greater (note that if recall is 17 or more the subject must recall items from all three categories and ACAT must be zero), and finally the zero value of STR with 23 items recalled (the category structure of 23 items remembered must be 8 items from two categories and 7 from the third). The assignment of zero to undefined scores makes some of the measures appear worse than they otherwise might be. This conservative procedure was used because, first, it is often used by researchers, and second, because being undefined for some list lengths *is* a problem that makes a measure less useful to the researcher.

These descriptive impressions of the behavior of the measures with list length are supported by the analysis of variance on the data described and a corresponding analysis of a 24-item list with eight categories. The factors in the analysis were organization (2) and list length (11) with 50 stat subjects per cell. The values shown in Table 3.4 are the proportions of variance accounted for in each of the measures by the factors and their interaction. Dashes represent nonsignificant effects and negligible amounts of variance.

Most of the variance of an ideal measure should be due to organization,

Table 3.4
Proportion of Variance Accounted for by Organizaton, List Length, and the List Length by Organization Interaction for 24-Item Lists with Three and Eight Categories

Measure	Three Categories			Eight Categories		
			Organization			Organization
	Organi-zation	List length	× List length	Organi-zation	List length	× List length
			RATIO			
LR	.559	.021	—[a]	.672	—	—
RR	.524	—	—	.621	.006	.015
MRR	.451	.053	—	.563	.031	—
ICI	.371	.331	.031	.603	.031	.011
PC	.471	.014	—	.670	—	—
			ORDER			
DS	.370	.167	.203	.448	.186	.180
Z	.420	.102	.126	.492	.146	.137
ARC	.265	.012	.013	.441	.023	.011
C	.247	.030	.056	.492	.065	.016
D	.342	.026	.030	.508	.045	.030
			STRUCTURE			
c	.060	.478	.075	.066	.835	.017
wpc	.010	.906	.011	.126	.598	.047
ACAT	.101	.135	.128	.373	.063	.062
STR	.132	.029	.028	.376	.036	.043

[a]Dashes denote effects that were not significant at the .05 level. These effects accounted for negligible amounts of variance.

and for the simple ratio measures, with one exception, at least 45% of the variance is due to organization. However, with the three-category list, ICI fared poorly, weighing almost as highly on list length as on organization. Analyses of other list structures have shown ICI to be strongly related to list length with 2, 3, and 4 categories and much less so with 6, 8, and 12 categories. The MRR measure's means looked to be strongly related to string length, but the effect controlled relatively small amounts of variance (less than 6%) as compared to organization (about 50%).

As a group the order measures came out somewhat less well than the ratio measures. In general less of their variance was due to organization, and a good deal of the variance in DS (37%) and Z (25%) was due to the list length and List length × Organization interaction effects. Looking at the means in Table 3.3, we can see that DS and Z, while unrelated to recall level with random recall, are highly related with constrained recall. Of the other three order measures, somewhat less of ARC's variance is due to organization, but considerably less is due to the confounding variables. Overall, whereas these measures are similar, ARC may be the best of the three.

Finally, the measures of category structure, as a group, appear to be by far the worst. The c and wpc measures are clearly not measures of organization at all. In no case is more than 15% of the variance of either one due to organization; 47 to 90% of their variance is due to the number of items recalled. The pattern of data shown here is supported by analysis of other list structures. In no case is the variance for either measure greater for organization than for list length. While c and wpc can certainly be viewed as components of recall, they are not measures of organization.

The other measures of category structure, ACAT and STR, fared less poorly than c and wpc, but a fairly small amount of their variance is due to organization (10–37%). With ACAT, 26% and 13% of the variance is due to list length and to the interaction in the three- and eight-category lists, respectively. While ACAT and STR seem similar in the eight-category case, STR appears clearly superior to ACAT when there are few categories in the list. This is not surprising since with few categories and fairly high levels of recall, items from each of the categories are recalled, leaving ACAT a score of zero, whereas there is still room for an unequal distribution of items that can be reflected as organization in STR.

The results of this analysis allow some fairly clear conclusions. The c and wpc measures are not measures of organization; they are measures of recall. The commonly used clustering measures ICI, DS, and Z are seriously confounded with recall level. If recall is organized, DS and Z may artifactually show subjects who recall more to be organizing more as well. The ICI measure is confounded with both random and organized recall if there are relatively few categories in the list. It appears that if recall levels are likely to vary in an experiment due to conditions or to the groups chosen (e.g., younger versus older children), these measures are less than optimal.

C. The Measures and the Number of Categories in the Input List

Just as some clustering measures are confounded with recall level, some may also be artifactually related to the number of categories in the study list. However, while the relation of the measures and recall level has been investigated extensively in the empirical literature, data on the relation of clustering and number of categories are available for only a few of the measures. In an effort to remedy this situation, an experiment varying number of categories was performed in parallel, with both real and simulated subjects. In the simulation, the degree of organization could be held constant so that artifactual variations in the measures could be observed. Our interest centers on the empirical relation obtained between the measures and the number of categories in real data, and in possible confoundings of number of categories and the clustering measures. Data on characteristics of the measures as a function of number of categories should also be useful to facilitate comparisons of results across experiments having different input list structures.

1. METHOD

In the study with real subjects being conducted in collaboration with C. R. Puff, different groups of college students received five trials on 24-item lists having either 2, 3, 4, 6, 8, or 12 categories. The exemplars in each category were either of high (e.g., *dog, tiger)* or low (e.g., *turkey, kangaroo)* strength. Subjects were then split into the highest and lowest thirds on clustering as defined by the ARC measure. There were, therefore, two levels of category strength, six category input list structures, and two levels of clustering with six subjects per group.

The simulation first involved a comparison of random and organized recall to allow assessment of the amount of variance due to organization. List length was also varied, but for purposes of economy, only list lengths 9 and 19 were used. The final variable was number of categories (2, 3, 4, 6, 8, or 12) in the input list. The design is then organization (2) by list length (2) by number of categories (6) with 50 stat subjects per cell.

2. RESULTS AND DISCUSSION

With the real data our initial interest is in the two measures, STR and ACAT, which are proposed in this paper. Is organization due to the items chosen for recall actually found in real subjects' data? The findings in the study provide a clear answer to this question—yes (sometimes). Specifically, when the list consisted of 2, 3, or 4 categories, no structure organization was found for either measure. However, as the number of categories increased from 6 to 12, subjects high in ARC clustering showed increases in both ACAT and STR.

With number of categories increasing from 6 to 12, ACAT increased from .15 to .53 and STR increased from .18 to .53. Although these data provide some encouraging evidence for category structure organization, we do not know yet whether the interaction with number of categories is real or whether it is built into the measures of category structure.

The real data means for each measure across number of categories are shown in Table 3.5. The main effect of number of categories was significant ($p < .01$) for all measures except recall level. However, there appear to be three different patterns of data. The ACAT and STR measures show increasing item selection organization with increasing number of categories. The measures DS, Z, ARC, D, and possibly ICI find an increase in clustering from two up to four or six categories followed by a decrease in organization with more categories in the list. Finally, the rest of the clustering measures—LR, RR, MRR, PC, and C—all show decreases in organization with number of categories. The finding that organization seems to increase, to decrease, or to increase and then decrease as a function of number of categories, depending on the measure chosen, is disconcerting. We will look next at the simulated data to see if they can aid in interpretation of these results.

Table 3.5
Real Data Means for the Measures as a Function of Number of Categories in a 24-Item List

Measure	Number of categories					
	2	3	4	6	8	12
n^a	16.19	16.67	17.48	16.86	17.16	16.13
r	11.54	10.55	10.33	8.73	6.34	4.02
			RATIO			
LR	.69	.60	.56	.47	.33	.23
RR	.74	.64	.60	.50	.35	.24
MRR	.79	.73	.74	.70	.57	.57
ICI	.52	.50	.52	.51	.42	.40
PC	.89	.81	.80	.71	.55	.46
			ORDER			
DS	4.28	5.78	6.77	6.57	4.87	3.27
Z	2.12	3.03	3.90	4.50	3.90	3.65
ARC	.56	.58	.62	.61	.48	.51
C	.77	.73	.74	.70	.57	.58
D	.29	.38	.46	.49	.41	.44
			STRUCTURE			
c	2.00	2.99	3.95	5.63	7.38	9.76
wpc	8.10	5.57	4.34	2.97	2.30	1.63
ACAT	.00	.00	.02	.10	.12	.34
STR	−.02	−.01	−.03	.19	.16	.30

[a] Mean differences for this variable are not significant at the .05 level. Differences for the other variables are significant at at least the .01 level.

The means for random and ordered simulated recall across number of categories are shown in Table 3.6. The results of the analyses of variance are shown in Table 3.7. Along with the columns for each of the effects and interactions, there is a total column that is the sum of the variance due to all of the effects *except* organization and error. Data in this column can be compared with the variance due to organization to provide an overall idea of the worth of each measure.

All of the simple ratio measures have a substantial portion of variance due to organization, and as expected, ICI also has a substantial variance due to

Table 3.6
Simulated Means for the Three Types of Measures with Random and Constrained Recall over Six Different Input List Structures

Measure		\multicolumn{6}{c}{Number of Categories–Input List}					
		2	3	4	6	8	12
\multicolumn{8}{c}{RATIO}
LR	R[a]	.42	.28	.21	.13	.09	.04
	O[a]	.69	.61	.55	.47	.40	.30
RR	R	.46	.30	.23	.14	.10	.04
	O	.75	.66	.60	.51	.43	.33
MRR	R	.50	.37	.32	.25	.21	.14
	O	.82	.77	.75	.73	.74	.72
ICI	R	.28	.19	.15	.11	.09	.05
	O	.46	.45	.45	.47	.46	.53
PC	R	.67	.48	.39	.25	.18	.07
	O	.91	.86	.81	.73	.67	.60
\multicolumn{8}{c}{ORDER}
DS	R	−.06	−.06	.24	.12	.23	−.04
	O	2.86	3.88	3.99	4.32	4.09	3.32
Z	R	−.10	−.02	.16	.10	.19	−.06
	O	1.68	2.30	2.59	3.17	3.53	3.74
ARC	R	−.06	−.00	.03	.02	.02	−.02
	O	.52	.58	.60	.63	.68	.66
C	R	.44	.36	.32	.25	.21	.14
	O	.69	.73	.74	.73	.74	.72
D	R	−.03	−.00	.02	.02	.02	−.01
	O	.31	.36	.39	.45	.52	.55
\multicolumn{8}{c}{STRUCTURE}
c	R	2.00	2.98	3.97	5.55	7.16	9.48
	O	1.95	2.71	3.45	4.74	6.10	7.97
wpc	R	7.00	4.70	3.52	2.49	1.91	1.44
	O	7.23	5.10	4.03	2.91	2.25	1.74
ACAT	R	−.00	.01	−.02	.03	−.04	.00
	O	.05	.28	.26	.45	.50	.76
STR	R	.00	−.09	−.07	.09	−.01	−.10
	O	.57	.68	.76	.75	.77	.80

[a]R = Random; O = Ordered.

Table 3.7
**Proportion of Variance Accounted for by Organization, List Length,
Number of Categories, and Their Interactions for the Clustering Measures**

Mea-sure	Organi-zation (O)	List length (N)	Category structure (S)	OS	NS	ON	ONS	Total of confounding variables
			RATIO					
LR	.449	.002	.310	.005	.003	—	—	.321
RR	.449	—[a]	.308	.005	—	.001	—	.317
MRR	.548	.018	.057	.019	.004	.001	—	.100
ICI	.526	.088	.020	.041	.033	.003	—	.187
PC	.481	.001	.248	.025	—	—	—	.277
			ORDER					
DS	.459	.133	.012	.006	—	.104	.006	.263
Z	.499	.075	.038	.029	.004	.055	.008	.209
ARC	.530	—	.008	—	.006	.002	—	.018
C	.501	.007	.022	.029	.018	—	—	.078
D	.520	.001	.025	.019	—	—	—	.049
			STRUCTURE					
c	.018	.085	.767	.009	.087	.005	.001	.954
wpc	.006	.181	.669	.000	.108	.004	.001	.963
ACAT	.250	.034	.083	.083	.027	.028	.032	.287
STR	.390	—	.005	.008	—	.000	.002	.019

[a] Dashes denote effects that were not significant at the .05 level. These effects accounted for negligible amounts of variance.

other factors such as list length. However, with RR and LR, both of which have come out well in previous analyses, over 30% of the variance is due to the category structure variable. As can be seen in Table 3.6, their means decrease with increasing number of categories in the input list. We can see why this occurs for random recall by looking at the chance expected values in Table 3.1. Both have number of category exemplars (E) only in their numerators. With increases in the number of categories, the number of exemplars decreases and so do the expected values of LR and RR. With MRR, c, which increases with the number of categories in the list, is subtracted from the denominator; this appears to compensate in part for the decrease in E.

It is now clear why organization (as measured by RR, LR, and PC) appeared to be decreasing with number of categories in the data from real subjects. These clustering measures are artifactually related to the number of categories in the input list. The negative correlation with number of categories is built into the measures and is relatively independent of the nature of the data.

With the order measures, results are less surprising as none are seriously confounded with number of categories. They all have a large amount of variance controlled by organization, but DS and Z have over 20% controlled by other factors, mainly the list length main effect and the List length × Organization interaction. Of the other three measures, ARC is again the least confounded with extraneous factors, with less than 2% of its variance due to effects other than organization.

Several of the category structure measures again came out badly, with c and wpc having less than 2% of their variance due to organization and over 66% now due to the category structure of the input list. This pattern would be expected since the range of each measure is determined by the number of categories and the number of items in each. Of the remaining measures, STR clearly came out better than ACAT. More of its variance is due to organization (39% versus 25%) and less than 2% is due to other factors as compared to ACAT's 29%.

With the exception of wpc and c, none of the order or structure measures are seriously confounded with number of categories in the input list. The simulation data then do not aid in interpreting the effect of number of categories for these unconfounded measures. Two measures of choice have emerged, however. Based on the simulations, ARC is the best order measure, and STR is the best structure measure. A problem is that STR finds organization to be increasing with number of categories, whereas organization increases and then decreases with ARC. A possible interpretation is that one of these results must be wrong. However, because these measures were constructed to tap different aspects of recall data, it is also possible that the two different patterns are real reflections of the two types of organization.

The separate measures interpretation can be correct only if ARC and STR are statistically unrelated in simulation data (where a real relation between order and structure is not present). The simplest way to find out is to correlate the values of the measures for the simulations. Four list structures were chosen, a 24-item list with 2, 4, 6, and 12 categories, and separate correlations were computed for random and ordered recall with list length varying from 3 to 23 items and with a total of 550 stat subjects contributing to each analysis. The results for three of the best measures, ARC, RR, and STR, are shown in Table 3.8. The most important aspect of these data is fairly clear. Both the order and

Table 3.8
Correlations of ARC, STR, and RR

Number of categories		ARC–STR	ARC–RR	STR–RR
2	R[a]	.002	.765	.295
	O[a]	−.121	.437	.397
4	R	−.036	.800	.013
	O	−.056	.421	.318
6	R	.039	.730	.255
	O	.142	.510	.420
12	R	.003	.745	.175
	O	.224	.853	.428

[a] R = Random; O = Ordered.

structure measures show positive correlations with RR while ARC and STR are not, in general, correlated with each other. The lack of correlation fits nicely with the theoretical desirability of having independent measures of order and structure. The correlations of RR with the other measures indicate that it is best viewed as a measure of both order and structure of the recall output. Since RR is more highly correlated with ARC than STR in all of the simulations run, RR may weigh more heavily on the order than the structure aspect of organization.

III. CONCLUSIONS: HOW THE RESULTS OF THE SIMULATIONS BEAR UPON THE ISSUES

A. Clustering and Number of Categories

Organization due to item order and item selection (category structure) was obtained in our data with real subjects. The simulation data showed the order measure, ARC, and the structure measure, STR, to be unconfounded with number of categories. Most of the simple ratio measures, along with wpc and c, were found to be artifactually correlated with number of categories. Thus, the decrease in clustering with number of categories found with the simple ratio measures in the real data is an artifact. It is due to their mathematical characteristics, not to a genuine relation between number of categories and organization in real subjects' data.

Measures such as LR and RR are thus not optimal if the category structure of the items in the input list is different for different subjects—as when longer lists are given to older than to younger children, or when category structure is a variable of interest in the study (e.g., Dallet, 1964; Earhard, 1967; Tulving & Pearlstone, 1966; Weist, 1970).

Interestingly, the relation between organization and number of categories seems to depend on the type of organization being looked at. Clustering due to item order increases and then decreases as number of categories increases, replicating the results of Weist (1970) and Dallet (1964), who used ARC and DS, respectively. However, clustering due to item selection is at chance with 2, 3, or 4 categories but then increases with number of categories. Thus, while ordering items by category seems to be a prevalent outcome with all list structures (although order clustering is lowest with 8 and 12 categories), organization of the items chosen appears only when a fairly large number of categories are present in the study list. There also seems to be a relation between the two types of organization in real subjects' data, because only groups high in order clustering were found to show item selection organization. Since findings such as these could not have been obtained using a single measure, the multiple-measures approach advocated by Pellegrino and Battig (1974) seems clearly appropriate.

B. Clustering and Recall Level

In the simulations, several measures (notably ICI, DS, and Z) were found to be highly artifactually related to level of recall under nonrandom conditions. We argued that these measures are inappropriate as tests of organization theory because the positive correlation between organization and recall is built into these measures and, therefore, cannot be assessed in the data. Similarly, a developmental theory predicting that organization should increase with age ought not be tested with these measures. The problem here is that recall level virtually always increases with age, so that comparisons of organization and age also involve comparisons of organization and recall level.

If some measures are importantly confounded with recall, their pattern of data should be to some degree predictable. That is, the measures that are artifactually correlated with recall should be most likely to show patterns of data similar to recall and show differences on variables that are related to recall. We will discuss several studies that allow for this type of test. It should be noted that we are ignoring the many instances when no differences between measures are obtained (e.g., Puff, 1973). Our interest here is in trying to make sense out of differences in patterns when these are obtained.

Moely and Jeffrey (1974) compared children trained in grouping and untrained children over two sessions on recall and five measures of clustering— DS, ICI, Z, RR, and MRR. Three of the five measures (ICI, DS, and Z) showed significant positive correlations with recall. Recall level was found to be related to the independent variables of training and session. All of the clustering measures showed an effect due to session, but only three showed a significant effect of training—ICI, DS, and Z. The similar findings with recall and the ICI, DS, and Z measures are exactly what would be expected based on the simulations. The close relation with recall obtained appears to be built into these measures rather than necessarily being present in the data.

Paris (1978) investigated recall and organization across trials for second- and sixth-grade children. Recall was found to increase with practice for the older but not for the younger children. Organization was assessed with RR, ARC, and Z, and significant increases in organization with practice were found with all measures. However, only the Z-score measure also showed an interaction identical to that found in recall—more improvement in organization for older than for younger children with practice. Again, the similar patterns, for the Z-score measure and recall are predictable from the simulation findings.

The data from Moely and Jeffrey and from Paris, while consistent with our conclusions, represent only two situations, and the generality of the measure-theory confounding is still open to question. Data that may help here are reported in Murphy, Puff, and Campione (1977). Studies that investigated organization as a function of age were divided into those using the measures found to be correlated with recall (ICI, DS, and Z), and those using measures less likely to be confounded (RR, MRR, and ARC). The key question was: Do older children organize more than younger children? For the 18 studies using a confounded measure, 94% found at least one significant increase in clustering as a function of age. Only 64% of the 14 studies using the unconfounded measures found such an increase. When measures that are confounded with recall level are used to test age differences in organization, the almost inevitable result is that older children appear to organize more. On the other hand, with the unconfounded measures, the findings are somewhat less consistent. These measures allow a test of the age–organization relationship rather than providing a certain confirmation of it. Since most studies with the good measures showed increases in clustering with age, the developmental–organizational theory is supported. However, the strength of the relation between these variables appears variable.

C. Subjective Organization and Recall Level

A recent and important paper by Sternberg and Tulving (1977) deals with the measurement of subjective organization. Because the measurement issues are similar in subjective organization and clustering, we will briefly outline Sternberg and Tulving's approach and contrast it with the type of approach adopted in this chapter. The basic unit of measurement for subjective organization (the intertrial repetition—ITR) is different from that in clustering, however a number of measures are similar in the two areas. A difference score, DS', can be constructed by subtracting an expected from the observed number of ITRs (Bousfield & Bousfield, 1966). This difference score can be divided by a maximum minus an expected value to form an ARC' measure (Pellegrino, 1971). In the simple two-trial case, Tulving's (1962) subjective organization measure (SO) becomes the observed over the maximum possible number of ITRs, which is analogous to the MRR clustering measure.

Sternberg and Tulving (1977) evaluated the measures of subjective organization using random simulations and real subjects' data. The measures were validated against organization theory so that a good measure was seen as one that was highly related to recall in real data, but not artifactually correlated with recall in the random simulations. DS' was found to be the best measure of subjective organization, and ARC' the worst.

Murphy, Sanders, and Puff (1978) argued that the procedure of validating the measures against organization theory may have led Sternberg and Tulving to choose, as best, a measure that is biased in favor of that theory. In a simulation similar to those in this paper, Murphy et al. investigated constant nonrandom organization, as well as data generated randomly. The difference score measure was found to be unrelated to recall under random conditions, but as with the clustering difference score, DS' varied strongly with recall under nonrandom conditions. In contrast, ARC' was sensitive to differences in organization, but did not vary with recall under random or nonrandom conditions as long as the level of organization was constant. Murphy *et al.* concluded that the correlation found by Sternberg and Tulving between DS' and recall with real subjects' data is artifactual because this correlation is also obtained in simulation data with organization constant. Murphy *et al.* argued that ARC' is the best measure and DS' the worst, conclusions exactly the opposite of those of Sternberg and Tulving.

Sternberg and Tulving's reanalysis of the Laurence (1966) study shows that one's choice of measures does make a difference. In the areas of both clustering and subjective organization, it is clear that small differences in evaluation criteria can have large effects on the outcome of the evaluation.

D. Conclusions

The approach adopted in this chapter is not a final solution to the measures problem in clustering. Such a solution awaits better theories. However, we have shown under which circumstances some of the measures are confounded with variables extraneous to organization, such as list length and the number of categories in the input list. Thus, the approach does help in deciding which measures not to use. Our approach should not be viewed as being atheoretical, because the constraining rule that generates nonrandom recall serves as a primitive theory. If one wishes to pick a measure that is unconfounded with such variables as recall level, however, it is unlikely that other rules would produce greatly different results. For example, since DS is computed by subtracting a relatively constant term $[E(r)]$ from a term that can greatly increase with recall level (r), any circumstances that lead to close to maximum organization or to a constant proportion of the maximum should lead DS to increase dramatically with recall. As Colle (1972) points out, Z also increases with recall level because DS is in its numerator.

We have argued that research on clustering can be of value, even though there is not a one-to-one correspondence between the processes underlying the production of clustering and the measures of it. At this point, an adequate process model has not been worked out, and direct measurement of many of the hypothesized underlying processes is difficult at best. The existing measures of organization can, however, provide information to aid in the development of better theories. Clearly though, the practice of arbitrarily choosing one measure of only one aspect of organization is less than ideal. The effects of organization on recall can be more fully understood by investigating as many different types of organization (i.e., subjective organization, priority of recall for newly remembered items, clustering), as possible on the same set of data.

If clustering is to be studied, an appropriate measure must be chosen. We have argued that this choice should be based on the mathematical characteristics of the measures and on how these characteristics are related to the research problem of interest. Probably the best procedure for selecting a measure at this point is to select from the measures that are not correlated with potentially confounding variables in the experimental situation. If only one measure is to be used, ARC, RR, or MRR might be a reasonable selection, depending on whether or not the number of categories in the input list is varied (either by the experimenter or by the subject in a sorting paradigm such as Mandler's, 1967). A much better approach would be to use both order and item measures—that is, ARC and STR. These measures are relatively unconfounded with extraneous factors and allow a two-dimensional look at organization. They also have the advantage of sharing the same measurement scale (0 = chance, 1 = perfect organization) as measures of subjective organization (Pellegrino, 1971) and priority (Flores & Brown, 1974), so that a number of different measures can be directly compared on the same data.

Research on organization in memory has made good progress since the early work by Bousfield. Understanding the restructuring of information in accord with what is already known in the semantic system is clearly an important aspect of understanding the functioning of memory. Organization theory is a key component of this understanding. It is hoped that work such as that reported in this chapter can help to alleviate difficulties with the choice of measures so that research on organization in memory can advance in a productive manner.

ACKNOWLEDGMENTS

Preparation of this chapter was supported by the Department of Psychology and the Computer Center at The University of Akron.

Thanks are due to R. Sanders and F. Schmitt for their helpful comments on several drafts of this chapter. C. R. Puff provided support and ideas throughout the course of this work as well as many helpful suggestions on earlier drafts of the chapter.

LIST OF ABBREVIATIONS

ARC—adjusted ratio of clustering
ACAT—ARC for categories
c—categories recalled
C—clustering index
D—deviation index
DS—difference score
ICI—item clustering index
ITR—intertrial repetition
LR—original ratio of repetition
MRR—modified ratio of repetition
PC—percentage clustering
r—repetitions
RR—ratio of repetition
SO—subjective organization
STR—structure

wpc – items per category
Z score – normalized repetition score
E – exemplars in a category
max – maximum possible repetitions
min – minimum possible repetitions
M – categories in the input list
n – items recalled
N – items in the input list

REFERENCES

Battig, W. F., Allen, M. M., & Jensen, A. R. Priority of free recall of newly learned items. *Journal of Verbal Learning and Verbal Behavior*, 1965, *4*, 175–179.

Bousfield, A. K., & Bousfield, W. A. Measurement of clustering and of sequential constancies in repeated free recall. *Psychological Reports*, 1966, *19*, 935–942.

Bousfield, W. A. The occurrence of clustering in the recall of randomly arranged associates. *Journal of Genetic Psychology*, 1953, *49*, 229–240.

Bower, G. H., Lesgold, A. M., & Tieman, D. Grouping operations in free recall. *Journal of Verbal Learning and Verbal Behavior*, 1969, *8*, 481–493.

Buschke, H. Two-dimensional recall: Immediate identification of clustering in episodic and semantic memory. *Journal of Verbal Learning and Verbal Behavior*, 1977, *16*, 201–215.

Cohen, B. H. Recall of categorized word lists. *Journal of Experimental Psychology*, 1963, *66*, 227–234.

Cohen, B. H. Some-or-none characteristics of coding behavior. *Journal of Verbal Learning and Verbal Behavior*, 1966, *5*, 182–187.

Cohen, B. H., Sakoda, J. M., & Bousfield, W. A. *The statistical analysis of the incidence of clustering in the recall of randomly arranged associates.* (Tech. Rep. No. 10). University of Connecticut, Contract NONR 631(00), Office of Naval Research, July 1954. (NTIS No. PB-117628).

Colle, H. A. The reification of clustering. *Journal of Verbal Learning and Verbal Behavior*, 1972, *11*, 624–633.

Dallett, K. M. Number of categories and category information in free recall. *Journal of Experimental Psychology*, 1964, *68*, 1–12.

Dalrymple-Alford, E. C. Measurement of clustering in free recall. *Psychological Bulletin*, 1970, *74*, 32–34.

Dalrymple-Alford, E. C. Some further observations on the measurement of clustering in free recall. *British Journal of Psychology*, 1971, *62*, 327–334.

Earhard, M. Cued recall and free recall as a function of the number of items per cue. *Journal of Verbal Learning and Verbal Behavior*, 1967, *6*, 257–263.

Flores, L. M., Jr., & Brown, S. C. Comparison of output order in free recall. *Behavior Research Methods and Instrumentation*, 1974, *6*, 385–388.

Frankel, F., & Cole, M. Measures of category clustering in free recall. *Psychological Bulletin*, 1971, *76*, 39–44.

Frender, R., & Doubilet, P. More on measures of category clustering in free recall—although probably not the last word. *Psychological Bulletin*, 1974, *81*, 64–66.

Gerjuoy, I. R., & Spitz, H. H. Associative clustering in free recall: Intellectual and developmental variables. *American Journal of Mental Deficiency*, 1966, *70*, 918–927.

Hays, W. L. *Statistics*. Chicago: Holt, Rinehart, and Winston, 1963.

Hubert, L. J., & Levin, J. R. A general statistical framework for assessing categorical clustering in free recall. *Psychological Bulletin*, 1976, *83*, 1072–1080.

Hudson, R. L., & Dunn, J. E. A major modification of the Bousfield (1966) measure of category clustering. *Behavior Research Methods and Instrumentation*, 1969, *1*, 110–111.

Hunt, E., Frost, N., & Lunneborg, C. Individual differences in cognition: A new approach to intelligence. In G. H. Bower (Ed.), *The psychology of learning and motivation* (Vol. 7). New York: Academic Press, 1973.

Lambert, W. E., Ignatow, M., & Krauthamer, M. Bilingual organization in free recall. *Journal of Verbal Learning and Verbal Behavior*, 1968, 7, 207–214.

Laurence, M. W. Age differences in performance and subjective organization in free-recall learning of pictorial material. *Canadian Journal of Psychology*, 1966, 20, 388–399.

Mandler, G. Organization and memory. In K. W. Spence & J. T. Spence (Eds.), *The psychology of learning and motivation* (Vol. I). New York: Academic Press, 1967.

Moely, B. E., & Jeffery, W. E. The effect of organization training on children's free recall of category items. *Child Development*, 1974, 45, 135–143.

Mueller, J. H., Carlomusto, M., & Marler, M. Recall as a function of method of presentation and individual differences in test anxiety. *Bulletin of the Psychonomic Society*, 1977, 10, 447–450.

Murphy, M. D., Puff, C. R., & Campione, J. C. Measures of category clustering in free recall. Paper presented at the Society for Research in Child Development, New Orleans, 1977.

Murphy, M. D., Sanders, R. E., & Puff, C. R. The measurement of subjective organization: A reply to Sternberg and Tulving. Unpublished manuscript, University of Akron, 1978.

Paris, S. G. Memory organization during children's repeated recall. *Developmental Psychology*, 1978, 14, 99–106.

Pellegrino, J. W. A general measure of organization in free recall for variable unit size and internal sequential consistency. *Behavior Research Methods and Instrumentation*, 1971, 3, 241–246.

Pellegrino, J. W. A reply to Frender and Doubilet on the measurement of clustering. *Psychological Bulletin*, 1975, 82, 66–67.

Pellegrino, J. W., & Battig, W. F. Relationships among higher order organizational measures and free recall. *Journal of Experimental Psychology*, 1974, 102, 463–472.

Postman, L. A pragmatic view of organization theory. In E. Tulving & W. Donaldson (Eds.), *Organization of memory*. New York: Academic Press, 1972.

Puff, C. R. The measurement of clustering in free recall. Paper presented at the Eastern Psychological Association, 1963.

Puff, C. R. Effects of types of input structure upon recall and different clustering scores. *Bulletin of the Psychonomic Society*, 1973, 2, 271–273.

Puff, C. R. A consolidated theoretical view of stimulus-list organization effects in free recall. *Psychological Reports*, 1974, 34, 275–288.

Robinson, J. A. Category clustering in free recall. *Journal of Psychology*, 1966, 62, 279–285.

Roenker, D. L., Thompson, C. P., & Brown, S. C. Comparison of measures for the estimation of clustering in free recall. *Psychological Bulletin*, 1971, 76, 45–48.

Rundus, D. Analysis of rehearsal processes in free recall. *Journal of Experimental Psychology*, 1971, 89, 63–77.

Rundus, D. Negative effects of using list items as recall cues. *Journal of Verbal Learning and Verbal Behavior*, 1973, 12, 43–50.

Shuell, T. J. Clustering and organization in free recall. *Psychological Bulletin*, 1969, 72, 252–274.

Shuell, T. J. On sense and nonsense in measuring organization in free recall—oops, pardon me, my assumptions are showing. *Psychological Bulletin*, 1975, 82, 720–724.

Sternberg, R. J., & Tulving, E. The measurement of subjective organization in free recall. *Psychological Bulletin*, 1977, 84, 539–556.

Tulving, E. Subjective organization in the free recall of "unrelated" words. *Psychological Review*, 1962, 69, 344–354.

Tulving, E. Episodic and semantic memory. In E. Tulving & W. Donaldson (Eds.), *Organization of memory*. New York: Academic Press, 1972.

Tulving, E., & Bower, G. H. The logic of memory representations. In G. H. Bower (Ed.), *The psychology of learning and motivation: Advances in research* (Vol. 8). New York: Academic Press, 1974.

Tulving, E., & Pearlstone, Z. Availability versus accessibility of information in memory for words. *Journal of Verbal Learning and Verbal Behavior,* 1966, *5,* 381–391.

Wallace, W. P., & Underwood, B. J. Implicit responses and the role of intralist similarity in verbal learning by normal and retarded subjects. *Journal of Educational Psychology,* 1964, *55,* 362–370.

Weist, R. M. Optimal versus nonoptimal conditions for retrieval. *Journal of Verbal Learning and Verbal Behavior,* 1970, *9,* 311–316.

CHAPTER 4

Methods for Finding Graphic Representations of Associative Memory Structures

For the last 20 years or so, cognitive psychology has made increasing use of concepts of mental structure as a principle of explanation. From the "tote hierarchies" of Miller, Galanter, and Pribram (1960) to hierarchical models of memory organization (Mandler, 1967, 1968), from "associative networks" (Deese, 1965) to "active structural networks" (Norman, Rumelhart & LNR, 1975), psychologists have applied the term structure to virtually every level of cognitive functioning that seems to depend on the interrelationships among informational entities. Indeed, it is difficult to think of areas of concern in cognitive psychology where, today, the notions of organization and structure play no role in theory or experiments.

MEMORY ORGANIZATION
AND STRUCTURE

Most experimental work on memory organization has been carried out in multitrial free recall (MFR), since this paradigm provides both operational and theoretical definitions of memory organization. At an operational level, organization is said to occur in MFR when the learner recalls list words in an order that becomes increasingly consistent or stereotyped as learning proceeds. Theoretically, this consistency reflects the grouping of distinct list items into functional memory units that are recalled as contiguous chunks.

Until recently, one of the major difficulties in testing and elaborating theories of organization has been the lack of ways to portray explicitly the multidimensional nature of organization in recall, that is, the actual memory structures assumed to underlie the consistent organization observed in free recall.

For a number of years I have worked on this problem of finding concrete, diagrammatic representations of memory organization—what I call a memory diagram, or *M-Gram* for short. The present chapter describes this work and contrasts it with that of others. Free recall is, however, just one example of the influence of cognitive structure in memory and learning, and I will also suggest how this work on organization in free recall can be applied to the study of cognitive structure in a more general, unified framework. I will begin with the basic data of free recall, before flights of generality overtake me.

I. STRUCTURE IN FREE RECALL

When a subject engages in free-recall learning, the raw results contain the information shown in Figure 4.1. For each trial we have the items recalled by the subject in the order they were recalled; when recall is spoken we can also record the temporal distribution of retrieval over the recall interval as shown in Figure 4.1 (times from onset of recall period, in seconds). Now there are two major types of information we may extract from these results (see Figure 4.2).[1]

Item information concerns the retrieval characteristics of particular to-be-remembered items. Examples of item information are the total number recalled, serial position curves, Tulving's (1964) CC and NC measures of intertrial and intratrial retention, and recall of high-frequency versus low-frequency words in a mixed list design. In general, item information tells us about the recallability of *individual* items, perhaps classified according to stimulus properties or previous response history.

[1] If we take a broader view of "item," which applies to letters, words, sentences, stories, and so forth, it can be argued that *all* data extracted from memory studies can be classified as either item information or relational information. Formally, both item information and relational information may be seen as measurement systems; for quantitative data, the former involves mapping a set O of objects ("items") into real numbers, the latter involves mapping pairs of items, $O \times O$ into the reals.

Output position	1 — Item	1 — Time	2	3	4	5	6	7	8
1	lettuce	00	mouth 00	celery 00	dog 00	potato 00	foot 00	leg 00	sheep 00
2	spinach	02	face 04	rice 03	cat 03	spinach 03	leg 02	arm 03	goat 02
3	yam	05	arm 05	yam 06	lion 07	lettuce 06	face 05	foot 08	lion 06
4	potato	08	leg 09	spinach 10	tiger 10	yam 13	mouth 12	finger 10	tiger 07
5	sheep	19	foot 12	potato 12	goat 15	celery 21	finger 15	mouth 12	cat 10
6	goat	23	spinach 15	lettuce 15	sheep 20	rice 28	arm 20	face 14	dog 12
7	lion	28	lettuce 19	finger 19	spinach 25	dog 32	lion 22	rice 19	arm 16
8	tiger	31	potato 22	face 22	celery 28	cat 38	tiger 26	yam 22	leg 17
9	leg	45	yam 26	arm 26	lettuce 32	sheep 44	cat 28	potato 25	finger 20
10	foot	50	rice 30	foot 30	potato 38	goat 47	dog 31	spinach 27	foot 24
11	arm	61	cat 37	leg 37	yam 44	lion 50	sheep 33	celery 30	mouth 26
12	face	82	dog 42	mouth 42	rice 47	tiger 53	goat 39	lettuce 33	face 27
13			lion 48	cat 46	finger 52	arm 60	celery 42	dog 38	potato 31
14			tiger 51	dog 48	mouth 54	mouth 64	spinach 45	cat 39	rice 33
15			goat 63	lion 51	face 59	leg 68	lettuce 48	goat 41	yam 35
16				tiger 63	arm 63	finger 70	potato 50	sheep 43	spinach 39
17				goat 70	leg 70	foot 72	yam 72	lion 45	celery 40
18				sheep 74	foot 74	face 75	rice 75	tiger 47	lettuce 41

FIGURE 4.1 Basic data in multitrial free recall. Each column lists the words recalled on a given trial, in output order, together with the output latency for each word.

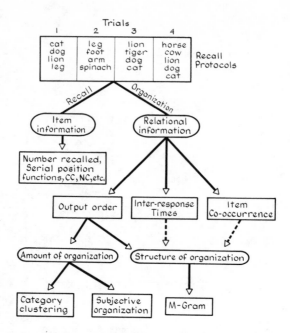

FIGURE 4.2 Classification of information available in free recall output.

Relational information: To investigate organization in recall we must turn to aspects of recall that indicate something about the *relations* among recalled items. Organization in free recall has been studied primarily in terms of the subject's order of recall. This focus is based on the notion that items that are grouped together in memory tend to be recalled closely together at the time of retrieval.

As indicated in Figure 4.2, there are at least two other possible sources of relational information—interitem response times (IRTs) and item cooccurrence (recall of sets of items on a given trial without regard to order of recall). For simplicity I will focus on the analysis of output order.

A. The Nature of Organization in Free Recall

Much of the research on organization of memory has been concerned with one or more of the following three problems:

1. To demonstrate the *existence* of oganization in recall—for example, to show that clustering or subjective organization is greater than chance under particular experimental conditions.
2. To assess quantitatively the true amount of organization in recall (the best measure problem).

3. To determine the effect of various stimulus variables (e.g., concreteness, associative strength), subject variables (e.g., age, verbal abilities), and procedural manipulations (blocking, instructions to organize, presentation rate) on organizational and recall scores. Included in this category are the studies of the effects of various types of organizational structure—associations, taxonomic categories, hierarchical grouping, and so forth.

These research problems are thus all concerned in one way or another with *amount* of organization in recall, considered as a property of free recall that can be scaled unidimensionally. However, organization is inherently multidimensional. It is natural to speak of the organization of memory for the same reasons that one can speak of organization in the web of a spider or in the arrangements of molecules within a complex chemical structure. That is, organization refers to the pattern of relations among the elements in a set.

Given this approach, it may be somewhat misguided to attempt to compress all of this information into a single number. If we think of organization as being analogous to some kind of multidimensional space, then measuring the amount of organization is a reasonable thing to do when there is some unique dimension in this space corresponding to amount. To the extent that different types or forms of structures vary in ways that cannot be arrayed along a unidimensional continuum, measures of organization by themselves are insufficient to provide a complete understanding of cognitive structure.

B. The M-Gram

The term *M-Gram* sounds perhaps like an acronym for something, and occasionally, for purely frivolous reasons, I have pondered what that something might be. Surprisingly, there is a description of this approach that fits the bill and that focuses on its salient attributes as well. Simply, M-Grams stands for *Methods* for *Graphic Representations* of *Associative Memory Structures*. Twc aspects of this description deserve some comment:

Graphic Representation. The term "representation" is intended to have a somewhat broader application than the term "model." By a representation of memory structure, I mean another data domain in which there exists an analogous, well-defined structure (either physical or conceptual) within which we can study the pattern of relations among elements in a memory set (e.g., to-be-remembered items). The principal value of a graphic representation is that it allows patterns to be grasped as a whole and focuses attention on relationships among items that might not otherwise have been noticed.

Associative Memory Structures. By associative memory structures I mean any systems of memory storage in which information concerning the relations among items is stored explicitly together with the internal representations of the items themselves. This class includes the relational models of memory structure characterized by the terms chunks, hierarchies, attributes, networks, seriations, taxonomic categories, and so forth. I wish specifically to exclude *nonassociative* memory structures such as buffer models and pushdown stacks, which conceive of memory as a collection of storage locations containing item representations, but which do not include the sort of relational information described previously.

Each type of associative structure just mentioned is an example of what I call a *structural framework*. My aim, then, is to describe how we may develop graphic representations of these distinct types of memory structures for organization in free recall and in other cognitive domains as well.

Once again, I will restrict my initial remarks to a hierarchical structure for organization in free recall in which it is assumed that TBR items are first grouped into subjective memory units that are in turn grouped into higher order units. Based on this structural framework, a hierarchical M-Gram is produced by some method for finding these subjective units and higher order units on the basis of a subjective order of recall. What is required is a procedure or a set of rules for mapping relations among items in output order into this graphic representation of the tree structure.

C. Proximity Analysis

The procedure that I have developed for representing memory structure is called proximity analysis. The mapping from recall output into an M-Gram is a two-step process as shown in Figure 4.3.

The first step assumes that the relevant aspects of free-recall organization may be summarized by the intraserial proximities between all pairs of items in the recall protocols. Given a definition of proximity, an item-by-item proximity matrix can be constructed with entries representing the degree to which each pair tends to occur in nearby (though not necessarily adjacent) output positions over some set of trials. In this way, questions concerning the organization of list items in memory can be reduced to corresponding questions concerning the structure of proximities between items in recall.

In the second step, a method of hierarchical cluster analysis may be applied to the proximities to produce an M-Gram representation of nested recall units. S. C. Johnson's (1967) diameter method is particularly appropriate to reveal the type of hierarchical structures considered by organizational theorists (Mandler, 1967; Tulving, 1962). The clusters found using this procedure are just those groups of items that are consistently recalled with high proximities among *all* items in the group. However, other clustering methods, which entail weaker assumptions or which allow clusters to overlap, may be more appropriate in some situations (Friendly, 1977).

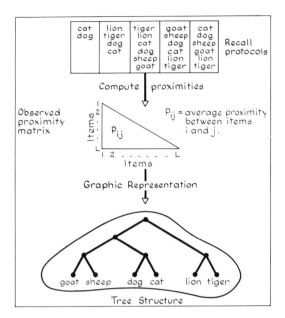

FIGURE 4.3 Mapping of recall–order consistency into a hierarchical representation as a two-step process: *(a)* assign interitem proximities; *(b)* hierarchical clustering of proximities.

To illustrate this procedure, the recall of a hypothetical subject is shown in Table 4.1. The items recalled on each of the 6 trials are shown in Panel 1 of the table, abbreviated by their initial letters. For each trial the proximities between all 15 possible pairs of words are shown in the lower panel. The proximity measure for items i and j is just the list length, L (= 6, here), minus the difference in output positions on that trial, for example, P *(apple, drum)* $= 6 - 2 = 4$ on Trial 1. The proximities for each pair are then averaged over trials and arranged in a matrix, as shown in Table 4.2.

Applying Johnson's clustering technique[2] to this matrix yields the tree structure shown in Figure 4.4. In this diagram the items appear as terminal branches of the tree. The relations of items within memory units and higher order memory units are represented by the sequence of mergings of the branches. In particular, a group of items consistently recalled together appears as a *compact* cluster, formed at a high proximity level. If this chunk is recalled independently of other chunks, it will also appear as an *isolated* cluster that does not merge with other clusters until a much lower proximity level is reached.

[2]In each step of this iterative process, the highest remaining entry in the proximity matrix is found. The items with that highest value are merged to form a cluster, and the entries for the merged items are collapsed by taking lowest values of corresponding pairs of cells. This process is continued until all items have been merged into one cluster and the matrix is reduced completely.

Table 4.1
Sample Data

I. WORDS
Apple, Banana, Carrot, Drum, Eye, Flower

II. RECALL PROTOCOLS

Output position	Trials					
	1	*2*	*3*	*4*	*5*	*6*
1	A	D	C	E	F	D
2	C	E	B	F	E	F
3	D	F	A	D	D	E
4	F	A	F	A	C	B
5	—	B	E	C	B	C
6	—	—	—	B	A	A

III. PROXIMITIES

Pair	*1*	*2*	*3*	*4*	*5*	*6*	*Sum*	*No.*	*Avg.*
AB	—	5	5	4	5	4	23	5	4.6
AC	5	—	4	5	4	5	23	5	4.6
AD	4	3	—	5	3	1	16	5	4.2
AE	—	4	4	3	2	3	16	5	4.2
AF	3	5	5	4	1	2	20	6	3.3
BC	—	—	5	5	5	5	20	4	5.0
BD	—	2	—	3	4	3	12	4	3.0
BE	—	3	3	1	3	5	15	5	3.0
BF	—	4	4	2	2	4	16	5	4.2
CD	5	—	—	4	5	2	16	4	4.0
CD	—	—	2	2	4	4	12	4	3.0
CF	4	—	3	3	3	3	16	5	4.2
DE	—	5	—	4	5	4	18	4	4.5
DF	5	4	—	5	4	5	23	5	4.6
EF	—	5	5	5	5	5	25	5	5.0

Table 4.2
Sample Proximity Matrix

Item:	*A*	*B*	*C*	*D*	*E*	*F*
Apple	×					
Banana	4.6	×				
Carrot	4.6	5.0	×			
Drum	4.2	3.0	4.0	×		
Eye	4.2	3.0	3.0	4.5	×	
Flower	3.3	4.2	4.2	4.6	5.0	×

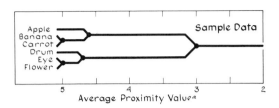

FIGURE 4.4 M-Gram for the sample data in Table 4.1.

Thus the figure shows that output organization for this data consists essentially of two clusters of three items each: *(apple, banana, carrot), (drum, eye, flower)*. Examining the recall protocols in Table 4.1, one can see that these clusters are perfectly consistent with the recall of this hypothetical subject. Each trial consists of recall of some or all of the items in one cluster followed by some or all of the items of the other cluster.

1. CATEGORIZED LISTS

The recall protocol shown in Figure 4.1 came from a small demonstration experiment. Subjects in this experiment learned an 18-item list consisting of 6 items from each of the categories *animals, vegetables,* and *body parts.* The proximity matrix for this subject is shown in Table 4.3. It can be seen that the entries within categories (the triangular blocks) are all considerably higher than entries between any pair in different categories (the rectangular blocks). Yet, if there is any more structure present in this table, it does not appear in any comprehensible form. In fact, the items were selected so that each category had a slightly different internal structure. The **vegetable** and **animal** categories contained, respectively, two and three subcategories; the **body parts** items were based on part–whole relations with three subcategories.

The hierarchical M-Gram derived from these data is shown in Figure 4.5. The most striking feature here is the strong grouping of the items into tightly knit, isolated clusters corresponding to the list categories. The items within the list categories merge at high-proximity levels, while separate categories do not merge until relatively low levels of proximity are reached.

In addition, however, interpretable subgroupings can also be identified within these categories. The **vegetables** divide into greens and starches, and the **animals** divide into farm, jungle, and domestic subcategories. The **body parts** category is composed of subclusters *(face, mouth, finger)* and *(arm, leg, foot),* which only partially preserve the part–whole relation.

It is worth noting that the proximity level at which all items merge into a single cluster is the smallest proximity among all items in that cluster. This is a useful (if stringent) measure of the strength or cohesiveness of that particular cluster. By this measure, the three categories appear equally strong in this

TABLE 4.3
Proximity Matrix for Recall Protocols of Figure 4.1

	1[a]	2	3	4	5	6	7	8	9	10	11	12	13	14	15	16	17	18
dog	×																	
cat	100	×																
lion	91	93	×															
tiger	88	91	100	×														
sheep	86	88	92	91	×													
goat	88	89	94	94	100	×												
face	55	57	57	57	52	51	×											
mouth	62	65	62	61	60	56	95	×										
arm	63	66	65	65	61	60	90	92	×									
finger	62	64	63	63	56	58	94	94	93	×								
leg	58	61	62	62	56	57	89	92	96	90	×							
foot	55	57	59	59	51	53	93	90	92	91	98	×						
celery	69	67	56	56	61	63	60	60	57	62	48	49	×					
spinach	69	68	60	58	65	64	61	62	60	62	56	57	96	×				
lettuce	70	69	60	58	64	64	60	61	59	62	54	55	94	97	×			
potato	68	67	60	59	64	65	65	65	64	67	60	60	87	95	93	×		
rice	66	65	54	53	53	58	66	66	65	70	58	60	88	86	85	92	×	
yam	66	65	57	56	60	62	63	64	62	67	58	57	91	93	92	97	99	×

[a]Numbers indicate item numbers.

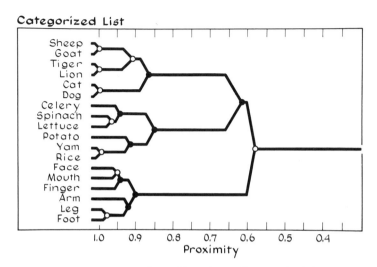

FIGURE 4.5. M-Gram derived from the recall protocols of Figure 4.1.

subject's recall. Had the categories differed in degree of organization, these differences would show up in the levels at which the categories formed.

These results demonstrate that proximity analysis can recover strong, categorical groupings in recall and can reveal something about the internal structure of categories (Rosch, 1975). However, I also wish to show that the method can distinguish among small or subtle variations in organizational structure. For this purpose I will briefly describe some results of an experiment concerning hierarchical lists (Friendly, 1972).

The experiment was designed to determine whether different subjects could be induced to organize a single list differentially by manipulating presentation order alone. The list contained 42 items grouped in nested categories. All of the items were edible substances (Level 1). At the second level, the items belonged to three 14-item categories **(seafood, farm produce, animal foods)**. Each of these major categories contained two 7-item subcategories (e.g., **farm produce** contained *fruit* and *vegetables* at Level 3).

Four groups of subjects received presentation blocked at different levels of the hierarchy, but for present purposes I will describe only two of these. For one of these, Group B2, the items were blocked into the major categories at Level 2 of the hierarchy; for Group 3 subjects, the items were blocked according to the six minor categories at Level 3. Each subject received 12 presentation–recall trials. The number of subjects per group ranged from 35 to 42. Average interitem proximities were computed for each group, averaging over subjects and trials. The cluster solutions for Group B2 and B3 are shown in Figures 4.6 and 4.7.

Whereas these figures look qualitatively similar, the differences in recall structure among the four groups are reflected quantitatively in the tree diagrams in the relative strengths of the category systems at Level 2 and Level 3 of the hierarchy. The dashed lines in Figures 4.6 and 4.7 show the average diameters of the Level 2 and Level 3 categories. The separation between these lines represents the (average) isolation of the Level 3 categories relative to the superordinate level. For Group B2, the clusters that are both compact and isolated are those at Level 2, corresponding to the blocking condition which that group received. In contrast, the compact, isolated clusters in the Group B3 M-Gram are those at Level 3 of the stimulus hierarchy. Again this corresponds exactly to the presentation condition of that group.

With such highly structured categorized lists, one would expect to find similar results with measures of category clustering. While category clustering measures are in fact consistent with the tree diagrams presented above, the latter provide a much more detailed picture of organizational structure.

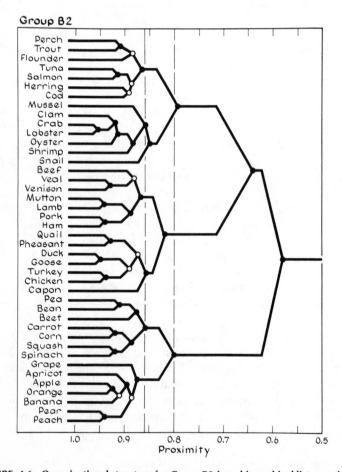

FIGURE 4.6. Organizational structure for Group B2 from hierarchical list experiment.

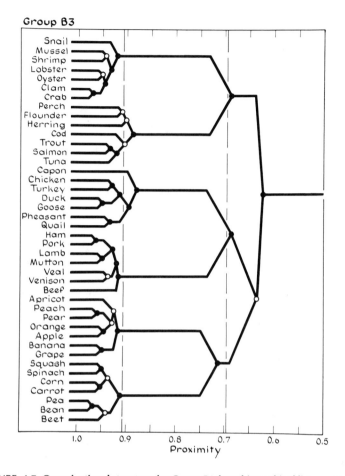

FIGURE 4.7 Organizational structure for Group B3 from hierarchical list experiment.

2. UNRELATED LISTS

Since proximity analysis is independent of any prior structuring of the items, it applies equally well to the recall of unrelated lists. This is particularly important, since SO measures cannot reveal *how* subjects are organizing an unrelated list, and it is perfectly possible for different subjects to obtain similar SO scores, while organizing the list in very different ways.

With unrelated lists, subjects do in fact differ among themselves in their organization groupings,[3] and the hierarchical M-Grams derived from their recall output show a "looser" structure. This is illustrated in Figure 4.8, which

---

[3]For this reason, it is often unwise to average proximities over subjects for unrelated lists (see Friendly, 1977).

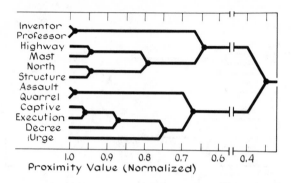

FIGURE 4.8. M-Gram for one subject learning an unrelated list. [*Data from Ornstein, 1970.*]

shows the tree structure diagram for a single subject from an experiment by Ornstein (1970). The organizational pattern in this subject's recall can be summarized by three principal clusters *(inventor, professor), (highway, mast, north, structure),* and *(assault, quarrel, captive, execution, decree, urge).* There are several tightly knit units, mostly pairs, such as *(inventor, professor), (assault quarrel), (captive, execution, decree).* However, the higher order units here are somewhat loosely structured—they merge at low-proximity levels, relative to typical results for categorized lists. In fact, the most striking differences in organizational structure between related and unrelated lists often appear in the extent and strength of higher order connections among organizational units.

D. Direct Grouping Methods

Other methods that attempt to discover organizational structure in free recall have recently been put forth. These methods generally appear to be more direct and in some vague, intuitive sense, more natural. They seem to be straightforward in that memory units are defined by direct examination of the recalled items, either by the subject himself (Allen, 1971; Anglin, 1970; Buschke, 1977; Marton, 1970), by the experimenter (Buschke, 1976), or by a computer algorithm (Monk, 1976; Reitman & Reuter, 1976; Zangen, Ziegel-baum, & Buschke, 1976).

The contrast between these methods and the M-Gram approach is illuminating, so I will describe briefly some of this work. Comparisons among the various approaches can be made in terms of both *validity* and *generality.* The thrust of my argument is to show that the directness that makes these alternate approaches seem so natural also makes them specific to the procedural details (and concomitant epiphenomena) that characterize organization in free recall. Hence, I claim that they are less suitable for studying organizational structure across varied cognitive domains and are limited in their application to free recall as well.

1. SUBJECTIVE GROUPING TASKS

In the simplest variants, the subject is essentially asked to indicate in some way those words that "went together in his memory." For example, Anglin (1970) simply had subjects scan their recall protocols and draw lines separating their subjective chunks. Allen (1971) and Seibel (1964) ignored recall order entirely and obtained independent memory unit data by asking subjects to write groups of list items that they remembered together in the cells of a grid. Others have embedded a memory grouping task into the free-recall procedure itself. Friendly (1974) had subjects sort the words into subjective categories instead of the normal presentation on each trial. To the extent that subjects actually know about the operation of their memories, one would expect a reasonable consistency among these subjective grouping tasks. Unless something is seriously wrong, the memory units they identify should be similar.

Buschke (1977) argued that the usual *sequential* recall may itself limit organization in recall order. So, in a two-dimensional recall procedure, Buschke's subjects wrote their recall responses on a two-dimensional response sheet, where items they remembered together were to be written in the same row. With this two-dimensional recall procedure, the subject could return to earlier clusters and write additional items there as they were remembered later in the series. This last feature is interesting because both recall order and subjective chunking can be observed simultaneously and compared. An example of the results from such a procedure is shown in Figure 4.9. Each column in this figure is merely an annotated transcription of the two-dimensional recall sheet for that trial, writing out each response sheet row by row, from the top down. The subject's output clusters (rows of the grid) are separated by solid lines, and consistent clusters of two or more items are denoted by letters, using capitals for the first recall of an item within a group.

The dashed lines indicate subsequent items written with previous clusters. To the extent that recall order actually reflects subjective grouping, there should be little reordering, and Buschke's data show this to be the case. About 99% of subject-defined recall clusters are output in strict sequential order.

For comparison, proximity analysis was applied to the recall protocols of Figure 9.[4] In doing this analysis, I have used the recall orders provided by Buschke allowing the few reordered items to remain where they are. However, information regarding the subject's own recall groupings has not gone into the analysis. The comparison allows a sensitive test of the ability of proximity analysis to recover these groupings from recall order alone. The hierarchical M-Gram derived from these data is shown in Figure 4.10. All of the clusters identified by this subject are recovered in the hierarchical clustering. These clusters are denoted by the same letters as in Figure 4.9.

[4]Dr. Bushke's permission to use these data is gratefully acknowledged.

R E C A L L S

List	1	2	3	4	5	6	7	8	9	10	smallest clusters
1 FIRE	FIRE	JOKE	TIME	ARCH F	ARCH F	CARE	CARE	TIME a	FIST b	ZONE	TIME a
2 TASK	LOAF	MOON A	SALT	DUKE F	DUKE F	JOKE	TIME a	YEAR a	KNEE b	JOKE	YEAR a
3 VIEW	TASK	LUCK A	JOKE	SALT	KNEE b	DESK	YEAR A	MOON a	NAIL b	TIME a	MOON a
4 DUKE	MOON	sign(↓)	KNEE b	TIME A	FIST b	MOON a	MOON a	LUCK a	BATH b	YEAR a	LUCK a
5 NAIL	BIRD	TASK	NAIL b	FIST b	NAIL b	LUCK a	LUCK a	HORN a	TIME a	MOON a	HORN a
6 HORN	PAGE	KNEE B	FIST B	MOON a	BATH b	HORN a	HORN a	DUKE f	MOON a	LUCK a	ROSE c
7 JOKE	PORT	NAIL B	BATH B	LUCK a	DESK	TIME a	ZONE	PAGE F	YEAR a	HORN a	BIRD c
8 FIST	sign(↑)	YEAR	DESK	BATH b	PORT d	ZONE	WARD D	ROSE c	LUCK a	ROSE c	PORT d
9 SHOP	VIEW	HOOD	HOOD	HORN a	CAVE d	KNEE b	PORT d	BIRD c	HORN a	BIRD c	WARD d
10 YEAR	WOOL	VIEW	VIEW	DESK	SALT	FIST b	CAVE d	WARD d	ROSE c	WOOL	CAVE d
11 TIME		HOOD(r)	MOON a	TASK	TIME a	NAIL b	ROSE c	PORT d	BIRD c	GOAL e	KNEE b
12 GOAL		BIRD C	LUCK a	NAIL b	MOON a	BATH b	BIRD c	CAVE d	WOOL	LOAF e	FIST b
13 GLUE		ROSE C	HORN A	BATH b	HORN A	ROSE c	FIST b	ZONE	LOAF e	MODE e	NAIL b
14 CAVE		CAVE D	TASK	HOOD	GOAL e	BIRD c	KNEE b	WOOL	GOAL e	TASK h	BATH b
15 LOAF		PORT D	BIRD c	WOOL	LOAF e	SALT	NAIL b	TASK h	MODE e	FIRE h	ARCH f
16 MOON		WOOL	ROSE c	BIRD c	MODE e	TASK h	BATH b	FIRE h	GLUE g	GLUE g/h	DUKE f
17 ROSE		PAGE	WOOL	ROSE c	WOOL	FIRE h	GLUE g/h	GOAL e	SHOP g	SHOP g	PAGE f
18 CARE		GOAL E	GOAL e	GLUE	VIEW	GLUE g/H	TASK h	LOAF e	VIEW	FIST b	WOOL
19 ARCH		MODE E	CAVE d	SHOP G	TASK H	SHOP g	FIRE h	MODE e	TASK h	KNEE b	SHOP g
20 BATH			PORT d	GOAL e	FIRE H	WOOL	WOOL	KNEE b	FIRE h	NAIL b	TASK h
21 KNEE			DUKE	MODE e	SHOP g	ARCH f	VIEW	FIST b	CARE	BATH b	GLUE h
22 PAGE				LOAF E	GLUE g	DUKE f	DESK	NAIL b	PORT d	VIEW	FIRE h
23 WARD				PORT d	BIRD c	CAVE d	LOAF e	BATH b	WARD d	CARE	ZONE
24 SALT				PAGE	ROSE c	PORT d	GOAL e	SALT	CAVE d	WARD d	DESK
25 ZONE				VIEW	HOOD	GOAL e	MODE e	DESK	SALT	PORT d	CARE
26 DESK				FIRE		LOAF e	PAGE	HOOD	ZONE	CAVE d	LOAF e
27 HOOD				CAVE d		MODE e	ARCH f	VIEW	ARCH f	DESK	GOAL e
28 BIRD				ZONE			DUKE f	GLUE g	DUKE f	HOOD	MODE e
29 WOOL							HOOD	SHOP g	PAGE f	ARCH f	
30 LUCK							JOKE	CARE	DESK	DUKE f	
31 MODE									HOOD	PAGE f	
32 PORT											

28 items recovered

FIGURE 4.5 Response protocol from two-dimensional free recall procedure, showing subject-defined clusters. Each of columns 1–10 represent a separate recall attempt [Data from Buschke, 1977.]

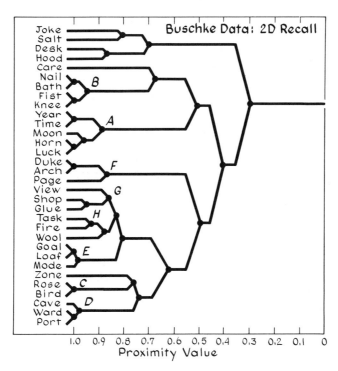

FIGURE 4.10 M-Gram derived from the two-dimensional protocol of Figure 4.9. The clusters marked with letters (A–H) correspond to the subject's own recall groupings, as shown in Figure 4.9.

Furthermore, most of these groups appear as compact clusters at high-proximity levels and do not merge with other clusters until a much lower level is reached. The only substantive differences I can discover between the two analyses are as follows:

1. Some items (e.g., *glue*) appear as parts of two different clusters in Buschke's results. In a hierarchy, clusters cannot overlap, so these items go into one cluster or the other. (Note that in the next step clusters *G* & *H* merge together, and are not isolated from each other.)

2. The items that this subject recalled singly (i.e., unclustered) do merge with other items, as they must in any complete hierarchy. These items (e.g., *zone, care, desk*), however, do not merge until a relatively low proximity is reached.

In addition to this "eyeball" comparison, Johnson's cluster statistic (S. C. Johnson, 1968; Fillenbaum & Rapoport, 1971) was applied to provide an approximate test of significance for each nontrivial cluster. The significant clusters include all save one of the subjective clusters and also indicate several reliable subclusters (e.g., *fist, knee*) as well as a number of reliable higher order groupings. The single cluster from Buschke's two-dimensional results that fails to reach significance is, interestingly enough, cluster H (task, fire). The first cluster to include H (task, fire, wool) is significant, however, and so is the cluster (G U H). These results are consistent with the foregoing eyeball comparisons and can be confirmed by visual examination of the protocols.

There is, however, an important difference between the two displays that deserves comment. Buschke's two-dimensional protocols appear to show, for this subject, clusters that develop by accretion over trials, e.g., ((((moon, luck), horn), time), year). Proximity analysis pools the recall data over trials and hence does not display any such changes. On the other hand, whereas two-dimensional protocols may suggest that clusters develop, by themselves they provide no summary or description of how these changes occur.

There are several possible ways to display changes in hierarchical structure, and I will mention just two[5]:

1. Perform several analyses of a given set of data, pooling over smaller blocks of trials.
2. Represent some changes in the organizational units graphically in the tree diagram. One possibility would be to use the size of the node drawn for a given cluster to depict the trial at which that cluster first appeared as a recall grouping.

2. GROUPING RULES

Though the subjective grouping techniques undoubtedly convey useful information regarding memory organization, workers in the area have tended to look for more objective methods. The remaining methods for locating recall units are distinguished from those just described in that a rule or algorithm for the method can be stated. Not only does this provide an objective method, but in addition the formal properties of these memory representations can be studied (e.g., Reuter, 1976), and the rules serve as an explicit specification of the structural framework represented, in this case, the hierarchy.

a. *Chunk rules.* In what is probably the simplest objective method, Buschke (1976) proposed that recall chunks can be found by direct examination of the recall protocols themselves. A chunk is defined as a group of items that occurs together in two or more retrieval attempts, bounded by different items or

[5]One source of difficulty here has to do with the level of our understanding of hierarchical structures and how they work. There are now several process models for learning and decision operations based on hierarchical structures (Boyd & Wexler, 1973; Feigenbaum, 1963; Yngve, 1961), and Reuter (1976) has outlined a mechanism for cued and noncued retrieval from a hierarchical memory tree. However, with the exception of the EPAM model (Feigenbaum, 1963), the hierarchical structures are themselves static, and it is less clear conceptually how such trees might grow.

chunks. Examining recall output orders for these clusters can be tedious, and it is probably easy to overlook some clusters, so Buschke and his associates have developed a computer program to do the job (Zangen et al., 1976). The results are displayed in a manner similar to that shown in Figure 4.9 and provide a relatively compact yet complete description of recall output that shows considerable insight into the recall process. However, the principal difficulty with this method is that the recall clusters are not characterized in theoretically useful ways. No structural model is presented to specify the form of structure within or between these recall units.

This observation points up a necessary tradeoff: Buschke's chunk rules probably describe the data closely, but it is difficult to use the chunks predictively or to construct well-defined comparisons across conditions. Imposing a model of organization allows for comparison and prediction, but does so at the expense of ignoring some of the details of the data. The argument for choosing the model is a standard one. To the extent that the model fits the data, small deviations can be treated as error, and the model-based summary is far more manageable, understandable, and useful than the raw data.

b. Hierarchical Grouping Rules. Monk's (1976) hierarchical grouping analysis (HGA) provides the first formal proposal I know of for directly identifying basic memory units in recall orders and then recursively applying the same algorithm to these basic units to determine a hierarchical structure. Monk's procedure can be understood most easily in relation to Pellegrino's (1971) intertrial repetition (ITR) measure. In both, memory units are classified on the basis of their internal order. Constant order, serial order, and variable order groups are distinguished. However, in Monk's HGA, these consistent groupings in the first-order analysis are identified rather than counted. The second stage is applied to these groups to eliminate redundant groups and find hierarchical (inclusion) relations among them. In application, a consistency criterion must be specified so that, in order to be counted, a group of items must be recalled contiguously on this specified number of trials. An example of Monk's HGA is shown in Figure 4.11, which shows a set of hypothetical recalls together with the hierarchical representation derived from these data. The method identifies *(goat, cow, horse)* as a three-item variable-order group—these items are recalled as a block on all four trials though their internal order varies. Another group is *(coal, fire, smoke),* but these items are recalled only in the order stated or its reverse. *Nought* and *zero* are recalled as a variable-order group, but are always followed by the items *one, two, three* in a constant order.

Monk's application of proximity analysis to these data is shown in Figure 4.12 for comparison. The results show that exactly the same subgroups are identified in both methods. However, Monk's procedure distinguishes among these subgroups on the basis of their internal ordering, and proximity analysis does not. The reason for this, of course, is that the proximities are defined symmetrically, so that information about response directionality is discarded at

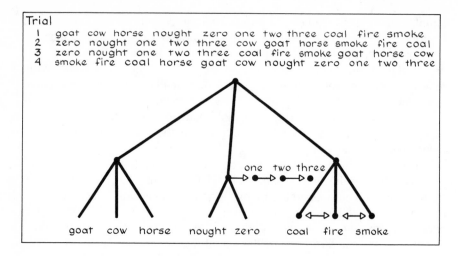

FIGURE 4.11 Example of Monk's (1976) hierarchical grouping analysis.

this stage. Whether this restriction is important cannot be determined in the abstract; however, the increasing reliance on bidirectional and unordered measures of organization (Pellegrino, 1971; Sternberg & Tulving, 1977) indicates that it may not be.

A similar procedure was presented by Reitman and Reuter (1976). However, Reitman and Reuter require that the list of items be completely learned before the method is applied. Then a series of additional recall trials is given in which the subject is cued to begin retrieval with specified items. In this way, all items are recalled, and the order of recall can be considered as a complete path through a memory tree generated in a top-down transversal of all branches. Formally, this simplifies the problem because one need not adjust for partial recall or deal with intrusions or repetitions in recall. Whereas a subject's organizational structure should be relatively stable by the time the method is

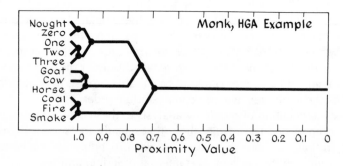

FIGURE 4.12 M-Gram for Monk's example.

applied, it provides no way to assess the way this organizational scheme develops as the list is learned, and so it completely bypasses any questions of the relation of organization to recall.

E. Proximity Analysis versus Direct Approaches

In contrast to these direct approaches, proximity analysis provides the basis for a far more general analysis of cognitive organization. The proximities among items in free recall output play the role of the middlemen. They represent a construction—a convenient device to bridge the gap between observed free-recall responses and a description of organizational structure. However, this indirect route through proximity allows this method to be applied rather broadly. This generally can be seen at two distinct levels:

1. Within free recall, a number of the methods I just described require a modification of the free-recall paradigm or use of a supplementary task to obtain the additional information about memory units. The sorting task used by Seibel (1964) and Friendly (1974) is confounded with the presentation phase of each trial. Buschke's two-dimensional recall does the same thing in the output phase. Reitman's algorithm requires that the list be recalled completely on every trial. Now, there is nothing sacred about the "standard" free-recall experiment, and I do not wish to suggest otherwise. However, the special experimental procedures introduced to identify memory units do place restrictions on the situations in which they can be applied. For example, it is hard to conceive of using Reitman's method developmentally or of studying the effects of presentation conditions with the sorting task.

Proximity analysis, in its general formulation (Friendly, 1972, 1977) requires only (a) that a measure of proximity or relatedness be defined for all pairs of to-be-remembered items, and (b) that there be sufficient data available to provide reasonably stable estimates of these values. The fact that proximity analysis can be applied to the sample data presented by Monk, Buschke, and others is one indication of this general applicability. However, even in free recall, proximity analysis is not limited to recall order alone. In the subjective grouping methods and in Buschke's two-dimensional recall, proximities can be defined in terms of the subject's classification of items that go together in his memory. Alternatively, a proximity measure could be based on other types of relational information (see Figure 4.2), such as interresponse times or coefficients based on item cooccurrence in recall (ignoring recall order).

For free recall, the proximity measure used here seems to work well, since it makes efficient use of the output order data (Friendly, 1972). This measure turns out to be fairly robust over a wide variety of situations including categorized versus unrelated materials, individual data versus group data, complete recall at criterion versus partial recall during learning (Friendly, 1977). However, in certain specialized situations, it is surely possible to tailor-make other measures of interitem relatedness that are either better empirically or more interpretable theoretically in that context. For example, other researchers (e.g., Anglin, 1970; Kintsch, 1970; Koh, Vernon, & Bailey, 1971; Schwartz & Humphreys, 1973) have used measures based on the frequency of *adjacent* recall. Since this measure discards much of the information available about organizational structure in output order, it requires more data to achieve equal reliability, and the results with such measures have sometimes been far from satisfactory (Friendly, 1977). It appears that the best results with the adjacency measures are obtained using group data and materials that have a fairly consensual structure across individuals. On the other hand, when the greater data requirement is met, an adjacency measure may be preferred, because its interpretation is often simpler. In a network model, for instance, the adjacency measure could be considered to index directly the strength of links between memory nodes.

2. At a second level, the M-Gram approach is not limited to hierarchical representations of memory structure. In free recall, hierarchical models for the organization of mnemonic information have been popular, but I suspect that this may be due more to the nature of free recall than to the nature of our memory. That is, performance in free recall depends on the subject grouping items together on some basis. A large proportion of the free-recall literature can be summarized by saying that subjects will use almost any explicit, logical structure in the list as a basis for this grouping or will invent their own subjective categories if no other basis is present. Given this characterization of organization in free recall, hierarchical models of this structuring are natural, and hierarchical M-Grams provide a methodology for making these structures visible and testable.

However, a hierarchy is just one type of memory structure, and for the sake of generality, I would like to be able to produce representations of memory structure within the context of other structural frameworks that have been suggested in the literature—dimensional or attribute models, networks, seriations (Mandler & Dean, 1969; Mandler & Anderson, 1971), and so forth.

I recently discussed how this can be done in the case of *dimensional* models and *networks* (Friendly, 1977). While I cannot go into these methods in detail, I can describe what is involved at a conceptual level (see Figure 4.13). All that is necessary to obtain (graphic) representations of other memory structures is to alter the second stage of the M-Gram approach and map the proximities into the appropriate structural framework. This is a general problem in the social sciences, and many techniques are already available under the rubric of "similarity scaling." There are in fact scaling methods corresponding to each of the structural frameworks shown in the figure. Table 4.4 shows some correspondences between memory models, structural frameworks, and scaling

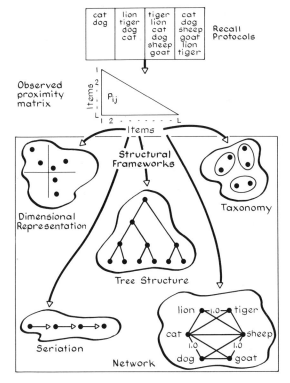

FIGURE 4.13 Structural frameworks: generalizing proximity analysis to other models for memory structure.

methods. It should be noted that whereas the calculation of proximities among items in recall is theoretically neutral, the particular scaling method adopted to represent the proximity structure implies the choice of the corresponding structural framework as a model for memory structure.

Table 4.4
Structural Frameworks and Corresponding Scaling Methods
for M-Gram Representations from Recall Proximities

Memory model	Structural framework	Scaling methods
Serial chain	Seriation	Guttman scale Hamiltonian path
Dimensions	Euclidean space Overlapping attributes	Multidimensional scaling ADDCLUS (Shepard & Arabie, 1978)
Tree structure	Strict hierarchy Overlapping clusters Free trees	Complete-link clustering Jardine & Sibson, 1971 Cunningham, 1978
Network	Undirected graph	Minimum spanning tree Maximal connected subgraphs

II. BEYOND FREE RECALL

In the last decade there has been a spreading of organizational research into far wider contexts than free recall. Among episodic memory tasks, organizational theories or explanations have been offered for effects in recognition memory (Bruce & Fagan, 1970; Mandler, 1972), paired-associate learning (Postman, 1971), and serial learning (Bower & Winzenz, 1969; Estes, 1972; N. F. Johnson, 1970; Martin & Noreen, 1974). Detailed models of storage and retrieval processes operating on memory structures have been described for free recall (Anderson & Bower, 1972; Rumelhart, Lindsay & Norman, 1972; Reuter, 1976) and serial learning (Estes, 1972, 1975).

At the same time, the study of semantic memory has produced elaborate theories describing how our knowledge of the world and of language is represented and structured internally (Anderson & Bower, 1973; Norman et al., 1975; Schank, 1975), and process models for performance in semantic tasks (e.g., Collins & Loftus, 1975). Finally, there is currently a concerted effort to understand memory for simple stories by analyzing the functional units of such stories and the structure of relations among them (Mandler & Johnson, 1977; Rumelhart, 1975; Thorndyke, 1977).

Yet, despite this expansive range of research on memory structure, the operational definitions of "organization," methods used for investigating it, and theories of memory structure tend to be task-specific and do not readily generalize across domains.

This is a particularly acute problem in cognitive psychology, which, in contrast with associative approaches to memory and learning, can be defined as the study of "unobservable mental events [Pachella, 1974]." However, whereas Estes spoke in 1960 of the new mental chemistry recent work on the structure of information in memory can be called "the new mental forestry." By talking about *structures* of unobservable mental events, we run the danger of moving even further from the concrete, operational definitions of theoretical terms that are necessary in an experimental science. I hope that the foregoing discussion demonstrates that we *can* talk sensibly about organization in multitrial free recall. The balance of this chapter is a discussion of a unified framework within which the concepts of organization and structure can be examined experimentally.

A. Organization and Structure

If we are to make headway, we need first of all to come to a clearer understanding of what we mean by memory "structure" and "organization." Whereas these terms have often been used interchangeably, there are two aspects of usage that must be distinguished. I intend to use *organization* to refer to observable regularities of cognitive behavior from which we infer something of an unobservable, internal *structure* that makes that regularity possible.

Organization is thus descriptive and operational, while structure is more explanatory and theoretical. This distinction is not the same as Pellegrino and Ingram's (see Chapter 2) disucussion of organization as a process or a product. Whereas my usage of organization here is cast in terms of an observable product, structure is more than a set of processes.

In these terms, then, the problem is to use the organization we observe in behavior to analyze, determine, and understand what we can about memory structure.

How are we to understand memory structure? The definition that I have found most useful asserts that *structure is determined by the pattern of relations among the elements in a set.* This definition depends on three terms, which I discuss in reverse order:

Elements of a Set. The elements are simply the basic units of theoretical discourse, which appear in experimental work as stimuli or as properties of stimuli. In memory tasks, the elements are usually words or verbal concepts, but the experimenter may be interested in the structure of events, episodes, propositions, sentences, stories, or even visual forms and scenes. The definition asserts that to talk intelligently about the structure(s) of any of these classes we must have in mind a well-defined set of objects whose relations are our concern. For example, a major problem in the analysis of text and simple stories is precisely to determine the units of analysis.

Relations. The emphasis on relations is primary here. It provides for a formal analysis of cognitive structure that avoids the pitfalls of both atomist associationism and the emergent wholes of Gestalt. From this perspective of operational structuralism (Piaget, 1968/1970), structure is determined neither from the elements according to to-be-discovered laws nor from the properties of wholes. Rather, it is the relations among elements and the processes, rules, or procedures by which cognitive structures arise that count (hence the earlier focus on associative memory structures). I fully realize that this orientation raises several further questions of epistemology and cognitive development that need to be addressed. However, I will bypass these in favor of a sharpening of cognitive structure viewed from a relational perspective.

Estes (1975) distinguished two senses of structure that I borrow here. By analogy with the computer, we may speak of memory structure in terms of the *physical* links among *hardware* components (or metaphors thereof), as is common in multistore memory models (Atkinson & Shiffrin, 1968). In this sense structure may refer to the configuration of these components and the transformations applied to information as it is transferred from one component to the next. Alternatively, we may speak of structure in terms of *logical* relations among informational units induced by the *software* that controls the processing. "Structure in this second sense refers to the way in which information entering in the system is organized relative to the procedures available for operating on it [Estes, 1975, p. 33]." Thus, while computer storage consists of sequential, linearly ordered storage locations in hardware terms, the data structures of high-level programming languages allow this storage to be accessed as if it were structured in terms of multidimensional arrays, list structures, networks, or hierarchies (see Winograd, 1975 for examples). It is such logical relations, which arise as incoming information is acted upon by the memory system, with which I am concerned here.

Patterns: Structural Frameworks. Relations among cognitive elements alone do not create structure. If every element is related to every other element in exactly the same way or to the same degree, we have at best a useless and uninformative kind of structure. Rather, the essence of cognitive structure is that, in any particular structural model, the relations are patterned and subject rules. Each of the structures depicted in Figure 4.13 is an example of a *structural framework,* which defines a particular kind of structure in terms of the types of relations and properties of these relations that are allowed in that structure. By considering exactly how one structural framework differs from another, we may be led to a taxonomy of structures themselves, ordering them perhaps in terms of relative power or embedding relations.

For example, the simplest structure framework examined as a memory model is the taxonomy, a set of membership structures that underlie the work on category clustering and unitization. At a slightly higher level, notions of category prototypes (Rosch, 1975) and fuzzy boundaries of cognitive categories (Oden, 1977; Zadeh, 1975) attempt to deal with the internal structure of such related groups. Ordered structures, including sequential orderings (seriation) and circular orderings (circumplex) have been discussed in the context of a variety of learning tasks (Mandler & Dean, 1969; Rothkopf, 1957). The digits 0 to 9, for example, display a (nonlinear) serial structure in various judgmental tasks (Shepard, Kilpatric & Cunningham, 1975), but confusion errors in learning the Morse codes for these digits are structured in a circumplex (Rothkopf, 1957). Finally, higher-ordered structures such as hierarchies and various network structures are by now quite familiar. Such orderings of structural frameworks can be made precise. It can be shown, for instance, that both the seriation and taxonomy are special cases of a tree structure, which in turn is a special case of a network structure. Thus any phenomenon which can be explained or modelled within a given structural framework can also be explained with a higher-order structural model. In this way relations among various frameworks for representing memory structure may be better understood.

B. Structure-Seeking

This definition of structure is meant to apply equally to a wide variety of laboratory and real-world settings. In what follows here, a further set of concepts and problems in this development is outlined.

Latent Structure. Human behavior in a particular memory-dependent task is assumed to be governed by an unobservable, latent cognitive structure. This structure reflects the individual's preexperimental knowledge base, together with the cognitive environment established by the task (instructions, set, expectations, etc.). A network model, for example, may explain the facilitative effects of blocking a categorized list by assuming that the cognitive environment induced by this manipulation (i.e., greater noticing of categorical relations) acts to increase the "flow" along paths connected to the category name of an $\langle isa \rangle$ relation.

Similarity. Of all relations among cognitive elements, it can be argued that similarity is the most fundamental. Every theory of behavior must deal with similarity in some way, most simply assuming it as an elementary undefined relation (Carroll & Wish, 1974). In memory theories, even the concept of the memory trace depends ultimately on some notion of similarity. For example, when we say that a subsequent presentation of the "same" item reactivates the trace laid down earlier, we cannot mean to assert an absolute identity between the two events. Rather, we must interpret such reactivation to mean that the two events are similar enough to generate a full or partial reinstatement of the original experience.

In the present approach, I assume that the effects of structure, in whatever form, can be explained in terms of the similarity between cognitive elements. Thus, for any structural framework, I assume that the relations among elements can be represented by a real-valued similarity function, $S(o_i, o_j, C)$, where o_i, o_j belong to the set O, and C reflects the effect of the cognitive environment. In what follows, C is dropped from this notation when a context is implicit in the discussion. However, cognitive elements only have a degree of similarity with respect to some aspect, situation, or task. In fact, the study of conditions under which the context does or does not affect similarity structure (Shepard & Chipman, 1970; Shepard et al., 1975) may provide valuable insights into the internal representations of verbal and nonverbal concepts (Shepard, 1975) and the relationship between memory and perceptual processes (Shepard & Podgorny, 1978). Ideally, the cognitive environment should be specified as part of the memory model, as it is in the megamodels of semantic memory and in Collins and Loftus's (1975) spreading activation model, where the context for each item includes the priming effect of earlier items.

Such similarity functions can be defined for virtually all theories of memory structure. In Tulving's (1962) theory of subjective organization, for instance, we may define

$$S(o_i, o_j) = \begin{cases} 1 & \text{if } o_i, o_j \text{ belong to the same subjective memory unit} \\ 0 & \text{otherwise.} \end{cases}$$

Or, if it is assumed that subjective units may themselves be grouped recursively into higher order units (Mandler, 1967), the similarity function can be specifed as,

$$S(o_i, o_j) = \begin{cases} k & \text{if } o_i, o_j \text{ belong to the same unit at depth } k \text{ in the hierarchy;} \\ 0 & \text{otherwise} \end{cases}$$

In each case, we may hope to explain the observed effects of structure in terms of suitable definition of similarity.

Proximity. When a subject engages in a memory task, it should be assumed that the latent structure becomes activated and results in certain regularity or consistent patterns in some observable aspect of performance, which may be called the *carrier* of structure (examples are output order in MFR, conditional error probabilities in serial learning and sentence learning). Thus, indices of associative strength, confusion frequency, and similarity judgments are all assumed to tap underlying cognitive relationships as activated in some task; and it is of some interest that these different measures typically relate highly among themselves, at least in an overall analysis (Henley 1969; Schwartz & Humphreys, 1973; Shepard & Podgorny, 1978). The basic step in the current approach is therefore to define a proximity function on the object set, $P(o_i, o_j)$, which captures the regularities observed in the carrier variable. Proximity is thus the observed counterpart to cognitive similarity. For a discussion of the properties of general proximity measures see Carroll & Wish (1974) or Shepard (1972).

Structure Seeking. Given some proximity index that can be computed from the data, together with a suitable structural framework, the structure-seeking problem is to provide a concrete representation of the proximity structure within the given framework. From the concepts of structure and similarity just introduced, it should be clear how the approach I described for free recall can be extended to other learning and memory tasks that depend on structure. The principal requirements for this are *(a)* to identify an appropriate carrier variable for organizational information that reflects memory structure and organizational processes, and *(b)* to define an index of proximity that measures (at least to an ordinal level) the relatedness of pairs of items. Having done these, the structure-seeking problem essentially reduces to applying various scaling methods to the proximities, as in the case with free recall.

Though this description has been somewhat sketchy, it does indicate how we can represent empirically the structure of unobservable mental events. At the same time, however, we must recognize that most work of this nature to date has been largely demonstrative, illustrating how some method works and showing that the results are in accord with other theory and data. The challenge now, I believe, is to use these methods to provide new insights into memory structure and its development (see Ornstein & Corsale, Chapter 7). One way to do this is to begin to examine memory structures systematically across a variety of tasks or performances and, in particular, to focus on invariances in the organization of responses across diverse tasks. For, if the proximities among a set of items are equivalent in two tasks, then we can assert some functional equivalence in the memory structures that gave rise to those proximities. Contrariwise, any lack of invariance can be interpreted as evidence that organization results from different logical structures or processes. The next two subsections illustrate some initial applications of this approach.

1. ENCODING STRUCTURE

Organization in free recall usually refers to consistent output order effects based on meaning or properties of the to-be-remembered items as words. Yet, it is well known that there are also factors that produce consistent organizational effects that are *independent* of the subject's preexperimental cognitive structure. For example, input serial position has an effect on recall order, where typically the subject tends to recall early- and late-presented items prior to other items (Deese & Kaufman, 1957; Rundus, 1971), regardless of any semantic relations among those items. By analogy with the distinction between primary and secondary memory, Tulving (1968) referred to the typical meaning-based effects as *secondary organization* and to the other effects as *primary organization*. Clearly, any complete account of recall organization must take account of organization that results from encoding structure, as well as from semantic structure.

Hogan (1975) presented a model of primary organization that details an encoding structure and a rule for the utilization of this structure in single-trial free recall. Hogan assumes that an encoding structure is developed during presentation based on contiguous rehearsal. The encoding structure may be characterized as a directed network whose links give the relative frequencies of transitions between list items during study. In retrieval, this structure is utilized as follows: The likelihood of a direct transition from the item in serial position i to the jth presented item is assumed to be given by the probability of the corresponding transition during encoding, and subsequent transitions are governed by a Markovian process operating on the transition network. The encoding transitions can be estimated simply by use of an overt rehearsal procedure yielding a matrix of conditional probabilities,

$$P(j \mid i) = \text{Prob (item } j \text{ is rehearsed} \mid \text{item } i \text{ occurs in the same rehearsal set)}.$$

With these data, the Markov model can predict the probabilities of retrieving an item from any serial position at each successive output. That is, the overall serial position curve can be decomposed into a set of such functions representing recall probability versus serial position for each output position. When estimated from the network model using overt rehearsal data, these curves show strong primacy and recency effects only for the first few items recalled. The predicted curves for the last few items recalled possess a primacy component, but show a *negative* recency effect that corresponds closely to experimental results of Craik (1970) and others.

Now, we can also attempt to map the encoding structure directly from the transition matrix **P** in a way that is independent of Hogan's encoding–retrieval model. To do this, we regard **P** as a matrix of encoding proximities that can be mapped into an M-Gram under a given spatial model.

For the present purposes, I have applied Kruskals' MDSCAL program (Kruskal & Carmone, 1969) to the matrix **P,** obtained from Hogan (1975, Table 1). MDS solutions were found for four dimensions down through one dimension. The stress values (Formula 2) obtained from these solutions were essentially equivalent for 2, 3, and 4 dimensions (.176, .158, and .158) but increased sharply to .266 when the configuration was constrained to a one-dimensional space. Accordingly, a two-dimensional fit was tentatively accepted. The two-dimensional configuration is shown in Figure 4.14. The orderly arrangement of the points (corresponding to input positions) in this figure shows clearly that rehearsals are highly structured: The points form a smooth spiral, starting near the origin.

Several features of this configuration are worth noting. First, the dimensions can be characterized by the two orthogonal directions shown on the plot. The first of these contrasts the primacy and recency items with those presented in the middle of the list. In recall, the primacy and recency items are, of course, recalled more often, and earlier in output, than items from the middle of the list, so this dimension reflects recall strength. The second direction contrasts the terminal (recency) items, considered to reflect recall from primary memory (Waugh & Norman, 1965), with prerecency items from the beginning and middle of the list, reflecting recall from secondary memory.

An alternative interpretation of this configuration focuses on the arrangement of points in a serial chain. (In two dimensions MDS achieves a better fit by drawing the ends of the chain together; see Shepard, 1974.) The implication of this is that for single-trial free recall at least, where semantic factors play a minimal role in primary organization, rehearsal probabilities depend strongly on the serial distance between items in the presentation list. The items rehearsed together are most likely to be items presented in nearby input loca-

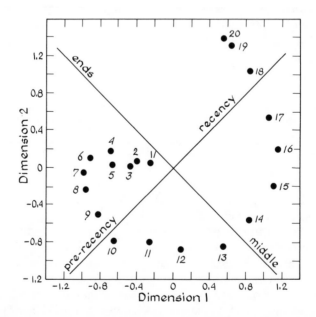

FIGURE 4.14 Two-dimensional MDS solution for Hogan's (1975) rehearsal data.

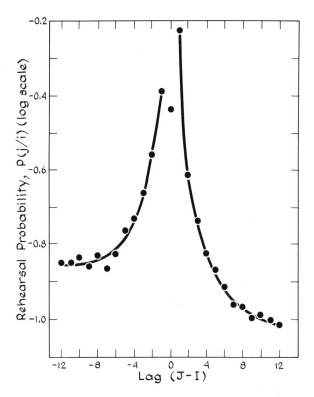

FIGURE 4.15 Rehearsal probability, *p(ji)*, plotted as a function of *(j−i)*, the lag between these items at presentation.

tions. It should also be noted that the spacing between consecutive points varies systematically, with wider gaps in the middle than at either end.

To look at this interpretation directly, Hogan's probability matrix can be averaged down the major diagonals to give probabilities that items are rehearsed as a function of the lag between them. Figure 4.15 shows the result of such an analysis. Given that item *i* appears in a rehearsal set, the probabilities that other items are rehearsed with it drop off sharply with increasing separation between them. This exponential decline in rehearsal probabilities in fact consistent with a network model in which transition probabilities combine multiplicatively, as in Hogan's Markov model. In any event, proximity analysis appears capable of representing structure in primary organization using rehearsal data or some other measure of proximity.

2. SINGLE-STRUCTURE HYPOTHESIS

In distinguishing between episodic and semantic memory, Tulving (1972) suggested that it would be useful, at least temporarily, to consider these as two separate systems with distinct storage structures. Several experiments performed by my students and I have explored the consequences of denying this separation. It has seemed more reasonable to us to consider the more parsimonious alternative that both semantic and episodic information are held in a single memory structure and that this structure is utilized in a variety of tasks that depend on interverbal relationships. This alternative can be termed the *single-structure hypothesis*. Some initial, exploratory tests of this hypothesis are reported below.

Consider the following two requests for retrieval:

1. Write down all the names of animals you can think of (free emission).
2. Write down all the names of animals you just saw on the screen (free recall).

According to the single-structure hypothesis, a subject's order of recall in these two tasks should reflect retrieval from the same memory structure, and hence organizational structures derived from such data should be highly similar.

Other questions could also be asked of the subjects. Retrieval in free recall is restricted to just those items that appeared on the current list. We could just as easily restrict retrieval to other subsets of the category **animals,** for example

3. African animals
4. Small animals
5. Brown animals
6. Animals whose names begin with *d, e, f,* or *g.*
7. Animals with names of eight or more letters.

Some of these queries are obviously easier and more natural than others. Questions (3), (4), and (5) call for subsets based on properties of location, size, and color, whereas appropriate responses to (6) and (7) are defined by lexical properties. However, subjects can respond to such questions and, as in free recall, their responses contain consistencies and regularities to the extent that retrieval is organized. This observed organization can be thought of as deriving from the individual's long-term memory structure, together with the cognitive environment established by the particular task. According to the single-structure hypothesis, we would expect recall structure to be largely invariant from semantic retrieval to episodic retrieval.

Shepard (1974) presented results from an experiment of (Shepard, 1957) type 1—free emission of animal names. Shepard selected the 16 most frequently listed animals, and for each pair of these he calculated a proximity measure based on the average distance between them in the written lists. Figure 4.16 portrays Shepard's results, obtained by applying MDS and hierarchical clustering to these proximity measures and embedding the clusters into the spatial representation. The clusters shown—*domesticated, pets, farm animal,* and so forth—appear to represent reasonable categories among animals, though of course other groupings are possible.

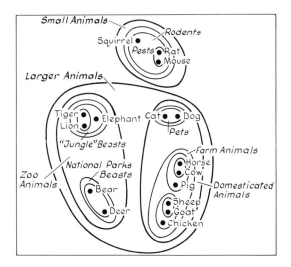

FIGURE 4.16 Two-dimensional representation of 16 animal names, with embedded hierarchical clusters. [*Data from Shepard (1957), based on a free emission task. (Figure from Shepard, 1974).*]

I used these same 16 items in a small free-recall experiment to see whether a similar structure would be recovered in free recall. There were just five subjects and each received eight study–test trials. The recall-order proximities among these items were averaged over both subjects and trials, and I performed the same analyses that Shepard had applied to his data. The result of this miniexperiment is shown in Figure 4.17. There are clear differences between my solution and Shepard's: *Squirrel* is positioned differently, joining the wild

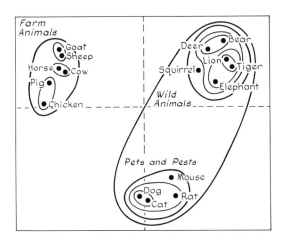

FIGURE 4.17 Two-dimensional representation of the 16 animal names, based on proximities from free recall. Pooled data from five subjects, each over eight trials.

animals in my configuration. Shepard's *pet* and *pest* clusters merge in the free-recall result to form a category that could be called (somewhat facetiously) "domestic pests," distinguished from the "wild pests" above them.

However, these are local discrepancies and overall, the two configurations are far more similar than they are different. The correlation between the clustering solutions (Friendly, 1977; Gruvaeus & Wainer, 1972) is .79, and a coefficient of congruence based on a best fit between the two spatial solutions is .94.

The results were encouraging, and a student of mine set out to test their reliability (Katz, 1976). One experiment compared organizational structures in free emission, free recall and several sorting tasks, using a slightly larger set of animal names. Three groups of subjects were tested. One group (Group A1; $N = 78$) was asked to list up to 50 animals. Following this, they were asked to sort the items they had produced into an arbitrary number of categories, based on "similarity." The 24 most frequently emitted words were selected and a second group (A2; $N = 33$) merely sorted these into subjective categories. A third group (A3; $N = 16$) was engaged in a free-recall task with six trials, followed by a sorting task in which they were asked to group together words that tended to go together in their recall.

We computed proximity measures for each task and applied hierarchical clustering to the group matrices. Again, there are some local differences among these clusterings (see Figure 4.18), but the correspondence across tasks is striking. This assessment is confirmed by correlations ranging from .78 to .91 among the cluster solutions derived from the various tasks (see Table 4.5).

Both solutions contain three major clusters, which can be loosely characterized as *domestic, zoo,* and *forest* animals. In free recall, *(rat, mouse)* merges with *(dog, cat)* as it did in the pilot experiment. Similar local differences in organization between free recall and semantic memory tasks have been observed by Caramazza, Hersh & Torgerson (1976) and may be attributed to the use of associative relations (e.g., *cat, mouse*) in addition to semantic subcategories in recall. Clearly, we need to look more closely at invariances in structure across semantic and episodic tasks.

Table 4.5
Correlations between Hierarchical Clusterings
Obtained from Different Tasks for the Animal List

			Task		
Task	FE	FES	Sort	FR	FRS
Free emission (FE)	×				
Free emission sort (FES)	.84	×			
Sorting (Sort)	.78	.90	×		
Free recall (FR)	.80	.86	.85	×	
Free recall sort (FRS)	.83	.92	.90	.91	×

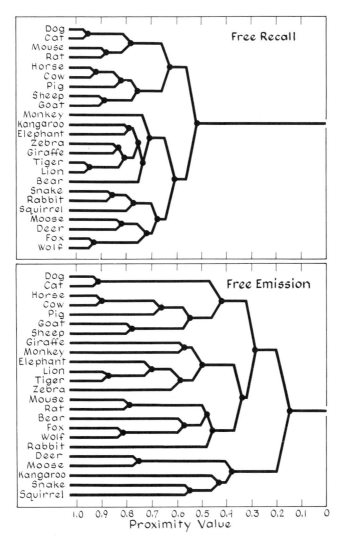

FIGURE 4.18 Hierarchical M-Grams derived from data in free-recall and free-emission tasks.
[*Data from Katz (1976).*]

C. Structure Testing

In contrast to the exploratory, model-fitting techniques used in structure seeking, there is also a need for confirmatory methods to test the correspondence between an observed structure and some hypothesized model. The measurement of category clustering and subjective organization are present-day, rudimentary examples of structure testing. In the former case, output order proximity is compared against a set membership structure (the list categories); in the latter, it is compared to output order on the previous trial. In both cases, the degree of correspondence is assessed relative to a "null" model of random recall.

However, we also need methods that enable us to express specific, detailed hypotheses concerning organizational structure and to test them quantitatively. By "express" I mean that the researcher should be able to state an organizational hypothesis that specifies any pattern of interitem relations; by "test" I mean that the method should provide a measure of correspondence between the data and the hypothesized model (such as X^2 or a correlation), together with enough distribution theory to obtain a probability value. Structure testing, in this sense, fulfills the need for a positive model of organization (Colle, 1972), which specifies the form that organization *has* rather than the form it does *not* have.

The hypothesized structure may reflect manipulations performed by the experimenter (e.g., list structure or presentation effects), or it may reflect some theory of performance. Equally, the comparison structure may come from another sample of the subject's performance in the same task or in some other task (e.g., memory structure in transfer tasks).

In the ideal situation, we would have a general theory of memory organization, stated as a model with a specified structure, and parameters identified with the functional components of the memory system. Together with this theoretical approach, there would be methods for testing the model that would allow some parameters to be estimated from the data, while others were fixed or constrained according to experimental hypothesis. Whereas most recent work on memory structure is principally exploratory, two recent proposals appear to point in useful new directions.

1. PATTERNS OF ITEM COOCCURRENCE

Rotondo (1977) developed a general model in which organizational hypotheses are stated in terms of membership in latent chunks. Each chunk is characterized by a *chunk strength* parameter that reflects the probability that the chunk itself is retrieved. Each item is also characterized in the model by its chunk *membership strength(s),* which reflect the conditional probability of recalling that item from a chunk to which it belongs, given that the chunk is retrieved. An item may belong to several chunks, so that chunks may overlap in various ways.

Another novel aspect of Rotondo's model is that it is fitted to data found from patterns of cooccurrence of items in recall, rather than from order of recall information. This choice simplifies the mathematics of the probability model, which relates the observed data (frequencies of cooccurrence of all possible item subsets) to the parameters of the model. Estimation and testing of the parameters are also simplified because the data are reduced to binary variables (recalled/not recalled) for which detailed distributional theory is available.

However, this reduction to binary variables requires huge amounts of data, since it entails estimating the probabilities of all of the possible 2^L response patterns (all possible subsets of items recalled) from the data. A 10-item list, for instance, would have $2^{10} = 1024$ response pattern probabilities, each requiring at least 20 to 50 observations. Further, Rotondo assumes that all recalls are statistically independent, which experimentally requires a single-trial recall procedure.

Whereas these restrictions may limit the practical application of the method, at least in free recall, the basic ideas of specifying and testing structural hypotheses are important and can be described with some simple examples.

Suppose we have a set of six items, $o_1, \ldots, o_6$, as shown in Figure 4.19. A hypothesis that the items belong to two mutually exclusive chunks can be specified with a structural diagram as shown in Panel A. Alternatively, a hypothesis of three overlapping chunks for these same items might be depicted as in Panel B. It should be noted that with overlapping chunks, an item o_i has membership strength parameters, e_{ik}, for each chunk to which it belongs. Any such hypothesis would presumably be derived on the basis of logical or semantic relations among the items or from prior use of structure-seeking methods for generating hypotheses. However, the data used to generate the hypothesis must be independent of the data used to test it. For example, one

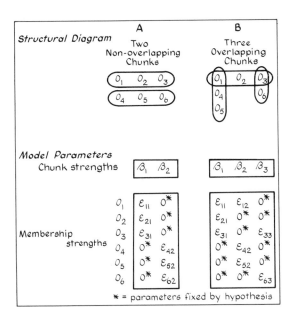

FIGURE 4.19 Two structural hypotheses for six items and the corresponding parameters according to Rotondo's (1977) model.

useful strategy is to fit overlapping clusters using Shepard & Arabie's (1978) ADDCLUS procedure on half of a sample and to test the clusters found using Rotondo's method on the other half.

Regardless of the source of the hypothesis, its effect is to restrict certain parameters in the model to *fixed* values (typically 0 or 1). In addition, some of the nonfixed parameters can be *constrained* to be equal (e.g., $e_{11} = e_{12} = e_{13}$ in Figure 4.19A would specify a chunk of equally retrievable items). The remaining parameters are considered *free*. The free and constrained parameters are then fit to the data, and the fitting process naturally yields a goodness of fit for the hypothesized model as well as for the parameter estimates. In addition, different models can be tested against one another, and this feature is particularly useful when one model is a restriction of another. For example, if a model with two independent chunks (Figure 4.19A) fits with all parameters free, we could specify equal membership strengths within chunks and examine the fit of the restricted model.

It also appears that Rotondo's method can be applied to serial learning, recognition, and other tasks where retrieval cooccurrence can be thought to index organization. Despite the practical limitations noted above, this is the first instance of a general probability model for organizational structure in which structural hypotheses can be specified as special cases. For dimensional frameworks, a method of specifying free, fixed, and constrained parameters of an MDS configuration has been developed by Bentler & Weeks (1978).

2. TESTS OF STRUCTURE IN PROXIMITIES

If structure in recall order can be represented in terms of a matrix of proximities, it may be easier to specify and test hypotheses on recall organization in terms of corresponding hypotheses on the entries in a proximity matrix. It turns out that this is indeed the case.

For concreteness, we can consider a simple free-recall experiment that pits two modes of organization against each other. The items are consistently presented in fixed spatial positions (on a computer-driven CRT screen, for example), so that they may be organized by spatial groups or as a visual memory image. Further, the list is composed of items from various thematic categories, so that the list might also be organized in clusters. How do we evaluate the recall data from such an experiment against these two a priori hypotheses?

Currently, we would represent the structure of proximities among these items in recall using MDS or cluster analysis or perhaps both. With luck, the obtained configuration might clearly conform to one hypothesized structure or the other, and the conclusion would be easily drawn. More likely, however, the scaling results might reflect a mixture of both organizational schemes, or it might be found that some subjects organize spatially, while others organize thematically. In any case, this eyeball approach provides no way to measure the degree of support for any such hypothesis.

An alternative approach, developed extensively by Lawrence Hubert and his collaborators (Hubert & Levin, 1976; Hubert & Schultz, 1976; Hubert & Baker, 1977), bypasses the scaling solutions and evaluates directly whether a particular hypothesis is reflected in the original proximities. The essence of this technique is that a specified structural hypothesis can be represented numerically in a hypothesis matrix **H**, where $H_{ij} = H(o_i, o_j)$ denotes the hypothesized strength of relation between items o_i and o_j. Then, we can measure how well the data match the hypothesis by correlating the entries in **H** with those in a proximity matrix **P**.

In the present example, a simple hypothesis index for a category structure could be defined as

$$H_{ij} = \begin{cases} 1 & \text{if } o_i \text{ and } o_j \text{ belong to the same category;} \\ 0 & \text{otherwise.} \end{cases}$$

This hypothesized structure, for a set of nine items, is shown in Panel A of Figure 4.20, together with the H matrix computed from the preceding definition. Similarly, the hypothesis that the subjects organized spatially could be represented numerically, as shown in Panel B, where

$$H_{ij} = \text{distance between } o_i \text{ and } o_j \text{ in the hypothesized spatial}$$
configuration.
$$= [(x_i - x_j)^2 + (y_i - y_j)^2]^{1/2}$$

where (x_i, y_i) denote the numerical coordinates of item o_i on the CRT screen.

Now, to evaluate the degree to which either hypothesized structure accounts for the pattern of recall organization, we have only to compute some measure of correlation between the observed proximity matrix **P** and each of the hypothesis matrices. Conceptually, the simplest statistic is the Pearson product–moment correlation,

$$r(\mathbf{P}, \mathbf{H}) = \frac{1}{n(n-1)} \sum_{i \neq j} \sum p_{ij} \bullet h_{ij}$$

where p_i and h_{ij} are expressed in standard score units. For hypothesis-testing purposes, the raw cross product, $\Gamma = \sum \sum P_{ij} \bullet H_{ij}$ is a sufficient statistic and simpler to compute.

Once this index is calculated, the next question is whether its value is large enough to reject an appropriate null hypothesis. The null distribution is generated by considering all possible reorderings of the rows and columns of the proximity matrix, **P**, while the **H** matrix is held fixed. For each ordering, a value of the correlation r(**P**, **H**) can be computed. The $L!$ correlations for all

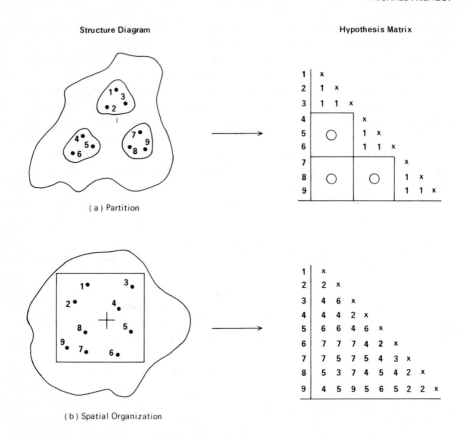

FIGURE 4.20 Alternative hypothesized memory structures and their representation as matrices, according to Hubert's quadratic assignment approach.

possible reorderings of **P** form a sampling distribution against which the correlation actually obtained can be judged for significance. In practice, it is not necessary to work out the entire sampling distribution, however. Hubert and Schultz (1976) showed how approximate tests can be carried out through formulas for the mean, $E[\Gamma]$, and variance, $\text{Var}[\Gamma]$, of the null distribution, which depend only on the **P** and **H** matrices.

In combination with the structure-seeking methods discussed earlier, this approach to structure testing provides a rigorous and flexible methodology for the analysis of cognitive structure.

III. CONCLUSIONS

The analysis of memory structure along the lines described here has a number of interesting and potentially fruitful consequences.

First, this approach attempts to characterize general types of memory structures (structural frameworks) and their properties. By doing so, it encourages the investigator to think about memory processes in terms of patterns or configurations of items and the relations among them.

Moreover, consideration of their properties may lead to a taxonomy of structural frameworks and thus of structural memory models in the same way that linguistic theory has developed ordering relations among grammars (Chomsky & Miller, 1965). A hierarchy, for example, is a special case of a network; the latter, therefore, is uniformly more powerful, but contains more free parameters.

Second, structural frameworks, like hierarchies, networks, and other configurations arise in a wide variety of physical as well as psychological contexts, which may suggest useful process models. The spreading activation model of Collins and Loftus (1975), for example, relies heavily on the analog of physical flow in a network. Hierarchical structures appearing in phrase-structure grammars and syntactic parsers suggest the two mechanisms of depth-first and breadth-first search for locating items in a tree structure.

Finally, the graphic representations of proximity analysis suggest the value of analyzing the detailed aspects of performance in a variety of standard memory tasks so that we may observe and possibly manipulate the structure generated by the learner in these tasks. There is an important practical corollary: If learning, in a general sense, is a matter of fitting new information into an existing and organizational scheme, then knowledge of an individual's memory structure may enable us to optimize this process. This is the ultimate test of any theory of learning, as Murdock, Anderson, and Ho (1974) have pointed out. Some initial steps in this direction were recently carried out (Friendly & Franklin, 1977).

REFERENCES

Allen, M. Graph theory, organization and memory. In C. N. Cofer (Chair), *Organization and memory: The influence of W. A. Bousfield.* Symposium presented at the meeting of the Eastern Psychological Association, New York, 1971.

Anderson, J. R., & Bower, G. H. Recognition and Retrieval Processes in Free Recall. *Psychological Review,* 1972, 79, 97–123.

Anderson, J. R., & Bower, G. H. *Human associative memory.* Washington, D.C.: V. H. Winston & Sons, 1973.

Anglin, J. M. *The growth of word meaning.* Cambridge, Mass.: The M.I.T. Press, 1970.

Atkinson, R. C., & Shiffrin, R. M., Human memory: A proposed system and the control processes. In K. W. Spence & J. T. Spence (Eds.), *The psychology of learning and motivation* (Vol. 2). New York: Academic Press, 1968.

Bentler, P. M., & Weeks, D. G. Restricted multidimensional scaling. *Journal of Mathematical Psychology,* 1978, 17, 138–151.

Bower, G. H., & Winzenz, D. Group structure, coding, and memory for digit series. *Journal of Experimental Psychology Monograph,* 1969, 80 (Pt. 2).

Boyd, J. P., & Wexler, K. N. Trees with structure. *Journal of Mathematical Psychology,* 1973, *10,* 115–147.

Bruce, D. & Fagan, R. L. More on the recognition and free recall of organized lists. *Journal of Experimental Psychology,* 1970, *85,* 153–154.

Buschke, H. Learning is organized by chunking. *Journal of Verbal Learning and Verbal Behavior,* 1976, *15,* 313–324.

Buschke, H. Two dimensional recall: immediate identification of clusters in episodic and semantic memory. *Journal of Verbal Learning and Verbal Behavior,* 1977, *16,* 201–215.

Caramazza, A., Hersh, H., & Torgerson, W. S. Subjective structures and operations in semantic memory. *Journal of Verbal Learning and Verbal Behavior,* 1976, *15,* 103–117.

Carroll, J. D., & Wish, M. Multidimensional perceptual models and measurement methods. In E. C. Carterette (Ed.), *Handbook of perception* (Vol. II). New York: Academic Press, 1974.

Chomsky, N. & Miller, G. A. Finite state languages. *Information and Contròl,* 1958, *1,* 91–112.

Colle, H. A. The reification of clustering. *Journal of Verbal Learning and Verbal Behavior,* 1972, *11,* 624–633.

Collins, A. M., & Loftus, E. F. A spreading–activiation theory of semantic processing. *Psychological Review,* 1975, *82,* 407–428.

Craik, F. I. M. The fate of primary memory items in free recall. *Journal of Verbal Learning and Verbal Behavior,* 1970, *9,* 143–148.

Cunningham, J. P. Free trees and bidirectional trees as representations of psychological distances. *Journal of Mathematical Psychology,* 1978, *17,* 165–188.

Deese, J. *The structure of associations in language and thought.* Baltimore, Md.: The Johns Hopkins Press, 1965.

Deese, J., & Kaufman, R. A. Serial effects in recall of unorganized and sequentially organized verbal material. *Journal of Experimental Psychology,* 1957, *54,* 180–187.

Estes, W. K. Learning theory and the new 'mental chemistry'. *Psychological Review,* 1960, *67,* 207–223.

Estes, W. K. An associative basis for coding and organization in memory. In A. W. Melton & E. Martin (Eds.), *Coding processes in human memory.* Washington, D.C.: V.H. Winston & Sons, 1972.

Estes, W. K. Structural aspects of associative models for memory. In C. N. Cofer (Ed.), *The structure of human memory.* San Francisco: W. H. Freeman & Co. 1975.

Feigenbaum, E. A. The simulation of verbal learning behavior. In E. A. Feigenbaum & J. Feldman (Eds.), *Computers and thought,* New York: McGraw-Hill, 1963.

Fillenbaum, S., & Rapoport, A. *Structures in the subjective lexicon.* New York: Academic Press, 1971.

Friendly, M. L. *Proximity analysis and the structure of organization in free recall.* Princeton, N.J.: Educational Testing Service, Research Bulletin RB72-3, 1972.

Friendly, M. L. Hierarchical organization in free recall and recognition. Paper presented at the meetings of the Eastern Psychological Association, Philadelphia, 1974.

Friendly, M. L. In search of the M-Gram: The structure of organization in free recall. *Cognitive Psychology,* 1977, *9,* 188–249.

Friendly, M., & Franklin, P. Facilitating learning in interactive free recall. Paper presented at the meeting of the Psychonomics Society, Washington, D.C., November, 1977.

Gruvaeus, G. T., & Wainer, H. C. Some notes on hierarchical clustering procedures. *British Journal of Mathematical and Statistical Psychology,* 1972, *25,* 200–206.

Henley, N. M. A psychological study of the semantics of animal terms. *Journal of Verbal Learning and Verbal Behavior,* 1969, *8,* 176–184.

Hogan, R. M. Interitem encoding and directed search in free recall. *Memory & Cognition,* 1975, *3,* 197–209.

Hubert, L. J., & Baker, F. B. The comparison and fitting of given classification schemes. *Journal of Mathematical Psychology,* 1977, *16,* 233–253.

Hubert, L. J., & Levin, J. R. A general statistical framework for assessing categorical clustering in free recall. *Psychological Bulletin,* 1976, *83,* 1072–1080.

Hubert, L. J., & Schultz, J. Quadratic assignment as a general data analysis strategy. *British Journal of Mathematical and Statistical Psychology,* 1976, *29,* 190–241.

Jardine, N., & Sibson, R. *Mathematical taxonomy.* New York: Wiley and Sons, 1971.

Johnson, N. F. The role of chunking and organization in the process of recall. In G. H. Bower (Ed.), *The psychology of learning and motivation* (Vol. 4). New York: Academic Press, 1970.

Johnson, S. C. Hierarchical clustering schemes. *Psychometrika,* 1967, *32,* 241–254.

Johnson, S. C. *A simple cluster statistic.* Unpublished manuscript, Bell Telephone Laboratories, 1968.

Katz, W. A. *The single structure hypothesis: A compairson of organizational structures derived from semantic and episodic memory.* Unpublished master's thesis, York University, 1976.

Kintsch, W. Models for free recall and recognition. In D. A. Norman (Ed.), *Models of human memory,* New York: Wiley and Sons, 1970.

Koh, S. D., Vernon, M., & Bailey, W. Free-recall learning of word lists by prelingual deaf subjects. *Journal of Verbal Learning and Verbal Behavior,* 1971, *10,* 542–547.

Kruskal, J. B., & Carmone, F. J., *How to use M-D-SCAL (Version 5M) and other useful information.* Murray Hill, N.J.: Bell Telephone Laboratories, March 1969 (mimeographed).

Mandler, G. Organization and memory. in K. W. Spence & J. T. Spence (Eds.), *The psychology of learning and motivation* (Vol. 1). New York: Academic Press, 1967.

Mandler, G. Association and organization: facts, fancies, and theories. In T. R. Horton & D. L. Dixon (Eds.), *Verbal behavior and general behavior theory.* Englewood Cliffs, N.J.: Prentice-Hall, 1968.

Mandler, G. Organization and recognition. In E. Tulving & W. Donaldson (Eds.), *Organization and memory.* New York: Academic Press, 1972.

Mandler, G., & Anderson, R. E. Temporal and spatial cues in seriation. *Journal of Experimental Psychology,* 1971, *90,* 128–135.

Mandler, G., & Dean, P. J. Seriation: Development of serial order in free recall. *Journal of Experimental Psychology,* 1969, *81,* 207–215.

Mandler, J. M., & Johnson, N. S. Remembrance of things parsed: Story structure and recall. *Cognitive Psychology,* 1977, *9,* 111–151.

Martin, E., & Noreen, D. L. Serial learning: Identification of subjective sequences. *Cognitive Psychology,* 1974, *6,* 421–435.

Marton, F. *Structural dynamics of learning.* Stockholm: Almqvist & Wiksell, 1970.

Miller, G. A., Galanter, E., & Pribram, K. *Plans and the structure of behavior.* New York: Holt, Rinehart & Winston, 1960.

Monk, A. F. A new approach to the characterization of sequential structure in multi-trial free recall using hierarchical grouping analysis. *British Journal of Mathematical and Statistical Psychology,* 1976, *29,* 1–18.

Murdock, B. B., Jr., Anderson, R. E., & Ho, E. Effects of presentation order on learning in multitrial free recall. *Journal of Verbal Learning and Verbal Behavior,* 1974, *13,* 522–529.

Norman, D. A., & Rumelhart, D. E., & LNR. *Explorations in cognition.* San Francisco: W. H. Freeman, 1975.

Oden, G. C. Fuzziness in semantic memory: Choosing exemplars of subjective categories. *Memory & Cognition,* 1977, *5,* 198–204.

Ornstein, P.A. The role of prior-list organization in a free-recall transfer task. *Journal of Experimental Psychology,* 1970, *86,* 32–37.

Pachella, R. G. The interpretation of reaction time in information-processing research. In B. Kantrowitz (Ed.), *Human information processing: Tutorials in performance and cognition.* Hillsdale, N.J.: Lawrence Erlbaum Associates, 1974.

Pellegrino, J. W. A general measure of organization in free recall for variable unit size and internal sequential consistency. *Behavioral Research Methods and Instrumentation,* 1971, *3,* 241–246.

Piaget, J. [*Le Structuralism.*] (C. Maschler, trans.) Basic Books, 1970. (Originally published, Paris: Presses Universitaires de France, 1968.)

Postman, Leo. Organization and interference. *Psychological Review,* 1971, *78*(4), 290–302.

Reitman, J. S., & Reuter, H. Discovering hierarchical memory structures from free recall. Paper presented at the meetings of the Psychonomics Society, St. Louis, Mo., November, 1976.

Reuter, H. Hierarchical memory structures from systematic aspects of free recall output orders. Unpublished manuscript, University of Michigan, 1976.

Rosch, E. Cognitive representations of semantic categories. *Journal of Experimental Psychology: General*, 1975, *1*, 192–233.

Rothkopf, E. Z. A measure of stimulus similarity and errors in some paired-associate learning tasks. *Journal of Experimental Psychology*, 1957, *53*, 94–101.

Rotondo, J. A. Discrete structural models of organization in free recall. *Journal of Mathematical Psychology*, 1977, in press.

Rumelhart, D. E. Notes on a schema for stories. In D. G. Bobrow & A. Collins (Eds.), *Representation and understanding: Studies in cognitive science*. New York: Academic Press, 1975.

Rumelhart, D. E., Lindsay, P. H., & Norman, D. A. A process model for long-term memory. In E. Tulving & W. Donaldson (Eds.), *Organization of Memory*. New York: Academic Press, 1972.

Rundus, D. Analysis of rehearsal processes in free recall. *Journal of Experimental Psychology*, 1971, *89*, 63–77.

Schank, R. C. *Conceptual information processing*. New York: American Elsevier, 1975.

Schwartz, R. M., & Humphreys, M. S. Similarity judgments and free recall of unrelated words. *Journal of Experimental Psychology*, 1973, *101*, 10–15.

Seibel, R. An experimental paradigm for studying the organization and strategies utilized by individual *Ss* in human learning and an experimental evaluation of it. Paper presented at meetings of the Psychonomic Society, Niagara Falls, Ontario, Oct. 1964.

Shepard, R. N. Multidimensional scaling of concepts based upon sequences of restricted associative responses. *American Psychologist*, 1957, *12*, 440–441. (Abstract)

Shepard, R. N. A taxonomy of some principal types of data and of multidimensional methods for their analysis. In R. N. Shepard, A. K. Romney, & S. B. Nerlove (Eds.), *Multidimensional scaling: Theory and applications in the behavioral sciences* (Vol. 1). New York: Seminar Press, 1972.

Shepard, R. N. Representation of structure in similarity data: Problems and prospects. *Psychometrika*, 1974, *39*, 373–421.

Shepard, R. N. Form, formation and transformations of internal representations. In R. Solso (Ed.), *Information processing and cognition: The Loyola symposium*. Hillsdale, N.J.: Lawrence Erlbaum Associates, 1975.

Shepard, R. N., & Arabie, P. Additive clustering: Representation of similarities as combinations of discrete overlapping properties. Unpublished manuscript, June 1978.

Shepard, R. N., & Chipman, S. Second-order isomorphism of internal representation: Shapes of states. *Cognitive Psychology*, 1970, *1*, 1–17.

Shepard, R. N., Kilpatric, D. W., & Cunningham, J. P. The internal representation of numbers. *Cognitive Psychology*, 1975, *7*, 82–138.

Shepard, R.N., & Podgorny, P. Cognitive processes that resemble perceptual processes. In W. K. Estes (Ed.), *Handbook of Learning and Cognitive Processes* (Vol. 5). Hillsdale, N.J.: Lawrence Erlbaum Associates, 1978.

Sternberg, R. J., & Tulving, E. The measurement of subjective organization in free recall. *Psychological Bulletin*, 1977, *84*, 539–556.

Thorndyke, P. Cognitive structures in comprehension and memory of narrative discourse. *Cognitive Psychology*, 1977, *9*, 77–110.

Tulving, E. Subjective organization in free recall of "unrelated" words. *Psychological Review*, 1962, *69*, 344–354.

Tulving, E. Intratrial and intertrial retention: Notes towards a theory of free recall verbal learning. *Psychological Review*, 1964, *71*, 219–237.

Tulving, E. Theoretical issues in free recall. In T. R. Dixon, & D. L. Horton (Eds.), *Verbal behavior and general behavior theory*. Englewood Cliffs, N.J.: Prentice Hall, 1968.

Tulving, E. Episodic and semantic memory. In E. Tulving & W. Donaldson (Eds.), *Organization and memory*. New York: Academic Press, 1972.

Waugh, N. C., & Norman, D. A. Primary memory. *Psychological Review,* 1965, *72,* 89–104.

Winograd, T. Computer memories: A metaphor for memory organization. In C. N. Cofer (Ed.), *The structure of human memory*. San Francisco: W. H. Freeman, 1975.

Yngve, V. H. A model and an hypothesis for language structure, *Proceedings of the American Philosophical Society,* 1961, *104,* 444–466.

Zadeh, L. A. Calculus of fuzzy restrictions. In L. A. Zadeh, K. S. Fu, K. Tanaka, & M. Shimura (Eds.), *Fuzzy sets and their applications to cognitive and decision processes*. New York: Academic Press, 1975.

Zangen, M., Ziegelbaum, P. & Buschke, M. CLUSTER: A program for identifying recurrent clusters. *Behavior Research Methods and Instrumentation,* 1976, *8,* 388.

PART III

PERSPECTIVES ON THE STRUCTURE OF SEMANTIC MEMORY AND SEMANTIC–EPISODIC RELATIONS

CHAPTER **5**

JANET L. LACHMAN
ROY LACHMAN

Theories of Memory
Organization and Human Evolution

The 1970s was a prime decade for semantic memory theories. A number of theories of semantic memory appeared, varying in size from single journal articles to book-length expositions. Some of these dealt more or less exclusively with semantic memory. The more ambitious included semantic memory as part of larger and comprehensive models encompassing memory, meaning, and knowledge. Whatever their scope, all attempted some account of the organization of permanent memory. All were computational theories, couching their accounts of mental structures and processes in terms of computational or information-processing concepts. Such theoretical efforts capitalize on conceptual commonalities between intelligent action as accomplished by human beings and the intelligent behavior of nonbiological systems. Not surprisingly, then, semantic memory theories in this tradition have emphasized the similarities between human and artificial intelligence rather than the differences. As yet, information-processing theories of semantic memory have not reached the point of examining the dissimilarities between information processing in human biological systems and in artifacts, much less exploiting these differences.

Pylyshyn (1978) compared extensively the methods and products of artificial intelligence and a broad class of cognitive theory. He concluded that although the two approaches—actually two disciplines—have different styles of research and different intellectual antecedents, the substantive knowledge that each approach produces shows no principled differences. Over 30 peer commentaries followed the original essay, yet not one mentioned the inescapable fact that human computational capacities are the product of an evolutionary history whereas those of automata are not. This observation brings us to the twofold purpose of this paper. We shall describe some of the conceptual orientation that has guided the current set of semantic memory theories and review their substantive achievements. At the same time we shall attempt a preliminary exploration of how current thinking in behavioral evolution might help distinguish theories of artificial intelligence from computational theories of human cognition and suggest constraints for the latter.

I. COMPUTATIONAL THEORIES OF COGNITION

The emphasis of contemporary theories of semantic memory on computational concepts derives from the intellectual ancestry of the information-processing approach to cognition. There are several lines of such ancestry, one of which stems from work in mathematical logic that inspired the concept of a Turing machine and related formulations (Church, 1936; Post, 1936; Turing, 1936). Turing's work, which eventually had major implications for cognitive psychology, was actually directed at the metamathematical issues of computability and proof. He was interested in a formal delineation of the class of mathematical problems that can be solved. In pursuing his own objectives, he analyzed the properties of an *effective procedure:* a fully specified set of steps that, if performed, will inevitably lead to the solution of a problem. An effective procedure is fully specified if it requires no appeal to human intuition, which is obviously the case if a simple machine without human intellect can follow the steps and achieve the solution. Turing further defended the thesis that any effective procedure that can be accomplished and characterized by human problem solvers can be achieved by a machine having only a small number of properties and capabilities. In this context, "machine" can be understood either as an abstract mathematical system or as a discrete set of processes whose states and changes of state can be described by a small number of elementary symbol-manipulating operations. Turing's system, called the *Universal machine* or *Turing machine,* could in principle solve a formidable range of mathematical problems with its small set of primitive operations. These operations are both abstract and concrete—abstract in that they are not tied inextricably to any particular physical implementation, but concrete in that they can be realized in a wide variety of physical devices. Among the physical devices could be biological organisms, an idea that later would have profound significance for cognitive psychology. However, this significance was not realized until Newell and Simon pulled together the concepts involved in Turing's formulation and the psychological concepts underlying intelligent action.

Perceiving, speaking, reading, comprehending, thinking, and remembering are all instances of intelligent behavior. They are also instances of symbol-manipulating procedures and therefore potentially describable in terms of the logical operations available to a symbol-manipulating automaton such as a Turing machine. The insight that the mind might be construed as a symbol-manipulating device is owed to Newell and Simon, as is the formal and empirical development of this insight (Newell & Simon, 1961, 1972, 1976). Their extension of the basic formulation of the Turing machine had profound impact on the study of cognitive psychology, because it effectively concretized the processes involved in symbol manipulations. Mathematical logicians had previously been able to demonstrate that symbols, and the operations performed on them, could be described in terms of explicit, concrete processes rather than intangible abstractions. The abstract symbols of formal logic could be copied, transformed, rearranged, and concatenated in much the same way as physical things. Moreover, formally objective standards of validity and consistency could be applied to these processes. This opened the way for Newell and Simon to show that at least some human ideation and various other cognitive processes could be represented symbolically and that these symbolic representations could be meaningfully altered by precisely defined symbol-manipulating processes.

Newell and Simon's metatheoretical work underlies much of the pretheory of information-processing psychology, including the semantic memory theories to be reviewed in this chapter. They proposed and developed the concept of a physical symbol system, which is made of entities (termed *symbols)* that are realized in various physical patterns. Sets of symbols make up more complex entities called *expressions* or *symbol structures.* Human intellectual systems and machines both may be expressed as a particular collection of symbol structures at a given instant in time. Symbol structures are operated on by a small number of information processes that alter the original expressions, reproducing, expanding, or destroying them, or creating new information in the form of new symbol structures (Newell & Simon, 1976). The most primitive set of symbol-processing operations that may ultimately be specified may be of the following form: create a symbol, store it, locate and retrieve it, modify it, compare it to a second symbol, and the like. These are *computational* or *information-processing* operations that are available to intelligent machines. The assumption that just such operations can characterize the mental activities of biological beings is an important basis of computational or information-processing theories of human cognition. This treatment of a complex set of issues is necessarily brief; however, a more detailed account is found in Lachman, Lachman, and Butterfield (1979). Minimally, the preceding discussion should make clear the sense in which theories of semantic memory are computational.

It should also serve to explain why information-processing theories of cognitive processes highlight the commonalities between biological and artifactual information-handling systems. Some theorists are explicitly committed to the view that human minds and computer programs are instantiations of a general-purpose machine with its symbol–system capability. For others, the commitment goes no deeper than the assumption that human minds and computer programs are analogous in some regards, whether or not they are parallel systems and therefore instances of the same higher order category. Either way, information-processing psychologists have found computational theory attractive and appropriate. Progress has generally been rewarding, and in our view, it has been no mistake to exploit the common properties shared by biological organisms and nonbiological information-processing artifacts.

The recognition of commonalities between parallel systems, however, does not imply an assumption of identity. Species of a genus, analogized entities, or instantiations of a higher order type are only partially governed by the same rules. Consideration of the differences between parallel systems is essential for several reasons. First and most obvious, an accurate account of any natural system encompasses its individual as well as its shared properties. Second, if identity between parallel systems is overassumed, apparent anomalies may arise that could be readily explained by reference to significant discontinuities between the systems. Ignoring major boundary conditions on the assumed parallels may lead to giving such anomalies too much weight—and may even be taken to impugn the assumption of any important parallels at all.

The efforts of Newell and Simon (1976) and others such as Pylyshyn (1978) have been directed toward discovering the continuities and similarities among intelligent systems whether biological or electronic. In the first part of this chapter we explore in a preliminary way an important discontinuity—the fact of human biological evolution—as part of an effort to specify the set of computational processes that are a product of the evolutionary history of the human species and the constraints these may impose on theories of semantic memory. In the second part of the chapter, we describe several of the most influential theories of semantic memory. We take special note of those aspects that derive from analogies with nonbiological artifacts and, where possible, suggest interpretation from an evolutionist perspective. The third section presents some of our own research, which, though not originally undertaken with evolution in mind, is readily interpretable in that light and leads us further in that direction.

II. THE SIGNIFICANCE OF PHYLOGENY

Few serious scientists question that the shape of the human hand, the structure of the human eye, and the organization of the human brain are the products of the evolutionary history of the human species, and that these can be understood and explained in an evolutionary context. Most information-processing psychologists would doubtless agree that human cognitive capabilities—including the computational capacities that figure in current information-processing theories of permanent memory—are also the products of evolution. However, while they might agree that the capacities they study have been determined by selection pressures just as bodily structures have, they seem implicitly to reject the idea that evolutionary considerations might figure in a worthwhile way in cognitive computational theories.

We consider this rejection to be a mistake. If information-processing theories cannot encompass those aspects of human cognition that differ from machine intelligence, they are unlikely to succeed as psychological theories. They will not provide satisfactory accounts of human thought, however elegant they may be otherwise. We believe that information-processing theories can and should take into consideration the evolutionary factors that have impacted human cognition for the following reasons. First, it may be possible to use evolutionary considerations to avoid dead-ends—to eliminate hypotheses that are clearly implausible for an evolved organism even though they make sense for artificial intelligences. Second, attention to evolutionary factors may suggest areas in which the information-processing formalisms available from the computational disciplines are patently inadequate. Third, the evolutionary history of the human being may contain the explanation of research results that are puzzling for theories relying too heavily on assumed parallels between human cognition and machine intelligence.

In undertaking this effort for information-processing theory, we are starting literally at the ground floor. Psychology has a long history of ignoring Darwinian theory, both in formulating hypotheses and in developing theoretical models (Hirsch, 1967; Razran, 1971). There have been occasional efforts to bring evolutionary issues to some aspects of general psychology (Goodson, 1973), perception (Gibson, 1966), and development (Fishbein, 1976); however, in the area of information processing in general and semantic memory in particular, no one has begun. We can therefore only offer a partial, tentative, and unordered set of observations about human evolution, with some suggestions as to how they might enter into the information-processing theories of semantic memory. We shall cast these observations as "evolutionary postulates"—a set of general statements that pertain to the phylogenesis of human intelligence. The statements involve selective pressures, species ancestry, order of emergence of various relevant characteristics, properties of the ecological niches occupied by recent ancestors, and other paleontological and phylogenetic events. We believe that postulates of this type can be valuable adjuncts to information-processing theories that aspire to model human cognition. We hope this particular set will give a sense of what such postulates might look like and encourage others to refine and add to it. We make no claims for the completeness or even the correctness of this particular set, except that it is extensible and corrigible. We believe that a well-developed set of evolutionary postulates in this domain will be essential in constraining cognitive theory and setting its boundary conditions. Ultimately, we hope that out postulates will serve as "major premises," to be taken in conjunction with other major premises (the essential statements of a cognitive theory) and minor premises (the particular conditions of an experiment) to predict experimental outcomes.

Broad evolutionary generalizations that provide a rationale for specific postulates are presented first, then the postulates themselves are presented.

EVOLUTIONARY GENERALIZATION A: *Human cognition is the product of biological evolution.*

It follows from this uncontroversial claim that the characteristics of human cognition reflect the evolutionary history of the human species, a history that began with the appearance of life on earth and proceeded through multicelled organisms and marine forms to terrestrial reptiles. The most interesting part of the story began with the emergence of placental mammals from an ancestral reptilian stock sometime during the Cretaceous period of 135 or so million years ago. This new mammalian form of reproduction probably evolved because it improved reproductive economy; but it was behaviorally significant in various ways. Not only did it favor the evolution of parental care of the young after birth, it permitted the transmission of learned behavior through observation and imitation (Campbell, 1974). In addition to instinctive behaviors and reflex learning ability, the infant mammal has a store of information available in the parent, who has at least survived long enough to reproduce. The little mammal who does what his mother does has a good chance of copying adaptive behavior, reducing the necessity for potentially fatal trial-and-error learning in each new animal. Mammalian reproduction, then, makes available a form of extragenetic information transmission and creates selection pressures favoring those who use it. We may further suppose that selection pressures favor *judicious* use of imitation—the later production of the *right* imitative behavior for the situation at hand. To accomplish this, an animal needs relatively analytic representations of information about environmental situations, a sophisticated memory to retain situational and behavioral data, and some range of choice. Some of the most basic human representational and decision-making mechanisms, then, may derive originally from the demands of mammalian life, having evolved to support judicious imitation.

Human cognition is also primate cognition and reflects the common history of humans and other primates. That common history dates from the Paleocene period, perhaps 63 million years ago, originating with a small shrewlike mammal that took up residence in trees. As a tree-dweller, it evolved important specializations for arboreal life: limbs adapted for tree-climbing and eyes adapted for improved vision. The dramatic improvements in the visual system of primates, including near-binocularity, are thought to derive from the demands of tree-swinging and leaping from branch to branch (E. T. Collins, 1921), although manual predation has also been suggested (Cartmill, 1972). Three-dimensional perception is a valuable asset to an animal who is about to leap out over thin air to a branch a few yards away. What is more, distant depth perception involves a high degree of visual discrimination; and the fine visual discrimination available to primates may thus be a by-product of arboreal life as well. Good visual discrimination is also preadapted for detailed object identification in an animal with the requisite memory abilities; indeed, the primates have evolved expanded temporal lobes (that presumably figure in memory) along with an enlarged visual cortex. At the same time, brain areas concerned with olfaction have contracted for primates; vision seems to have taken over as the primary mode of picking up information about the environment. These developments, possibly at their base adaptations to life in the trees, may be the prerequisites for the conceptual capabilities of later primates, including *Homo sapiens*.

From the primate order there evolved the superfamily Hominoidea, which includes man, the living great apes, and a number of fossil genera. Perhaps 15 or 20 million years ago, toward the end of the Miocene period, there emerged from the Hominoidea the new family Hominidae; the only living member of this family today is man. Although the classification is still somewhat controversial, most authorities (Simons & Pilbeam, 1972) consider *Ramapithecus* to be the first genus of the Hominidae. This creature, though small and apelike, differed from apes specifically in the direction of man (Campbell, 1974). It appears that *Ramapithecus* moved from the forest to the forest edges and took up ground feeding as a result (Jolly, 1970; Simons & Pilbeam, 1972). He thus represents the transition from arboreal to terrestrial life, with many of the concomitant adaptations: bipedalism, changed dentition, and, probably, altered social structures. There is also reason to believe that *Ramapithecus* took somewhat longer to reach adulthood than do apes (Simons & Pilbeam, 1972). Regrettably, we do not know *Ramapithecus'* cranial capacity, since the genus is known only by remains of teeth and jaws; no fossil skulls have been identified as Ramapithecine.

Ramapithecus (Simons & Pilbeam, 1972) is probably the ancestor of a later genus, *Australopithecus,* of which two species have been identified. One, *A. boisei,* became extinct; the other, *A. africanus,* is almost surely the ancestor of the later genus *Homo* and of modern man (Campbell, 1974). *Australopithecus africanus* lived between 5.5 and 1.2 million years ago. He was small in both stature and brain; however, he evidently walked upright with a gait resembling that of modern man (LeGros Clark, 1966, 1967). During his time—through the Pliocene into the Pleistocene—the earth was undergoing drastic climatic changes. The northern latitudes were becoming cooler and drier, winters more severe. By the end of Australopithecine times, the well-known ice ages of the Pleistocene period were underway. These changes in environment presented important challenges to all life forms, including *A. africanus.* These animals had definitely left the forest and adopted an omnivorous diet; to obtain meat they may have engaged in limited cooperative hunting (LeGros Clark, 1967). Although they apparently never discovered fire, they made and used simple tools (LeGros Clark, 1966). During the latter part of the Australopithecine period, there began a period of strikingly rapid brain enlargement; the changing environment doubtless created selection pressures for improved wit. Cranial capacities of *Australopithecus* range from about 435 cm³ (which is close to the average value for a chimpanzee) to 815 cm³ (LeGros Clark, 1964). The increase in brain size suggested by these changing cranial capacities shows a substantial increase in the ratio of brain weight to body weight. It seems likely that this increase in brain size supported the improved behavioral flexibility and adaptability necessary to survive in the increasingly cold northerly latitudes. The enlarging brain and cranium also had important implications for the timing of human birth, which apparently reflects a compromise between infant needs and maternal architecture (Campbell, 1974; Montagu, 1965). Ideally for the infant, birth would occur after brain development was relatively complete; however, the extended time required for such development would result in an infant too large for a mother to carry and deliver. The organization of the brain during this period of rapid expansion must have occurred in such a way as to permit much development to occur while the newborn and young child is in active contact with the environment. What is more, the long immaturity of human young must have created strong pressures for a social organization in which they could be nurtured over protracted periods.

The increase in brain size continued and accelerated in *Australopithecus's* successor, the new genus *Homo.* The first species of this genus, *Homo erectus,* had a variable cranial capacity averaging about 1000 cm³. It appears to have been *H. erectus* who discovered fire and perfected cooperative hunting (LeGros Clark, 1966). *H. erectus* may also have introduced such evidences of civilization as representative art, tents, clothing, and ritual burial. *H. erectus* was the ancestor of *Homo sapiens,* who has been in existence for about half a million years—for the last 300,000 years pretty much as he is today. The general speculation is that language came into being gradually and was rather complete by half a million years ago.

The foregoing account of human phylogeny is not entirely uncontroversial, but there is good agreement on its major claims (Campbell, 1974). Details, such as whether *Ramapithecus* is correctly classified as a hominid, need not concern us. The kinds of considerations that are important include the cognitive implications of imitation, the importance of the visual system to primates, the environmental demands that accompanied the rapid increase in brain size, the nature of cognition required by birth timing and long infancy, the significance of primate social organization to evolving cognitive structures, and the relationship between conceptual thought and earlier adaptations.

EVOLUTIONARY GENERALIZATION B: *Human higher mental processes preceded Western civilization.*

This seems obvious when baldly stated, but it is seldom mentioned and seems sometimes to be overlooked. Presumably, the kind of conceptual ability we wish our cognitive theories to capture was available to early *Homo sapiens* and is now available to persons who have not been educated in Western schools. Our cognitive computational processes did not evolve to support sentence verification, list learning, and other popular laboratory tasks—few of which show conspicuous ecological validity (Neisser, 1976). The limitations of such tasks in discovering truly universal human cognitive abilities are virtually never addressed. For example, some researchers (e.g., Medin & Cole, 1975) have found that common verbal learning tasks are not performed similarly by literate and nonliterate people. Although there may be methodological problems with the studies, it is possible that literacy, not the organization of human cognition, produces the pattern of results that we are attempting to interpret. Few of the most common laboratory tasks in semantic memory research could be performed by illiterates. This is not to say that such tasks should be immediately abandoned and our future studies on semantic memory be conducted with aboriginals. However, it suggests that researchers should keep the limitations on generality clearly in mind. From an evolutionary viewpoint, it makes sense to ask what a particular cognitive capacity evolved *for*, as well as what contemporary educated Western adults can do with it.

Theoretical statements as well as experimental tasks seem to equate human cognitive organization with Western school-learning. For example, it has been common to suppose that "mental organization" has as one if its main features the hierarchical organization of things: *Fido, terrier, dog, mammal, animal, living thing,* and so on. Some linguists (Katz & Fodor, 1963) have suggested that word meanings are built out of such hierarchies. It is true that hierarchical taxonomies have been useful in advancing Western science, and people certainly can learn to use them. Set-inclusion may even be a general principle that can be appreciated by modern apes, and we can easily see that grouping elements with common properties (e.g., *deer* and *cow* as *prey*) would be adaptive. However, most hierarchies run out of natural utility after two or at most three levels, after which they seem best suited to the rather recent pursuit of systematizing large bodies of information. Relating *deer* and *rock* as common instances of *physical things,* for example, seems more suited to the pursuits of philosophers than to the life-style of *Homo erectus.* We shall return to this observation in connection with the model of Smith, Shoben and Rips (1974) and the work of Rosch (1978).

EVOLUTIONARY GENERALIZATION C: *Human higher mental processes are a late adaptation and are not discontinuous with the prior adaptations of the animal in whom they evolved.*

It should be obvious that a new trait will have the best chance of persisting in a population if it is consistent with the existing organization of the population members. For example, a trait that makes an animal appear fearsome will have little adaptive value in a species that responds to predators by playing possum. Because each evolutionary advance occurs in the context of earlier ones, existing adaptations enormously constrain the kind of innovation that can prove adaptive, and thereby persist, in the evolving species.

Given the progression we have sketched—from reptile to mammal to primate to man—what does this observation suggest about cognition? Among other things, it suggests that mammalian innovations such as imitation and improved memory evolved in part to serve reptilian needs. Primate capacities— improved vision and object identification—supported the needs of small mammals. In addition, the capacity for abstract thought served the adaptive demands of a primate life-style. The human brain actually has a tripartite character, with three different sets of structural and chemical features. MacLean (1962, 1964, 1973) has suggested that these represent inheritances from our reptilian, old mammalian, and recent mammalian forebears, respectively. He has paid special attention to the "old mammalian" brain, corresponding to the limbic system, to which he ascribes an important role in emotional behavior. The particulars of MacLean's account may or may not be correct. Still, it is worth emphasizing that the emotional concomitants of defense, aggression, sexuality, parenting, and sociality predated abstract reasoning as we see it today. The nature of semantic memory was doubtless shaped by the existence of these motivational forces as well as by the particular set of environmental demands that attended its emergence.

With these broad generalizations as background, we are ready to present our preliminary set of evolutionary postulates. Most follow readily from the previous discussion, and some require additional assumptions. Some of the postulates are general in nature, and further development is needed to generate specific situations in which they apply. As previously stated, this set is tentative and incomplete; hopefully, it will become more refined with time and with resulting empirical investigations.

POSTULATE 1. *Human learning is not unitary.*

Nature has provided a number of mechanisms for producing adaptive behavior, and human beings have an evolutionary history that implicates all of them. The potential to produce responses by reflex, by conditioning, by imitation, and by symbolic means are all available and are probably all cognitively significant. However, because these learning modes evolved at different times, it is likely that there is some "division of labor" among them. Reflex behavior, classical and instrumental conditioning, and some degree of imitation are available to other mammalian forms and may involve primarily those systems we share with other mammals, e.g., basic appetitive and emotional systems. Symbolic learning, in contrast, requires conceptual thought; this in turn may require the ability to form permanent and detailed representations of environmental objects and events. If primate vision and manipulative skill supported (and hence preceded) the evolution of detailed representational ability, symbolic learning is likely to be well suited to complex social behavior patterns, cooperative hunting, protracted child-rearing, and the like. Indeed, emotions are virtually impossible to control through the symbolic medium of language. We cannot simply instruct ourselves to feel love, not to be afraid, and so on. Yet one traumatic "conditioning" experience can instill a lifelong phobic response, which is easier dispelled by counterconditioning than by symbolic verbal means. Conversely, conditioning is an inefficient way to produce behaviors (such as language) normally controlled by the higher mental processes, unless these processes are also implicated (Spielberger & deNike, 1962). Postulate #1 also implies that symbolic learning should have a strong visual bias, because it relies on the detailed representational ability provided by primate vision. This observation leads to our next postulate.

POSTULATE 2. *Human cognition reflects the centrality of primate vision.*

Ideas that are visually encoded, or whose maintenance and retrieval can be mediated by the visual system, will be relatively easy to process. Visual, or visually mediated, information should be relatively detailed, rapidly encoded, and facilely retained and retrieved. The empirical evidence indicates that it is (Shepard, 1967). If mechanisms for processing visual information can be implicated in processing information from other modalities, it should be facilitative to do so. The languages of the world suggest that this happens. Porzig (cited by Lorenz, 1977) has noted that languages commonly translate abstract concepts into visual–spatial terms. His examples include temporal relationships (e.g., *within* 2 years) and others (*besides* his work; *depths* of the soul). The word for *seeing* is closely related to those for *knowing* and *understanding* in many different languages. Empirical data are consistent with these observations of language; "imageable" words and sentences are easier to comprehend and recall (Paivio, 1969, 1971), which may reflect the importance of vision. Visual processing mechanisms may be especially fast and efficient, and visual information may be stored in great detail and with great permanence. If verbal inputs can be imaged, it may be possible to "parasitize" visual processing mechanisms, thereby gaining access to their greater manipulability. These assumptions would explain people's superior performance with such content, as well as their phenomenological reports of its visual-like status. Phenomenological reports about the visual "feel" of images, and their good performance with imageable material, may reflect the ability to process such material by means of mechanisms linked to vision.

POSTULATE 3. *The human representational system is not neutral with respect to content.*

Some concepts, percepts, and relationships should be easier to process than others because they have a longer history of adaptive salience. Adaptive demands on prehuman species may have required particular forms of ideation, e.g., concepts having to do with sociality and survival, sexuality and parenting. Such concepts may have a more fundamental status than other, derivative ones and may have fed into the development of symbolic thought and language. Other concepts may have only become available with the capacity for language and may thus be available *only* in symbolic form. Logical analysis does not suffice to identify a set of elemental concepts, for the set would reflect the relatively particular adaptive demands to which pre-human species were subjected. The set is thus content-determined rather than logically organized. Identification of such elemental concepts is an empirical enterprise, which would be importantly guided by evolutionary considerations.

POSTULATE 4. *Human cognition reflects the importance of primate social organization.*

A number of conceptualizations are essential to an animal living in a social troop. It must be able to recognize particular individuals and remember his own relationship to them, such as dominance or submission. It must have a self-image, a sense of "place." It must be able to recognize some kinship relations; even among wild chimpanzees, mutual bonds between siblings have been observed, and mother–child bonds last well into the adulthood of the child (Goodall, 1976). Moreover, position in dominance hierarchies is familially transmitted to some extent. The social animal must be able to reconcile the earlier legacy of adaptations to solitary survival, such as competitive aggression, with demands of the new, cooperative form of social survival; this resolution may be implicated in the intrapsychic conflict model of Freudian theory. Since many ape species live in highly organized social troops, at least some such adaptation preceded the neocortical expansion that began in late Australopithecine times. The nature of the cognition that expansion produced was therefore impacted by, among other things, the social demands of life in a primate troop. In this connection it is possible that some of the concepts of sociobiology (Wilson, 1975) may prove cognitively relevant.

POSTULATE 5. *The origins of human cognition were shaped by emotional factors already present.*

Emotional states provide the motivation for action, and human cognition guides the organization of the action. There must, therefore, be an intimate relationship between them. It is extremely difficult at this time to specify the nature of that relationship, because emotions and cognition have typically been treated by very different groups of scholars. No current information-processing theory of adult cognition gives any role to affective factors; and students of affect rarely consider the complex cognitive system through which emotions are expressed. Several hypothetical relationships can be suggested, though all are highly speculative. One suggestion is that abstract and symbolic capacities provide an alternative form of expression for emotional states, releasing the organism from the relatively restricted repertoire of responses to those states. Another view is that abstract ideas served to meet emotional needs in even more successful fashion than earlier-evolved, "hard-wired" responses. Still another view is that human cognition supported the transition from the emotional states that served a solitary life-style to those required by a social cooperator. This last view has a distinctly Freudian flavor, giving the "higher mental processes" the role of ego—mediating the conflicting demands of self-seeking, solitary survival (id) and cooperative, altruistic sociality (superego).

This area of relationship between prehuman emotional states and the emergence of human intelligence is clearly underinvestigated. Even though specific suggestions are difficult to make, it is worth reminding ourselves occasionally that "higher" processes exist in the same system with "lower" ones, and cannot function entirely independently.

POSTULATE 6. *Human logic is nonstandard.*

Theories of semantic memory somehow need to explain how people can draw logically unwarranted inferences, believe logically contradictory things at the same time, and categorize the same object differently on different occasions. Such flexibility must have been directly or indirectly adaptive. Human reasoning did not evolve to solve complex syllogisms or do trigonometry. Though it contains the capacity to do these things, its basic organization reflects the uses to which it was initially put. One current dilemma in semantic memory models is that computational theories involve efforts to describe the organization of permanent memory by means of existing logical formalisms. However, these formalisms were developed to *improve* and *extend* human reasoning processes; without modification, they can only be descriptive of a "cleaned-up" (and possibly distorted) version of cognition. What is needed is an effort to develop computational models that will capture the inconsistencies and irregularities of everyday, informal human reasoning. Development of a formalism of potential use in such models was undertaken by Zadeh (1975) in "fuzzy logic"; however, psychologists have not constructed detailed models based on the formalism.

POSTULATE 7. *The human cognitive system is organized to support a long period of extrauterine development.*

We have alluded to the timing of human birth as a compromise between infantile and maternal needs. This compromise produces an organism whose intellectual processes must continue to mature in active contact with the environment and while its representations of the world are being formed. If reorganizations and restructurings occur after the nine months' gestation period, the child must be able to accommodate changing ways of apprehending external reality. This situation may give rise to the seeming discontinuities captured in the notion of Piagetian stages. It may also be related to the flexible logical capabilities noted above; the world may look very different to a child before and after an important restructuring has taken place, but he must be able to make the transition. The ability to accommodate different—even incommensurate—conclusions about the same universe may be essential to cognitive development and may continue to characterize the adult if there is nothing maladaptive about it.

Semantic memory theorists seldom emphasize that the adult's representations of the world emerge in an orderly way from those of a child. However, evolution is intimately concerned with childhood. Evolutionary developments that favor growing up will be selected for even if they are suboptimal for the adult. By contrast, developments that are optimal for adults will never evolve if they prevent the organism from reaching maturity. The capabilities available to the child, and required by it, thus limit the capabilities that are likely to become available to the adult. Some of the flexibility in human adult cognition may therefore reflect the developmental demands of human infancy and childhood. However, dependence of adult cognitive organization on the requirements of ontogeny is neither acknowledged in semantic memory theory nor calculated into its construction.

We shall now review the substantive achievements of recent and current semantic memory theories. We shall indicate where the theories might take guidance from one or another of the evolutionary postulates. It is important to reemphasize that none of these theories were constructed to be responsive to evolutionary considerations, and therefore it is rare for our postulates to relate directly to theoretical particulars. The same is true for data; the studies done to develop and test the theories were not designed to be interpreted in phylogenetic terms. Even so, we shall attempt to interpret experimental outcomes and theoretical puzzles by reference to the postulates whenever possible.

III. CONTEMPORARY STUDY OF PERMANENT MEMORY

Like other information-processing theories, those of semantic memory have made extensive use of computational concepts; they emphasize the commonalities rather than differences between human mental organization and that of automata. The major intellectual ancestor of most current theories of permanent memory organization is the Teachable Language Comprehender (TLC). Its author is recognized as an artificial intelligence theorist rather than a psychologist (Quillian, 1968). In our view, this approach and emphasis are fundamentally sound, and computational theories are entirely proper. However, we suggest that better psychological models may emerge if greater sensitivity is shown to the phylogenetic history of the human cognitive system.

Current theories of human permanent memory organization fall into three classes. Those we shall describe in this chapter focus on the relatively static structure of permanent memory. A second group, which we call "global theories," additionally address permanent memory modification through new inputs, usually linguistic. We have described global theories elsewhere (Lachman et al., 1979). The third kind of organizational theory derives from the classical verbal learning tradition; it is well represented in this volume, especially in Section II.

A. Experimental Tasks in Semantic Memory Research

The type of theory we have called "semantic memory" developed earlier than the global theories. It clearly reflected the blending of traditions from experimental psychology with conceptualizations drawn from the field of artificial intelligence. There are two major sources of empirical data for these models: normative data concerning the relatedness of pairs of words designating conceptual entities or classes, and latencies from a variety of laboratory tasks on speeded classification and verification. Various procedures for collecting normative data have been used. Subjects typically rate the "semantic relatedness" of category–instance pairs such as *horse* and *animal,* or produce all the instances they can of a given category. Commonly supplied instances are considered "highly related" to the superordinate category. Speeded classification procedures have two defining features: They yield measures of response speed; and people must use their everyday knowledge of objects and events—their meanings and categorical entailments—in order to respond correctly. A typical speeded classification experiment requires a person to indicate whether a given word is a member of a specified category. In some studies, subjects are required to give category names in response to words, for example, respond *animal* if shown a *horse.* In other studies, the subject might respond "same" or "different" to item pairs based on their category membership or verify that a category–item pair such as *red–color* is or is not valid as a subset–superset relationship. Another arrangement requires people to respond "true" or "false," either orally or by pressing switches, to statements like *A typhoon is a dwelling* or *A watermelon is a fruit.*

Whichever arrangement is used, the cognitive demands of the task are the same: People must use their knowledge of the entailments of conceptual categories in order to respond. This requirement need not involve mention of a category; the sentence *Canaries are related to finches* does not mention birds, but a person could not verify it without knowing that canaries and finches are both birds.

Many semantic memory experiments have required people to say "true" or "false" to propositional expressions that have the form subject–verb–predicate. The proposition may be explicit, as it is in the *typhoon, watermelon,* and *canaries* examples above. The proposition may also be implicit in the experimental instructions. For example, a subject who says "yes" to the pair *dog–animal* has implicitly verified the proposition *A dog is an animal.* Semantic memory researchers assume that all speeded classification and speeded verification procedures depend on the same underlying cognitive structures and processes. Since about 1970, variations on these procedures have been used in the vast majority of semantic memory experiments. The dependent measure is usually reaction time. Reaction times have been used to justify inferences about such matters as the distance between elements in the layout of semantic memory, inferences about the operations involved in the retrieval of those elements, and inferences concerning the relationships among these operations.

Although the speeded classification–verification task did not originate with semantic memory models (see, e.g., Pollack, 1963; Schaeffer & Wallace, 1969), Landauer and Freedman (1968) were the first to use explicitly the task in its contemporary manner, to address the general problem of how information is retrieved from human long-term memory. They noted, for example, that when one sees a sparrow and decides that it is a bird, one has somehow consulted a store of memories to determine the appropriateness of the class name for the stimulus. In developing the rationale for their task and the interpretation of their outcomes, Landauer and Freedman were clearly guided by analogies with nonbiological information retrieval systems. They varied the size of the categories whose instances subjects were judging. They reasoned approximately that, if verification time increased with category size, then subjects must scan their memories serially rather than in parallel, because parallel models typically do not predict time differences for searching long versus short lists or other data structures. Thus, because there are fewer types of *dogs* than of *animals,* it should take less time to judge *Collie is a dog* than *Collie is an animal* only if semantic memory searches have a serial component. This type of argument assumes parallels between human mentation and nonbiological computational systems. Landauer and Freedman's results, which showed a category size effect, are somewhat controversial. However, their statement of the problem and their interpretive framework are consistent with the current set of semantic memory theories.

B. TLC: A Pioneering Formalization of Semantic Memory

Although Quillian's TLC is published primarily in computer science outlets (Quillian, 1968, 1969), it motivated much of the initial research in semantic memory. Quillian's computational theory was designed to answer questions. A primary requirement of such theory construction is the selection of a memory structure to represent, in an absolutely unambiguous way, the information that would be the source of answers. For his program, Quillian had to function as nature has for man—of all the possible ways one might represent knowledge, he had to pick exactly one. Then, given this structure, he had to work out exactly how the information in it was to be utilized and to specify each step of the process. It is, of course, certain that Quillian's decisions about structure and process were not independent; he developed them to be as efficient as possible and mutually compatible. A program of this sort, in our view, becomes a psychological theory as soon as one claims that it functions *like a human being* in carrying out its task. It was a short step from Quillian's (1968) original artificial intelligence program to the psychological theory of propositional verification that was proposed and tested in the work of Collins and Quillian (1969).

1. QUILLIAN'S MODEL,
THE "TEACHABLE LANGUAGE COMPREHENDER"

Quillian's (1968) theory was conceived as a model of language and expressed in a computer simulation program that aspired to the comprehension of English text. Quillian hoped, as he said,

> to develop a computer program that could comprehend newspapers, textbooks, encyclopedias, and other written text. That is, the program should be able to extract and somehow retain meaning from natural language text it has not seen before, ... Therefore, while the reader who disagrees or who has no interest in human behavior can read TLC's strategy strictly as program specification, we choose to regard this strategy also as psychological theory and will speak of a computer and a person interchangeably as our example of the mechanism carrying it out. [p. 459].

Quillian's theory defined comprehension as the relating of input assertions to information previously stored in memory as general world knowledge. Each piece of information, or "element," had to be represented in a precise, unambiguous code. Yet there had to be sufficient flexibility to permit the code to be extended to represent any concept expressible in natural language. The structure Quillian used was a data structure called a *network of finite automata,* a piece of which is shown in Figure 5.1. The network consists of inter-connected elements called *nodes,* which are represented by dots in the figure. Each node is connected to at least one other by a *link,* or pointer as it may also be called, which designates the relationship between the pair of nodes. Although this may look complicated (and it is, at the level of actually writing a program to store it in a computer memory), the general principles are straightforward. All that is meant by the diagram in Figure 5.1 is that the programmer sets up the computer's memory so that whenever it has *bird* represented in its central processor, it also has all the necessary instructions to retrieve the information that a bird *has feathers, can fly, has wings,* and *is an animal.* Once this related information is retrieved, new concepts are available to the central processor—i.e., *feathers,*

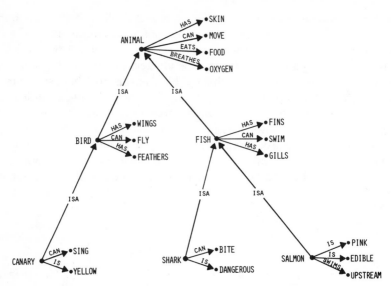

FIGURE 5.1 How the network data structure of Quillian (1968) can represent a part of semantic memory.

fly, wings, animal. Their availability supplies the necessary instructions to retrieve any information stored with (linked to) these concepts and so on until the central processor reaches a concept that has no further linked concepts. In Figure 5.1, the concept *bird* might be input (on cards, tape, teletype, or any input device), which would make available the information that *bird is an animal,* which in turn would make available the information that an *animal can move.* This is as far as the machine could go with the part of the structure shown in the figure, but it incorporates the important capacity of inference. Quillian was explicitly attempting to build inferential ability into his program. Indeed, when we know that a *bird has skin* because *birds are animals* and *animals have skin,* we have made an inference; and this was how TLC was designed to "know" more than it had explicitly stored in memory.

In interpreting how these concepts may be used in psychology, it is important to remember that they have concrete meanings in the computer programming of artificial intelligence; however, the meanings become more abstract when we speak of people. The computer analogy supplies a shorthand for saying "Perhaps the way people represent a concept like *animal* is by keeping together in their memories all the information directly relevant to the animals they know about, such as the facts that *they can move,* that *they breathe air* and *eat .food,* and so on. Perhaps when they are asked about *animals,* they bring into their working memories constellations of related information, which permits them to answer the question." It is useful to say that the person has "accessed a node," even though the terms "node" and "access," in some theoretical contexts, may have neither precise psychological meanings nor known physiological correlates. Such terms can only be understood by analogy with the logicomathematical systems and computer programs from which they were borrowed. Such terminology is not incommensurate with evolutionist thinking. It would be perfectly possible to formulate a theory based on evolutionary considerations and express it in the language of nodes and links. One might, for example, distinguish the adaptive salience of various properties or subordinate classes and express the differences in salience by different weights on the links. In fact, as we shall see, the data have necessitated the inclusion of weighted links in more recent theories (Anderson, 1976; Collins & Loftus, 1975). However, Quillian originally created all links equal.

To return to the way Quillian set up the semantic memory, the first link of a concept node is connected to the node representing its immediate superordinate. The other links connect the concept with its properties or attributes—these correspond to adjectives, possessions, and other predictions such as *is dangerous, has wings, swims upstream*. Quillian distinguished between the semantic memory and the natural language lexicon; in other words, these nodes were not intended to represent the words in a person's vocabulary, but the concepts in his mind. Often, of course, there are words that represent the concepts, such as *robin, tulip, park, hippie*, or *beauty*. However, there can be concepts that have a single node in the memory, but no single-word name in English. For instance, an art historian's semantic memory might contain a single node for *French impressionist painter* even though English has no single name for the concept. The semantic network, which is that part we are most interested in, was designed to represent the conceptual knowledge system. Quillian also limited TLC to relatively common knowledge about which most Westerners would be likely to have the same memory structure. Presumably, for members of the same culture at least, there is considerable overlap; and it was the overlapping knowledge that Quillian attempted to represent.

One can see that each node potentially connects with everything else in the system. For example, in Figure 5.1, *shark* is connected to *fish*, which is connected to *animal*. Although it is not shown in the figure, a more complete drawing would show a link from *animal* to *living thing*, which in turn would connect downward to all the living things a person knows about, as well as all the information he has about each one. *Living thing* is itself a subset of *physical object*: Therefore, *shark* is linked via *fish, animal, living thing*, and *physical object* to every physical object known. The theory thus accounts for the fact that people can verify a statement like *A shark is composed of matter* whether or not they have ever thought about sharks in this way before.

C. Psychological Implications of TLC

TLC embodies a psychological theory that suggests that people's knowledge of the world is organized rather like the data structure shown in Figure 5.1 and that the retrieval operations performed by the computer in answering questions by reference to its data structure are similar, at some level of abstraction, to those performed by people in a similar situation. Quillian thus began a tradition of giving all concept nodes and links in the memory equal status except for a hierarchical level. This is inconsistent with our Postulate 3, which asserts that some concepts should be intrinsically more accessible than others. Quillian's work also led to a tradition of representing memory information in propositional notation, which does not take account of possible differences in the representational status of visual and linguistic information, implied by our Postulate 2. This practice is still universal among semantic memory theorists, although there is some controversy about it (Pylyshyn, 1973; Kosslyn & Pomerantz, 1977). Quillian also made his theoretical memory exceedingly logical and hierarchical, contrary to our Postulate 6; subsequent data collection has required that later models increase the flexibility of the memory representation. These observations are not to be taken as an indictment of Quillian's effort; he had to start somewhere. However, they serve to highlight areas where the evolved nature of the human memory may deviate from efficient organizational principles for automata.

An empirical research program was implemented to test TLC as "a valid model of human semantic memory and language comprehension [Collins & Quillian, 1972b, p. 119]." Collins and Quillian assumed that traversing the nodes and links of semantic memory takes time, and in their first study (Collins & Quillian, 1969), they made bold predictions of the time that would be required for subjects to verify the truth of simple statements such as *A canary is yellow* and *A salmon is an animal*. Based on the number of intervening hierarchical links, they assumed that people would take longer to verify that *A canary is an animal* than *A canary is a bird* and that it would take more time to confirm that *A canary can move* than that *A canary can fly*. Figure 5.1 suggests how they derived these predictions. The information *can fly* is directly accessible from *canary*, but *can move* is not. To retrieve *can move*, it is necessary to traverse the link between *canary* and *bird* and that between *bird* and *animal*. Thus, while only one link must be traversed to confirm that *A canary can fly*, three are necessary to confirm that *A canary can move*. Collins and Quillian found that a version of the speeded classification task involving propositional verification provided an experimental way to test the Quillian model. Subjects in their first experiment were presented simple, three-element sentences such as those in our examples. They quickly pressed one button if the sentence was generally true, another button if it was generally false. Their sentences contained either property relationships (P sentences) or superordinate relationships (S sentences). They also counted the number of hierarchical links necessary to make the response. Thus, in Figure 5.1 *A canary is a bird* would be an S1 sentence because it involves a superordinate relationship one link up. *A shark can move* would be a P2 sentence because it involves a property and two hierarchical links.

Collins and Quillian's (1969) famous results are shown in Figure 5.2;

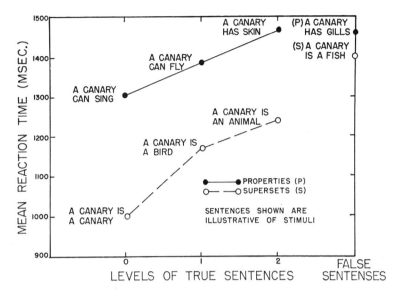

FIGURE 5.2 Average reaction time to confirm or deny sentences designating set inclusion or property nodes at varying hierarchical distance. [*After Collins & Quillian, 1969.*]

indeed, verification time did increase with the hierarchical distance between subject and predicate. Strictly speaking, the model predicts parallel lines for the superordinate and property relations. S0 sentences were verified somewhat faster than predicted, perhaps because such sentences involved repeating the word (*A canary is a canary*). Otherwise, each additional hierarchical link increased verification time roughly 75 msec, and property relations required about 200 msec more than superordinate relations. The authors concluded that retrieving property relations at a node takes more time than moving from one node to the next and also that a subject can proceed to a superordinate node while he is still searching for the predicate among properties at the subordinate node.

The results for false sentences did not readily support any single plausible hypothesis. Collins and Quillian considered several, none of which could fully accommodate their data. Collins and Quillian, unsurprisingly, did not include in their considerations any speculation about the evolution of mechanisms to support falsification. We shall take a moment to do so here. First, hard-wiring can substitute for falsification in lower animals. The stickleback, who fights in response to seeing a certain kind of red spot, needs no analyzers or processes to note "This is not an enemy." The exclusion is more passively accomplished. Second, a statement may be true in a limited number of ways, but it can be false in an infinite variety of ways. True propositions are, therefore, generally more informative action guides than false ones. It is reasonable to conjecture, then, that encodings of the form *X is Y* have a longer phylogenetic history than those of the form X *is not* Y. If we may equate a conditioning trial with the affirmative information and an extinction trial with negative information, the operant-conditioning literature provides additional support for this analysis. Conditioning may occur quickly, even in a single trial, while extinction is much slower (Skinner, 1953). This suggests that for such animals as pigeons, rats, and dogs affirmative information is more relevant behaviorally than negative information—which would make it reasonable to find asymmetries in encoding ease.

The point at which negative information takes on behavioral relevance is when an animal is able to form a relatively specific expectation. If the animal *expects* prey, food, or other event and the event fails to occur, this fact (a negative proposition, in effect) may be worth encoding and retaining. Even more importance attaches to falsification when cooperators must dispel misapprehensions on the part of significant others, and this is also the point at which language is important. Wason's (1965) findings on the context of plausible denial indicate that negation is primarily useful for such dispelling. One does not, for example, say "The train was not late this morning" when the train is normally punctual. We may, therefore, hypothesize that falsification is a late arrival, perhaps the result of sociality and an epiphenomenon of symbolic language, rather than a capacity that has been directly selected for. If so, falsification behavior should be more variable than verification behavior, since strong selection pressure and a long evolutionary history tend to favor uniformity. This was true of Collins and Quillian's data; people were more variable in their response times to false sentences than to true ones. It appears generally true of those sentence verification studies in the literature that have reported variability data (e.g., Anderson & Reder, 1974). No theory satisfactorily handles falsification at present, though some have that objective (Glass & Holyoak, 1975).

The first paper (Collins & Quillian, 1969) stimulated a rash of studies. Some were direct tests of the TLC, others proposed alternative ways to interpret the data, still others simply picked up the task as a way to infer permanent memory organization. Partly to accommodate the results of these studies, Quillian's (1968) model has been elaborated and revised. The most recent version of it, presented by Collins and Loftus (1975), is described later.

D. Semantic Distance

Schaeffer and Wallace (1970) were among the first to respond to the Collins and Quillian (1969) paper. They focused on one of its major weaknesses: the inability of the TLC to predict the pattern of negative responses to sentences such as *A canary is purple*. Schaeffer and Wallace (1969) had previously used the speeded classification task to study semantic similarity, which they defined as common subcategory membership (two animals are more "semantically similar" than an animal and a plant). They had shown that the more semantically similar word pairs from the same category were, the faster they could be judged the "same." In their 1970 experiment, subjects pressed one button if the two words belonged to the same superordinate (e.g., both birds), another button if they did not. This permitted the authors to obtain reaction times (RTs) to two kinds of "different" responses: those where the two words belonged to the same higher superordinate (e.g., both animals, but not both birds) and those where even the higher superordinate category was different (e.g., one plant and one animal). On the basis of semantic similarity, they predicted that the more semantically similar the word pairs were, the more difficult it would be to judge them "different."

Their results accorded with their predictions; it was harder to judge *parrot* and *giraffe* different than to judge *parrot* and *elm* different, for example. The semantic distance effect thus works two ways. "Same" judgments are facilitated by closeness of semantic relationship and retarded by distance. "Different" judgments are facilitated by distance and retarded by closeness. This effect, which has been repeated many times, demanded revision of the Quillian model and must be accommodated by any theory of semantic memory. As we shall see, the exact nature of the semantic distance effect remains an unsolved problem.

Wilkins (1971) attacked Collins and Quillian from a different perspective, but his outcomes are closely related to the semantic distance effect. According to Collins and Quillian's model, the first link of any concept leads directly to its immediate superordinate. The initial link of *canary, sparrow, chicken, ostrich,* and *stork* all lead directly to *bird*. There is no reason, then, why any bird should be categorized faster than any other. However, Wilkins showed systematic differences in classification speed for different category instances. The differences were predictable from normative data on categorization similar to the widely used Battig and Montague (1969) norms. These norms supply information on what instances people think of when they are given a category name. For example, 377 people gave *robin* as an instance of a *bird,* and of those, 189 wrote *robin* first among the birds they gave. By contrast, only 10 people gave *stork* at all, and only one listed it first.

Wilkins called the relationship reflected in the norms "conjoint frequency," but it has also been called "semantic distance," "category dominance," and "production frequency." Whatever it is called, it suggests the same prediction: Items high in the list such as *robin, sparrow,* and *cardinal* should be easily classified as birds, while items low in the list such as *warbler, pelican,* and *stork* should be harder to classify. Using similar norms published earlier, Wilkins selected items high and low in the tables, matched on frequency of occurrence in written English. Under speed and accuracy instructions, subjects assigned high words to their appropriate category on an average of 589 msec; low words took 632 msec. Thus, high conjoint frequency combinations of instance and category were verified faster than low conjoint frequency combinations. Level in a hierarchical network, alone, does not account for these results. In some sense, a *robin* and a *sparrow* are better instances of *bird* than *warbler* or *pelican,* and are more quickly categorized. This fact suggested that it would be necessary to modify the Quillian model. Collins and Loftus (1975) have addressed this problem in the development of their spreading activation theory.

E. Cognitive Economy

The Wilkins [i] (1971) study addressed the relationship that Collins and Quillian called *superordinate,* that of category inclusion. Conrad (1972) found a parallel result for property attributes. No preexisting norms were available as to how often people might think of *has feathers* for *bird,* for example; but Conrad's intuitions were that some attributes might come to mind more quickly than others. If so, these might be verified faster. Conrad collected her own norms by asking students to write descriptions for categorical concepts such as *animal, bird, shark, canary, airplane,* etc. She arranged the responses by the percentage of her subjects supplying each; as an example, over 75% of her subjects supplied "can move" as a property of *animal,* but only 12% supplied "has ears." She then conducted an experiment paralleling that of Collins and Quillian, timing her subjects as they verified sentences like *An animal can move* and *An animal has ears.* Like Wilkins, she found that the production frequency norms predicted verification times. Frequently given properties took 1080 msec to verify, on the average, whereas infrequently given ones took 1140 msec.

Conrad argued that her results contradicted a major assumption of Collins and Quillian, that of "cognitive economy." Stated strongly, the hypothesis of cognitive economy holds that each property is stored at *only one node.* That is, if *has wings* is stored with *bird,* it cannot be stored again with *canary.* This would make property verification extremely sensitive to hierarchical level, since no property could be verified until the system accessed the single storage node for that property. However, Conrad found that verification RTs were fast for properties high in her norms, regardless of how many hierarchical levels intervened between the subject node and the most efficient storage node for the property. She therefore challenged the strong hypothesis and even concluded that "properties are stored in memory with every word which they define and can be retrieved directly rather than through a process of inference [p. 154]." Although TLC was set up using strong cognitive economy, this assumption was not necessarily a central feature of the associated psychological theory. A weaker version, holding that some properties are stored at multiple nodes but that many are verified by inference, is more palatable on numerous grounds. For one thing, at least some cognitive economy is required for inference-making capacity, and one of Quillian's major objectives was to model such inference-making. On the other hand, Conrad's data do imply that TLC structured excessive cognitive economy by restricting property links to a single node. Evolutionary considerations suggest *partial* cognitive economy, based on our

Postulate 3 that the representational system is not neutral with respect to content. It seems likely that some properties are highly salient to the objects they characterize, whereas others are irrelevant from an adaptive viewpoint. For example, the skin of edible animals and fruits is likely to be more salient than the skin of inedible or inaccessible ones. Thus, a system that directly stored *A buffalo has skin* might do well to leave to inference the fact that *A hawk has skin*. The mechanism mediating differential salience is a matter for empirical and theoretical scrutiny; however, one possibility may be suggested. Properties that are perceptually associated with a concept may be retrieved directly with it, whereas those that are known abstractly may require inference. That is, one may know that a chicken has skin from having seen, felt, plucked, removed, or eaten the skin. *Skin* may thus be directly stored with chicken. The fact that a hawk has skin may be available only through the abstract knowledge that birds—many never experienced by the knower—have skin. It also seems likely, though no extant model explicity posits such a mechanism, that many Westerners verify *A hawk has skin* by analogizing unfamiliar hawks and familiar chickens, rather than by invoking the category *bird*. If so, similarity ratings between such concepts should predict how rapidly a highly available property of one could be asserted of the other. This reflects the supposition, in our Postulate 6, that human logic is not as deductive as standard formal logics, but may be predicated on a loose kind of perceptual similarity. The a priori assessment of "similarity" is, of course, difficult—but may be essential to a predictive semantic memory theory. The theory of Smith *et al.* (1974) comes closest to accommodating this possibility; their theory is discussed later.

The cognitive economy issue is an example of how overreliance on an analogy with automata can transcend not only evolutionary implications, but also common sense. It is absurd to suppose that a biological system would reflect either complete cognitive economy or none at all; it is organized to deal with life, not to be simply characterized. Such overreliance can also lead one to ignore important aspects of the data; Conrad's own norms support partial cognitive economy. The property *is liquid* was given by 50% of her subjects for the concept *drink*, but not at all for *Coca-Cola, coffee, lemonade,* or *beer*. Similarly, every one of her subjects supplied *has wings* for *bird*, but none of them supplied it for *canary, owl,* or *ostrich*. How, then, can subjects verify the statements *Coffee is a liquid* and *An owl has wings?*

F. Semantic Distance and Memory Organization

What is it that the production frequency norms of Wilkins (1971) and Conrad (1972) measure? Whatever it is, it seems to be a powerful predictor of reaction time in classification and verification tasks. Rips, Shoben, and Smith (1973), who named it "semantic distance," operationalized the concept in two different ways. In one experiment, they used norms to select the most frequently given noun members of the concept categories *animal, mammal, bird, vehicle,* and *car.* As the hierarchical Collins and Quillian model would predict, *cardinal, eagle, robin,* and so on were verified as *birds* faster than as *animals.* However, the *mammal* category was inconsistent with predictions from a hierarchical model. It should be at the same level as *bird,* as shown in Figure 5.3; but it was easier for subjects to verify *bear, cat, cow, deer,* and the like as animals rather than as mammals. This suggests that the logical taxonomic categories of a hierarchical model may not represent the categories people actually use, as might be expected from our Postulate 3 (some categories are more salient than others) and Postulate 6 (that the system does not conform to the requirements of formal logic). Thus, the actual hierarchical and lateral organization of memory must be sought in prior learning and possible in primate adaptation. Rips *et al.* also observed considerable variation for the decision times of hierarchically identical propositions; for instance *A pig is a mammal* took considerably longer on the average (1476 msec) than *A cow is a mammal* (1258 msec).

In a second experiment, Rips, Shoben, and Smith defined "semantic distance" in terms of norms collected explicitly to determine how "distant" people judged particular category instances to be from each other and from their superordinate category name. People were asked, for example, to rate the distance between the concept *mammal* and its various instances such as *cow, goat, horse,* and so on. They also rated the distance between *cow* and *horse; horse* and *goat,* etc. Rips *et al.* found that the obtained ratings were excellent predictors of reaction time to verify statements such as *A cow is a mammal, A goat is a mammal, A horse is a mammal,* etc. By use of multidimensional scaling procedures, they also determined that distance ratings appeared to reflect organization along two dimensions, size and predacity, for both mammals and birds. *Birds* and *mammals* that were unusually large or small, or unusually predatory or meek, tended to be rated as more distant from the category name than those of intermediate size and predacity. Rips *et al.* interpret their results as contrasting with hierarchical distance models such as that of Collins and Quillian and interpret them in the context of the Smith *et al.* (1974) model to be presented in detail later.

Subjects in these experiments are typically raised in urban environments and have little or no experience with predation, either as hunter or as victim.

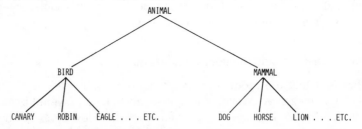

FIGURE 5.3 A network like that of Collins and Quillian (1969) but including the node MAMMAL. Reaction times predicted by this structure were not found by Rips, Shoben, & Smith (1973).

Yet size and predacity leap from the data as memory vectors for classifying animals. One can think of numerous other dimensions that would be equally useful as bases of animal classification for modern city dwellers, such as rarity, utility, domestication, or beauty. The appearance of size and predacity may be coincidental. However, for a predatory yet relatively defenseless primate such as early man, size and predacity together appear to be felicitous classifiers of animals. They also figure prominently in children's stories ("the big, bad wolf"). They are exactly what we might predict on the basis of evolutionary considerations. Thus, one hypothesis that may be put forth is that some aspects of classification, even among the literate, are phylogenetically determined.

G. Typicality and Basic Level

We have described several ways of operationalizing semantic distance—from experimenter's intuitions to normative measures reflecting the judgments of large pools of subjects. However collected, the norms have some common dimensions. All correlate in varying degrees with the time needed to classify subordinates and properties or verify subject–predicate propositions. An interesting view of what these norms measure is represented in the work of Rosch (1973, 1975, 1978). Rosch originally approached the problem from a perspective different from that usually used by semantic memory theorists; she wanted to discover the principles people use in dividing up the perceptual world. Interestingly, Rosch began her research program in a cross-cultural setting, and her outcomes and interpretations tend to comport well with our evolutionary postulates. For example, she found that some colors are perceptually salient across cultures despite the apparent arbitrariness of how different languages place boundaries in the color spectrum (Rosch, 1977). From color perception, Rosch's work quickly extended to the study of natural-language concepts, or categories, such as those commonly used in semantic memory studies. She argued that speakers of English living in urban America know how *typical* an instance is of its superordinate category. They know, for instance, that *bed* is more typical of the category *furniture* than is *hammock,* and that *robin* is a more typical *bird* than is a *penguin.* This observation was unlike previous psychological research in concept formation, where natural categories were usually treated as all-or-none. Rosch proposed that most natural categories are actually *analogue* in nature; that is, a category's internal structure represents the degree of relatedness of various category members to the category itself. The category members, in other words, are organized around prototypical instances and vary in their proximity to the prototype. The organization exists *in the minds* of the people of a common cultural background who use the category.

Rosch also distinguished prototype and nonprototype members for some categories. Prototype category members are the clearest cases, or most typical instances; *chair, bed,* and *table* are prototype members of the category *furniture.* Nonprototype members, such as *ashtray, drapes,* and *vase* for *furniture,* vary in their representativeness of the category. *Lamp* and *stool* are "better" examples of *furniture* than are *ashtray* and *picture.*

The prototype structure of natural-language semantic categories has been called *typicality.* Rosch has shown that people can reliably rate how typical the various members of familiar categories are, and their ratings predict various aspects of performance in a task requiring people to match words or pictures (Rosch, 1975, 1978). Prototypical instances of a category appear to be more accessible and to require fewer inferences or decision processes in property verification (Ashcraft, 1978). Prototypical members of a superordinate, moreover, show the greatest family resemblance to other members of the superordinate category. Thus, Rosch and Mervis (1975) suggest that family resemblances rather than criterial features may provide the most cogent definition of a category. Either way, one senses that some members are more significant than others in describing a category and that such special significance may reflect the prior adaptive salience of these members. This suggestion is strengthened by the observation of Berlin (1978), based on substantial evidence from folk classification research, that "prescientific man brings order to his biological world in essentially the same ways [p. 24]."

Typicality also affects rate of learning. It is possible to make up artificial categories, in which some category members are more typical than others; when this is done, the more typical instances are easier to learn (Rosch & Mervis, 1975). This does not contradict the evolutionary premise, however. Once the machinery of categorization evolved, based on the adaptive significance of a few instances, it would support a new mechansim for creating novel categories. This observation as well as many of our other suggestions accords with the position of Rozin (1976). He argues that intelligence evolves as the organism gains generalized access to behaviors that originally served as specific solutions to specific problems. Categorization, followed by novel category construction, could be such a case.

Rosch's work leaves room for analogical classification and is thus consistent with Postulate 6 in not "overlogicalizing" memory structures. She states that her research "was not intended either as a model of semantic memory or as a verification or refutation of any particular theory of semantic memory [1975, p. 225]." Still, her results are difficult to incorporate in any theory of semantic memory that posits sharp category boundaries, such as one proposed by Glass and Holyoak (1975). The findings are much more compatible with theories positing flexible conceptual structures and with some nonstandard logics such as "fuzzy set" theory (Zadeh, 1975). "Fuzzy" sets appear capable of representing flexible conceptual structures (e.g., Oden, 1977).

Rosch made another significant contribution to psychological semantics. She discovered a *basic level* type of category membership (Rosch, Mervis, Gray, Johnson, & Boyes-Braem, 1976). Most objects fit into a hierarchy of categories having increasing generality. For example, *Colonial kitchen chair* is less general than *kitchen chair,* which is less general than *chair, furniture, artifact (man-made object), inanimate object,* and *physical object.* Rosch observed that many such hierarchies contain one level that is special in terms of descriptive salience. At this level, people can describe what the object is for, what actions can be performed upon it, draw a silhouette of it, and supply its characteristics. At higher levels, they cannot do these things because the category is too abstract; and at lower levels there is no difference from basic level in what they can say about the object. For example, it is possible to draw a silhouette of a chair, but not of furniture; it is possible to describe what is done with a colonial kitchen chair, but this is no different from what is done with chairs in general. For this hierarchy, *chair* is at the basic level; it is the highest level in the hierarchy that is descriptively salient.

Rosch suggested that most object properties may be stored at the basic level. From an evolutionary or ecological standpoint, it is not at all unreasonable to suppose that the perceptual and utilitarian integrity of object categories should determine their psychological significance. Basic level may have its counterpart in two concepts from a very different area of psychology, the effort to develop an ecologically based theory of perception (Gibson, 1966, 1977; Shaw & Bransford, 1977). Gibson suggested the concept of "affordances" for environmental configurations that are adaptively significant with respect to a given animal. Thus, for a small animal a hole provides the affordance of hiding; for an animal who preys on the same small animal, the hole provides the affordance of possible prey. Both animals stand in some utilitarian relationship to the hole, and its perceptual relevance is contingent on that utility. An animal that neither hides in small holes nor preys on others that do has no reason to organize a percept of the hole—his "effectivities" do not take advantage of the affordances of the hole. Effectivities—what a given animal can do with a given environmental event—and affordances—what the environmental event permits a particular kind of animal to do with it—are significant factors in Gibson's perceptual theory. We are sympathetic to the ecological thrust of Gibson's enterprise (if not to all its associated claims), and we think the concepts of affordances and effectivities may prove useful in cognitive theory. Although it is admittedly speculative, we offer the suggestion that affordances and basic-level concepts may be related. The effectivities and affordances of early hominids might be expected to have perceptual and conceptual salience for us, their descendants. Affordances in particular remind one of basic level, defined as it is in terms of perceptual integrity (e.g., silhouettability) and utility (what one can do with it). The relationship may be worth developing.

Rosch's work has partly motivated a new approach to the general concept of psychological similarity. Tversky (1977) and Tversky and Gati (1978) describe a set-theoretic approach to similarity that encompasses the Rosch data as well as people's similarity judgments of faces, personality traits, and other semantic and perceptual stimuli.

IV. THEORIES OF SEMANTIC MEMORY

In this section, we describe three theories of semantic memory. These are sufficiently well developed to be characterized in detail; several other theories are mentioned briefly. The first model to be discussed, the Theory of Spreading Activation, is an updated version of Quillian's original model as presented by Collins and Loftus (1975). It has been revised to take account of the semantic distance effect, storage of properties at multiple nodes, and other data its authors considered relevant. The structure of the network has been considerably modified, and the processes involved in a search for information within the network have been elaborated and extended.

At about the same time Collins and Quillian began to publish their work, Meyer undertook a research program to develop an independent theory of semantic memory (Meyer, 1970, 1973, 1975). He used a version of the speeded classification task including *quantifiers* in his stimulus sentences, such as *all, some, no,* and the like. Based on data from experiments in which subjects verified such statements as *All stones are rubies* and *No men are nurses,* Meyer formulated a two-stage category search model that was initially quite different from Quillian's. However, Meyer had to modify his model to take account of later data, including the semantic distance effect, and the most recent version (Meyer & Schvaneveldt, 1976) is much more like Collins and Quillian's model than the earlier version.

Smith *et al.* (1974) felt that the semantic distance effect and other data would prove much too difficult for the original Quillian model. They considered that it would be more productive to formulate a completely new model than to patch up the old one. Unlike Meyer, they formulated their model explicitly as an alternative to Collins and Quillian and have contrasted their approach with those of both Collins and Quillian (1972 a, b) and Meyer (1970). The semantic distance effect has been a central factor in their theory, which is the most serious rival at present to the Collins and Loftus theory.

A. Spread of Activation Theory

1. ASSUMPTIONS CONCERNING MEMORY ORGANIZATION

The revised theory, like the original, represents the contents of permanent memory in network notation with concept nodes and links between the nodes. However, the new version is not hierarchically organized. Instead, concept relatedness (semantic distance) is the central organizational principle in the memory network. We have redrawn Figure 5.1 following Collins and Loftus (1975) and have extended it in a notation that is more congenial to the new network structure; the drawing is shown in Figure 5.4. The difference in length of lines is intended to capture the fact that different concept pairs are related by links of different strengths. In Figure 5.4, for example, both *ostrich* and *canary*

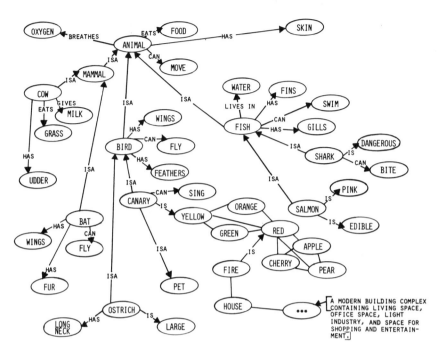

FIGURE 5.4 Graphic representation drawn to capture the essentials of the Collins and Loftus (1975) network.

are subsets of *bird* (a relationship designated by the term *isa* as the definition of the superordinate link from *ostrich* to *bird* and *canary* to *bird*). However, *ostrich* is positioned further from *bird* than is *canary* to accommodate the difference in the relatedness of the two concept pairs. The proper length of the lines can be determined in the various ways that semantic distance is measured. The *isa* link between *bird* and its subordinates, for example, reflects the percentage of subjects who supplied *ostrich* and *canary* as instances of a *bird* in the Battig and Montague (1969) category norms. One could also use the Rosch (1975) measures of typicality, or normative ratings of semantic distance. Of course, it is not the actual length of the individual lines that is important to the theory, but what length symbolizes—the strength of the relationship or accessibility of information that underlies the reaction time data in proposition verification experiments. At present, the variety of measures of that relationship poses a major challenge for semantic memory theory in general and for Collins and Loftus in particular. The method used to estimate link strength influences the fit one's theory can achieve to the data. Even if the theory were correct in many particulars, it would predict reaction times poorly if a poor measure of link strength guided the assignment of numerical values to the links. Solutions to the problem of what nodes are linked and what determines the strength of a link (accessibility to a node) will be incorporated into all the extant theories of semantic memory.

The semantic memory network links concepts, not words. Some of the concepts in the network can be labeled by words, others cannot. In Figure 5.4, most of the concepts happen to have single-word names, and we have placed them in the ovals to identify the concepts. However, two exceptions in the figure show examples of how some concepts have no single-word name. Near the bottom of the figure are the concepts for *long neck* and for a certain type of building, both of which must be communicated by descriptions rather than names—even though they may function well as unitary concepts. The vocabulary, or lexicon, constitutes a separate system in the spreading activation theory, as it did in Quillian's original version. Other semantic memory theorists have argued for a similar distinction (e.g., Lachman & Lachman, 1980; Loftus, 1977, 1976; Rumelhart, Lindsay & Norman, 1972). In the spreading activation theory, each name in the lexicon is linked to at least one concept in the semantic memory. The lexicon is also a network structure, but it is organized differently from the semantic memory. What determines proximity of nodes in the lexical network is primarily the phonotactic similarity of words (how similar they sound). This organization is justified partly by the work of Brown and McNeill (1966), who showed that people have systematic memories for certain aspects of the sound of a word that they cannot quite recall, but have "on the tip of the tongue."

Quillian's original set of links has been extended in the newer version to accommodate both intuitive and empirical considerations. A kind of link that has been added is the "negative superordinate," which we will designate *isnota*; it could be drawn in Figure 5.4 between *bat* and *bird*. Holyoak and Glass (1975) extensively studied false sentences and found that many such decisions can be made faster than would be possible through inferential processes. This implies that sometimes the category–exclusion relationship must be directly available. Indeed, such a conclusion accords with our suggestion that some categories are universal and phylogenetically determined. Exceptions to these categories may have to be directly learned. Examples are *A bat is not a bird, A whale is not a fish,* and *An eel is not a snake.*

2. PROCESSING ASSUMPTIONS

Perhaps the best analogy for understanding the spreading activation mechanism that is central to the processing component of the system is by thinking of a set of tuning forks sharing the same fundamental frequency. If you strike the first fork, its intensity is highest right after it is struck, and then decreases and eventually becomes silent. Adjacent forks also vibrate, but at a lower level than the original; and the intensity of the ring they produce also decreases with time. If you strike one of a roomful of tuning forks, vibration will spread outward from the first fork. Concept nodes act in an analogous fashion.

According to the theory, a concept node is activated when a person sees, hears, reads, or thinks about a concept. "Activation" is a term whose meaning in the context of a computer simulation, or analogy with tuning forks, is clearer than its psychological implications; however, one might think of it as a change of state. When activated, a node changes state so that it is more likely to be brought into consciousness or working memory than it was before it was activated. Activation of a node produces activation in all its adjacent nodes, which in turn produces activation in all their adjacent nodes. In this way activation "spreads" through the system. However, like the vibration of the forks, activation decreases in strength over time and distance. Thus, when the single node *fish* is activated, perhaps by mention of the word *fish,* the adjacent concepts *water, fins, gills, shark, salmon,* and *animal* will be activated, the strength of the activation depending on distance from *fish. Water,* for example, will be more strongly activated than *salmon.* Activation of *shark* will produce activation in *dangerous* and *bite,* though this activation will be relatively weaker than that of *shark.* Activation of *salmon* will activate *pink* and *edible,* but at a weaker level than *salmon.* For all nodes, activation is highest initially, "fading" with time.

To explain how spreading activation makes it possible to verify a proposition, it is necessary to add some assumptions. First, consider the case in which a subject is asked to verify the proposition, *A fish eats food.* The word *fish* occurs first, and therefore the node *fish* is activated first. Activation begins to spread from *fish* to adjacent nodes. An instant later, the word *food* occurs, and activation begins to spread outward from the *food* node. The *animal* node will be the point where activation, spreading from the two originating concepts, intersects. At this point, the system must make a decision whether the relationship represented by the path of nodes and links connecting *fish* and *food* are consistent with those represented by the relational operator or verb of the proposition.

To keep track of the path connecting the two originating nodes, it is assumed that as activation spreads, it leaves "tags" at each intermediate node. These tags designate the originating node and the just-preceding node. Activations spreading outward from *fish* and *food* and intersecting at the node for *animal* will sum together. In addition, the activation level at the intersection node will depend on how many links the activation has had to traverse and how strong these links were. Strength is inverse to length in Figure 5.4. Short links, for example, are stronger and "transmit" activation more easily than longer "weak" links. Thus, the proposition *A mammal eats food* should result in a higher activation level for *animal* than *A fish eats food* (see Figure 5.4). Activation level at the intersection node *(animal,* in our example) must reach a certain threshold for decision mechanisms that are involved in path evaluation to come into play. This assumption is required because spreading activation will no doubt result in a number of intersections that are not the intended ones. Since everything in semantic memory is linked by some path or other to everything else, the system would be constantly evaluating irrelevant paths if there were not some cutoff level to designate the potentially relevant intersections.

3. DECISION ASSUMPTIONS

In deciding if a sentence is true or false, the system first determines the path through the spreading activation process just described. The relations between subject and predicate must then be evaluated to decide whether the relationships stored in semantic memory are the same as those in the proposition to be verified. There are several kinds of evidence, some constituting positive evidence and some constituting negative evidence. All sources figure in the evaluation, and negative evidence exceeding a "false" decision criterion leads to a "no" or "false" response whereas positive evidence exceeding a "true" decision criterion leads to a "yes" or "true" response. For example, the theory says that an *isa* superordinate will immediately push the positive evidence over the criterial level for propositions of the form subject *isa* predicate, whereas a negative superordinate *(isnota)* will push the negative evidence over the criterial level. For all propositions, links contribute evidence according to their strength. For instance, strong positive evidence for *A canary can sing* is contributed by the link between *canary* and *sing,* which is strong (based on the percentage of subjects, 88%, who gave *can sing* as a property of *canary* in Conrad's [1972] norms). Weaker positive evidence is supplied by the link between *salmon* and *edible* for the proposition *A salmon is edible,* on the same basis (57%). A mismatch on a strong link, that is, a highly criterial property, constitutes strong negative evidence. For instance, a person who knows that porpoises have no gills will be able to reject *A porpoise is a fish* on the basis of the strong *has* link between *fish* and *gills.* For such a person, the path of strongest activation will be from *porpoise* through *has no* to *gills,* and from *fish* through *has* to *gills,* which will supply the mismatch negating the proposition. A person whose semantic memory does not contain the information that porpoises have no gills may deny the proposition on the basis of an *isnota* link directly from *porpoise* to *fish.* When two subsets have the same superordinate, this generally supplies strong negative evidence for the *isa* relationship. That is, denial of *A mammal is a fish* may be accomplished by the fact that both *mammal* and *fish* are subsets of *animal,* and therefore have a relationship of mutual exclusion constituting negative evidence for the decision-making mechanism. This source of negative evidence may also supply the negative evidence for a person who must judge the truth of *A porpoise is a fish,* if he knows that a porpoise is a mammal.

Altogether, Collins and Loftus describe five kinds of evidence that may be utilized by the semantic decision system, alone or in combination. The resulting configuration of possible bases for decisions is complex. This complexity is fully consistent with information-processing pretheory, reflecting the effort to deal with a large number of human capacities in terms of a small group of basic operations. As theories of semantic memory mature, the field will no doubt attempt to identify the minimum set of elementary or primitive decision rules that can handle the most extensive range of judgments of which humans are capable. To date, the selection of rules has been motivated primarily by computational considerations. Collins and Loftus have suggested those that will make the system work and that fit sentence-verification latencies. Evolutionary premises have not been invoked; however, it is possible they might provide a valuable heuristic method in the modeling effort.

B. Meyer's Category Search Model

So far, the propositional form "subject—relationship (verb)—predicate" has been the central factor in the experiments and theories described. The various experimental tasks converged on the same basic requirement. Subjects had to compare two internally represented concepts and determine whether their relationship was, or was not, that specified by the stimulus terms. There are obviously many ways one might add complexity to the simple stimuli that have been used. Meyer (1970) extended the simple proposition by adding *quantifiers* to the beginning of sentences. Quantifiers suggest "how many," such as *all, some, few, many, nineteen, nine-hundred, no.* Quantifiers have implications for the truth value of propositions containing the *isa* relationship, the only ones used in Meyer's experiments. One can consider the two concepts *sharks* and *fish* in a forward *isa* relationship, *Sharks are fish,* and a reverse *isa* relationship, *Fish are sharks.* The truth value of these sentences can change depending on the quantifier used. *All sharks are fish* is true, but *No sharks are fish* is false. *All fish are sharks* is false, whereas *Some fish are sharks* is true. Meyer (1970) proposed a theory to explain how people evaluate *existential affirmative* sentences (those using "some") and *universal affirmative* sentences (those using "all"). Later, he reported research designed to extend the theory to negative sentences like *No fish are sharks* (Meyer, 1973, 1975). The theory can be understood without reference to negative sentences, however, and our discussion will only consider affirmatives.

Meyer originally divided his sentences into four types based on the set-theoretic relationship between the subject noun and the predicate noun. These are shown in Figure 5.5: subset, superset, overlap, and disjoint. These correspond essentially to what we have earlier called *isa, reverse isa, can be,* and *isnota,* respectively. Assignment of noun pairs to one or another type of relationship has depended upon the experimenter's intuitions about the populations represented or implied by each category.

Meyer proposed a model of how people verify such simple quantified sentences. He did not intend his model to have the scope of Quillian's, and it was not designed as a competitor. It was designed to account for performance in a restricted laboratory task that was, hopefully, representative of human information processing in general. The relatively limited context in which he

RELATIONSHIP OF SUBJECT (S) TO PREDICATE (P)	VENN DIAGRAM	EXAMPLE		TRUTH VALUE	
		S	P	UNIVERSAL AFFIRMATIVES "ALL" SENTENCES	EXISTENTIAL AFFIRMATIVE "SOME" SENTENCES
SUBSET (ISA)		SHARKS	FISH	TRUE (ALL SHARKS ARE FISH)	TRUE (SOME SHARKS ARE FISH)
SUPERSET (REVERSE ISA)		STONES	RUBIES	FALSE (ALL STONES ARE RUBIES)	TRUE (SOME STONES ARE RUBIES)
OVERLAP (CAN BE)	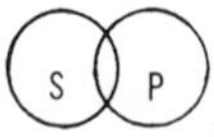	STUDENTS	SCHOLARS	FALSE (ALL STUDENTS ARE SCHOLARS)	TRUE (SOME STUDENTS ARE SCHOLARS)
DISJOINT (ISNOTA)	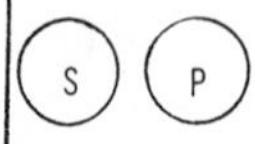	TREES	FISH	FALSE (ALL TREES ARE FISH)	FALSE (SOME TREES ARE FISH)

FIGURE 5.5 Set relations and logical truth values of universal and existentially quantified sentences [*Adapted from Meyer, 1970.*]

worked led Meyer to make a number of simpler assumptions than Quillian had to make to develop TLC, which had the ambitious goal of answering questions. Meyer's model contained only the limited set of relationships and properties that had to be accessed to verify the quantified sentences he used (although presumably he intended the model to be extensible to other kinds of materials that might be stored). Further, Meyer did not propose separate storage systems for words and concepts, but confined his theory to concepts that had single-word names.

Meyer's model was designed to account for verification latency data obtained for samples of simple quantified sentences differing on three variables. These were (a) the four types of set relations, (b) the type of quanitifer (all or some) and (c) the relative difference in the estimated size of the subject and predicate categories—that is, the number of exemplars estimated to be a part of each or of both. All possible combinations of the first two variables, type of set relation and quantifier, can be seen in the example sentences in Figure 5.5.

1. ASSUMPTIONS CONCERNING MEMORY ORGANIZATION

Meyer considered that the names of categories were stored in semantic memory, along with two kinds of information. First, the memory contains information about how concept categories intersect with other categories. For example, the concept *shark* intersects the other concepts *fish, animal, food, soup* (sharkfin), *predator*, etc., and this information is retrievable from semantic memory. Second, the memory contains information about the properties of the category members. Only those properties that are essential to the meaning of a category are represented. The essential features of the category *shark* might include *is dangerous, is animate, swims,* and *has teeth.* This was the kind of structural information incorporated in Meyer's original model, to which our discussion is confined. His most recently adopted structural assumptions are identical to those of the Collins and Loftus network (Meyer and Schvaneveldt, 1976).

2. PROCESSING AND DECISION ASSUMPTIONS

The original model proposed a two-stage decision sequence, shown in Figure 5.6. The system attempts to make a decision in Stage 1 and only executes the second stage if necessary; that is, the stages are serial. This means that those decisions that require two stages should take longer than those that require only one stage, by whatever amount of time is necessary to execute Stage 2 decisions.

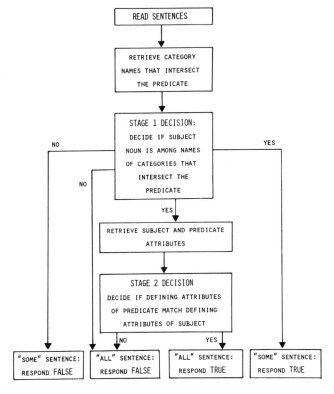

FIGURE 5.6 Meyer's Predicate Intersection Model for verifying quantified sentences [*Adapted from Meyer, 1970*]

In the first stage the names of concepts that intersect the predicate are retrieved in an order reflecting their extent of overlap with the predicate. For example, in any sentence having *fish* as its predicate, the system will retrieve the names of those concepts that intersect with *fish,* for example, *trout, bass, shark,* . . . *eel,* . . . *food,* . . . *pet.* Each retrieved name is compared to the subject name. If all intersecting categories are examined and no match is found, the system will respond "false," regardless of whether a *some* or *all* sentence is being evaluated. This happens for disjoint categories. Given, for example, *Some trees are fish,* or *All trees are fish,* the name *trees* will not be found among the categories that have exemplars in common with *fish,* and the system can decide "false" on this basis alone. If a match is found, no further decision making is necessary in the case of a *some* sentence; this will occur in all except disjoint sentences. Sentences like *Some sharks are fish, Some stones are rubies, Some students are scholars* can all be judged "true" without further analysis. The subject must proceed to a Stage 2 decision whenever an *all* sentence is under evaluation and a match is found. In Stage 2, the defining attributes of subject and predicate are compared, and if every attribute of the predicate matches an attribute of the subject the system can decide "true." If any attribute of the predicate is not among attributes of the subject, the system responds "false." This will happen in *all* sentences with superset or overlap relations. Each of the following would require a Stage 2 decision: *All sharks are fish* (subset), *All stones are rubies* (superset), and *All students are scholars* (overlap). Only the first sentence will be judged "true," because every defining feature of *fish* is also a defining feature of *shark.* However, *rubies* have defining features (e.g., *is red)* not shared by all *stones,* and *scholars* have defining features not shared by all *students.* On the basis of the Stage 2 comparison and decision, the subject will judge the latter two sentences "false."

Predictions from the model take into consideration whether one or two stages are required for a decision. Where only Stage 1 is needed, the number of instances in the predicate category, the subject category, and their intersection can be used to generate predictions, as can the hypothesized search order. The model thus offers a relatively complex set of predictions, but certain ones are obvious. First, *some* sentences should generally be evaluated faster than *all* sentences because, as can be inferred from an examination of Figure 5.6, *some* sentences never require the Stage 2 decision. The two stages are serial, so decisions requiring Stage 2 generally take longer than those requiring only Stage 1. The overall results of Meyer's experiments (Meyer & Schvaneveldt, 1976) agreed with this prediction. *Some* sentences were verified faster than *all* sentences. However, *all* sentences having disjoint categories (e.g., *Some/All trees are fish)* are also supposed to be completed in Stage 1, so the model predicts no difference in response time for *some* and *all* versions of these sentences. The data showed that they are not quite equal.

A second source of predictions is category size. Disjoint sentences (either *some* or *all)* can be judged "false" in Stage 1. However, the judgment cannot be made until the subject has exhaustively searched every concept that intersects the predicate. Consequently, the speed of such responses should be sensitive to the number of elements in that intersection population. The model predicts that disjoint sentences with a small number of intersecting categories should be judged "false" more quickly than disjoint sentences with many intersecting categories. The concept "solids," for example, contains a large intersect population including, among other things, *mountains, stones, rubies, tables, chairs, books, windmills,* . . . etc., while "rubies" contains a considerably smaller one. Therefore *All/Some oceans are solids* should take longer than *All/Some oceans are rubies.* Although the experimental outcomes described by Meyer were complex, this tended in general to be the case.

The more precise a theory, the more quickly it runs into trouble. Meyer's theory was very precise, and it soon began unraveling. It was developed before the importance of semantic distance was realized, and consequently Meyer did not attempt to control the semantic distance between categories in the four set relations and two quantifier types. Rips (1975) showed a powerful effect of subject–predicate semantic relatedness on verification time in disjoint sentences, and the studies of Rips et al. (1973) and Smith et al. (1974) suggest that category size effects in general may reduce to semantic distance effects. Meyer's prediction about disjoint sentences, which he attributed to the number of elements that had to be exhaustively searched before a "false" response could be made, may have been confirmed only because larger categories are likely to be less semantically distant from subject terms than smaller categories (e.g., *solids* is semantically closer to *oceans* in the preceding example than *rubies* is). This relative closeness would generally produce more difficulty for a subject responding "false."

Second, Meyer arranged his experiments so that subjects verified a group of *some* sentences at one time, and a group of *all* sentences at another time. This experimental arrangement permits a subject to adopt different strategies for the two quantifiers by capitalizing on semantic distance as follows. From Figure 5.5 it can be seen that *some* sentences are always "true," except when the category relations are disjoint, whereas *all* sentences are always "false," except when the subject is a subset of the predicate. This means that when the subject must judge only *some* sentences, he need only ascertain whether the categories are disjoint. If they are, he can respond "false," otherwise he can respond "true." However, disjoint categories tend to be semantically unrelated. The subject need only sense some relatedness to respond "true." This strategy does not work for sentences containing *all.* When other investigators ran studies with the *some* or *all* quantifiers mixed together in the same time block so that subjects could not use semantic relatedness as a cue, the effects of quantifier type were attenuated or eliminated (Glass & Holyoak, 1974; Glass, Holyoak & O'Dell, 1974; Holyoak & Glass, 1975; Rips, 1975; Butterfield, 1974. Further, according to Meyer's model, true sentences in which the subject is a subset of the predicate require either one or two stages depending on the quantifier. *Some* sentences such as *Some robins are birds are* evaluated in Stage 1; *all* sentences such as *All robins are birds* require Stage 2. These sentence types, therefore, provide a test of Meyer's model when semantic-distance strategies are removed. Butterfield (1974) did so, and found no differences in processing times between *some* and *all* sentences with subset relations.

Where does this leave us? First, the Predicate Intersection Model is untenable, at least with respect to its most important processing and decision assumptions. Second, the effect of category size remains controversial; it is still unclear whether all category size effects are reducible to semantic distance or whether category size exerts effects, but only under still-obscure limiting conditions. Third, a variety of strategies are apparently available to subjects verifying simple quantified sentences that the original model cannot accommodate. In the most recent revision of the model, Meyer and Schvaneveldt (1976) have discarded many of their earlier assumptions and added a number of new assumptions including activated network path evaluation for judging *some* sentences.

Meyer's work directed other investigators to the effects of quantifiers, which have been used in a number of studies. The most complete data are those of Glass, Holyoak, and O'Dell (1974) and Holyoak and Glass (1975). When they removed the confounds of the pioneering studies, they found no difference between the quantifiers *all, many,* and *some.* The best predictor of RT in such sentences was the semantic distance between the subject and predicate as measured by production frequency norms. The quantifier *no,* as in *No dogs are horses,* was somewhat slower, perhaps for the same reasons discussed earlier in connection with negation and falsification.

C. The Feature Comparison Model

The semantic distance effect appears to reflect a general human capacity that is suggested by a large number of studies. People can sometimes judge quickly if two words are related or not without inferring or retrieving the nature of the relationship. This capacity remains even if the two words are embedded in simple sentences as subject and predicate. Smith *et al.* (1974) capitalized on semantic distance and constructed a theory that bears a superficial resemblance to Meyer's. In judging the truth of simple sentences, the theory holds, people first make a global comparison between subject and predicate nouns. If the concepts are highly related, the sentence is immediately judged true (e.g., *A robin is a bird*). If virtually no relationship is felt to exist, the sentence is speedily disconfirmed (e.g., *A ruby is a bird*). In the middle range of relatedness (e.g., *A chicken is a bird*), processing moves to the second stage where the important features of each concept are compared. The model attempts to account for the verification times of subset, disjoint, and property statements; and in so doing it suggests a possible psychological basis for the meaning of nouns.

1. ASSUMPTIONS CONCERNING MEMORY ORGANIZATION

Smith *et al.* consider that concepts are represented in semantic memory as sets of features. The concept *robin* for example, is represented by the extent to which it is avian, winged, red-breasted, large or small, common, etc. Strictly speaking, Smith *et al.* regard features as the *value* the concept takes on for each of a set of dimensions. Thus, the features of *robin* would be its value on the dimensions avianness, wingedness, red-breastedness, size, commonness, etc. Features are ordered, or weighted, by their importance to the definition of the concept. The features just listed are all important to the definition of *robin* and therefore have high weights. In addition, the concept *robin* includes in its feature set other features that are not defining but nevertheless figure in most people's idea of *robin,* such as *is undomesticated, is edible, eats bread*. These features have low weights, because they are accidental (though characteristic) features of *robin*. Smith *et al.* consider that semantic memory contains the feature list that defines each concept and that a weight is associated with each feature indicating how essential it is to the definition of the concept. The memory also contains a cutoff level for weights, above which features are *defining* and below which they are merely *characteristic*.

2. PROCESSING AND DECISION ASSUMPTIONS

Like Meyer, Smith *et al.* postulate two basic decision stages; some decisions can be made without the second stage, others cannot. However, the stages are actually unlike Meyer's. Figure 5.7 depicts the processing and decision sequence that Smith *et al.* assume. In Stage 1, a global comparison is executed to determine the semantic relatedness of subject and predicate terms. This is done by retrieving all the features, both defining and characteristic, of the two concepts and comparing the two feature lists *in toto*. Smith and his colleagues are not deeply committed to any of the variety of formulas that might enter into this global comparison; however, they propose that the comparison yields a *similarity index* for the two feature lists. The exact set of features that define a concept, as well as the importance of various features to the definition, may vary between individuals (and even in the same individual from time to time). Therefore, the similarity index will not be identical every time it is computed. In fact, the model assumes that the value of the similarity index for any given pair of concepts will be normally distributed—sometimes higher, sometimes lower, but falling most of the time around some characteristic mean level. The Stage 1 decision processes are based on a signal detectability theory for recognition tasks and are formally similar to those in the Atkinson and Juola (1974) word recognition model.

Before each trial, two values are set, against which the similarity index is compared. One represents the high-similarity criterion and the other, the low-similarity criterion. If the computed feature similarity index is above the

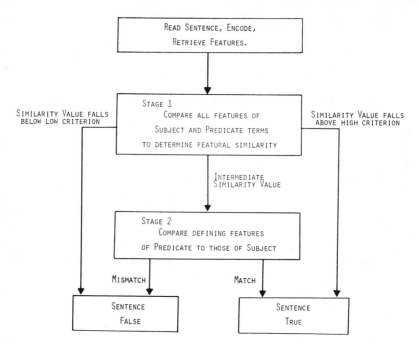

FIGURE 5.7 **The Feature Comparison Model of Smith, Shoben and Rips (1974).** [*Adapted from Smith, 1978*]

high-similarity criterion, the subject immediately responds "true." This will happen with sentences like *A collie is a dog* and *A shark is a fish*. If the similarity index falls below the low-similarity criterion, the subject can immediately respond "false." This will happen with sentences like *A banana is a mountain* and *A rabbit is a computer*. When the subject and predicate are neither extremely related nor extremely unrelated, the feature similarity index will fall between the high and low criteria; and it is under these circumstances that the system will proceed to Stage 2.

In Stage 2, the distinction between defining and characteristic features becomes important. Only the defining features are compared in Stage 2. If some defining features of the subject fall outside the range of allowable values for defining features of the predicate (as in *A man is a woman*), the subject can respond "false." Otherwise, the defining features of subject and predicate are compared, and a "true" response is made if all defining features of the predicate are also defining features of the subject, as in *A chicken is a bird*. Likewise, a "false" response is made if some defining features of the predicate are not also defining features of the subject, as in *A bat is a bird*. Smith and his colleagues point out that Stage 1 is holistic, intuitive, and error-prone, since it considers similarity of feature lists as a whole without taking into account *which* features are similar. It is possible that a fast "true" response could be made in State 1 to *A bat is a bird,* for example.

Stage 2 is selective, logical, and relatively error-free. Smith *et al.* suggest that these two stages correspond to the two ways literate individuals understand subset relations, which might be described as "loosely speaking (a bat is a bird)" and "technically speaking (a chicken is a bird)." We are inclined to think this interpretation is on the right track. However, we propose an extension of it that reflects our Evolutionary Generalization B—human higher mental processes preceded Western civilization (and schooling). Perhaps Stage 1 reflects a universal, preliterate categorization mode characteristic of the species *Homo sapiens* — based, as Smith *et al.'s* model has it, on similarity. It may therefore involve phylogenetically prior and more fundamental processes than Stage 2, which may be an artifact of Western education. In school we learn, for example, that a bat is not a bird—despite considerable perceptual evidence to the contrary and similar affordances of bats and birds to prescientific humans. School-learned taxonomic divisions may rest on information not perceptually available to most people, such as the classification of whales as mammals. Such divisions may have to be abstractly stored and linguistically mediated; and they may map badly onto "natural categories." It should be no surprise if these taxonomic divisions should be less accessible than more intrinsic ones. Our suggestion is in the spirit of Smith *et al.'s* observation that Stage 1 involves a kind of "loosely speaking" categorization, while Stage 2 involves a kind of "technically speaking" categorization, although we might suggest the terms *perceptually* and *scientifically* speaking as substitutes. We also find their characterization of Stage 1 as holistic and intuitive acceptable; however, to call it "error-prone" seems to miss the mark. By what standards is it an "error" to call a bat a bird or a whale a fish? There are obvious cross-cultural predictions to be made, but the method typically used heretofore to test the model requires literate subjects and would require modification to perform the proper studies.

The initial presentation of a scientific theory is never its final form; and this is certainly true of the present model. Several mechanisms in the theory are either completely unspecified or remain amenable to several different specifications. For example, the model does not specify the mechanism for partitioning a word's semantic features into "defining" and "characteristic." The theory has been criticized on grounds that philosophers have tried for centuries to separate defining and characteristic features of concepts to determine their meanings. This criticism might be appropriate if Smith *et al.* were building a philosophical model to instruct us what the proper meaning of a well-defined concept *should* be. However, their theory has a different objective—to reflect how people actually do make judgments of category membership. Such a theory need not suggest *the correct* decision rule, it only need capture the decision rules that people use. If our Postulate 6 is taken seriously, the philosophical and psychological objectives are incommensurate, since philosophers must conform to the demands of formal logic, whereas psychologists must transcend such demands. Furthermore, the evolutionary point of view suggests that the problem is not to find a demarcation line that distinguishes characteristic features from defining ones; it is to find the *kind* of features that enter into similarity relations and those that enter into abstract taxonomies. One obvious possibility presents itself: Those features that have been perceptually experienced and/or have functional significance, such as *can fly* and *has wings* in the case of *bat* or *can be sat on* in the case of *chair,* may figure in Stage 1 decisions. Features that have been abstractly stored such as *gives birth to live young* may figure in Stage 2 decisions. The philosophical problem may thus be simply moot.

Second, Smith *et al.* leave open the possibility for a variety of different formulas for computing the similarity index in Stage 1 processing. They have suggested certain constraints that they feel will guide the choice of formula; however, within these constraints there are a multitude of possibilities. More data are needed to select among several equally plausible options.

The theory was initially formulated to deal with subset and disjoint relations, and this it does well. It predicts the outcomes of most extant experiments in the field, including many we have not presented because of space limitations. It can predict most effects of typicality, semantic relatedness, and category size. The theory proposes that the same feature weights determine production or rating behavior in normative tasks and verification RTs.

In the verification task, it is the overlap of characteristic features that is responsible for so-called errors. Since the decision making in Stage 1 makes its judgment on the overall similarity index, there will be occasional fast but "erroneous" judgments when accidental features are in conflict with school-learned categories. This is how typicality exerts its effect in the Smith *et al.* model. Atypical instances of a category (e.g., *penguin* in the case of *bird)* may share too few characteristic features to push the similarity index above the low criterion. The result is a fast "false" response to *A penguin is a bird.*

Will the Smith *et al.* theory be extensible to encompass other tasks besides sentence verification of category–membership sentences? Rips (1975) has shown that the theory does a reasonable job of predicting RTs to quantified sentences. Beginnings have been made in extending the theory to the study of analogies and the verification of definitional properties. It remains to be seen whether the sentence verification task is truly prototypical of knowledge retrieval; and the extensibility of the model will depend on the extent to which it is. The theory, however, has made important inroads into the problems of semantic memory and psychological semantics. It is perhaps the most congenial among the semantic memory theories to the perspective of this paper. The Stage 1 and Stage 2 processes may neatly distinguish what is essentially human from what is only human potential in the organization of permanent memory.

D. Two Additional Models of Semantic Memory

Two additional models (Fiksel & Bower, 1976; Glass & Holyoak, 1975) are described briefly. Glass and Holyoak's theory was developed as a rival to that of Smith, Shoben, and Rips, while that of Fiksel and Bower was developed as an alternative to extant semantic memory theories.

Glass and Holyoak made certain observations of "false" verification times that did not accord well with predictions from the Smith et al. model; they felt that an alternative theory was needed. Their own position supplies explicit mechanisms to account for sentence falsification. They abandoned the probabilistic nature of the Smith et al. model, substituting a network model notation.

Concepts are represented in the network structure by *markers,* or meaning elements, a notion imported from linguistic semantics (Katz, 1972). For each concept, one *defining marker* represents the concept's essential properties. For example, the defining marker for *robin* represents information essential to the conceptualization of a robin at just that level of particularity. The defining marker for *robin* will differ from the defining marker of a concept at a more particular level (e.g., some specific robin) or at a less particular level (e.g., all birds). However, the defining marker for *robin* implies or, in Glass and Holyoak's terms, *dominates* markers such as *Avian* (bird), *Animate* (animal), and *Feathered*(having feathers), and perhaps others. The defining marker plus those markers dominated by the defining marker constitute the marker set that will be searched when a person accesses the concept *robin.* Because a concept's defining marker may dominate defining markers for other concepts (as *robin* dominates *avian),* the concept for *robin* relates by implication to all markers for the concept *avian* (bird). This supplies the inferential potential of the model and defines a structure in some ways similar to the Collins and Loftus network. The marker structure that Glass and Holyoak have described can, in the initial formulation, accommodate only quantified sentences that are not anomalous and whose verb is *is, are,* or *has.* When a person verifies a sentence, he ostensibly searches the markers related to the subject for information that either confirms or disconfirms the entire proposition.

Much of the processing component of the model is unspecific in its initial formulation; however, at the core is a search through the markers. The order of the search is critical to predicting verification *RTs,* and Holyoak and Glass propose that the best estimate of actual search order is normative production frequency in a sentence completion task. To obtain the necessary normative data, Glass et al. (1974) gave subjects sentences of the general form, *Quantifier–subject noun–are* ____, and asked for completions. Five different quantifiers—*all, some, many, few,* and *no*—were used. Thus, subjects might be asked to complete statements like *All robins are* ____ , *Many airplanes are* ____ , *No flowers are* ____ . Production frequency of the predicates supplied by their subjects was a good predictor of RT when a new sample of subjects verified the completed sentences as "true." Glass and Holyoak believe that this predictive power stems from the fact that both verification latency and production frequency reflect the same thing: the order of searching the markers related to the subject-noun concept.

As soon as the subject locates confirming or disconfirming evidence in the subject concept-marker set, a decision is made. Thus, for "true" sentences such as *All robins are birds, Some robins are birds,* and *Most robins are birds,* a response can be made as soon as the *avian* marker is located among the set of markers that relate to *robin*.

Glass and Holyoak have been particularly explicit in their explanation of how two kinds of "false" sentences are judged. As we mentioned, they excluded anomalous false propositions such as *All birds are chairs* from consideration. The remaining kinds of false sentences that they have discussed in detail are *contradictory* and *counterexample* sentences. Contradictory sentences are those such as *All robins· are sparrows* and *Some birds are reptiles*. These false sentences are high in "semantic similarity" and should, therefore, be disconfirmed slowly, but their RTs were fast. Glass and Holyoak account for the rapid falsification of such sentences by supposing that the relation of incompatibility is directly represented in memory. In this way, the defining marker for *robin* immediately implies incompatibility with the defining marker for *sparrow*, because *robin* and *sparrow* are disjoint divisions of the category *bird*.

The second type of "false" sentence is the *counterexample* sentence. These are "false" only when quantified by *all*, but remain "true" when quantified by *some* (e.g., *All birds are sparrows*). In searching the marker for the subject *bird*, no contradiction to *sparrow* will be found. The rejection of this type of false *all* sentence, according to Holyoak and Glass (1975), is based on accessing a counterexample to the predicate such as *robin* or *canary*. Several experimental outcomes support this view.

The future of the Glass and Holyoak model depends primarily on two factors: how well they can fill in the many gaps that now exist in the model, and how well they can extend it. At present, a number of structural and processing issues are left unclear. For example, the notion of a "defining marker," their central meaning postulate, is not particularly satisfying. The defining marker for *canary* is "an abstract concept roughly equivalent to 'possessing the essential properties of a canary' [Glass & Holyoak, 1975, p. 321]." Further, Glass and Holyoak postulate the creation of redundant paths in order to accommodate certain overly fast reaction times. For instance, *A canary is an animal* is verified faster than the inferential process of going from *canary* to *avian* to *animal* would suggest. The model allows for a redundant direct link from *canary* to *animal* to accommodate this, an arrangement that is formally similar to partial cognitive economy. However, they are well aware that explicit specification of such redundancy rules is hazardous; they can be postulated between any pair of conceivable concepts to account for any observed verification data. This can rob the theory of predictive power, as can specification of multiple property storage just when necessary to account for reaction times. What is needed is a principle to suggest the set of redundant links or, in the case of partial cognitive economy, the probable locations of multiply-stored properties. Evolutionary considerations, if taken seriously by semantic memory theorists, may be heuristically useful in suggesting such a principle. Finally, Glass and Holyoak have not specified a search process, except that the markers are searched in a fixed order. Of course, greater breadth of sentence types must be accommodated if the theory is to prosper.

Fiksel and Bower's (1976) model is a deeply mathematical theory, developed as a question-answering automaton. Like Collins and Quillian, Fiksel and Bower have set their theory the task of modeling the actual psychological mechanisms involved in human question-answering. The model was specifically formulated for the data we have covered in this chapter; it incorporates mechanisms for these tasks that are designed to predict the outcomes actually obtained. It goes beyond Quillian's (1969) model in that it specifies certain conceptual and mathematical properties of *nodes* and *links* in considerable detail.

It will be recalled that nodes are the representational locus for concepts or meaning units, and links are the labeled relations between nodes. Fiksel and Bower conceive each node as a finite state *automaton*. This means each node has states, or transitory conditions, that depend on inputs from adjacent nodes in the network. By virtue of transitions from state to state, a node and its neighbors can respond to inquiries independent of other parts of the network and without global control. The model formalizes the details of signal propagation through the network and includes a path intersection method for answering questions and verifying propositions. It is compatible with most of the extant data on sentence verification, including quantification and negation. It also allows for the storage of transient, episodic information and the interaction of semantic and episodic information. Probably because of its highly technical formulation, it is not yet the subject of any detailed research effort.

V. WORD PRODUCTION AND MEMORY ORGANIZATION

The work heretofore described is concerned with the organization of conceptual memory. The major experimental task used does not require the subject to produce any concepts, only to evaluate those that are presented to him by the experimenter. Sentence verification is somewhat analogous to comprehension: The subject must use the words input by the experimenter to access the relevant concepts. Another approach, more analogous to production, has also been used in the effort to determine the organization of permanent memory. Subjects are shown a picture or given a definition, and their job is to produce its name. Thus, Brown and McNeill (1966) gave people definitions and asked them to produce the words they defined. Carroll and White (1973) and Lachman (1973) presented pictures and asked for names.

Production researchers have studied word frequency, word codability, and age of acquisition, whereas verification researchers have studied semantic distance, sentence quantifiers, and subject–predicate relations. Verification studies have either ignored or controlled—but not varied—word frequency, codability, or acquisition age (e.g., Wilkins, 1971). When word frequency has influenced verification speed, it has been treated as a consequence of semantic similarity (e.g., Smith *et al.,* 1974). The use of production norms in verification studies naturally biases them toward high-frequency words. The stimuli in production tasks, by contrast, have involved systematic variation of frequency, codability, and acquisition age.

Researchers who use the production task are also more likely than verification researchers to be interested in the organization of lexical memory. In both fields, there is general agreement that words and the concepts they name reside in different systems, differently organized. Verification researchers can afford to defer the study of lexical memory organization and concentrate on the conceptual store. Production researchers cannot; the organization of lexical memory figures too centrally in the outcome of production studies to be ignored.

Seventeen years ago, Oldfield (1963) posed a major question for theories of lexical memory organization. He estimated that young, university-educated people know the meaning of perhaps 55,000 to 90,000 discrete words. How, then, is the store of words in memory organized and indexed, and how do we access them at the rate of two words a second that is typical of normal speech production (Oldfield, 1966)? Specific answers to these problems have proved elusive; and today, after much research, the complexity of the issues is apparent. The organization of words in an internal storage system is part of the larger problem of *lexicalization:* the attachment of meaning to words and the appropriate use of those words in speech and speech-related behaviors.

Some words, whatever their meaning, take longer to produce than others. This differential accessibility probably reflects the organizational structure of the memory system that stores lexical items internally and relates them to the concepts they designate. It is reasonable to suppose that efficiency influences that organizational structure: Words of high ecological salience should be readily available, while less salient words should be harder to access. However, in order to develop and maintain efficiency, there must be some mechanism for accommodating changes in the salience of particular lexical items. The variables that influence word production latency, then, should provide clues to two important questions. First, how is the lexical memory system organized to facilitate efficient word production? Second, how does the system reorganize itself to maintain efficiency in the face of changing patterns of word salience? The variables of interest fall into two broad classes.

One class of variables reflects the conventional nature of language—what people of a particular language community need to converse about. Frequency of particular words, the age at which they are learned, and the amount of consensus in their usage (codability) are three such variables that have been studied. These variables may directly reflect memory organization in individuals; however, they are communal in nature and must be measured by means of samples from the language community. Their impact on the individual language user may be estimated, indirectly, from the community's collective behavior. A second class of variables is experimentally manipulated. These variables are presumed to exert a direct effect on the internal computational processes occurring within the individual during the access of lexical items, and include repetition, the prior presentation of a word, picture, or other event that alters the subsequent accessibility of a given word.

A. Communal Variables: Frequency, Acquisition Age, and Codability

Frequency is usually estimated from word counts of printed language and refers to the frequency of occurrence of the name labels for pictures (Oldfield, 1966; Oldfield & Wingfield, 1965). Uncertainty, or codability, reflects the diversity of names given to an object (Lachman, 1973; Lachman, Shaffer, & Hennrikus, 1974). Age of acquisition is based on estimates of how early in life an object's name is first encountered (Carroll & White, 1974). These factors appear to be permanent vectors of memory organization (Lachmen et al., 1974).

Wingfield (1966) studied extensively the role of frequency in picture-naming. A major finding was that the time it takes to name an object is a linear function of the log frequency of occurrence of the object's name in written English (Oldfield & Wingfield, 1965). Objects with the highest frequency names, for example, have average latencies of about 600 msec, while those with the lowest have average latencies of about 1300 msec, a sizable difference. However, Oldfield and Wingfield (1965) selected pictures that met certain strict conditions, one of which was that each stimulus picture possess a "single commonly-acknowledged name [p. 277]." It seems likely that this condition would be easily met by very high frequency objects, such as *book, chair, shoe,* and *key.* But what of objects with low-frequency names, e.g., *stethoscope, gyroscope, bagpipe,* and *syringe?* To check the intuitions that such objects are relatively unlikely to have a single, commonly agreed upon name, students in a class were shown a series of pictures and asked to write the first name they thought of for each. As anticipated, the frequency of the dictionary name was inversely related to the number of different names the students supplied. For example, everyone responded "book" to a picture of a book; but to a gyroscope, they supplied "spinner," "top," "machine," "whirler," and "rotator," as well as "gyroscope." In a series of formal studies (Lachman, 1973), additional facts emerged to undermine the notion that frequency is a unitary variable that alone determines memory organization and naming latency. The most damaging observation was that high-frequency names, when given to "low-frequency objects," had reaction times that were generally indistinguishable from those for low-frequency names given to the same objects. In other words, the latency to name a picture of a gyroscope was high whether the subject called it "gyroscope," which is low frequency, or "machine," which is high frequency. It appears that the long latencies for such pictures are determined at least as much by properties of the object as by properties of the name. Hence, a variable such as frequency, which is defined entirely by properties of the linguistic code, cannot be solely responsible for differential naming latencies and memory organization. It seems likely that different naming latencies do not stem exclusively from either object properties or name properties, but from the process by which people map language onto the categories that they find or impose upon the world.

Much of the current research on classification of objects into categories was presented above. A quarter of a century ago, Brown and Lenneberg (1954), in their work on codability, recognized that words are labels for categorization processes. However, people differ in the way they categorize objects in the world—from culture to culture, subgroup to subgroup, family to family, and even person to person. The mapping of linguistic labels onto categories can be no more determined than the categorization process itself; it must be at least as variable. One theory of codability suggests that the tightness of mapping—what Brown and Lenneberg called codability—depends on the social and biological salience of objects (Lachman & Lachman, 1980). "Salience" may derive from prior adaptive demands on the species, such as we have suggested underlies the differential status of concepts (in Postulate 3). It may also be learned, as a result of the cultural importance of some objects vis-à-vis others. The most salient objects have a one-to-one mapping with words; they are linguistically well coded. The most salient objects in all cultures probably include items of food, clothing, shelter, and such objects as are necessary for adaptation and survival. These salient objects should have high-frequency, well-coded names. Other objects, of low salience, are likely to have names of low written and spoken frequency, and the name-to-object mapping is apt to be many-to-one (many words to one object). This is shown by an increase in name diversity as object frequency declines—that is, as the amount of commerce or interaction with the object becomes more rare. The salience of categories may be a major clue to memory organization. Some categories may actually be universal; the phylogenetic history of the species may have resulted in some environmental configurations being part of the conceptual organization of everyone. Such categories might be expected to be well coded in all cultures, and there is some evidence in support of the idea (Berlin, 1978). However, other categories are obviously culturally determined; their salience (and even their existence) reflects nonuniversal or specialized cultural demands.

The salience of categories in a culture varies over a wide range. In our culture, *autos, cups,* and *chairs* are exceedingly salient. *Buddhas, pueblos,* and *gyroscopes* are considerably less so. Some categories are of such low salience to the majority of speakers that, if there is a single-word name, most people do not know it (e.g., technical terminology). If uninitiated persons must communicate about such categories, they construct multiword descriptors. On the other hand, objects of sufficient salience have names that are stored in the memories of virtually all mature and intact individuals in the language community.

Codability is measured normatively. When naming norms are collected under time constraints, common and salient objects are given the same name by all subjects. As salience and codability decrease, the object-to-name mappings become increasingly one-to-many. Rare, infrequent objects yield a distribution of various names. Such distributions of name diversity can be measured by several statistics such as the number of different names the object elicits or the uncertainty (Shannon, 1948) of the name distribution. Codability is a theoretical concept for object-to-language mappings; uncertainty is a quantitative, operational definition of codability. Actually, codability and the other two communal variables of frequency and acquisition age are probably all manifestations of the more fundamental factor of *ecological salience*—not of the name-word but of the named object. Codability captures object properties more directly than does name frequency or age of name acquisition. This should indicate why stimuli are calibrated on uncertainty rather than on the more familiar frequency variable in many studies (e.g., Lachman & Lachman, 1980; Butterfield & Butterfield, 1977).

Details of a theory of codability and elements of a process model for picture naming are presented elsewhere (Lachman & Lachman, 1980). The usual effects of uncertainty on picture-naming latency are shown in the upper curve of Figure 5.8. Pictures with zero uncertainty, for which everyone gives the same name, yield short latencies. At higher levels of uncertainty, where several names are given to the same object, latencies increase dramatically. Sophisticated subjects have reported that the names of some objects somehow seem to be directly accessed; other objects (usually uncommon ones) seem to engender a conscious and deliberate effort, and the name given is sometimes selected from several possible alternatives. These two modes of production occur disproportionately at low and high uncertainty: Low-uncertainty pictures tend to produce "automatic" naming, whereas high-uncertainty pictures are more likely to result in conscious searches. Thus, names at low average uncertainty, $U < 2.0$ *bits*, appear to be retrieved directly by an algorithmic process. However, the concepts underlying high-uncertainty objects have no algorithm for locating a particular name, and hence one must be selected heuristically. Butterfield and Butterfield find that the increase in latency with greater uncertainty can be explained by subjects' increasing use of deliberate search strategies. Direct access of internally stored names clearly decreases with higher values of uncertainty. This would be consistent with efficient retrieval. If algorithmic capacity is costly or limited, it would make sense to allocate it to those environmental events that are likely to be labeled most often—highly salient and well-coded events. The assumption that the system works efficiently can be made either from the evolutionary perspective offered in this paper or from the analogy with automata. However, more qualitative hypotheses regarding the nature of efficient functioning will emerge from an evolutionist perspective.

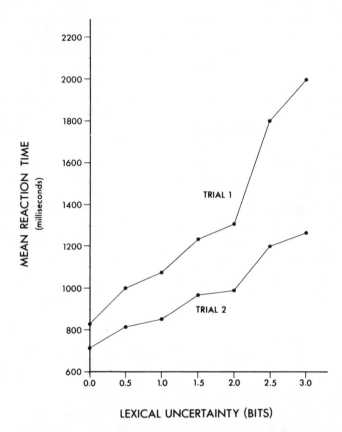

LEXICAL UNCERTAINTY (BITS)

FIGURE 5.8 Naming latency as a function of uncertainty of the distribution of name–word responses obtained from a normative sample. [*From Lachman, Shaffer, & Hennrikus, 1974.*]

B. Manipulated Variables: Repetition

When a set of pictures is named a second time, in a single experimental session, a substantial drop in latency occurs on the second naming. Figure 5.8 shows the phenomenon: Naming latencies drop about 100 msec at $U = 0$ and more than 800 msec at $U = 3$ bits. This pervasive effect even occurs, though it is somewhat attenuated, when the language is shifted (English–German) from the first to the second naming (Lachman & Mistler-Lachman, 1976).

It is possible that the repetition speed-up effect reflects a reordering of priorities within the semantic and lexical systems, in order to deal efficiently with concepts and words that have become topically more current. A word that has already occurred once in speech is more likely to be needed again soon than a word that has been long unused. The repetition speed-up effect may be one mechanism mediating the speed and efficiency of word production in fluent speech. However, one must consider the internal memory systems that must mediate the experimental task. When a person sees and recognizes a picture, contact is made with a visual code. If the viewer can report properties of the object, contact has been made with a conceptual or semantic code. If he can name the picture, contact has been made with a lexical code. This entire sequence happens faster the second time. The question then is this: Which of the three codes and their corresponding memory networks was activated, or changed to a more accessible state, by previous presentation and naming of the picture? A series of studies to address this question was undertaken in our laboratories, and the details of many of the experiments can be found in Lachman and Lachman (1980). Our initial hypothesis was that the repetition speed-up effect implicated primarily the lexical or semantic systems, or the link between them; we assumed that the visual system was only minimally involved. The reasoning was based on several observations concerning the effects of uncertainty. Some tasks, such as picture matching, require no internal name location; such tasks are insensitive to uncertainty. This suggests that the long latencies at high-uncertainty levels are due to effortful name location and/or production processes. Figure 5.8 shows, further, that the repetition speed-up effect is greatest at high-uncertainty levels. Taken together, these observations suggested to us that the repetition speed-up effect was localized in name-finding processes, becoming most conspicuous when these processes are initially effortful. Since we considered name location to involve the mapping of a name–word onto a conceptual code, our initial view was that the semantic and lexical codes, primarily, were implicated in the repetition speed-up effect.

Our general approach was to devise tasks that were designed to tap only selected subsystems and to present the stimuli in these tasks prior to a demand for standard picture naming. The no-drop baseline was represented by first-trial naming; the maximum-drop baseline was represented by renaming. Latencies in the experimental conditions were compared to these two baselines to determine what percentage of the drop was due to the system or systems presumably implicated in the experimental task. For example, a subject might be shown *no* pictures in Stage 1, but merely asked to read words projected one at a time. The words were the names most frequently given to a set of our stimulus pictures. Subsequently, the subject would be shown the stimulus pictures, and his task would be to name them. The Stage 2 naming latencies could then be compared to the no-drop and maximum-drop baselines to determine the extent to which reading the names of the pictures influenced speed of producing those names upon seeing the pictures. If the additional assumption is made that name-reading implicates only the lexicon, the size of the effect in this experimental condition can be interpreted as reflecting the contribution of the lexical network to the repetition speed-up effect. Various experimental arrangements along these lines were developed to activate selectively one or another subsystem or pair of subsystems (Lachman & Lachman, 1980). We expected that it would be easy to demonstrate that the contribution of the visual subsystem to the repetition effect was nonexistent or minimal.

However, the results of a number of studies in the series (Lachman & Lachman, 1980 converged clearly on the following conclusions: When prior processing of a picture activates a visual code and primes the visual network, it produces a latency drop of 30–40% on subsequent naming—even when there is every reason to suppose that lexical memory has been left unactivated. Moreover, brief visual presentations leave their tracks; subjects are no longer "naive" with respect to pictures they have viewed for as little as 200 msec. We neither expected nor desired these outcomes. Since the visual identification phase of picture-naming should be so fast, most of the naming time should be devoted to searching for a name. Sheer visual processing should therefore account for a small proportion of the name search and therefore, for a small proportion of the latency drop at renaming. However, priming the visual network appeared to reduce subsequent naming latencies by as much as 40%. Several other studies are consistent with this conclusion. Bartram (1974) found clear reductions in latency due to prior visual processing, and Poon and Fozard (1978) showed that familiar pictures of objects are named faster than unfamiliar exemplars. This convergence, and our own studies, led us to question our hypothesis that the visual system is not implicated in the repetition speed-up effect. It now appears that all three systems—visual, semantic, and lexical—are involved.

It has been argued that it is virtually impossible to isolate a visual code since the effects of semantic processing are ubiquitous (Klatzky & Stoy, 1978). Certainly meaning and understanding are extremely potent factors in human information processing. However, semantic priming alone cannot account for the data reported in Lachman and Lachman (1980). If semantic priming accounted for the entire latency drop, then any task involving a semantic code should produce the drop in its full magnitude. This did not happen. Two independent conditions in which the semantic network was primed resulted in a speed-up about half the size obtained when all three codes were accessed. The semantic network alone can account for, at most, half the repetition speed-up effect. The visual and/or lexical systems must be invoked to deal with the remainder.

It seems likely that the relationship between the visual network and the other two is not as independent as our initial views would have it. The lexical network, and the semantic network as well, may develop in intimate congress with the perceptual system. This possibility is intuitively reasonable, since vision is phylogenetically and ontogenetically prior to language. Humans, like other primates, are heavily dependent on vision for their knowledge of the environment; and the visual system may importantly determine semantic and lexical categories. Research that we have conducted with coordinate bilingual subjects highlights the potential developmental intertwining of visual and lexical networks. Priming of the visual system alone produced a subsequent naming-latency drop in the native language—but not as much in a second language learned after puberty (Lachman & Mistler-Lachman, 1976). This suggests that the visual system may be tied to linguistic long-term memory, but only that of the first language learned, the mother tongue. If this is correct, the visual system may produce its effects on later naming by virtue of "pulling in" semantic and lexical systems. That is, the visual system may implicate these systems and thereby update *them,* rather than directly update a visual code.

The outcome of our own research program, which converged on the findings of others (Bartram, 1974; Poon & Fozard, 1978) suggests that there is something special about visual information processing. It is fast, since 200 msec worth of viewing can leave a record that is detectable an hour later. As we have suggested, the visual system may be inextricable from the conceptual and lexical systems; it may be that these systems have developed parasitically on vision.

This latter conclusion is bolstered by the considerable work on imagery. It is well known that conscious efforts to create images can render a list of unrelated items more memorable (Bugelski, 1968), and imagery ratings are predictive of memorability of words (Paivio, 1969, 1971). Moreover, people can perform mental rotation tasks (Shepard, 1967; Shepard & Metzler, 1971) in which they literally provide themselves new information by creating visual images and manipulating them. In language comprehension, there is ample evidence that the imageability of sentences is related to their comprehensibility and recallability (Begg & Paivio, 1969; Holmes & Langford, 1976; Jorgensen & Kintsch, 1973; Thorndyke, 1975). Why should this be so? We have already suggested the possibility, in the spirit of Evolutionary Postulate 2 concerning vision, that mechanisms available for visual processing are faster and more efficient (due to their longer history of adaptation) than those available for symbolic processing of linguistic symbols. However, if these mechanisms can somehow be invoked in service of symbolic language, linguistic processing can take advantage of their greater manipulability. The act of imaging may somehow involve the mapping of linguistic material onto visual processing mechanisms, producing both a subjectively visual experience and better comprehension and memory.

If it is possible to localize certain effects in the visual system, we should expect these to show less variability than effects residing in the lexicon. The visual system, having evolved earlier, is the result of a longer adaptive history and is probably hard-wired to a greater extent than the lexical system. It will be interesting to compare these to the semantic system. We have recently obtained evidence of system update in a question-answering task, which should provide the basis for interesting comparisons to picture-naming.

VI. SUMMARY AND CONCLUSIONS

We have presented a set of evolutionary generalizations and postulates, in preliminary form, and suggested that they may be used in semantic memory both for theory construction and for the interpretation of experimental data. Where possible we have tried to exemplify their use. We will refine and extend the list; hopefully other scholars will help by critical analyses and direct refinement.

There are a number of issues that attend any discussion of behavioral evolution, which are too complex for detailed discussion in this paper. However, they may be mentioned briefly for the reader who wishes to explore them further. Wilson (1975, 1978) offered a theory of the genetic basis of social behavior under the rubric "sociobiology." There have been a number of vigorous critical attacks on his work, for a variety of reasons. Hampshire (1978) appears to object to the fundamental thesis of sociobiology from the viewpoint of a mind–body dualist; and indeed, sociobiology implies a monist point of view. However, monism is certainly not unknown in psychology and can be readily defended (see Uttal, 1978 for a lucid review of the mind–body question in psychology and particularly psychobiology). Some critics charge that it is wrongheaded to postulate "a gene for every behavior" (Washburn, 1978); however, this need not imply that behavior is totally resistant to analysis in genetic terms. Other critics appear to come from a political rather than a scientific perspective, expressing concern about the extensions of biological imperatives to human behavior; such critics cite the excesses of social Darwinism and seem to fear that the discovery of biological imperatives for undesirable social action somehow justifies such action. However, sociobiology has also some highly distinguished defenders (Boulding, 1978; Holton, 1978).

It may also be asserted that efforts to relate cognitive behavior to evolutionary considerations involve premature neurologizing. This is not the case, since we may postulate the origin and function of various systems without reference to the structures that contain them. It is possible to couch the discussion of evolutionary factors in logical and computational terms without reference to neurology, although of course a better knowledge of neurology would be invaluable if it were available.

Finally, it may be argued that evolutionary factors without consideration of the neurological structures involved will of necessity be too vague and general to be much use in either theory construction or interpretation of data. To this we would reply that cognitive theory and the neurosciences of higher mental processes are themselves at a vague and general stage of formulation, despite the apparent precision of some of the formal models that appear and then disappear virtually uncited into the archives. The ultimate test of whether evolution can provide a sound heuristic for cognitive theory will be the effort to use it as such. This effort has not yet been made. We hope that the suggestions contained in this chapter will encourage others to begin the attempt.

ACKNOWLEDGMENTS

We wish to extend special thanks to Kenneth R. Burstein, Mary Carol Day, Arnold L. Glass, Alexander Siegel, and Edward E. Smith for extensive commentary on an earlier draft. They are to be credited only with making the product better; any deficiencies are the responsibility of the authors. Several experiments described were supported by NSF Grant BNS 7725657.

REFERENCES

Anderson, J. R. Language, memory and thought. Hillsdale, N.J.: Lawrence Erlbaum Associates, 1976.

Anderson, J. R., & Reder, L. M. Negative judgments in and about semantic memory. Journal of Verbal Learning and Verbal Behavior, 1974, 13, 664–681.

Ashcraft, M. H. Property dominance and typicality effects in property statement verification. Journal of Verbal Learning and Verbal Behavior, 1978, 17, 155–164.

Atkinson, R. C., & Juola, J. F. Search and decision processes in recognition memory. In R C. Atkinson, D. H. Krantz, & P. Suppes (Ed.), Contemporary developments in mathematical psychology. San Francisco: W. H. Freeman & Company, 1974.

Bartram, D. J. The role of visual and semantic codes in object naming. Cognitive Psychology, 1974, 6, 325–356.

Battig, W. F., & Montague, W. E. Category norms for verbal items in 56 categories: A replication and extension of the Connecticut category norms. Journal of Experimental Psychology Monograph, 1969, 80, 1–46.

Begg, I., & Paivio, A. U. Concreteness and imagery in sentence meaning. Journal of Verbal Learning and Verbal Behavior, 1969, 8, 821–827.

Berlin, B. Ethnobiological classification. In E. Rosch & B. B. Lloyd (Eds.), Cognition and categorization. Hillsdale, N.J.: Lawrence Erlbaum Associates, 1978.

Boulding, K. E. Sociobiology or biosociology? Society, 1978, 15, 28–34.

Brown, R., & Lenneberg, E. H. A study in language and cognition. Journal of Abnormal and Social Psychology, 1954, 49, 454–462.

Brown, R., & McNeill, D. The "tip of the tongue" phenomenon. Journal of Verbal Learning and Verbal Behavior, 1966, 6, 325–337.

Bugelski, B. R. Images as mediators in one-trial paired-associate learning. II: Self-timing in successive lists. Journal of Experimental Psychology, 1968, 77, 328–334.

Butterfield, G. B. The effects of semantic variables and context on the retrieval of information from semantic memory. Unpublished doctoral dissertation, University of Kansas, 1974.

Butterfield, G. B., & Butterfield, E. C. Lexical codability and age. Journal of Verbal Learning and Verbal Behavior, 1977, 16, 113–118.

Butterfield, E. C. & Butterfield, G. B. Retrieval strategies as a function of name uncertainty. In press.

Campbell, B. A. Human evolution. Chicago: Aldine Publishing Company, 1974.

Carroll, J. B., & White, M. N. Word frequency and age of acquisition as determiners of picture-naming latency. Quarterly Journal of Experimental Psychology, 1973, 25, 85–95.

Cartmill, M. Arboreal adaptations and the origin of primates. In R. Tuttle (Ed.), The function and evolutionary biology of primates. Chicago: Aldine-Atherton, Inc., 1972.

Church, A. An unsolvable problem of elementary number theory. American Journal of Mathematics, 1936, 58, 345–363.

Clark, W. H. LeGros. Fossil evidence for human evolution (2nd ed.). Chicago: University of Chicago Press, 1964.

Clark, W. H. LeGros. *History of the primates.* Chicago: University of Chicago Press, 1966.

Clark, W. H. LeGros. *Man-apes or ape-men? The story of discoveries in Africa.* New York: Holt, Rinehart & Winston, 1967.

Collins, A. M., & Loftus, E. F. A spreading-activation theory of semantic processing. *Psychological Review,* 1975, *82,* 407–428.

Collins, A. M. & Quillian, M. R. Retrieval time from semantic memory. *Journal of Verbal Learning and Verbal Behavior,* 1969, *8,* 240–247.

Collins, A. M., & Quillian, M. R. How to make a language user. In E. Tulving & W. Donaldson (Eds.), *Organization and Memory.* New York: Academic Press, 1972a.

Collins, A. M., & Quillian, M. R. Experiments on semantic memory and language comprehension. In L. W. Gregg (Ed.), *Cognition in learning and memory.* New York: Wiley & Sons, 1972b.

Collins, E. T. Changes in the visual organs correlated with the adoption of arboreal life and with the assumption of erect posture. *Transactions of the Opthalmological Society of The United Kingdom,* 1921, *41,* 10–90.

Conrad, C. Cognitive economy in semantic memory. *Journal of Experimental Psychology,* 1972, *92,* 149–154.

Fiksel, J. R., & Bower, G. H. Question-answering by a semantic network of parallel automata. *Journal of Mathematical Psychology,* 1976, *13,* 1–45.

Fishbein, H. D. *Evolution, development and children's learning.* Pacific Palisades, Ca: Goodyear Publishing Co., 1976.

Gibson, J. J. *The senses considered as perceptual systems.* Boston: Houghton-Mifflin Co., 1966.

Gibson, J. J. The theory of affordances. In R. Shaw & J. Bransford (Eds.), *Perceiving, acting and knowing: Toward an ecological psychology.* Hillsdale, N.J.: Lawrence Erlbaum Associates, 1977.

Glass, A. L., & Holyoak, K. J. The effect of *some* and *all* on reaction time for semantic decisions. *Memory and Cognition,* 1974, *2,* 436–440.

Glass, A. L., & Holyoak, K. J. Alternative conceptions of semantic memory. *Cognition,* 1975, *3,* 313–339.

Glass, A. L., & Holyoak, K. J., & O'Dell, C. Production frequency and the verification of quantified statements. *Journal of Verbal Learning and Verbal Behavior,* 1974, *13,* 237–254.

Goodall, J. Continuities between chimpanzee and human behavior. In G. L. Isaac & E. R. McCown (Eds.), *Human origins: Louis Leakey and the East African evidence.* Menlo Park, California: W. A. Benjamin, Inc., 1976.

Goodson, F. E. *The evolutionary foundations of psychology: A unified theory.* New York: Holt, Rinehart & Winston, 1973.

Hampshire, S. The illusion of sociobiology. *The New York Review of Books,* 1978, *25,* 64–69.

Hirsch, J. Behavior-genetic, or "experimental" analysis: The challenge of science vs. the lure of technology. *American Psychologist,* 1967, *22,* 118–130.

Holmes, V. M., & Langford, J. Comprehension and recall of abstract and concrete sentences. *Journal of Verbal Learning and Verbal Behavior,* 1976, *5,* 559–566.

Holton, G. The new synthesis? *Society,* 1978, *15,* 15–22.

Holyoak, K. J., & Glass, A. L. The role of contradictions and counterexamples in the rejection of false sentences. *Journal of Verbal Learning and Verbal Behavior,* 1975, *14,* 215–239.

Jolly, C. J. The seed-eaters: A new model of hominid behavioral differentiation based on a baboon analogy. *Man,* 1970, *5,* 5–26.

Jorgensen, C. C., & Kintsch, W. The role of imagery in the evaluation of sentences. *Cognitive Psychology,* 1973, *4,* 110–116.

Katz, J. J. *Semantic theory,* New York: Harper & Row, 1972.

Katz, J. J., & Fodor, J. The structure of a semantic theory. *Language,* 1963, *39,* 170–210.

Klatzky, R. L., & Stoy, A. M. Semantic information and visual information processing. In J. W. Cotton & R. L. Klatzky (Eds.), *Semantic factors in cognition.* Hillsdale, N.J.: Lawrence Erlbaum Associates, 1978.

Kosslyn, S. M., & Pomerantz, J. R. Imagery, propositions, and the form of internal representations. *Cognitive Psychology, 1977, 9,* 52–76.

Lachman, R. Uncertainty effects on time to access the internal lexicon. *Journal of Experimental Psychology,* 1973, 99, 199–208.

Lachman, R., & Lachman, J. L. Picture naming: Retrieval and activation of long-term memory. In L. W. Poon, J. L. Fozard, L. S. Cermak, D. Arenberg, & L. W. Thompson (Eds.), *New directions in memory and aging: Proceedings of the George Talland Memorial Conference.* Hillsdale, N.J.: Lawrence Erlbaum Associates, 1980.

Lachman, R., Lachman, J. L., & Butterfield, E. C. *Cognitive psychology and information processing: An introduction.* Hillsdale, N.J.: Lawrence Erlbaum Associates, 1979.

Lachman, R., & Mistler-Lachman, J. L. Dominance lexicale chez les bilingues. In S. Erlich & E. Tulving (Eds.), *La Memoire Semantique.* Paris: Bulletin de Psychologie, 1976.

Lachman, R., Shaffer, J. P., & Hennrikus, D. Language and cognition: Effects of stimulus codability, name–word frequency, and age of acquisition on lexical reaction time. *Journal of Verbal Learning and Verbal Behavior,* 1974, 13, 613–625.

Landauer, T. K., & Freedman, J. L. Information retrieval from long-term memory: Category size and recognition time. *Journal of Verbal Learning and Verbal Behavior,* 1968, 7, 291–295.

Loftus, E. F. Organization and retrieval of attribute and name information. In S. Erlich & E. Tulving (Eds.), *La Memoire Semantique.* Paris: Bulletin de Psychologie, 1976.

Loftus, E. F. How to catch a zebra in semantic memory. In R. Shaw & J. Bransford (Eds.), *Perceiving, acting and knowing.* Hillsdale, N.J.: Lawrence Erlbaum Associates, 1977.

Lorenz, K. *Behind the mirror.* New York: Harcourt, Brace, Jovanovitch, 1977.

MacLean, P. New findings relevant to the evolution of psychosexual functions of the brain. *Journal of Nervous Mental Disease,* 1962, 135, 289–301.

MacLean, P. Man and his animal brains. *Modern Medicine,* 1964, 32, 95–106.

MacLean, P. *A triune concept of the brain and behaviour.* Toronto, Canada: University of Toronto Press, 1973.

Medin, D., & Cole, M. Comparative psychology and human cognition. In W. K. Estes (Ed.), *Handbook of learning and cognitive processes (Vol. 1).* Hillsdale, N.J.: Lawrence Erlbaum Associates, 1975.

Meyer, D. E. On the representation and retrieval of stored semantic information. *Cognitive Psychology,* 1970, 1, 242–300.

Meyer, D. E. Correlated operations in searching stored semantic categories. *Journal of Experimental Psychology,* 1973, 99, 124–133.

Meyer, D. E. Long-term memory retrieval during the comprehension of affirmative and negative sentences. In R. A. Kennedy & A. L. Wilkes (Eds.), *Studies in long-term memory.* London: Wiley and Sons, 1975.

Meyer, D. E., & Schvaneveldt, R. W. Meaning, memory structure, and mental processes. *Science,* 1976, 192, 27–33.

Montagu, A. *The human revolution.* Cleveland: The World Publishing Co., 1965.

Neisser, U. *Cognition and reality.* San Francisco: W. H. Freeman, 1976.

Newell, A., & Simon, H. A. The simulation of human thought. In *Current trends in psychological theory.* Pittsburgh: University of Pittsburgh Press, 1961.

Newell, A., & Simon, H. A. *Human problem solving.* Englewood Cliffs, N.J.: Prentice-Hall, 1972.

Newell, A., & Simon, H. A. Computer science as empirical inquiry: Symbols and search. *Communications of the ACM,* 1976, 19, 113–126.

Oden, G. C. Fuzziness in semantic memory: Choosing exemplars of subjective categories. *Memory & Cognition,* 1977, 5, 198–204.

Olfield, R. C. Individual vocabulary and semantic currency. *British Journal of Social and Clinical Psychology,* 1963, 2, 122–130.

Oldfield, R. C. Things, words and the brain. *Quarterly Journal of Experimental Psychology,* 1966, 18, 340–353.

Oldfield, R. C., & Wingfield, A. Response latencies in naming objects. *Quarterly Journal of Experimental Psychology,* 1965, *17,* 273–281.

Paivio, A. Mental imagery in associative learning and memory. *Psychological Review,* 1969, *76,* 241–263.

Paivio, A. *Imagery and verbal processes.* New York: Holt, Rinehart and Winston, 1971.

Pollack, I. Speed of classification of words into superordinate categories. *Journal of Verbal Learning and Verbal Behavior,* 1963, *2,* 159–165.

Poon, L. W., & Fozard, J. L. Speed of retrieval from long-term memory in relation to age, familiarity, and datedness of information. *Journal of Gerontology,* 1978, *33,* 711–717.

Post, E. L. Finite combinatory processes—Formulation I. *Journal of Symbolic Logic,* 1936, *1,* 103–105.

Pylyshyn, Z. W. What the mind's eye tells the mind's brain: A critique of mental imagery. *Psychological Bulletin,* 1973, *80,* 1–24.

Pylyshyn, Z. Computational models and empirical constraints. *The Behavioral and Brain Sciences,* 1978, *1,* 93–99.

Quillian, M. R. Semantic memory. In M. Minsky (Ed.), *Semantic information processing,* Cambridge, Mass. : MIT Press, 1968.

Quillian, M. R. The teachable language comprehender: a simulation program and theory of language. *Communications of the ACM,* 1969, *12,* 459–476.

Razran, G. *Mind in evolution.* New York: Houghton-Mifflin, 1971.

Rips, L. J. Quantification and semantic memory. *Cognitive Psychology,* 1975, *7,* 307–340.

Rips, L. J., Shoben, E. J., & Smith, E. E. Semantic distance and the verification of semantic relations. *Journal of Verbal Learning and Verbal Behavior,* 1973, *12,* 1–20.

Rosch, E. On the internal structure of perceptual and semantic categories. In T. E. Moore (Ed.), *Cognitive development and the acquisition of language.* New York: Academic Press, 1973.

Rosch, E. Cognitive representations of semantic categories. *Journal of Experimental Psychology: General,* 1975, *104,* 192–240.

Rosch, E. Human categorization. In N. Warren (Ed.), *Advances in cross-cultural psychology (Vol. 1).* London: Academic Press, 1977.

Rosch, E. Principles of categorization. In E. Rosch & B. B. Lloyd (Eds.), *Cognition and categorization.* Hillsdale, N.J.: Lawrence Erlbaum Associates, 1978.

Rosch, E., & Mervis, C. B. Family resemblances: Studies in the internal structure of categories. *Cognitive Psychology,* 1975, *7,* 573–605.

Rosch, E., Mervis, C. B., Gray, W., Johnson, D., & Boyes-Braem, P. Basic objects in natural categories. *Cognitive Psychology,* 1976, *8,* 382–439.

Rozin, P. The evolution of intelligence and access to the cognitive unconscious. In J. M. Sprague & A. N. Epstein (Eds.), *Progress in psychobiology and physiological psychology (Vol. 6).* New York: Academic Press, 1976.

Rumelhart, D. E., Lindsay, P. H., & Norman, D. A. A model for long-term memory. In E. Tulving & W. Donaldson (Eds.), *Organization of memory.* New York: Academic Press, 1972.

Shannon, C. E. A mathematical theory of communication. *Bell System Technical Journal,* 1948, *27,* 379–423; 623–656.

Shaw, R., & Bransford J. *Perceiving, acting and knowing: Toward an ecological psychology.* Hillsdale, N.J.: Lawrence Erlbaum Associates, 1977.

Schaeffer, B., & Wallace, R. Semantic similarity and the comparison of word meanings. *Journal of Experimental Psychology,* 1969, *82,* 343–346.

Schaeffer, B., & Wallace, R. The comparison of word meanings. *Journal of Experimental Psychology,* 1970, *86,* 144–152.

Shepard, R. N. Recognition memory for words, sentences, and pictures. *Journal of Verbal Learning and Verbal Behavior,* 1967, *6,* 156–163.

Shepard, R. N., & Metzler, J. Mental rotation of three-dimensional objects. *Science,* 1971, 701–703.

Simons, E. L., & Pilbeam, D. R. Hominid Paleoprimatology. In R. Tuttle (Ed.), *The functional and evolutionary biology of primates.* Chicago: Aldine-Atherton, Inc., 1972.

Skinner, B. F. *Science and human behavior.* New York: MacMillan, 1953.

Smith, E. E. Theories of semantic memory. In W. K. Estes (Ed.), *Handbook of learning and cognitive processes (Vol. 5).* Hillsdale, N.J.: Lawrence Erlbaum Associates, 1978.

Smith, E. E., Shoben, E. J., & Rips, L. J. Structure and process in semantic memory: A featured model for semantic decisions. *Psychological Review,* 1974, *81,* 214–241.

Spielberger, C. D., & deNike, L. D. Operant conditioning of plural nouns: A failure to replicate the Greenspoon effect. *Psychological Reports,* 1962, *11,* 355–366.

Thorndyke, P. W. Conceptual complexity and imagery in comprehension and memory *Journal of Verbal Learning and Verbal Behavior,* 1975, *14,* 359–369.

Turing, A. M. On computable numbers, with an application to the Entscheidungs problem. *Proceedings of the London Mathematics Society* (Series 2), 1936, *42,* 230–265.

Tversky, A. Features of similarity. *Psychological Review,* 1977, *84,* 327–352.

Tversky, A., & Gati, I. Studies of similarity. In E. Rosch & B. B. Lloyd (Eds.), *Cognition and categorization.* Hillsdale, N.J.: Lawrence Erlbaum Associates, 1978.

Uttal, W. R. *The psychobiology of mind.* Hillsdale, N.J.: Lawrence Erlbaum Associates, 1978.

Washburn, S. L. Animal behavior and social anthropology. *Society,* 1978, *15,* 35–41.

Wason, P. The context of plausible denial. *Journal of Verbal Learning and Verbal Behavior,* 1965, *2,* 7–11.

Wilkins, A. J. Conjoint frequency, category size, and categorization time. *Journal of Verbal Learning and Verbal Behavior,* 1971, *10,* 382–385.

Wilson, E. O. *Sociobiology.* Cambridge: Harvard University Press, 1975.

Wilson, E. O. *On human nature.* Cambridge: Harvard University Press, 1978.

Wingfield, A. The identification and naming of objects. Unpublished doctoral dissertation, University of Oxford, 1966.

Zadeh, L. A. Calculus of fuzzy restrictions. In L. A. Zadeh, K. S. Fu, K. Tanaka, & M. Shimura (Eds.), *Fuzzy sets and their applications to cognitive and decision processes.* New York: Academic Press, 1975.

Semantic Memory: A Free-Elements System

I. INTRODUCTION

One of the important characteristics of behavior is that it is organized. To explain this organization, we generally assume that memory is itself organized. Moreover, we assume that there exists an analogical, structural, and/or functional correspondence between the organization of memory and the organization of behavior and that the former determines, at least in part, the latter.

A number of different models have been proposed to describe the organization of memory. Some of them represent memory in the form of an asso-

MEMORY ORGANIZATION
AND STRUCTURE

ciative network (e.g., Anderson, 1972; Anderson & Bower, 1973); in others the hierarchical character of the organization is stressed (e.g., Mandler, 1968; Quillian, 1968); in still others, a multidimensional organization is defined (e.g., Smith, Shoben, & Rips, 1974). All these models and many others rest on the postulate that memory is organized.

It is possible that this postulate is not a good point of departure for the study of memory and that the opposite postulate has a greater heuristic value. It should be noted initially that organized behavior only signifies that memory is capable of producing organization as it produces information: It is capable of producing categorical hierarchies or algebraic or trigonometric organizations, which does not imply that it is organized in a categorical, algebraic, or trigonometric mode. It seems preferable to define memory as a set of potential organizations, that is, possible and optional; or, to be more precise, as a system capable of generating organized structures.

What should be expected of memory?

1. It must permit the production of extremely varied behavior because the situations and the problems to be solved vary considerably. To achieve this goal, the subject's knowledge should be arranged in diverse organizational systems, some of which are frequently realized and some of which can be entirely new. For these multiple arrangements to be possible, it must be assumed that the elements of memory are free and mobile. This requirement is contrary at first sight to the postulate of a memory fixed in a definite organization.[1]

On the other hand, if memory is defined as a set of free elements, great importance must be accorded to the set of processes that permits the reconstitution or construction of the organized structures. The subject's cognitive operations, as well as all the contextual information relative to the task and the situation, play a decisive role.

2. However, the subject must also, particularly in usual situations, be able to produce behavior that is appropriate, rapid, and precise, such as driving a car or utilizing a transitive relation. These requirements do not seem compatible with the constructive processes that are always relatively long and groping. They assume structures prepared in advance, rigorously determined in their content and organization, functioning in an almost automatic fashion.

Thus it is considered that memory should respond to two apparently contradictory requirements: mobility and adaptative flexibility, which imply a free-elements memory, and efficacy, which assumes an organized memory. Whatever the theoretical solution that is envisaged, it is clear that one cannot

---

[1]In introducing a sufficient number of supplementary mechanisms and in forming the hypothesis of a sufficiently complex organization, it is possible to explain a certain variety of possible behaviors starting with the classical postulate: Memory is organized. However, these models are not economical, and their generality, beyond some particular experimental situations, is difficult to establish.

deal with the problem of organization of memory without also dealing with that of freedom.

Biologists have some interesting ideas about an analogous problem: the relations between order and chance in the phylogenetic evolution of species and in the ontogenetic evolution of nervous structures (Atlan, 1972; Paillard, 1978).

It is assumed that each species possesses a certain potential for freedom that is also its evolutive potential. Each species can construct its specific organization(s) by drawing upon its potential for freedom. This construction implies exchanges between the organism and environment and calls forth complex autogenerative processes. Piaget's (1952) theory on the construction of the schemes of intelligence provided a good psychological example of these processes. For the biologist, the freedom potential of a species represents in a way its capacity to adapt to variations of environmental conditions. When this potential is entirely consumed, the species can neither adapt itself nor evolve further. It is thus condemned to die out if environmental conditions continue to change.

The problem can be faced in similar fashion at the level of the organism. Each individual possesses at birth a certain genetically determined potential for freedom. This potential is utilized in the construction of organized structures, for example, neurophysiological, which respond to the conditions of the physical, biological, and social environment. Although the psychological problems arise in a different fashion, several interesting ideas can be borrowed from this general biological model.

In what follows, an attempt is made to show how a child progressively acquires a certain potential of cognitive freedom in learning to know situations, objects, events, and their properties. It is assumed, and this is an initial difference from the general model, that the potential for freedom is not bestowed at the start, but is acquired as a result of experience. I attempt to show that the adult cognitive system—memory—involves two parts, one free and the other organized. I do not attempt to judge their respective importance. The organized part is itself a result of certain experiences. Contrary to the general model, however, development of the organized part does not appear to be detrimental to the free part. Instead, one is led to assume a simultaneous development in two directions: growth of free structures and growth of organized structures.

What is memory and how can it be described?

On this point, too, biologists can provide us with several interesting suggestions. Since the mid 1960s, psychologists have been accustomed to consider memory as an informational machine, taking as a model the functioning of a computer: The memory receives, analyzes, processes, stores, retrieves, restitutes, . . . information. It is assumed that these operations are carried out within specialized subsystems or at different stages of memory functioning. This type of model is characterized by the fact that the information that is processed is physical information defined outside of the subject, whether at the level of the stimulus received or at the level of the responses produced.

However, there is another way to view these matters and a completely different language for describing them. Initially, one can assume the existence of specifically psychological information, just as there is genetic or physical information. Psychological information can only be defined in terms of the elements and structures (necessarily hypothetical) of memory, which one can assume represent specific knowledge acquired by the subject. When the subject carries out a task, the psychological information is reconstituted or constructed within memory. Like the biologist, I define the units of memory as elements and organized groups of elements, that is, structures. The units of memory are more or less "differentiated" and "structured." They are transformed during genetic development and learning that involves certain modifications of the structural and functional properties of memory. They exercise different functions: (a) memory function, or the capacity to store acquired knowledge; (b) instrumental function, or the capacity to produce behavior; and (c) cognitive function, or the capacity to generate new knowledge. We can distinguish further the informative function, or the capacity to mark specific knowledge relative to specific events; the relational function, or the capacity to connect several different kinds of knowledge, etc. These general areas are treated fully in earlier papers (Ehrlich, 1968, 1975; see also, Lockhart, Craik & Jacoby, 1976).

The last point that I would like to raise briefly concerns semantic memory in particular. Psychologists (who elaborate psychology) are generally adult logicians. Being logicians, they tend to consider that all human memories are organized in the same economical and rational manner as their own and that, if they are not as yet, for example, that of the young child, genetic evolution will inevitably bring about that organization.

For example, several years ago two opposing theories were proposed to explain the formation of categorical hierarchies in the child. According to one hypothesis, learning goes from the particular to the general (Anglin, 1970); for example, the child first acquires the concept of a *pigeon,* then that of a *bird,* and then that of an *animal.* According to the other hypothesis, the opposite is true (Clark, 1972). Both these hypotheses are based on the same logical principle: The child begins by learning that which is the simplest. Unfortunately what is "simple" in an "extensive" definition of categories (*pigeon* is simple and *animal* is complex) becomes "complex" in a "comprehensive" definition; thus, the two opposing hypotheses.

In fact, it now seems established that the concepts acquired first are not the most "simple" but the most "useful" for the child in his current activities: In the preceding example, it is *bird* that is learned first (Rosch, 1976). Moreover, it is doubtful that the adult memory, or a part of it, would be organized in the form of a categorical hierarchy. Semantic memory is capable of producing categorical organizations when the situation requires it, as for example in the experiment by Bower, Clark, Lesgold, and Wizenz (1969); however, this does not mean that it (memory) is organized in this way.

Another example of the logician's approach is evident in an experiment by Gentner (1975) regarding acquisition of verbs of transmission of possession. This study attempts to support the model of Norman and Rumelhart (1975), which leads to the hypothesis that some action verbs are simpler than others and that they should thus be learned first by children: *give* and *take* are simpler than *pay* and *exchange*, which are simpler than *buy, spend,* and *sell.* For example, *buy* implies the "*acquisition of something*" but it also implies *paying,* which in turn implies *giving.* Thus the order of complexity and the order of learning of verbs by children should be: *give,* then *pay,* then *buy.* This is approximately what was indicated by Gentner's research with children ages 4–8. On the other hand, research conducted by Bernicot (1978) with similar material but in a different task[2] and with children ages 6–9 brings different results: The "complex" verbs and the "simple" verbs give rise to the same percentage of correct responses and this for each age; the percentage varies according to age and is never greater than 80% at 9 years for the most familiar verbs. Knowing a "complex" verb like *buy* does not imply knowing a "simple" verb like *give;* there are sensible differences between verbs, but this is not due to their "complexity." For example, the knowing of the verb *take* is inferior at any age to the knowing of the verb *buy.* Above all, what the experiment points out is that the semantic content of verbs is different and much richer than what was assumed by Norman and Rumelhart's theory.

The logical a priori assumption about what is most "economic" or "simplest" or about the nature of responses that the subject "should" produce presents serious disadvantages because it reverses the order of priorities. The first question is whether or not the subject's cognitive system allows itself to adapt to such an experimental situation, conforming to the theoretical model of the psychologist.

The first step is to identify the knowledge effectively acquired by the subject. These acquisitions are not based on logical necessity, but on practical requirements. These requirements vary according to age, sociocultural class, and situations and problems habitually encountered. Identification of the subject's effective knowledge requires long and expensive preliminary testing. However, this approach increases the chances of attaining pertinent theoretical models, which in the end is perhaps the most economical approach.

Psychology has not benefited as have physics or biology from several centuries of observations that have contributed to identifying the most important

[2]In Gentner's experiment, the subjects must mime the action, which raises serious problems of interpretation. In Bernicot's experiment, children are asked to say if two sentences are the same or different and to indicate why, for example, *Mr. Tino buys an eraser; Mr. Tino borrows an eraser.*

biological and physical problems. The study of psychology was prematurely involved in overly theoretical and experimental systematization. This is perhaps a disadvantage.

II. GENERAL PROPERTIES OF SEMANTIC STRUCTURES

A. Informative Function and Relational Function

Semantic organization occurs where there is a group of semantically related elements. This kind of group is called a semantic structure. Related signifies two things: (a) that the elements of the group are organized according to a particular configuration and (b) that the elements of the group are functionally dependent. The concept of relation is thus central because it defines the structural and functional relationships between the elements of the group (cf. Miller, Galanter, & Pribram, 1960).

What is a semantic relation? This is a difficult question that occupies an important place in most theories. Indeed, most often, a relation is defined as an element or a structure of a special type whose role is to link together other elements or other structures. Thus two kinds of elements are distinguished: those that are linked and those that link. Piaget's (1952) theory of intelligence provides an example of this. Piaget's "schemes of intelligence" are defined as relational structures. Their function is to organize other structures: perceptions, images, memories.

I have developed a different point of view in which each element of semantic memory is considered capable, by rights, of performing two different functions: the *informative function* and the *relational function* (Ehrlich, 1977).

Let us take for example the sentence *The boy is eating the apple*. It concerns an organized semantic group with three principal elements: *boy, eat,* and *apple*. Each of these elements performs a specific informative function in the sentence: *boy* is different from *girl* or *worm; eat* is different from *pick* or *peel*, etc.

Now let us consider the element EAT. It performs an informative function like the two others. In addition, however, it performs a relational function: It establishes a specific relationship between the two other elements and organizes the entire propositional group. This relational function derives from a property of the element *boy: He could eat something* and from a property of the element *Apple: It could be eaten*. These two properties have something in common, and this commonality is synthesized at the level of the element EAT. Later, it will seem that this synthesis requires a long learning period for children. However, when it is ended for adults, the element *eat* is capable of performing a relational function of the general form *A eats O:* agent *A eats* object *O*. The relating of *A* and *O* is only possible if *O* belongs to those objects that can be eaten by *A*. From this point of view, the sentences *The boy is eating nettles* or *The English eat frogs* raise many problems.

The relational function should be envisaged under two different aspects: *(a)* during the operation of relating, when the subject constructs the propositional group: this defines the *operative function* of *eat; (b)* when construction is realized and the relational element fixes the organization of the group: this defines the *organizational function* of *eat.* The former aspect concerns the activity of the subject in a production or comprehension task for example. The latter concerns the product of this activity when it is ended.

Several points should be clarified:

1. I call *referents* those objects, events, actions, states, or qualities that can be known. I call *referential properties* physical characteristics, the use, the function, etc, of the referents. Semantic structures are psychological units (hypothetical) that mark in memory knowledge of the subject relative to referents and to referential properties. For example, an adult knows generally that *to drink* is to carry a liquid to the mouth and swallow it; thus he knows the constituents of the action: *mouth, swallow,* . . . he also knows the objects to which it is done: *wine, milk, Coca-Cola,* etc.; he knows the instruments of the action: *bowl, glass, bottle,* . . .; the possible agents: *men, animals, plants;* their more or less direct conditions: *thirst, heat, boredom,* etc.

Each semantic structure corresponds to a definite referent: The structure is thus specific. When used in a task it performs a specific informative or relational function, that is, relative to a definite referent. However, it can occur in very diverse activities: identification, matching, classification, . . . and in different types of tasks: learning, memorization, comprehension. Briefly, semantic structure is specific in its content but polyvalent in its psychological functions.

2. By rights, all semantic structures should perform an informative and a relational function. In fact, things are more complex:

2.1. The same semantic element sometimes performs the informative function only and sometimes the informative function and the relational function: The elements *large* and *moving* are simply informative in *The truck is large* and *The truck is moving.* They are informative and relational in *The truck is larger than the car* and in *The truck is moving down the road.*

2.2 The informative capacity of semantic structures varies by degrees. It is inversely proportional to the generality of the referent. It is thus higher for *wine* than for *liquid* (Ehrlich, 1977). It is also proportional to the richness of semantic structures, and this richness depends on learning: When a subject has acquired extensive knowledge relative to a referent, he possesses a rich structure with a great informative capacity. Richness also varies depending on the level of the structures utilized. A suprapropositional structure like *The cat spilled the milk because the dog barked* possesses a greater informative capacity than a propositional structure like *The cat spilled the milk;* this is itself more informative than a structure of lexical level like *milk.* This involves variations in learning and memorization performances (see, e.g., Craik & Tulving, 1975).

2.3. There are structures whose informational capacity is relatively high, but whose relational capacity is weak. Structures corresponding to objects and concrete events like *house, tree, meal,* . . ., are often of this type. There are also structures whose informative capacity is close to zero but whose relational capacity is high. These are structures that mark and coordinate general referential properties. This is the case of logicomathematical structures in general. However, the semantic domain also includes logical connectors, markers of causality, spatial and temporal relations like *and, with, in, on, beside, after, because, thus,* . . .; indeed, all *x* could be *the cause* of numerous *y*; and *x* could be located *before, beside,* or *on* numerous *z.* The informative capacity of these structures is thus relatively weak because of their generality. On the other hand, they perform a specific relational function: A causal relationship is totally different from a spatial relationship. Finally, there are structures that possess both a strong informative and relational capacity. This is notably the case of structures corresponding to actiõns: for example, *spill* in the sentence *The cat spills the milk.*

Thus we conclude that the informative and relational functions of a semantic structure vary by degrees: according to the nature of the referent and its properties; according to the nature of the situation and the task; and according to the experiences of the subject.

B. The Real and the Possible from a Psychological Point of View

1. As was just stated, each referent possesses certain properties that characterize its form, its function, its constituents, its qualities, etc. As for the subject, he has acquired certain knowledge relative to the referent and its properties. What is this knowledge?

1.1 First of all, there is the set of possible properties and those that are not possible. For example *A plane can fly, travel,* even *palpitate,* but it cannot *saw, sweep,* or *smile;* we can *munch on a candy, fruit, vegetables* but not on a *tree,* a *baker,* . . .

1.2 Among the set of possible properties there are those that are known and those that are unknown by the subject. *Penguins live in Brittany,* but not everyone knows this. Thus, we establish here an initial distinction between properties that are physically and logically possible and those that are known by the subject. Only the latter have psychological reality and could be utilized in activities of the subject.

1.3 Among the known properties certain ones are particularly specific, that is, remarkable or dominant:

Remarkable because of their physical or functional singularity: That which characterizes the *sheep* is *wool,* the *rabbit, long ears.*

Remarkable too because they correspond to the major interests of the subject, to the most important problems with which the subject is habitually confronted.

Dominant, in a general fashion—and this includes the two preceding effects—because they are involved more frequently than others in the activities of the subject. If we ask someone to say what characterizes a *tree,* he would more frequently say *branches, trunk,* or *leaves* than *bark* or *roots.* If he were asked to say what *moves, car* is more frequently a response than *wheelbarrow* or *plane* (cf. Ehrlich & Philippe, 1976).

2. Under certain conditions referential semantic structures can be composed in organized groups. However, a double distinction must also be established here between possible organizations and probable organizations and between possible organizations and effective organizations.

2.1 The large collection of possible organizations depends on the referential knowledge acquired by the subject and particularly on those that could perform a relational function. This defines the potential organizational capacities of memory, or if you prefer, the organizational capacities of the subject.

Among the collection of possible organizations there are those that are only rarely used or that even have never yet been realised, for example, *The shepherd pushes the airplane.* They are called *circumstantial structures.*

There are also organizations that correspond to highly probable referential combinations and/or those frequently utilized by the subject: for example *The shepherd tends the sheep.* They are called *permanent structures.* There are in addition all the intermediaries between circumstantial and permanent structures (see p. 210).

2.2 However, one must also distinguish the possible organizations and the organizations effectively realized in the course of the task. Only the latter can be detected at the level of behavior. These are the structures that are momentarily active. They are reconstituted if they are permanent structures; they are constructed at the time of the task if they are circumstantial structures.

In short, a subject's referential knowledge and organizational capacities can be seen at different levels: *(a)* The unbounded set of knowledge and capacities that could eventually be acquired, notice taken of the events that could be encountered; *(b)* the limited set of acquired knowledge and possible organizations that defines the potential capacities of semantic memory; *(c)* the fairly limited set of current knowledge and organizations; and *(d)* the set of knowledge and organizations effectively utilized during a task.

Of the preceding levels, *(a)* conveys the theoretical competence of a robot; *(b), (c),* and *(d)* concern the psychological subject. However, because these distinctions are not always made, confusion and misunderstanding are frequent. Indeed, the psychological theory, the methods, and the empirical data differ, depending on whether theoretically possible capacities, really acquired capacities, or the capacities utilized in a task are being studied.

3. It is assumed that an adult's referential knowledge is free and can be related, that is, inserted according to extremely variable combinations. Memory is thus not defined as an organized system but as a set of possible and

optional organizations (b). Among these organizations some are more probable than others, indeed, are highly probable. These are preferential organizations qualified as permanent structures; later I will show which of these are particularly effective (c).

Observed behavior merely reflects the organization of several structures utilized in the course of the task (d). It does not depend solely on (b) and (c), but also on the subject's constructive activities and on the characteristics of the particular situation. This raises methodological difficulties in the study of semantic memory.

III. GENESIS OF SEMANTIC STRUCTURES

The preceding discussion concerns adult semantic memory. A particularly important question is: How does the child and then the adult come to acquire a set of free and reliable semantic structures?

A. The First Referential Structure

One must begin from the initial state where the child has as yet no referential knowledge. At this stage all of his perceptive and motor activities require a physical support. The object's presence is essential: It produces the stimulation that elicits perceptive exploratory activities and manipulations. During these activities a perceptual image of the object and/or a percep-tual–motor image of the subject's action is formed. However, these images are unstable; they disappear when the object disappears and when the perceptual and motor activities it has caused disappear. Thus, all cognitive activity is impossible in the absence of the referent.

However, it is also assumed that in the course of repeated encounters between the subject and objects, images become more and more lasting. In the end, they are preserved in the form of permanent representations. Thus, some cognitive activities are possible even when the referent is not present.

When these representations are able to be verbalized explicitly, that is, during the child's second year, they form the first structures of semantic memory. These structures are global and poor. They correspond at first to general situations within which different referents are not distinguished. For example, when the child says gone, he does not differentiate among a departure, a disappearance, the cessation of a stimulation (cf. Bramaud du Boucheron, 1979). Later, when the different referents of a situation begin to be individualized, it is in a global form: a bird, for example, is first represented in the form of a dark mobile state; it does not have wings.

In short, the first semantic structures are global and undifferentiated, and their informative capacity is limited. They mark cognitions relating to complex situations. They mix with some confusion representations of objects of the outside world and representations of the subject himself, his affects, and his actions. However, they constitute the point of departure of a fundamental process: The subject begins to free himself from the constraints of the immediate physical presence of objects. Previously, his perceptual and motor activities were tied to objects actually present; after now, certain activities are possible without objects.

B. Differentiation of Concrete Referential Structures

The global structures become progressively differentiated in many constituents. These constituents correspond to referential properties: spatial and temporal localization of the referent *(The shoe is on the foot)*; function and use *(The spoon is for eating)*; constitutive parts *(The doll has a head)*; physical and psychological qualities *(The dessert is good; The house is large)*, etc. (cf. Ehrlich, Bramaud du Boucheron, & Florin, 1978).

This differentiation is realized during the subject's analytical activities. Initially, these have a perceptual and motor nature and are realized in the referent's presence. However, the products of these analyses could be transferred to the level of semantic structures.

Let us imagine a child who finds himself in a good position to examine a *bird* up close (even to handle it, if it is a toy). He could identify the *wings*, the *legs*, the *head*, . . . These referential properties identified in a perceptual plan could then be marked under certain conditions, at the level of the corresponding semantic structure. This is thus qualitatively transformed and enriched in the sense of a larger differentiation.

When the child makes use of differentiated semantic structures, he can effectuate, in the absence of the referent, many activities that previously were impossible: *(a)* The child can name the properties of a referent: If we ask a child to tell what he knows about a *rooster*, we obtain, even from a 3–4-year-old child, pertinent responses: *It has a comb, It has a tail, . . .; It crows, It is on a farm, . . . (b)* The child can name the referents having this or that property: If we ask him to say what *rolls* he could reply *balloon* or *car*; if we ask him what has *leaves*, he could reply *flower* or *salad*. These responses show that the child is able to go from the whole to the part (from the referent to its properties) and from the part to the whole (from the referential properties to the referent).

It should be emphasized that these tests are strictly verbal. We present neither objects nor pictures of objects to the child. The comparison of two referents is equally possible but solely in a negative way. Their similarity is denied; they are considered different according to their respective properties. Bramaud du Boucheron and Cotillon (1978) presented children of different ages (4½–7½ years) with pairs of words designating more or less similar referents; for example, *pancake–brioche; yogurt–brioche; sausage–brioche*. The children were asked to say whether *pancake* and *brioche* are "somewhat alike" or "not at all alike" and to say why. At 4½ years, the majority of replies obtained are replies of difference even in the case of similar referents: *pancake and brioche are not alike; A pancake is flat. A brioche is not flat.* It is also about this age that children refuse to allow that the same person could be a *father* and a *doctor* (Saltz & Medow, 1971).

At the stage just described, semantic structures are already differentiated because they mark certain referential properties. However, these structures correspond to concrete referents connected to the particular contexts and to the experiences particular to the subject: *The apple on the tree,* and *The apple that is eaten* give rise to two different representations. In other words, the generic concept of *apple* with these two possible properties *(We can eat it; It can be on a tree)* is not yet formed.

The problem is the same at the level of referential properties. Each property appertains to a determined referent and cannot be detached from it. There are the *leaves* of every *tree* known by the subject (P1) and the *leaves* of every other *tree* (P2). P1 and P2 have not yet been identified as a property common to several trees. Their synthesis in the form of a generic concept *(leaves* in general) is not yet realized. It follows, and this is important, that the semantic elements corresponding to referential properties cannot yet perform a relational function.

In the experiment of Bramaud du Boucheron and Cotillon just described, children 4½ years old affirmed in general that *sausage and pâté are not alike.* However, some moments before or after, they were perfectly able to say that pâté is edible and that sausage is edible. However, *to eat pâté is one thing, to eat sausage is another;* in the plan of semantic structures, there is no identity of the element *eat* as a property of *sausage* and as a property of *pâté;* for that reason *eat* cannot be identified as common to *pâté* and to *sausage* and cannot perform a relational function.

In short, at the end of the second stage, semantic structures are differentiated and enriched. Their informative capacity is increased appreciably. Meanwhile, they always remain particular (concrete), and they are impervious with regard to each other and can neither be connected nor composed. In his activities the subject cannot yet detach himself from the contingent aspects of his semantic structures. His semantic memory is not yet a system of free and connectable elements.

C. Abstraction and Functional Autonomy: The Genesis of Referential Concepts

The third stage is characterized by a double transformation: that of properties and that of referential structures.

1. ABSTRACTION AND AUTONOMY OF REFERENTIAL PROPERTIES

Referential properties detach themselves from the semantic structures to which they belong and become functionally autonomous: There is an abstraction in the etymological sense (separation, isolation). This process develops from the time when the child compares several referents and notices that they have something in common. This comparison is made at first in the presence of referents, in the form of perceptual and motor activities realized on objects. The subject notices that *Two trees that he sees have the same leaves; that when his father and his mother drink, it looks alike.* When a property has been identified as common to the plan of perceptions or actions, it can be labeled as common at the level of corresponding semantic structures.

In the beginning, there are specific and distinct referential properties. For example, *the bramble pricks (Ax),* a specific property of the *bramble (X); scissors prick (Ay),* a specific property of *scissors (Y).* The subject discovers that *(Ax)* and *(Ay)* have something in common *(prick).* There is a synthesis of *(Ax)* and *(Ay)* at the level of the common element (A). When the synthesis is realized, *(A)* loses this particular and variable aspect according to how it appertains to *X, Y, Z* . . . It is detached from *X* and *Y.* In short, *(A)* has become an abstract semantic element, general and functionally autonomous, capable of performing at the same time an informative and relational function. All semantic structures possessing the property *(A)* can be connected. Thus, many semantic constructions organized by *(A)* become possible.

At the same time (but sometimes before or after), referential properties differentiate themselves in specific constituents. The child learns that *prick* is to *be stuck by something pointed, which hurts.* The process is the same as that described previously at the level of the second stage.

The semantic structures whose successive transformations have just been described can have two different origins: perceptions and actions (cf. Bramaud du Boucheron, 1979). In the first case, they develop from perceived objects or events and their properties: *The chair has legs; the bird flies,* . . .. It is especially this case that was envisaged in the foregoing examples. In the second case, they develop from the subject's own actions. This is notably the case of structures corresponding to the most important and current actions of a young child: *eat, play, sleep, run,* . . . We no longer assume here that *eat* is synthesized from two different referential properties: *Eat an apple* (Ax); *Eat cheese* (Ay). We assume that the child begins by acquiring global knowledge of action centered around himself: (I *eat).* This structure is then differentiated during the second stage into several referential properties, which include the objects to which action is performed *(cheese, apple);* the agent who performs it *(me, Papa, the dog);* the instruments of the action *(mouth, fork);* and so forth. During the third stage, referential properties are detached from the action as just shown.

2. FORMATION OF REFERENTIAL CONCEPTS

The abstract and functionally autonomous properties that characterize a referent can be reconstructed. Thus, a referential concept is formed, that is, a general and abstract semantic structure that characterizes types of objects, events, or actions: *the tree* in general. These concepts realize the synthesis of all the referential properties common to the collection of *trees* (cf. also Nelson, 1974). The genesis of concepts does not suppress primitive referential structures but adds a degree of supplementary knowledge. The child does not forget the knowledge he has of his *house* when he has learned the general concept of *house*.

Referential concepts do not mark a particular group of necessary properties anymore, as was the case of particular and concrete semantic structures until the end of the second stage. They mark a group of possible properties that represent a considerable modification of semantic memory.

In the second stage, structures remain impervious to each other. It is impossible to connect them and to compose them. They are differentiated into several referential properties, but these cannot be detached and therefore necessarily function together. Thus, memory consists only of necessary functional groups, all others being impossible. This indicates a certain rigidity of semantic memory.

In the third stage, referential properties and concepts are general and functionally autonomous structures. Semantic memory has become a system of free and connectable elements. The subject's activities are no longer connected to the contingent aspects of the primitive (concrete) semantic representations. A dichotomy between necessary structures and impossible structures no longer exists; it took its place in a large set of possible optional structures. All of this indicates a great mobility and a great adaptive flexibility of memory, conditions of creativity.

An experiment on comprehension illustrates the preceding (Bramaud du Boucheron & Perez, 1978) ideas. Children of about 6, 7, and 8 years were presented orally with three types of assertions: *I mash the banana with a fork,* an action considered "normal"; *I mash rocks with a fork;* an action considered "impossible"; *I mash the banana with a ladle,* an action considered "eventually possible." For each assertion presented, subjects were asked to indicate whether it was "normal," "impossible," or "eventually possible" and to justify their response. We are assured beforehand that these notions were well understood.

The results showed that the majority of children of all ages identified without difficulty the "normal" and "impossible" actions: The mean correct responses varied between 75% and 90%. In contrast, the mean percentage of correct responses for "eventually possible" actions varied considerably as a function of age: 19% at 6 years, 34% at 7 years, and 82% at 8 years. For the youngest children most of the actions "eventually possible" were considered "impossible": 62% at 6 years; 58% at 7 years; 16% at 8 years.

Examination of justificative arguments is instructive. It shows that among the youngest children, the instrument of action cannot be detached from its most common use: *The ladle is used to serve soup.* Not being detachable from this situation, *the ladle* cannot be inserted in another construction: *I mash the banana with the ladle.* We are still in the second stage, the stage where the element *ladle* is already differentiated but where it remains attached to one particular situation (SERVING SOUP) and cannot be utilized in any other.

The older children have crossed over to the third stage. *The ladle* is detachable from the original situation and can be inserted in other constructions, even if unusual. *The ladle* has acquired a certain autonomy and a proper firmness as an object that is *heavy, hard, fairly large, . . .* capable of *mashing something;* justificative arguments clearly indicate it.

IV. STRUCTURAL PERMANENCE AND EFFICACY

After a child's first learning experiences, semantic memory appears in the form of a large set of free and connectable structures. These structures can be qualified as permanent because they keep themselves and remain constantly available as basic elements of the subject's semantic constructions. Later on, memory can be further enriched and differentiated when the subject acquires new referential knowledge. This augments his constructive and organizational capacities and permits him to face more and more varied problems.

Yet, the situations and problems by which individuals are confronted do not only require a great adaptive flexibility and great constructive capacity. Certain tasks require responses that are adequate, precise, and rapid, incompatible with a constructive activity generally long and groping. It must thus be assumed that certain semantic constructions are prepared in advance and that they function automatically.

It is assumed that within the collection of possible semantic constructions some are more probable than others: whether because they correspond to particularly remarkable and/or important events for the subject or whether (and) because they correspond to habitual events and are frequently utilized by the subject. For example, *The butcher cuts meat with a knife* is a more probable construction than *The butcher is reading Voltaire on the train.*

After appropriate learning experiences, that is, particularly after a frequently repeated utilization, these constructions are fixed in memory in the form of permanent structures. These are groups of knowledge maintained in a defined organization. The pattern of organization is preserved and is constantly available for any new utilization. When the situation calls for it, they are instantly reconstituted with the effect of an activator process emanating from the situation. They do not thus need to be constructed by the subject, which does away with the long procedure of research, composition, and decision that characterizes the operations of construction. They function in a unitary fashion and are revealed to be particularly effective in all sorts of tasks: comprehension, short-term memory, long-term memory. This effectiveness has been illustrated in many experiments (see for example, M. F. Ehrlich, 1977; Bert-Erboul, 1978).

In an experiment of this kind (performed in collaboration with A. Bert-Erboul), four lists of 16 simple sentences were used. Sentences in the first list corresponded to permanent structures, for example, *The hairdresser cuts hair* (A). Sentences in the second list corresponded to circumstantial structures, for example, *The hairdresser looks at the roast* (C). It is a matter here of constructions realized by the subject that correspond to a relatively improbable event. In the other two lists, the sentences corresponded to intermediary structures, neither totally permanent nor totally circumstantial, for example, *The hairdresser cuts the roast* (B1), *The hairdresser looks at the hair* (B2). This material was chosen from a preliminary study, designed to elicit for each agent *(hairdresser)* actions and objects that were highly probable *(cut* and *hair)* and improbable *(look at* and *roast).*

Four groups of 14 adult subjects learned the four lists during three cued recall trials (CL). The 16 sentences were presented in writing; then the agent of each phrase *(The hairdresser)* was presented and the subject had to recognize the corresponding action and object. Immediately after the last learning trial, the subjects took a test of free recall (short-term memory, FR-ST). Three weeks later, the subjects took a new, long-term free recall test (FR-LT), then a test of cued recall over the long term (CR-LT).

The mean number of entirely correct sentences reproduced during the three learning trials (Curve CL), of short-term free recall (Curve FR-ST), of long-term free recall (Curve FR-LT), and of long-term cued recall (Curve CR-LT) is represented in Figure 6.1. The analysis of variance shows that the differences among the three types of materials A, B, and C are always significant. One can see that the permanent structures are more effective than the others for learning and retaining verbal material. In addition, there are degrees of permanence to which variations of performance correspond. Finally, it is established that CR-LT variations as a function of the material are much more important than FR-LT variations. This shows that permanence, especially, found expression in great consistency within structures: The probability of retrieving the action and

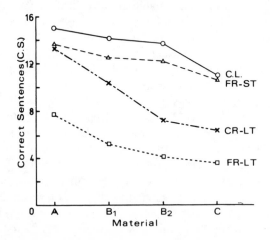

FIGURE 6.1 Mean number of correct sentences (C.S.) in learning (C.L.) in short-term free recall (FR-ST), in long-term free recall (FR-LT), and in long-term cued recall (CR-LT) for four types of materials (A, B1, B2, C).

the object in the presence of the agent is particularly high in the case of permanent structures. On the other hand, accessibility to structures estimated by FR-LT varies much less as a function of a material.

V. CONTEXTUAL DETERMINATIONS AND STRUCTURAL PREDETERMINATIONS

Until now, the context in which psychological activities take place has not been treated. Fortunately for him, the subject does not work in empty situations but in situations that furnish him with more or less precise indications of what he should do. "Situation" is taken here to be large scale, that is, nature of the task, instructions, nature of the material treated. In short, it concerns the collection of information provided by the verbal and nonverbal context.

Context, especially, contributes to removing the indetermination concerning the semantic structures that should be used by the subject to carry out the task. Among the collection of possible structures, context indicates those that are temporarily *useful* according to the requirements of the task. In traditional experiments on semantic memory, the verbal material presented to the subject plays a particularly important role. It either activates directly the useful semantic structures, which is what occurs when the subject utilizes permanent structures that it suffices to reconstitute, or it activates certain semantic elements that must then be dealt with by the subject and composed according to a specific organization. This is what occurs when the subject utilizes more or less unusual circumstantial structures that should be constructed.

It is clear that the determination of temporarily useful semantic structures among the collection of possible structures depends on three classes of factors: (a) the subject's knowledge resulting from his experiences; (b) activating effects of the actual context; and (c) treatments and cognitive operations of the subject for constructing the useful semantic structure, the instrumental basis of expected behavior. Unfortunately, psychology still lacks theories that take into account simultaneously these three groups of factors in treating them as a system of interaction.

Meanwhile, in some cases, presentation of the material suffices in determining the useful semantic structures even when they are circumstantial. This is what happens when the subject is asked to comprehend or to learn texts or sentences like The gardener is washing his shirt. Presentation of the sentence activates the corresponding semantic group, and the subject's constructive activity is limited to verifying that this group is semantically coherent (possible).

The situation is similar when material is presented in a test of cued recall. However, it is different in the case of free recall where the subject is generally induced to restructure the list according to a particular subjective organization (cf. e.g., Puff, Murphy, & Ferrara, 1977). The constructive activities can be equally important in tasks like those of Bransford and McCarrell (1974); in this case the material presented cannot be directly integrated and the subject must search in his memory for the supplementary semantic elements that can bring about this integration.

Thus, it must be considered that in the determination of useful structures, among the collection of possible structures, the respective parts played by context, by prior knowledge, and by cognitive operations of the subject vary appreciably from one task to another.

This is why research that considers only one or another of these factors raises serious discussions. There is for example the work of Craik (1976) in which principally cognitive operations are involved. There is also the work of Tulving (1976) on encoding specificity and episodic memory that is principally involved with the role of context.

In its concrete and somewhat provocative form, the theory of encoding specificity has been widely contested. Contrary to Tulving's (1976) assertion, a cue can be effective in recall even when it has not been encoded with the critical stimulus at the time of learning (cf. Bahrick, 1970; Postman, 1975).

However, this theory has a much more general scope if it is understood as follows: It is the context of encoding and, in particular, the nature of the items presented that determines the semantic structures the subject should use now (when encoding) and later (when recalling); it is the context that selects and activates a small number of useful structures among the collection of possible semantic structures.

Even in this general form, Tulving's theory of encoding specificity remains insufficient if two other groups of factors are not taken into account: the nature of cognitive operations realized in the encoding and recall, and the subject's prior experiences.

To study this question, we repeated Tulving and Thomson's (1973) cued recall experiment. In this experiment (Ehrlich & Philippe, 1976), three conditions of encoding were crossed (only the target word is presented; with a cue-word strongly associated with it; with a cue-word weakly associated with it) and three conditions of recall (no cue is presented; a strong cue is presented; a weak cue is presented). In Tulving and Thomson's experiment, recall occurred immediately after presentation of the items (short-term memory, ST). In our experiment, we added a situation of long-term (LT) recall two weeks after the learning experience. Eighteen groups of subjects were used: nine in ST and nine in LT. In our experiment, material was changed also. Instead of using pairs, cue word–target word, characterized only by their associative strength, we chose pairs of words having a specific semantic relation, the part–whole relation whereby the cue is always a part of the target word: mane–*lion;* tail–*fish* . . . This is designed to neutralize or at least to limit the effect of one of the factors: the nature of encoding operations. It is assumed that in situations of cued recall, the subject's activity consists essentially of establishing a specific semantic relation between the cue and the target word in encoding and retrieving this relation at the time of the recall. This activity is not useful in our experiment since the cue–target word relation is the same for the 24 items used.

On the whole, the results that we obtained clearly weakened the hypothesis of encoding specificity. However, what interests us more here is the relationship that exists between the effects of context and prior experiences of the subject. Our hypothesis is the following: The effects of context (encoding specificity) are proportionately more important where the subject's prior experiences are weak. If the items to be remembered correspond to permanent structures, the effect of context is weak or null. This is what occurs with items such as toe–foot. These structures are predetermined and fixed in the subject's memory in the form of strong functional units.[3] They can be reconstituted whenever one of the terms is presented (e.g., cue: toe) and when the subject knows the semantic relation with the other term, which is the case in our experiment. In this case, the presence or absence of the cue in encoding does not change anything; what is important is that it be presented at the time of recall.

On the other hand, if the items to be remembered correspond to circumstantial structures, the presentation of the cue in encoding is necessary to determine the useful structure and to mark it in the semantic memory; this is the case with items where the cue is not a specific property of the object, for example, dressmaking–shoes.

The results of Ehrlich and Philippe's (1976) experiment were reanalyzed with only three of nine conditions:

O–O: The cue is presented at neither encoding nor recall

O–C: The cue is presented only at recall

C–C: The cue is presented at encoding and recall

Moreover, we only consider here that the situation or the cue (C) is a relatively specific property of the target word (T); this is the situation which, in Tulving and Thomson (1973), corresponds to a strong association between (C) and (T).

For each of the 24 items, two estimations were calculated at first: (a) an estimation of the structural predetermination, or retrieval effect, of the cue (P) and (b) an estimation of the contextual determination, or encoding effect of the cue (E).

For each time (i) there is: $P_i = OC_i - OO_i$ and $E_i = CC_i - OC_i$. Here, OO_i is the rate of recall obtained by presenting only the target word in the encoding; OC_i and CC_i are the rates of recall obtained in the two other situations considered here; P_i represents the cue's own effect for retrieving the target word and is considered directly proportional to the subject's experiences—structural predetermination; E_i represents the supplement effect due to the presence of C at encoding and is an estimation of the effect of encoding specificity—contextual determination.

Our hypothesis makes the provision that P_i and E_i will be inversely

---

[3]These units are strong because of the subject's experiences. These experiences fixed the toe in the semantic memory in the form of a highly specified property of the foot; more specific than skin, for example (cf. p. 202).

Table 6.1
Means of Values of OO_i, of Encoding Effects (E_i), and Retrieval Effects (P_i) in Short-Term Recall (ST) and Long-Term Recall (LT) for Three Types of Materials (A, B, C)

	A		B		C	
	S.T.	L.T.	S.T.	L.T.	S.T.	L.T.
OO_i	.550	.200	.585	.228	.562	.225
E_i	.212	.362	.067	.314	−.039	.125
P_i	−.012	.050	.243	.228	.375	.487

proportional. To verify that, the 24 items are divided into three groups A, B, and C as a function of the values of P_i.

1. For each item, two values of P_i were calculated, one for short-term memory (STM) and one for long-term (LTM). There was no significant difference between the means of P_i for STM and LTM. Then, for each of the 24 items, the sum of the two values of P_i $(S_i = STM + LTM)$ was calculated. It is from (S_i) that the three groups A, B, and C were made up: eight items of which the values of S_i are the strongest (Group A); eight items of which the values of (S_i) are the weakest (Group C); the rest forms Group B.

2. For each of the three groups of items, the means of OO_i, of P_i, and of E_i were calculated for STM, and LTM (Table 6.1).

3. Relative means were also calculated by dividing the values of P_i and of E_i of Table 6.1 by the values corresponding to OO_i. These relative means are presented in Figure 6.2.

It is evident that the encoding effect (E_i) and the retrieval effect (P_i) are inversely proportional. The results are similar in short-term and in long-term memory. However, they are much more accentuated in long-term memory, in relative value, notably because of the decrease of OO_i when going from the short term to the long term.

Tulving's hypothesis of encoding specificity thus appeared as a particular case that should be incorporated into a more general theory. It is verified when the subject utilizes circumstantial structures[4]; it fails when the task permits utilization of permanent structures. However, because permanence varies by degrees as a function of experience, all the intermediary cases are possible.

Similar results were obtained in a study of the sentence comprehension (experiment conducted by J.M. Passerault and G. Personnier). Children of about ages 8, 10, and 12 were given in writing 20 incomplete sentences, for example, the dealer . . . merchandise; The smoker . . . butt. The subjects had to retrieve the verbs (sell and throw away). The responses produced by these subjects were divided in two groups of 10 sentences: (a) those for which the

[4]We could perhaps speak of "episodic structures" but giving a meaning to the term other than Tulving's (1976).

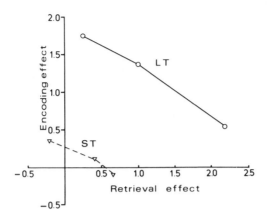

FIGURE 6.2 Variations of relative encoding effect (E_i/OO_i) and of relative retrieval effect (P_i/OO_i) for short-term recall memory (STM) and long-term memory (LTM).

expected response was given most frequently and that thus corresponded to relatively permanent structures (A) and *(b)* those for which the expected responses were least frequent and that corresponded to relatively circumstantial structures (B). Then, a supplementary contextual element was added to each sentence in the form of a causal or instrumental clause inducing either the expected verb ($\overset{+}{V}$) or another verb ($\bar{V}$), for example, *because the cigarette is finished, the smoker . . . butt* ($A\overset{+}{V}$); *With his foot the smoker . . . butt* ($A\bar{V}$). We then had four types of sentences ($A\overset{+}{V}$, $A\bar{V}$, $B\overset{+}{V}$, $B\bar{V}$) that were presented to three new groups of subjects of 8, 10, and 12 years of age.

We shall now consider just the 8-year-old children and situations $A\bar{V}$ and $B\bar{V}$[5]. In the controlled situation (first group of children) in the absence of the causal clause, the expected response was produced with a frequency of .41 for material (A) and with a frequency of .14 for material (B). When we added the causal clause (second group of children), the frequency of the expected response was .56 in the AV (an increase of about 37%) and .49 in BV (increase of about 250%).

It is clear that the role the added context plays is much greater in the case of circumstantial structures than in that of relatively permanent structures. In short, in the preceding discussion, we started with the idea that semantic memory is a system of free elements, capable of generating many possible structures. In this perspective, it is essential to understand how, among all possible structures, the several structures useful for the execution of each particular task are determined. This determination depends on three orders of factors: structural predetermination resulting from certain experiences; the

[5]The results obtained with the other groups of children are otherwise similar. We find an inhibition effect in situations $A\bar{V}$ and $B\bar{V}$; this effect is particularly important in the $A\bar{V}$ situation, which is understandable.

selective and activating action of the context; and the subject's cognitive operations.

Most tasks simultaneously call forth these three factors according to a combination that is complex and variable from one situation to another. However, we have been able to show in the two experiments just described that contextual action can tend toward zero when structural predetermination becomes important and that the reciprocal is also true.

VI. CONCLUSIONS

Our starting point was the general hypothesis that adult semantic memory gives shape to a system of free elements. These elements are defined by their structural and functional properties. They mark knowledge acquired by the subject relative to events, objects, actions, qualities, . . .; they perform an informative and relationally specific function; they can be connected and composed according to extremely varied structural combinations, presenting a permanent or circumstantial character; they form the instrumental basis of the subject's behavior in an extended series of tasks production or comprehension, learning and memorization, resolution of problems with or without inferential constructions, and so forth.

Next, an attempt was made to show that semantic memory is progressively built up in a child according to a long process of learning in which three stages can be distinguished. The first stage marks the appearance of primitive semantic structures that are both complex and global. It liberates the subject from the constraints of the physical element actually present. The second stage is indicated by differentiation and enrichment of the primitive semantic structures. However, the differentiated structures continue to mark particular and concrete knowledge relative to particular referents: They cannot be connected. In his activities, the subject remains dependent on the contingent aspects of his structures that can be neither generalized nor composed. The third stage is characterized by the appearance of conceptual structures that are general, abstract, functionally autonomous, and connectable. It is at this time that semantic memory becomes a system of free elements. At first limited to several contingent and necessary structures, the subject's activities can now diversify considerably, with learning based on the large collection of possible semantic constructions.

Finally, an attempt was made to determine what becomes of this semantic memory of free elements, so dearly acquired, but so well adapted to diverse situations and to the requirements of creative activity.

Among the collection of possible circumstantial constructions, some become more probable than others and tend to become fixed in the memory in the form of permanent structures. It is only in this sense that we can speak of the organization of memory: among the extremely vast collection of possible structural organizations, some of which are permanently fixed in the memory following appropriate learning experiences. These permanent structures are particularly effective in executing rapid and precise behavior because they are prepared in advance and because they function in a quasi-automatic mode. This permits the subject to economize on a constructive activity always relatively long and tentative. This efficacy is attested by several experimental studies.

However, these studies demonstrate as well that when the task permits utilization of permanent structures, the role of the context in encoding becomes minor. Indeed, permanent structures are determined in advance in their informative content and their organization; in opposition to circumstantial structures, they do not need to be determined by the context. This leads us to emphasize the importance, but also the relative nature, of Tulving's theory of encoding specificity.

REFERENCES

Anderson, J. R. FRAN: A simulation model of free recall. In G. H. Bower (Ed.), *The psychology of learning and motivation* (Vol 5). New York: Academic Press, 1972.

Anderson, J. R., & Bower, G. H. *Human associative memory*. New York: Wiley and Sons, 1973.

Anglin, J. M. *The growth of word meaning*. Cambridge, Mass.: M.I.T. Press, 1970.

Atlan, H. *L'organisation biologique et la théorie de l'information*. Paris: Hermann, 1972.

Bahrick, H. P. Two phase model for prompted recall. *Psychological Review*, 1970, *77*, 215–222.

Bernicot, J. Etude génétique des représentations sémantiques: connaissance de verbes de transmission de possession par des enfants de 6 à 9 ans. Poitiers, 1978 (unpublished).

Bert-Erboul, A. Le rôle de la pemanence et des niveaux hiérarchiques des structures conceptuelles dans l'apprentissage des phrases. *Année Psychologique*, 1978, *78*, 79–92.

Bower, G. H., Clark, M., Lesgold, A. M., & Wizenz, D. Hierarchical retrieval schemes in recall of categorized word lists. *Journal of Verbal Learning and Verbal Behavior*, 1969, *8*, 323–343.

Bramaud du Boucheron, G. Le développement de la mémoire sémantique chez l'enfant. Poitiers, 1979 (unpublished).

Bramaud du Boucheron, G., & Cotillon, J. M. Les enfants organisent-ils hiérarchiquement les concepts d'objets? *Cahiers de Psychologie du Sud-Est*, 1978, *21*, 17–35.

Bramaud du Boucheron, G., & Perez, C. Les enfants comprennent-ils des phrases décrivant des événements inconnus? *Psychologie Française*, 1978, (in press).

Bransford, J. M., & McCarrell, N. S. A sketch of a cognitive approach to comprehension. In W. B. Weimer & D. S. Palermo (Eds.), *Cognition and the symbolic processes*, New York: Wiley and Sons, 1974.

Clark, E. V. On the child's acquisition of antonyms in two semantic fields. *Journal of Verbal Learning and Verbal Behavior*, 1972, *11*, 750–758.

Craik, F. I. M. La profondeur de traitement comme prédicteur des performances de la mémoire. In S. Ehrlich & E. Tulving (Eds.), *La mémoire sémantique*. Bulletin de Psychologie, 1976, numéro spécial, 133–142.

Craik, F. I. M., & Tulving, E. Depth of processing and the retention of words in episodic memory. *Journal of Experimental Psychology General*, 1975, *104*, 268–294.

Ehrlich, M. F. Apprentissage et mémoire à long terme de phrases: le rôle de la cohésion sémantique des éléments. *Année Psychologique*, 1977, *77*, 41–62.

Ehrlich, S. *Les mécanismes du comportement verbal*. Paris: Vrin, 1968.

Ehrlich, S. *Apprentissage et mémoire chez l'homme*. Paris: Presses Universitaires de France, 1975.

Ehrlich, S. La notion de spécificité dans l'étude de la mémoire sémantique. *Journal de Psychologie Normale et Pathologique*, 1977, *3*, 307–333.

Ehrlich, S., Bramaud du Boucheron, G., & Florin, A. *Le développement des connaissances lexicales à l'école primaire*. Paris: Presses Universitaires de France, 1978.

Ehrlich, S., & Philippe, M. Encoding specificity, retrieval specificity or structural specificity. *Journal of Verbal Learning and Verbal Behavior*, 1976, *15*, 537–548.

Gentner, D. Evidence for the psychological reality of semantic components: the verbs of possession. In D. A. Norman & D. E. Rumelhart (Eds.), *Exploration in cognition*. San Francisco: Freeman, 1975.

Lockhart, R. S., Craik, F. I. M., & Jacoby, L. Depth of processing in recognition and recall: some aspects of a general memory system. In J. Brown (Ed.), *Recognition and recall*. New York: Wiley and Sons, 1976.

Mandler, G. Association and organization: facts, fancies and theories. In T. R. Dixon & D. L. Horton (Eds.), *Verbal behavior and general behavior theory*. New York: Prentice Hall, 1968.

Miller, G. A., Galanter, E., & Pribram, K. *Plan and the structure of behavior*. New York: Holt, Rinehart and Winston, 1960.

Nelson, K. Concept word and sentence: interrelations in acquisition and development. *Psycholocical Review*, 1974, *81*, 267–285.

Norman, D. A., & Rumelhart, D. E. *Exploration in cognition*. San Francisco: Freeman, 1975.

Paillard, J. Système nerveux et fonction d'organisation. In J. Piaget, J. P. Bronckart & P. Mounoud (Eds.), *La psychologie*. Paris: Gallimard, Encyclopédie de la Pléiade, 1978.

Piaget, J. [*The origins of intelligence in children*] (M. Cook, trans). New York: International University Press, Norton, 1952.

Postman, L. Tests of the generality of the principle of encoding specificity. *Memory and Cognition*, 1975, *3*, 663–672.

Puff, C. R., Murphy, D. M., & Ferrara, R. A. Further evidence about the role of clustering in free recall. *Journal of Experimental Psychology, Human Learning Memory*, 1977, *3*, 742–753.

Quillian, M. R. Semantic memory. In M. Minsky (Ed.), *Semantic information processing*. Cambridge, Mass.: M.I.T. Press, 1968.

Rosch, E. Classifications d'objets du monde réel: origines et représentations dans la cognition. In S. Ehrlich & E. Tulving (Eds.), *La mémoire sémantique*. Bulletin de Psychologie, 1976, numéro spécial, 242–250.

Saltz, E., & Medow, M. L. Concept conservation in children: the dependence of belief systems on semantic representation. *Child Development*, 1971, *42*, 1533–1542.

Smith, E. E., Shoberr, E. J., & Rips, L. J. Structure and process in semantic memory: a featural model for semantic decisions. *Psychological Review*, 1974, *81*, 214–241.

Tulving, E. Rôle de la mémoire sémantique dans le stockage et la récupération de l'information épisodique. In S. Ehrlich & E. Tulving (Eds.), *La mémoire sémantique*. Bulletin de Psychologie, 1976, numéro spécial, 19–25.

Tulving, E., & Thomson, D. M. Encoding specificity and retreival processes in episodic memory. *Psychological Review*, 1973, *80*, 352–373.

PETER A. ORNSTEIN
KATHLEEN CORSALE

CHAPTER **7**

Organizational Factors in Children's Memory

Since the late 1960s there has been an explosion of interest in memory development in children. This interest can be seen in the flood of review chapters (Brown, 1975, 1979; Hagen, Jongeward, & Kail, 1975; Naus & Halasz, 1979; Ornstein & Corsale, 1979) and books (Kail & Hagen, 1977; Ornstein, 1978) on this topic that are now available. A major outcome of this

MEMORY ORGANIZATION
AND STRUCTURE

219

research on memory development has been a documentation of the conditions under which children's memory seems to improve with age, and the factors that appear to be responsible for this mnemonic development. In general, it can be argued that improvement is most clearly seen in the context of those memorization situations that require the deliberate deployment of information-handling strategies and techniques. Thus, age differences in memory performance are more clearly seen in deliberate recall tasks than in either recognition situations (see, e.g., Perlmutter & Lange, 1978) or incidental learning settings (see, e.g., Brown, 1975; Naus & Halasz, 1979; Ornstein & Corsale, 1979). Although young children often have the capabilities to do so, their performance in deliberate memory tasks frequently reflects the lack of strategic deployment of these skills.

The present chapter is devoted to an in-depth consideration of children's memory performance in free-recall tasks involving both unrelated and categorically related sets of items, situations in which the deliberate use of mnemonic techniques is important in mediating developmental changes. This chapter focuses on the extent to which age-related recall improvements are due to corresponding changes in subjects' organizational attempts. Organization is viewed in terms of the regularities that are observable in the order of recall output and of the grouping that might be discernible as to-be-remembered materials are studied. The fact that developmental changes in organizational activities might be at least partially responsible for age-related improvements in recall is suggested by current views of the role of organization in human memory (see, e.g., Bower, 1970; Tulving & Donaldson, 1972), as well as by recent models of the memory system. The multistore (e.g., Atkinson & Shiffrin, 1968) and depth of processing (e.g., Craik & Lockhart, 1972) models differ in the mnemonic metaphor used to describe performance (see Naus, Ornstein, & Hoving, 1978; Naus & Halasz, 1979; Ornstein & Corsale, 1979), but both would nonetheless be in basic agreement concerning the importance of organization and other strategies in mediating developmental changes in recall.[1]

Although the present chapter focuses on the use of organizational strategies, the operation of these techniques cannot be understood without a consideration of additional knowledge that children have available in permanent

---

[1]Although the operation of organizational variables in children's memory can be viewed within the context of both the multistore and levels of processing models, it should be emphasized that neither of these frameworks for mnemonic analysis represents an adequate model of memory development. Neither theoretical position specifically addresses those situations in which recall improvement with age does not seem to be correlated with age changes in the tendency to organize. Nor does either position speak to the complexities involved in the child's developing use (or lack thereof) of organizational techniques in memory situations. Indeed, both types of models represent attempts to characterize the relatively static adult memory system, and both fail to account for significant aspects of the growing and changing memory of children. There are currently no comprehensive models of children's memory available, although Naus and Halasz (1979) and Ornstein and Corsale (1979) discuss these issues.

memory.[2] One can consider, for example, what may be involved in the recall of a list of taxonomically related items presented for a few trials in a recall task. In this situation, recall increases with age, as does one measure of organization, that of category clustering, the tendency to order recall according to the categorical structure implicit in the set of to-be-remembered items (see Bousfield, 1953; Moely, 1977; Lange, 1978). Those children who cluster in recall are utilizing semantic information that they have available in permanent memory. This information—knowledge of semantic categories and the interrelationships among verbal stimuli—may be combined with certain rules for operating upon memory, a repertoire of potential strategies (including clustering) for committing material to memory.[3] These strategies themselves are represented in some fashion in permanent memory, but they cannot be effectively employed unless the child has the relevant semantic and conceptual knowledge about the to-be-remembered items and, under some conditions, the knowledge that their implementation would be useful. Thus, it is necessary to study the collection of mnemonic strategies under the child's control, his fundamental semantic and conceptual knowledge, and his "metamemory," or knowledge concerning the operation of memory (see Kreutzer, Leonard, & Flavell, 1975; Flavell & Wellman, 1977). All of these aspects of permanent memory may be undergoing developmental change and may contribute to the observed increases in recall and category clustering.

One final set of considerations must be noted. To understand developmental changes in memory performance, it is necessary to explore the situational constraints that govern the utilization of information from permanent memory and the implementation of deliberate memorization techniques. To a greater extent than is true of adults, children present us with discrepancies between behavior in different mnemonic settings. Often a child may have certain semantic knowledge, but he or she may fail to utilize this information in the

[2]In some sense, the present stress on both mnemonic strategies and other information available in the knowledge base can be interpreted within the framework of Tulving's (1972) distinction between semantic and episodic memory. According to Tulving, episodic memory represents the memory for temporally tagged events or episodes, whereas semantic memory comprises that memory that is necessary for language comprehension. For Tulving, semantic memory represents a type of mental thesaurus, although it has been used by many to refer to the general knowledge base described here (but see Nelson & Brown, 1978, for a critique of this use of the term). If one argues that deliberate memory tasks tap episodic memory, then the present point of view would suggest that performance in these tasks requires the utilization of information available in semantic memory. However, it is unlikely that the semantic–episodic distinction is precise enough to contribute significantly to an understanding of children's free recall. See Nelson and Brown (1978) and Naus and Halasz (1979) for a consideration of these issues.

[3]It must be added that under some conditions the effects of semantic information available in the permanent knowledge base seem to be observed without the corresponding implementation of deliberate strategies for memorization. Thus, for example, strong associative connections among to-be-remembered items may result in a type of nondeliberate or automatic clustering (Lange, 1973, 1978). For additional demonstrations of the effects of the knowledge base, see recent papers by Chi (1978) and Myers and Perlmutter (1978).

context of the memorization task per se (see Ornstein & Corsale, 1979, for a discussion of these "production deficiencies"). This failure may occur because a child does not realize that such information would be useful, as for example in the situation in which a subject is unaware that the deliberate deployment of strategies is necessary for remembering (see Appel, Cooper, McCarrell, Sims-Knight, Yussen, & Flavell, 1972; Corsale & Ornstein, 1977). Or, this failure may result because of motivational or other reasons, as in the situation in which a child does not utilize appropriate techniques in a formal laboratory task but may do so in an informal play setting (see, e.g., Istomina, 1975). Regardless, in order to understand the developing memory performance of the child, it is necessary to explore memory strategy utilization in a variety of different types of deliberate and nondeliberate memory tasks.

In the present paper, these various issues are addressed. First, children's use of organizational strategies in the context of deliberate memory tasks is assessed. This discussion focuses on several general topics: (a) age changes in the use of organization in recall (i.e., at output) and as stimuli are presented (i.e., at input), (b) the conditions under which children of different ages utilize organizational techniques and the factors affecting young children's failure to employ these strategies in many contexts, and (c) the linkages among organization at input and at output and recall performance. The second section of the paper is devoted to an examination of permanent memory (i.e., the knowledge base) and its role in the development of organizational strategies. This section includes the topics of generalized domain-related knowledge, metamemory knowledge, and knowledge of semantic concepts.

I. DELIBERATE MEMORY TASKS: THE USE OF ORGANIZATION

During the school-age years, children demonstrate increasing sophistication in the use of many mnemonic skills. Age-related changes in attention (e.g., Hagen & Hale, 1973) and rehearsal (e.g., Ornstein, Naus, & Liberty, 1975; Ornstein & Naus, 1978) as well as in organization (e.g., Cole, Frankel, & Sharp, 1971; Lange, 1978) seem to contribute to the improved recall performance that is commonly observed. The development of organizational efficiency requires both the knowledge of semantic relationships and the availability of strategies. Use of organizational strategies can be assessed at output (i.e., in the actual recall of items) in terms of ordered patterns of items recalled. In addition, organization can be assessed as to-be-remembered items as presented (i.e., at input) by having subjects sort or group the stimulus materials.

A. Output Organization

Measures of output organization are derived from the order in which to-be-remembered items are recalled in memory tasks. Sequential constraints in the recall order are thought to represent subjects' attempts at structuring the to-be-remembered material at stimulus input or during the actual retrieval of the items. Traditionally, two types of output organization, clustering and subjective organization, have been studied. With taxonomically related items, category clustering (Bousfield, 1953; Bousfield & Bousfield, 1966) reflects the extent to which recall is structured according to the categories provided by the experimenter. In contrast, with unrelated items, subjective organization (Bousfield & Bousfield, 1966; Tulving, 1962) reflects the imposition of a personal structure upon the materials. However, both clustering and subjective organization are measures of the *amount* of organization present in a set of recall protocols, and they do not provide information concerning the *quality* or type of the organization present. Friendly (1977) developed a technique that permits an assessment of the fine structure of organization present in recall protocols, and the usefulness of this approach to the question of children's output organization is demonstrated later.

B. Clustering

In general, one can state that category clustering increases with age over the elementary school years. Thus, when young children are presented with a list of randomly arranged examples from several taxonomic categories, they are not particularly strategic in terms of recalling the words in sequences of related items. Older children and adults are likely, however, to cluster the category instances in their recall. Bousfield, Esterson, and Whitmarsh (1958), for example, demonstrated that adults clustered more than third or fourth graders in a single-trial recall task. Subsequently, Cole, Frankel, and Sharp (1971) showed that eighth graders clustered more than either first or third graders and that there were no clustering differences between the first and third graders, with children at both grades exhibiting relatively low levels of output organization.

Although it is clear that clustering does increase with age, there is little agreement among investigators concerning when such tendencies to structure recall are first observed. Several groups of experimenters (e.g., Furth & Milgram, 1973; Lange, 1973) found that age-related trends in clustering are not linear and that, in fact, substantial clustering is not observed until late in the elementary school years. In contrast, other investigators seem to find significant clustering in the recall protocols of children below the age of five (e.g., Rossi & Rossi, 1965; Myers & Perlmutter, 1978; Rossi & Wittrock, 1971). It seems likely, as Lange (1973, 1978) has argued, that the discrepancy between these various studies is to some extent a function of the characteristics of the to-be-remembered items. Inspection of the materials used in the studies demonstrating clustering with young children suggests that category clustering in these instances may reflect high interitem associations. In fact, Lange (1978) claims that "When precautions are taken to insure that same-category instances are not strong natural associates, preadolescent children do not cluster their recall output under standard free recall conditions. [p. 106]." In contrast, Lange argues that when there are strong interword associations among the category members chosen for the recall task, even very young children demonstrate clustering.

Although there is not a great deal of experimental evidence in support of Lange's position, two other studies have indicated that the hypothesis is plausible. Haynes and Kulhavy (1976) presented exemplars of taxonomic categories serially to 7-, 9-, and 12-year-olds who were instructed to look for similarities among the items. For half of the children, the examples of the categories were highly associated, while for the remaining children, the examples of any particular category were not strong associates. Haynes and Kulhavy (1976) demonstrated that at all age levels, clustering in recall was greater for the high-associated list than for the low-associated list. Corsale (1978), in a study to be discussed later, also showed higher clustering for high-associated taxonomic exemplars than for low-associated examples among kindergarteners and third graders. Such findings lend some support to Lange's hypothesis and to the growing concern with the role of knowledge base in memory performance.

Lange's position, although speculative, is most intriguing because it helps to order the discrepant findings in the literature concerning the onset of clustering in recall. Further, the position advocated by Lange leads to a somewhat altered analysis of clustering performance. In contrast to the view that clustering always involves the conscious deployment of a deliberate strategy, Lange suggests that under conditions in which the child is familiar with the stimulus materials, clustering may not reflect higher order strategies. Rather, it may be the case that

> the subject is "struck" by the organization he perceives, and he encodes and stores organizational units as a direct and automatic function of their perceived structure. Assuming the validity of this analysis, it is reasonable to posit further that the recall organization we sometimes see in preschool and elementary school children . . . occurs through a series of involuntary actions that can operate at both the perceptual-encoding and retrieval phases of processing [Lange, 1978, p. 107].

C. Subjective Organization

The clustering literature indicates that older children are able to use categorical organization present in the to-be-remembered material to structure recall. In addition, it seems likely that younger children may be able to take advantage of the stimulus properties of lists in which there are strongly associated category members. In contrast to these conditions in which there is a degree of structure provided by the experimenter, subjective organization experiments explore the child's performance with relatively unrelated items. Subjective organization is measured by observing the extent to which pairs of items are recalled contiguously on two successive recall trials. In this situation, although the literature is not entirely consistent, the bulk of the available evidence suggests that there are minimal tendencies on the part of children to impose a personal structure on the to-be-remembered materials.

Laurence (1966), for example, with children ranging from 5.5 to 10.5 years of age, observed substantial age differences in recall, but none in measured subjective organization. Comparable findings of recall differences but equivalent subjective organization have been reported by Nelson (1969) with children of 5 and 8 years of age, by Shapiro and Moely (1971) with children between 9 and 13 years of age, by Ornstein et al. (1975, Experiment I) with subjects between 8.5 and 13.5 years, and by Ornstein, Hale, and Morgan (1977) with 8-and 12-year-olds. In addition, Kokubun (1973) reported no difference in measured subjective organization until the final trials of a 16-trial sequence. However, since the recall performance of his 8-, 11-, and 14-year-old subjects seemed to differ prior to the final trial block, it would be difficult to argue that subjective organization was the critical factor in determining the age differences in recall. To date, only one experimenter has reported evidence of a significant age difference in children's subjective organization. The recall and subjective organization of Rosner's (1971) first graders were less than those of her fifth- and ninth-grade subjects (although it should be added that these two groups of older subjects had equivalent organization but different degrees of recall).

Given Lange's (1978) interpretation of developmental changes in clustering, it would be expected that only minimal amounts of subjective organization would be observed when children are presented with unstructured lists. However, the task of measuring subjective organization is more difficult than that of assessing category clustering, and, therefore, it might be appropriate to inquire as to whether the absence of age changes in subjective organization might be due to measurement problems. Two pieces of recent evidence are relevant to this question.

First, Ornstein, Hale, and Morgan (1977) reasoned that the failure to obtain developmental trends in subjective organization might be due to the fact that typical measures of such organization involve the observation of pairwise sequential dependencies. To the extent that older children form higher order subjective units, age trends in such organization might be underestimated. Ornstein, Hale, and Morgan utilized Pellgrino's (1971) indices of subjective organization, which measure not only intertrial repetition of adjacent items, but also higher order consistencies. However, these investigators were still unable to obtain any evidence for developmental changes in organization. Second, Sternberg and Tulving (1977) examined the available measures of subjective organization and argued that a bidirectional intertrial repetition measure, modified from that initially proposed by Bousfield and Bousfield (1966), is the most appropriate index currently available. When Sternberg and Tulving (1977) applied this measure to Laurence's (1966) data, they were able to obtain evidence for developmental changes in organization. However, the bidirectional intertrial repetition measure is correlated with level of recall, and, accordingly, the reported increase of subjective organization with age may have been an artifact of age changes in amount of recall (see also Murphy,

Chapter 3).[4] Therefore, the bulk of the existing data is consistent with the view that children's output organization is most clearly seen with highly structured materials.

D. Hierarchical Clustering

A more complete picture of the organization present in children's recall protocols both with related and unrelated materials may be obtained by applying Friendly's (1977) proximity analysis techniques. It can be argued that measures of taxonomic clustering and subjective organization are both incomplete in that they are single indices that summarize the *amount* of organization thought to be present. In contrast, Friendly (1977) has developed a technique for examining the overall *structure* of such organization. The analysis quantifies the structure of recall organization, using information concerning the ordinal separation or proximity between pairs of items in the recall protocols. An item-by-item proximity matrix is constructed with elements representing the degree to which each pair of items is recalled contiguously over trials and/or subjects. Various scaling solutions can be applied to the proximity matrices (see Friendly, 1977), but most frequently, a hierarchical clustering procedure (Johnson, 1967) is utilized. This procedure results in the generation of a tree structure diagram that indicates nested clusters of items that correspond to the item–pair proximities.

By reanalyzing several previously obtained sets of recall data, Friendly, Ornstein, and Bjorklund (1976) demonstrated the usefulness of this approach for an analysis of developmental data. Analyses of sets of related words are presented first, since these can be most straightforwardly interpreted. Figure 7.1 presents tree structure diagrams that were obtained from Ornstein et al. (1977). These diagrams are from third and seventh graders who were given taxonomically related items to learn. There were a total of 25 items, 5 each from five categories, and these items were presented for five trials. The ordinate scale in these figures represents the degree of proximity among items averaged over recall protocols. For example, in a 25-item list, if all subjects recalled items A and B in adjacent positions, on every recall trial, the proximity of items A and B would be 25. The results were in accord with the fact that the older children demonstrated greater amounts of category clustering, but they present a more detailed picture of the structure of recall organization. Inspection of the figure indicates that the recall groupings of the younger subjects show a considerable degree of clustering by the list categories, but they generally fail to include all the items within a category. In contrast, for the seventh graders, all of the items seem to be grouped according to the list categories.

---

[4] Murphy, Sanders, and Puff (1978) discuss these issues in an important reply to the Sternberg and Tulving (1977) paper. Further, as will be discussed later, Murphy (Chapter 3) and his colleagues (e.g., Murphy, Campione, & Puff, 1977) have pointed out problems in interpretation when clustering measures are correlated with levels of recall.

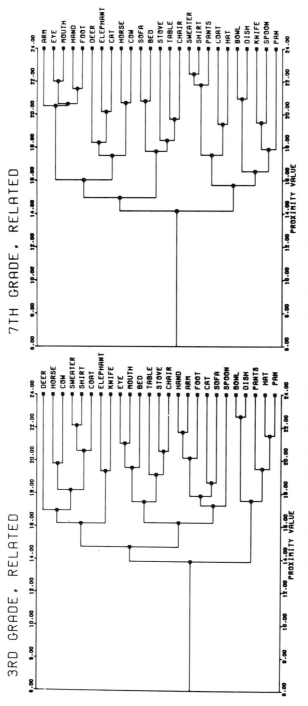

FIGURE 7.1 Hierarchical clustering solutions, based on interitem recall proximities, for third and seventh graders given categorized words. [From Friendly, Ornstein, and Bjorklund (1976).]

For both age groups, the list categories appear to vary in cohesiveness, and this tends to be related to recall differences across categories. For example, for the third-grade subjects, the category **utensils** is least cohesive; the members of this category emerge in four separate clusters, and this is also the least well recalled of the five list categories. For the seventh graders, **utensils** is also the least cohesive category; its members merge together at the lowest proximity value, and this category is also poorly recalled. In contrast, the **body-parts** category is most cohesive and is best recalled by the seventh graders.

Friendly, Ornstein, and Bjorklund demonstrated that the proximity analysis method was responsive to differences in the salience of categorical relations. Bjorklund and Ornstein (1976) constructed lists of to-be-remembered items composed of either highly salient examples from familiar categories or less salient examples of these same categories. Categories on the high-saliency lists consisted of the four items judged most "typical" of their respective categories by independent samples of same-age children; low-saliency items had been rated as less typical examples. The tree structure diagrams for third-grade children who learned these lists are shown in Figure 7.2. For the children learning the high-saliency items, the pattern is similar to that of the third graders in the Ornstein, Hale, and Morgan study discussed previously. All four items from the category **animals** are clustered early, a single pair is found for the category **clothes**, and no cohesive groupings are found for the remaining two categories of **tools** and **food**. For the low-saliency materials, however, only two categorical pairs are found across all categories (eggs–candy; glove–necklace). Further, there is little higher order organizing of any kind found with these items.

When the proximity analysis techniques were applied to lists of unrelated items learned by subjects studied by Ornstein et al. (1977), the resulting structures were in some sense like those obtained with the low-saliency list. Examples of these solutions are shown in Figure 7.3 in which it can be seen that the items clustered together by both the third- and seventh-grade subjects appear to be classified on a number of different dimensions. It should be noted, however, that the two grades do differ in terms of the overall higher order structure represented in the solutions. The third graders' diagram contains two major clusters that do not merge together, whereas that of the seventh graders indicates a greater number of higher order units, with all items merging into a single cluster. Consistent with inspection of this figure, measures of goodness-of-fit suggest that the overall fit of the data to an underlying hierarchical model was better for the older subjects.

These demonstrations suggest that proximity analysis is a useful procedure for identifying changes in the form of children's organizational patterns. The technique is a useful supplement to existing measures of output organization and, as well, can be used in conjunction with comparable assessments of input organization, that is, that organization that is visible in the groupings subjects form as to-be-remembered materials are presented.

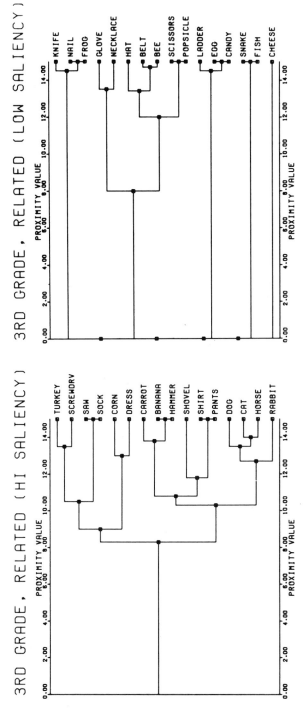

FIGURE 7.2 Hierarchical clustering solutions, based on interitem recall proximities, for third graders given high- and low-saliency category exemplars. [*From Friendly, Ornstein, and Bjorklund (1976).*]

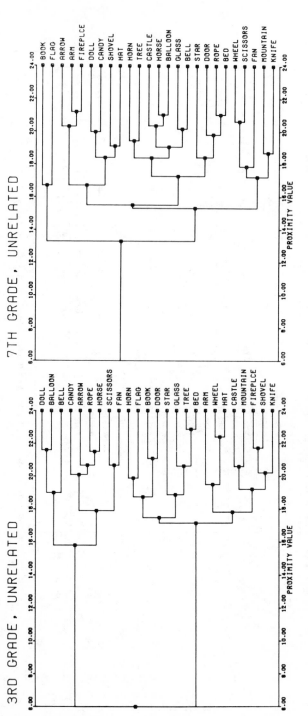

FIGURE 7.3 Hierarchical clustering solutions, based on interitem recall proximities, for third and seventh graders given unrelated words. [From Friendly, Ornstein, and Bjorklund (1976).]

E. Input Organization

All measures of output organization, including the proximity measures just discussed, provide a relatively indirect assessment of the mnemonic processing presumed to be carried out by subjects. In addition, indices of output organization make inferences about organization based upon the same data that are used to measure recall level. This problem can be further aggravated, as Murphy (Chapter 3) has indicated, if the measures of output organization (e.g., clustering) utilized are mathematically dependent upon amount of recall. In contrast to these measures, organizational attempts may be directly observed as items are being presented for study, providing an assessment that is not linked to the recall protocols. For example, Mandler (1967) introduced a procedure in which subjects were asked to sort to-be-remembered items into groups prior to recall. Recall performance was shown to vary as a function of the degree to which the subjects grouped the items. Within a restricted range, recall increased with each additional sorting group formed.

A number of investigators have utilized sort–recall procedures with children of different ages. The general findings are consistent with those seen in clustering and subjective organization paradigms in that young children do not appear to be employing task-appropriate strategies. However, it must be noted that under some conditions (reflecting manipulations of instructions and materials), children readily demonstrate the use of organizational strategies in a sorting task. Sort–recall studies with relatively unrelated items in which children are asked to sort in preparation for subsequent recall will be presented initially. This task is directly analogous to the free-recall studies of subjective organization, except that subjects are asked to sort items actively at the time of presentation. The young child's lack of organizational attempts in these situations will then be contrasted with his deployment of more active strategies in other contexts.

Liberty and Ornstein (1973) demonstrated developmental differences in sorting (i.e., input organization) and recall with fourth graders and college students who were presented with 28 unrelated items for alternating sort–recall trials. Free-sorting subjects were permitted to sort items together on any basis, while other subjects at each age level were provided with specific sorting patterns to "learn." Figure 7.4 presents the free-sorting data for fourth graders and adults in the form of tree structure diagrams, similar to those described previously that were generated from recall data. The axis in this figure indicates the proportion of subjects who sorted various groups of items together. As can be seen, free-sorting fourth graders tended to make random, nonsemantically constrained groupings, whereas the adults tended to make highly organized groups based upon the meanings of the items. Further, fourth graders' sorting patterns were relatively idiosyncratic, whereas the adults were consistent with one another on the specific groupings formed (i.e., the proportion of subjects grouping particular clusters together is higher for adults than for fourth graders).

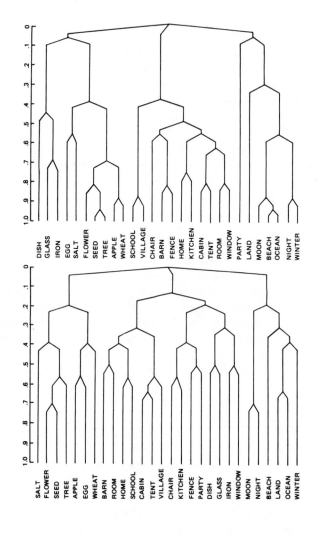

FOURTH GRADERS   ADULTS

FIGURE 7.4 Hierarchical clustering solutions, based on intersubject sorting agreement, for fourth graders and adults given unrelated items. [From Liberty and Ornstein (1973).]

The lower degree of semantic organization present in the children's sorts is reflected in the poorer recall performance of these subjects. Further, those constrained fourth graders who learned sorts generated by adults recalled more items than same-aged subjects who grouped items according to patterns developed by other fourth graders. Similarly, adults required to learn the sorts of free-sorting fourth graders exhibited lower recall scores than those learning the sorts of other adults. These data indicate that the semantic characteristics of the sorts, that is, the input organization, are related to recall success.

Although the fourth graders in the Liberty and Ornstein experiment did not use underlying semantic relationships to form their sorting patterns, they were nonetheless aware of these relationships. In post-task questioning, some fourth graders were asked to group "things that go together." Under these conditions, the children sorted like the adults. That is, their sorts were highly constrained semantically, and subjects tended to be consistent with one another on the placement of items. The postrecall sorts of the adults did not differ from the patterns generated during the recall experiment. These data demonstrate that subjects of both ages were aware of the semantic relationships among the items, but only the older subjects spontaneously used this information to organize the to-be-remembered material during the sort–recall portion of the task. Most importantly, these findings suggest that the fourth graders have not yet learned to make strategic use of the information that they already possess.

These findings were supported by a series of experiments by Bjorklund, Ornstein, and Haig (1977) that further explored the developmental relationship between recall and input organization. In Experiment I, for example, free-sorting third, fifth, and seventh graders' sorting performance with relatively unrelated items was examined and related to recall performance. Subjects' sorting patterns were evaluated as high semantic (obvious semantic basis consistent over trials), low semantic (semantic basis with some variability over trials), orthorgraphic (based on physical features of words), or random (no systematic groupings). The majority of the third graders' sorts were best classified as random (86% of all subjects), whereas the seventh graders' groups were most often semantically (high or low) constrained (61%). Fifth graders were more variable in the kinds of groupings that they made. Recall increased with age and with sorting style such that even though more older children than younger children sorted semantically, third graders who sorted semantically (high or low) recalled more than orthographic and random sorters at any age and, on the average, as well as fifth and seventh graders who sorted by meaning.

All subjects learned adult sorting patterns in a second phase of the experiment. Under these conditions, only the fifth graders tended to increase their recall performance. The third graders were unable to learn the adult sorting patterns in the four trials they were given, and as a result, their recall was not facilitated. Also, seventh graders, already near ceiling in terms of semantic sorting style in the initial free sorting, showed no sorting or recall improvement in the second phase. All subjects were asked to free-sort in a third phase of the experiment, so that transfer could be assessed. Consistent with the fact that only the fifth graders modified their performance as a result of learning adult strategies, only these subjects showed sorting and recall improvement in the transfer task.

These data, as well as those of Liberty and Ornstein (1973), indicate that young children have knowledge of semantic relationships that could be applied strategically in recall, but is not. Such findings parallel those in studies of subjective organization where children often fail to organize unrelated items in their recall output. These results are consistent with Lange's (1978) hypothesis that under typical conditions children do not strategically organize on a conceptual level in recall until the later school years.

F. Conditions under Which Children Organize in Recall

The previously cited literature suggests that children have knowledge of semantic relationships, but that this knowledge often is not reflected in the implementation of organizational strategies. For example, Liberty and Ornstein's (1973) fourth graders could sort as adults did at the conclusion of a recall experiment, but did not do so spontaneously when the task was to sort so that recall would be facilitated. Indeed, the fact that the learning of adult sorts facilitated recall indicates that the children had some knowledge of the basis of those sorting patterns in permanent memory. The same argument could be applied to the fifth graders in the Bjorklund, Ornstein, and Haig (1977) experiment. Similarly, Kobasigawa and Middleton (1972) demonstrated that young children can have explicit knowledge of taxonomic categories but that this does not guarantee that such knowledge will be evidenced in taxonomic clustering.

What are the conditions under which young children can be induced to use organizational information they already possess? Several studies have shown that under certain conditions children as young as 5 years of age can be led to process actively to-be-remembered words according to semantic information available in permanent memory. For example, Bjorklund et al. (1977), in a second experiment, determined that third graders could make use of an organizational strategy when they were explicitly made aware of the semantic relationships among the to-be-remembered items. Following an initial free-sorting period, third graders sorted according to adult-defined groupings and were also told to search for semantic relationships among the items grouped together. Relative to a free-sorting control group, these third graders showed elevated recall. In a third experiment, Bjorklund, Ornstein, and Haig demonstrated that constraining subjects to sort according to adult patterns was not necessary for recall facilitation to occur. Third and fifth graders were permitted to free-sort, but were given explicit instruction in the use of an organizational strategy. The results indicated that under these conditions subjects sorted in a semantically based fashion and that they showed recall improvement relative to a control group. Further, the magnitude of the improvement was equivalent to that obtained by additional constrained sorting groups.

A study by Moely, Olson, Halwes, and Flavell (1969) also used a training procedure to demonstrate that young children could be guided to use information they already possess in permanent memory in the service of memorization. Kindergarteners, and first, third, and fifth graders were shown a list of taxonomically related pictures. At each grade level, subjects in a control condition were told to move the pictures around, whereas those in a naming condition were asked to name the exemplars of each presented category. Finally, subjects in a teaching condition were asked to sort items together that "went together," to name the groups, to count the number of items per group, and to structure their recall according to the groups. Thus, the teaching condition explicitly forced the children to use their knowledge of semantic relations in recall. The kindergarteners and first graders in this condition sorted like the fifth graders, and the clustering scores based upon the sorts for each grade level were equivalent. Recall for these groups was also similar, indicating that the children could sort items into meaning-based groups and that this strategy effectively mediated recall. Kindergarteners in the control and naming conditions did not cluster and recall at the level of the children in the teaching group. However, at the completion of the experimental session, these subjects were asked to sort the items on the basis of meaning. Here, a clustering measure of the sort showed that these kindergarteners grouped as much as the fifth graders, providing further support for the notion that young children possess knowledge of semantic relations but do not spontaneously use it in a memory task.

Other studies (e.g., Worden, 1975; Corsale & Ornstein, 1977) have shown similar effects with more subtle prompting than that used by Moely et al. (1969). For example, in a task similar to that of Liberty and Ornstein's (1973), Worden (1975) simply instructed second and fifth graders and adults to sort a set of unrelated items into groups of things that "go together" and told them that they would have to remember the items. The subjects were not given explicit instructions in organizational grouping, although they had been given an initial period of time to examine all of the items before sorting was begun. The subjects were then told to group items by meaning and to think about why the items went together. When a stable sorting criterion had been reached, the subjects were given a single recall trial. The results indicated that under these conditions of stimulus prefamiliarization and sorting, the children and the adults sorted in a similar fashion. As would be expected, given the establishment of equivalent organizations, there were no differences in recall among the three age groups.

In another study, Lange and Griffith (1977) showed that instructions in semantic grouping can reduce age differences in recall. Lange and Griffith (1977) presented subjects with unrelated items for three free-recall trials, followed by a task in which sorting according to meaning was required. Sorting trials continued until the preschoolers, first, fourth, and seventh graders, and adults tested reached a stable organization (i.e., identical sorting for two trials in a row). Subjects were then given a final recall trial, with performance (both recall and clustering) on this trial being markedly superior to that on the presort recall trials. Although there were still age differences in recall, young children's performance increased enough to diminish the absolute differences among age levels. Thus, the attainment of a stable organizational criterion, as a result of instructions to group meaningfully, can lead to recall facilitation.

G. What Underlies Young Children's Lack of Strategy Usage in Deliberate Memory Tasks?

The preceding studies clearly indicate that when children are led to sort in a sophisticated fashion according to semantic information they already possess, recall facilitation is observed. Under typical stimulus presentation conditions, however, young children do not do this. What is it that they are doing in the context of standard free recall and related experiments? One possibility might be that young children react to the recall context in such a way that they are not even cognizant of the interrelationships existing among the to-be-remembered words.

This question was recently addressed by Bjorklund (1976) in a series of experiments designed to assess the extent to which children recognized and tagged to-be-remembered items as category members. In a first free-recall experiment, kindergarteners and third and sixth graders were presented with two categorized lists (thematic and taxonomic). In one condition, items were presented randomly, but subjects were informed of the categorical nature of the list; in two other conditions, subjects were not so informed, and the items were either blocked by categories or were randomly presented. All subjects were given a single serial presentation of each list, and, prior to recall, they were asked if they noticed any groups of similar items. When the children had finished recalling the items, they were asked either to sort the list into groups of things that were "alike or go together in some way," or were given a category name and asked to choose the corresponding exemplars.

The mean numbers of categories identified prior to recall are shown in Figure 7.5. All subjects noticed more taxonomic than thematic categories.[5] However, the number of categories recognized increased with age, and for the kindergarteners and third graders, the uninformed-blocked and informed-random groups recognized more categories than the uninformed-random subjects. Sixth graders were able to recognize nearly all of the categories regardless of

[5]The finding that even kindergarteners showed greater recognition of the taxonomic categories is particularly interesting, given the classification literature (e.g., Denney, 1972; Inhelder & Piaget, 1964), which would suggest that young children are less sensitive to this type of categorical organization. The issue of the linkage between underlying categorical structures and the use of organization in recall is discussed later.

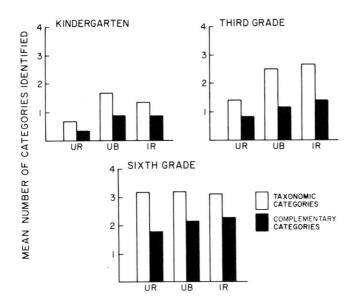

FIGURE 7.5. Mean number of correct identifications of taxonomic and thematic categories for kindergarteners and third and sixth graders prior to recall. Subjects were either uninformed about the categorical nature of the materials and received items in random (UR) or blocked (UB) fashion or were informed of the categorical nature of the lists and received the items in a random pattern (IR). [*From Bjorklund (1976).*]

presentation condition. Thus, it seems that in the context of the recall task, younger children do not recognize the categorical nature of the items. When subjects had finished recalling the items and were asked to sort or to choose the category members, kindergarteners and third graders indicated that they were aware of a greater number of categories than they previously had identified. When asked to sort the items, age differences in category identification were still apparent, but these were eliminated in the situation in which subjects were asked to select exemplars of particular list categories.

To determine whether the kindergarteners' failure to identify categories within the recall task was due to lack of categorical tagging of the items at input, Bjorklund (1976) used a cueing technique in a second experiment. Kindergarten children were presented with a list of 16 pictures, four items from each of four taxonomic categories, and the presence of category labels at input and output was manipulated. If kindergarten children "tag" individual items according to their categories as each item is presented—regardless of whether or not the overall categorical structure of the list is detected—then presentation of category cues at the time of recall should facilitate recall performance (see Tulving & Thomson, 1973). Similarly, presentation of category labels at input but not at output should not alter young children's recall performance if they already spontaneously encode items according to category labels. In this experiment, four groups of subjects were formed by the factorial combination of the cue-at-input and cue-at-output variables. As can be seen in Figure 7.6, the kindergarteners' recall was facilitated when the category labels were presented as retrieval cues, regardless of whether or not the labels had been presented initially. These data are consistent with the view that the young subjects were tagging the to-be-remembered material with categorical information at stimulus input. Bjorklund argued that the failure of kindergarten-aged children to organize recall along categorical dimensions at output spontaneously is due to their failure to link together items of the same category, rather than their failure to encode individual items categorically. Studies of encoding using release-from-proactive-interference (e.g., Cann, Liberty, Shafto, & Ornstein, 1973; Esrov, Hall, & LaFaver, 1974) and recognition (e.g., Hall & Halperin, 1972) paradigms also suggest that children as young as 4 or 5 years of age encode individual items categorically, even, in some conditions, when the categories are abstract, such as Osgood's evaluative classification (Douglas & Corsale, 1977).

The preceding data suggest that even young children possess organizational information, but that this information is not fully utilized when remembering is requested. Indeed, it seems as if these children have not yet learned just what it means to remember, in contrast to older children and adults who behave as if "to organize is to remember" (cf. Ornstein, Trabasso, & Johnson-Laird, 1974, and also Appel et al., 1972). Corsale and Ornstein (1977) investigated some of the conditions under which young children will demonstrate organizational sophistication in the context of the recall task. Their results indicate that third graders perform differently, both in terms of the form of the sorting patterns generated and the levels of recall, depending upon the kinds of instructions that preface the administration of the task.

Corsale and Ornstein (1977) found that third graders, when instructed to

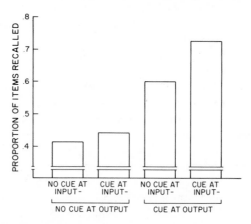

FIGURE 7.6 Recall probability for kindergarteners under various conditions of cues being present at stimulus input and recall output. [From Bjorklund (1976).]

sort relatively unrelated items into groups of things that are similar or alike, formed hierarchically organized groups based on the semantic nature of the items. Further, these children showed enhanced levels of recall, even when recall was unexpected, relative to subjects not instructed to sort the materials by meaning. Indeed, same-aged subjects tended to sort randomly and exhibit low levels of recall when asked to sort in preparation for recall (cf. Bjorklund et al., 1977). Moreover, it does not seem to be the presence of the recall instruction, per se, that inhibits the third graders from using their knowledge of semantic relationships; subjects who were instructed to sort items based on their meaning and who were also informed of a subsequent recall trial, performed almost identically to the third graders who were not expecting a recall test. In contrast, the sorting and recall performance of seventh graders was equivalent regardless of instruction. These findings suggest that older children are aware that an organizational strategy can be appropriately employed to aid recall and engage in such strategies spontaneously. In contrast, third graders use an organizational strategy in recall only when explicitly asked to do so. They do not seem to realize that such a strategy would be a useful mnemonic device.

The experiments discussed here suggest that children may fail to organize in preparation for recall, in part because they do not understand what it means "to remember." However, even though young children may not fully understand the specific task requirements of recall, it is possible that some sets of materials (e.g., highly related items) may elicit organization-like activities. As described previously, Lange (1973, 1978) suggested that young children's clustering in recall may be more a function of the associations among the items themselves than the result of the deliberate use of a memory strategy. Although the use of organization at stimulus input would appear to reflect a deliberate decision by the child, and in this sense be somewhat different from Lange's automatic clustering, it is nonetheless possible that the kinds of materials (i.e., related versus unrelated) used would affect the tendency to utilize these strategies.

Corsale (1978) sought to investigate the joint effects of materials and instructions on children's use of an organizational strategy at input and whether organizational strategies would also be observed at output (i.e., in clustering). In a task similar to that of Corsale and Ornstein (1977), kindergarteners and third graders were asked either to group items that go together or to group in preparation for recall. The materials to be sorted represented taxonomic categories, although the salience of the category exemplars was varied. Half of the subjects received highly salient and associated examples of the categories (e.g., cat, dog, horse, rabbit as examples of **animals),** whereas the others received less salient and low-associated examples (e.g., frog, bees, snake, and elephant, as examples of **animals).**

When presented with the highly salient categorical materials and asked to group things that go together, both third graders and kindergarteners formed taxonomic categories. However, when asked to group so as to facilitate recall, only the third graders tended to sort in this fashion. This tendency of third graders to use a task-appropriate strategy (i.e., forming semantically related groups when not explicitly instructed to do so) contrasts with Corsale and Ornstein's (1977) third graders who did not sort based on meaning when presented with relatively unrelated items under similar instructional conditions. Thus, the kinds of materials used will influence children's spontaneous use of an organizational strategy. This finding is also supported by the data of children sorting the low-salient categorical materials. Again, only the third graders formed taxonomic categories when asked to sort in preparation for recall. It should be noted, however, that even though third graders *in general* tended to form taxonomic categories with the low-salient items, there was more variability in sorting patterns than with the high-salient materials. On the other hand, with both high- and low-salient category exemplars, the kindergarteners were similar to Corsale and Ornstein's (1977) third graders, failing to create semantically based groups in preparation for recall.

These results are consistent with Lange's (1973, 1978) assertion that young children's clustering may be "automatically" determined by the associative structure of the materials, except that the use of an organizational plan at stimulus input suggests that operation of a deliberate mnemonic strategy. Corsale's (1978) sorting data indicate clearly that the use of an organizational strategy at stimulus input can be a function of the nature of the relationships implicit in the materials. Corsale and Ornstein's (1977) third graders recalled more on an incidental test of recall when they sorted on the basis of meaning than when they sorted in preparation for recall. In contrast, the third graders in Corsale's (1978) study tended to sort, recall, (and cluster) similarly under both instructional conditions. However, paralleling Corsale and Ornstein's third graders, and their own sorting data, the kindergarten children in the present study recalled more after instructions to sort for meaning than they did when preparing for recall. Further, Corsale's data dovetail with Lange's (1973, 1978) position in an additional way. Regardless of the type of sorting elicited prior to recall (by means of instructions to sort for recall or to sort for meaning), the associative characteristics of the materials can be shown to influence the level of clustering in recall. Thus, for example, Corsale's (1978) kindergarteners who did not form taxonomic groups even with the highly salient category exemplars (when instructed to sort for recall) exhibited *higher* levels of clustering in recall than did peers who did form taxonomic categories with the low-salient materials (when instructed to sort for meaning). These clustering data suggest that under some conditions a subject's activities at stimulus input are less important in determining clustering than the nature of the materials being committed to memory; in contrast, level of recall in these tasks seems to be influenced primarily by sorting activities.

H. Linkages among Input Organization, Output Organization, and Recall

The Corsale (1978) data indicate several inconsistencies between the use of organization at stimulus input and at output. In contrast to what might have been expected, the organization present at input is not always reflected at output, and vice versa. Under some conditions, Corsale's subjects exhibited relatively high levels of category clustering in recall when they did not initially sort the to-be-remembered items taxonomically. This would seem to be the result of relatively automatic processes reflecting interitem associations (cf. Lange, 1978), but it points up the independence, at least under some conditions, of input and output organization. Similarly, Corsale (1978) demonstrated that the use of taxonomic organization at input did not always lead to taxonomic clustering in recall. Consistent with these findings, Corsale and Ornstein (1977) also failed to detect any relationship between subjects' use of input and output organization with unrelated materials, even among seventh graders. These asymmetries between input and output organization clearly raise many questions of interpretation.

A further complexity is added by the issue of the linkage between these two types of organization and actual recall performance. Consistent with other data (e.g., Bjorklund et al., 1977; Corsale & Ornstein, 1977), Corsale's (1978) findings suggest that recall varies as a function of the degree of structure imposed at stimulus input. Moreover, this relationship between input organization and recall held regardless of the level of output organization present, raising the critical question of whether output organization serves to mediate children's recall performance; similar issues have also been raised in the literature on adult memory (see Puff, 1970; Puff, Murphy, & Ferrara, 1977). Given the findings that recall did not vary as a function of degree of clustering, is it possible that output organization is only incidentally related to actual memory performance? Does output organization contribute anything to recall above and beyond that due to subjects' activities at input? Variations in clustering have often been associated with different degrees of recall, but it seems possible that in some situations, at least, both output organization and recall levels reflect the outcome of other mnemonic processes.

The relationships among input and output organization and actual memory performance would thus appear to be complex, with the interpretation of output organizational phenomena being the most difficult. At a minimum, measures of output organization provide information about the sequence in which items are retrieved from memory, but the processes underlying this organization, and indeed its consequences, seem to vary from context to context. In many situations, this retrieval process reflects the application of a deliberate strategy, whereas in others it seems to be an automatic by-product of semantic knowledge. Further, in some situations, the retrieval sequence is closely related to the subjects' organizational activities at stimulus input, whereas in other contexts, it is independent of input organization. Finally, in some settings, the output organization that is observed seems to be associated with enhanced recall, whereas in other situations it is not.

Currently there are not sufficient data available to resolve these complexities. Little is known, for example, about the conditions in which output organization might facilitate recall beyond that caused by input organization. However, it is possible to speculate that output organization might facilitate recall when the retrieval sequence is coordinated with the subject's encoding activities at stimulus input (cf. Tulving & Thomson, 1973). Output organization might thus be maximally effective when it reflects an organized search of the structures established when the to-be-remembered materials were presented. Preliminary support for this view was seen in a second experiment reported by Corsale (1978). All subjects in this study sorted items prior to recall, but some were also instructed to recall according to the groupings formed initially. The results indicated clear effects of constraining such that under conditions of equivalent sorting, recall was facilitated when subjects were asked to recall according to the input groupings. These data are consistent with the view that facilitation due to clustering might occur when such organization serves as a deliberate coordinated retrieval strategy, but they would also suggest that automatic types of clustering (Lange, 1978) might influence recall if there were a chance coordination with the subjects' encoding activities.

Additional experiments are clearly needed to test these views about the mnemonic consequences of output organization. Similarly, it is necessary to gather data concerning (a) the factors that might lead subjects to coordinate their retrieval patterns with schemes established at stimulus input and (b) the different roles of output organization as an automatic process and as a deliberate strategy. It seems likely that information concerning these important questions can probably be found in studies in which the subjects' knowledge of the relationships among stimulus items is manipulated. For example, although children's attempts at input–output coordination might vary with age, they might also depend to some extent upon the degree to which the to-be-remembered items are clearly structured. Similarly, the automatic uses of output organizational strategies, regardless of whether or not these influence recall level, would appear to rest upon the subjects' knowledge of the organizational structures implicit in the materials.

The issues raised here suggest the important role of the knowledge base in memory performance. In the past decade, research on the development of memory has focused almost entirely on strategy usage and on its relation to recall performance. It is becoming increasingly evident that the knowledge base, both in the sense of the amount of knowledge and in the structure of that knowledge, is important in understanding memory processing (Chi, 1978). This would especially seem to be the case developmentally since the knowledge base undergoes dramatic change during childhood. It thus seems most essential to investigate the role of the underlying knowledge base, its influence on strategy usage and coordination, and its effect on the level of recall.

II. CHANGES IN THE KNOWLEDGE BASE

The literature discussed previously indicates that with increases in age children become more likely to utilize appropriate strategies in the context of memory tasks. It has also been suggested that a subject's permanent memory or knowledge base strongly influences recall performance and the use of mnemonic strategies. However, there is also evidence (e.g., Liberty & Ornstein, 1973; Corsale & Ornstein, 1977) that suggests that children sometimes have organizational information in permanent memory that is not spontaneously employed in the service of memorization. These factors, in combination with the complex relations among input organization, output organization, and recall just discussed, necessitate a detailed examination of the development of the knowledge base.

There are three aspects of knowledge that seem relevant to the study of memory development: general knowledge about particular topics, knowledge about strategy usage and the operation of one's own memory system (i.e., metamemory), and knowledge about semantic relationships among linguistic concepts (i.e., semantic memory). Each of these areas is examined in turn.

A. Generalized Knowledge

Although little is known about the relationship between generalized knowledge about particular topics and memory performance, Chi (1976, 1977, 1978) and Voss and his colleagues (Chiesi, Spilich, & Voss, 1979; Spilich, Vesonder, Chiesi, & Voss, 1979) have begun to explore these issues. For example, Chi (1977) attempted to determine whether developmental differences in memory span were due to differences in knowledge about stimuli, capacity of working memory, or strategy variables. By controlling the familiarity of the stimuli and the degree to which adults were able to use strategies, differences in memory span performance between adults and children were almost completely eliminated. As a result, Chi (1977) concluded that developmental differences in actual capacity of working memory were minimal and that adults' typically higher performance is the result of their greater familiarity with the stimuli and their greater facility with task-appropriate strategies.

In a subsequent study (Chi, 1978), the effects of the knowledge base were probed more deeply. Subjects were required to remember the positions of chess pieces in modified memory-span tasks. Degree of knowledge about the game of chess was manipulated by comparing a group of expert chess players with a group of relatively novice players; however, all subjects had some knowledge of chess. The manipulation of *developmental* interest here was the knowledge variable: The expert players were children and the novice players were adults! Two different tests of memory for the positions of chess pieces were given. In the first, subjects were allowed one trial to reproduce the legitimate arrangements (i.e., possible arrangements given the rules of chess) of chess pieces that had been presented. In the second, subjects were given feedback on errors and they continued with the task until the correct solution was reached.

Chi's (1978) data strongly support the notion that knowledge plays a critical role in memory performance. The children, who in this case were good chess players, remembered the locations of more pieces than did the adult subjects and required significantly fewer trials to arrive at a correct solution on the second task. To demonstrate that these effects were the result of knowledge about chess, all subjects performed memory-span tasks in which the location of digits rather than of chess pieces was probed. Results of this digit-span task were exactly reversed from those of the chess task. That is, developmental trends were obtained, with adults recalling more digits and taking fewer trials to reach perfect recall than did the children.

Voss and his colleagues (Chiesi, Spilich, & Voss, 1979; Spilich, Vesonder, Chiesi, & Voss, 1979) investigated how individuals differing in their knowledge of a particular topic also differ in the manner in which they process this domain-related information. Although adult performance was studied, the implications of the results are relevant to developmental issues of the knowledge base and its influence on mnemonic processing. In this research, groups of subjects differing in their knowledge of the game of baseball were identified. The performance of high-baseball-knowledge (HK) and low-baseball-knowledge (LK) subjects was then compared in terms of the manner in which baseball-related information is processed, stored, and retrieved. These data suggest that although HK and LK subjects do not differ in their awareness of the goal structure of the game, the performance of the HK subjects was superior to that of LK subjects. Specifically, HK subjects were better able to (a) attend to and remember information that was critical vis-à-vis the goals of the game, (b) unitize series of game actions, and (c) monitor action and changes in game "state" in the context of the goal structure. Thus, Voss and his colleagues showed that strategies such as chunking, information monitoring, and selective attention can be influenced by the degree of subjects' knowledge of the content area.

The work of Chiesi, Spilich, and Voss (1979), of Spilich, Vesonder, Chiesi, and Voss (1979), and of Chi (1978) indicates that memory performance is a complex interaction of knowledge about particular topics, about strategies and their implementation, and about particular task requirements. Probably of equal importance is the implication that the use of a mnemonic strategy is not an all-or-none event and may not follow a steady course of development. Rather, usage of a strategy seems highly dependent on task variables and subject variables (e.g., knowledge).

B. Metamemory: Children's Knowledge of Mnemonic Rules

In order for a child to apply his knowledge of semantic relationships in a recall task, he must have stored in permanent memory mnemonic rules of operation. Flavell (1970) uses the term "metamemory" to refer to the development of intelligent monitoring and knowledge of active storage and retrieval skills in memory. Kreutzer et al. (1975) indicate that knowledge of how to operate one's memory system involves information on a number of levels. In addition to being aware of particular strategies, one must be aware of particular task situations, of which strategies best fit the task, and of how one's own memory performance will relate to particular strategies. Flavell and Wellman (1977) formalized the components of metamemorial knowledge in terms of person variables, task variables, and strategy variables. Person variables include such things as knowledge of one's own capabilities and limitations. Task variables concern knowledge of relevant and irrelevant dimensions of a task such as differentiating between related and unrelated materials (relevant) or the color that to-be-remembered items are printed in (usually an irrelevant dimension). Finally, strategy variables concern knowledge of various strategies that might be appropriate in various memory tasks.

To investigate children's perceptions of their own memory capabilities (person variables), Yussen and Levy (1975) asked 4-, 8-, and 20-year-olds to predict how well they would perform on a short-term memory task. Predicted recall significantly differentiated the age groups linearly, with the 4-year-olds predicting the highest recall ability! Actual recall also differentiated the ages linearly, with the adult group recalling the most items. Adults actually recalled the amount of material that they had predicted they could recall, whereas the 4-year-olds fell far short of their predicted performance. Consistent with these data is Chi's (1978) demonstration that ability to predict performance is, in part, a function of knowledge of the stimuli. Using her expert–novice chess player dichotomy described above, Chi divided adults into expert and novice player groups and had them predict the number of chess piece positions they could recall when a legitimate chess configuration was used and when the same pieces were arranged randomly. Novices predicted the same number for random and legitimate chess configurations while experts predicted greater recall with the legitimate arrangement. In terms of actual recall, novices recalled the locations of more pieces from the legitimate than from the random configuration, although not as many as did the experts. The experts' recall paralleled their predictions. Thus, in this case, the experts were more accurate than novices in predicting their recall. Perhaps the developmental differences that have been observed in recall prediction are also in part due to differences in knowledge base. It may be that "knowledge variables" underlie to some extent the operation of Flavell and Wellman's person variables.

In terms of task variables, Kreutzer et al. (1975) showed that kindergarteners and first graders are not as aware as older children that related items may be easier to remember that unrelated ones, that interpolated events may interfere with retrieval, and that a series of pictures making a story may be easier to remember than an equal number of unrelated pictures. However, even these young children are aware that spacing of pictures (close versus far spacing) should not affect recall. In a related study, Tenney (1975) asked kindergarteners and third and sixth graders to generate lists that would be easy to remember. Older subjects generated to-be-remembered lists that contained an overall explicit organizational scheme (often taxonomic), whereas younger subjects tended to free associate from one item to another in the generation of lists. These studies seem to indicate that young children are not aware of the task demands in recall.

The study of Kreutzer et al. (1975) provides normative data on strategy variables by detailing what children of different age groups know about mnemonic techiques and the appropriateness of various strategies for different tasks. Consistent with the recall literature, older children are more strategically planful and have a variety of internal strategies available, whereas younger children may rely on external sources such as reminders from others. It seems that older children are aware of task requirements and possess rules in the knowledge base concerning the operation of a number of strategies. Younger children, although capable of efficient strategies (e.g., Corsale & Ornstein, 1977), may lack rules of operation, resulting in a failure to employ spontaneously such strategies in the recall task. However, it is important to add that children's use of strategies and one's assessment of subjects' knowledge of strategies may vary depending upon task conditions. Although young children seem to lack knowledge of study strategies in formal memorization situations, they may show evidence of their abilities in less structured, gamelike settings. Wellman, Ritter, and Flavell (1975) engaged preschoolers in a game, the object of which was to remember under which teacup a stimulus was hidden. Subjects were asked to "remember where X is" or "wait here with X" while the experimenter left the room for 45 seconds. "Remember" subjects performed better than "wait" subjects, indicating that under appropriate task conditions (i.e., games), even preschoolers know something about how to remember.

Although much work has been done on metamemory and its development, an issue of critical concern is how children's metamemory knowledge relates to their ability to apply this knowledge. That is, how does metamemory relate to actual performance? This would seem to be a central question because, as illustrated above, children often possess a great deal of knowledge that they do not employ spontaneously. To explore this issue, Salatas and Flavell (1976) compared performance on a recall task in which the subject was free to categorize a set of taxonomic items with the subject's performance on a series of metamemory questions involving the use of organization in memory. Although no relation was found between subjects' categorization behavior and metamemory performance, or between recall and metamemory performance, for subjects instructed to "look" at the items (cf. Appel et al., 1972), such relationships were found in the "remember" condition. It seems that just having been engaged in a recall task makes children aware of the usefulness of an organizational strategy.

Although the linkage between metamemory knowledge and recall performance was found under certain conditions by Salatas and Flavell (1976), other investigators have found little or no* correlation between metamemory and recall. Flavell and Wellman (1977) caution that this relationship is complex and variable because it depends not only on the subject's metamemorial knowledge, but also on the situation at hand and on the number of possible strategies available. In addition, the child may not elect to use what he knows about memory in a recall task for motivational or other reasons. Finally, as strategies become overlearned and "automatic" in later development, the correlation between knowledge of strategy usage and recall performance may be attenuated. Much more research is needed in the area of metamemory and its relationship to recall performance.

C. Semantic Memory

In the last 10 years, a large body of findings has emerged concerning the structure of adult semantic memory. Reaction time tasks, sorting paradigms, judgment procedures, and word-association tasks (e.g., Collins & Quillian, 1969, 1972; Miller, 1969; Fillenbaum & Rapoport, 1971; Rumelhart, Lindsay, & Norman, 1972; Smith, Schoben, & Rips, 1974; Rosch, 1973) have been employed in a variety of ways in an attempt to map the structure of semantic memory. These varied approaches have resulted in a proliferation of models of different types (e.g., network models, set-theoretic models) that are thought to be useful in terms of exploring the structure of the permanent memory system (see E. E. Smith, 1978, for an overview). Taken together, these models represent an important research direction, but they have serious limitations in terms of their usefulness as descriptions of both adult semantic memory and the growing knowledge base of children (see Bransford, Nitsch, & Franks, 1977; Brown, 1979; Naus & Halasz, 1979; Ornstein & Corsale, 1979). On the whole, it is a rather static view of semantic memory that is described by the various models, with no real treatment of how new information becomes integrated within the existing knowledge structures or of how these structures are modified by experience. These are important concerns for an understanding of the mature' cognitive system, and they are *critical* for an assessment of the growth of this system. Thus, the models of adult semantic memory do not provide guides for developmental analysis.[6]

Paralleling the emergence of interest in models of semantic memory has been a growing concern with issues of children's semantic development. Clark (e.g., 1973) and Nelson (e.g., 1974a), for example, have provided important leads concerning the acquisition of individual verbal labels and their relationships to underlying preverbal concepts. Clark (1973) has argued that the early items in children's lexicons are defined in terms of a relatively small number of semantic features and that semantic growth involves the acquisition of more complete sets of such features. Nelson (1974a) has called attention to the fact that in many cases children already possess preverbal concepts onto which linguistic terms must be mapped. Although this early research has focused on the development of individual verbal concepts, it is currently leading to more in-depth explorations of the structural interconnections among such concepts. Several recent papers introduced by M. D. Smith (1978) deal with these questions of semantic development.

One source of data for an investigation of the interconnections among young children's verbal concepts is in samples of spontaneous speech, particularly situations in which errors in usage (according to adult standards) occur. For example, Nelson, Rescorla, Gruendel, and Benedict (1978) analyzed one class of these errors, namely, overextension data (e.g., the child's application of the label "dog" to other four-legged animals in addition to dogs). These investigators argue that the occurrence of overextension does not always imply that a child is making mistakes; for example, a child may recognize that a cow is not like the dog with which he is familiar, but that it shares some common properties. Lacking the correct label, the child uses one that has been correctly applied in the past to similar concepts, in effect using the label to categorize the environment. In support of this hypothesis, Nelson et al. (1978) indicate that the linquistic label that is "incorrectly" applied is usually related conceptually to the correct label. In addition, they (see also Anglin, 1978) argue that the discrepancy between children's production (i.e., labeling) and comprehension (i.e., ability to confirm or deny exemplars as category members) indicates that very young children have some rudimentary knowledge of category and similarity relationships.

This stress on early categorization is also seen in Bowerman's (1978) report of the substitution errors of 2- and 3-year-old children. These data indicate that children often make errors in which a contextually correct word is replaced by one that is semantically similar, even under conditions in which both words had previously been used correctly. Bowerman's findings are not examples of overextensions, but they do suggest semantic confusion, implying

[6]Of course, developmental findings can be interpreted within the context of these models. Thus, Clark's (e.g., 1973) theory of lexical growth in terms of the acquisition of semantic features can be related to feature–list theories of semantic memory. The important point, however, is that extant models of semantic memory are not sensitive to the essential developmental issues.

the beginnings of semantic organization. Her hypothesis is that errors of semantic substitution will not occur before a child has linked the words together in semantic memory. ·

The importance of the findings of Nelson et al. (1978) and Bowerman (1978) lies in the fact that they provide insights into the origins of semantic memory. These demonstrations of early semantic organization tie in nicely with those carried out with older children in which some interesting trends in the structure of children's categories have been recorded. One line of research with older children (e.g., Rosch, 1973; Jacobowitz, 1974) uses judgment tasks in order to assess the relationships among stored concepts in children's category structures. A second set of studies explores age-related changes in the criteria that children use in defining categories (e.g., McCauley, Weil, & Sperber, 1976) and whether these criteria affect recall performance (e.g., Denney & Ziobrowski, 1972; Worden, 1976).

In assessing the development of category structures, preschoolers and school-age children are usually asked to select, name, or respond to questions concerning examples of various taxonomic categories. The available evidence suggests that some category instances are commonly judged to be "better" examples of the categories in question than are other examples. These "good" examples of categories have been termed "central' or "core" category members (Rosch, 1973; Saltz, Soller, & Sigel, 1972), in contrast to the peripheral or noncore category members. As an example, a "lion" is a core member of an animal category, whereas a "fly" is a peripheral instance of this category. Age changes in the clustering and recall of category instances such as these, which differ in degree of salience, have been described previously in the work of Friendly, Ornstein, and Bjorklund (1976) and Corsale (1978).

Rosch (1973) has shown that children make more errors than adults in judging whether peripheral (i.e., noncore) exemplars are members of a category. These findings are consistent with those of Saltz et al. (1972) and of Anglin (1977) in that children were found to be aware of "core" items as being category members, but were less sure of the boundaries that differentiate categories. Evidence from a number of researchers is consistent with this conclusion, although as Nelson (1974b) and Bjorklund and Ornstein (1976) indicate, categories develop at different rates. For example, these investigators found no developmental changes in the naming or identification of instances of the **animal** category, whereas there were age-related changes in the use of **tools, furniture,** and other categories.

The preceding findings suggest some of the ways in which semantic memory changes with age. These approaches can be usefully supplemented by psychometric analyses of judgmental data. Preliminary steps in this direction have been taken by Jacobowitz (1974), who has used hierarchical clustering and multidimensional scaling techniques to assess qualitatively children's categories. For example, Jacobowitz presented children and adults with names of body parts and asked them to judge the degree of similarity among items. Using multidimensional scaling procedures (see, e.g., Carroll & Chang, 1970; Young, 1974), Jacobowitz found that children's representations of a "body-parts" category differed from and were more variable than those of adults. The scaling solutions of adults showed more systematic internal organization linking individual category members than did those of the children. Jacobowitz's study indicates that scaling procedures can be an effective tool for the study of age changes in the internal lexicon.

An alternative approach to the study of children's category structures has been used by McCauley et al. (1976). These investigators attempted to demonstrate the criteria (associative and/or categorical relatedness) children used in defining categories. A list of picture pairs was constructed in which the second picture was related to the first in one of four ways—the four possibilities resulting from the factorial combination of high–low associative relatedness and high–low categorical relatedness. Children were shown the pictures in each pair, one at a time. Latency to name the second picture was measured on the assumption that pairs considered strongly related by the subject (either by associative or categorical criteria) would be named faster because the category would have already been accessed or primed in permanent memory by the naming of the first picture in the pair. McCauley et al. (1976) found no differences at the kindergarten and second-grade levels in latency to name pictures that varied in degree of associative relatedness: All children named high associates faster than low associates, indicating that associative relationships represent an important aspect of children's semantic memory. However, when pictures differed along the categorical dimension, only the second graders differentiated between high and low category-related pictures, indicating that, for kindergarteners, categorical relatedness is a less salient dimension.

The data of Rosch (1973), Jacobowitz (1974), and McCauley et al. (1976) suggest interesting age changes in the categorical structure of semantic memory. These findings relate nicely to word association (e.g., Brown & Berko, 1960) and classification (e.g., Denney, 1972; Inhelder & Piaget, 1964) studies, indicating developmental changes in classification style. Although the literature is not completely consistent, with increases in age there are greater tendencies for children to group according to taxonomic principles. Given these trends, it is important to determine the extent to which the changing cognitive structures affect the use of organization in recall. A strong position (e.g., Piaget & Inhelder, 1973) would hold that the memorization performance of children would be seriously influenced by the category structures in semantic memory. Impairment of recall performance would be predicted in those situations in which the organization present in the to-be-remembered materials did not correspond to that in permanent memory.

An initial exploration of the relationship between internal structure and recall was reported by Denney and Ziobrowski (1972). Drawing upon the literature suggesting age changes in style of classification, Denney and Ziobrowski predicted that young children would show recall and clustering facilitation when presented with functional or "complementary" categories (e.g., *pipe, tobacco*), as opposed to taxonomic or "similarity" categories (e.g., *ruler, king*). In contrast, it was felt that adults would demonstrate the reverse pattern. Although the rationale underlying this study was interesting, the data provide only mixed support for these predictions. In fact, the first graders showed greater clustering on the complementary list than they did on the similarity list, and adults did the opposite. However, Denney and Ziobrowski (1972) reported that the children showed greater clustering than did the adults with the complementary materials and that the adults were superior with the similarity list. Close inspection of the data, however, suggests that the differences between the first graders and adults on the complementary list was slight and that the levels of clustering for both age groups probably did not differ from chance.[7] In summary, Denney and Ziobrowski's results provide only partial support for the linkage between underlying semantic structures and organization in recall.

In an additional investigation of this linkage, Worden (1976) asked second and fifth graders to sort items that could be classified along either taxonomic or thematic dimensions. Children were required to classify according to one or the other dimension or were permitted to free-sort in any desired fashion. Although free-sorting second graders showed a greater tendency to form thematic (as opposed to taxonomic) groupings than did fifth graders, the interaction between grade level and type of categories formed did not reach significance. Similarly, second graders constrained to sort thematically tended to recall more than second graders who sorted taxonomically. However, this trend was also obtained for fifth graders, and the critical interaction between grade level and sorting conditions was thus not significant. Consequently, Worden's findings are not definitive in regard to the role of underlying structure in recall.

Although different methods were used in the two studies, neither Denney and Ziobrowski (1972) nor Worden (1976) was able to provide strong support for the view that there are qualitative developmental changes in the use of organizational criteria in recall. These data imply the need for a more detailed specification of the postulated linkage between conceptual structure and recall performance. It is clear that the use of taxonomic versus nontaxonomic organizing principles is not an all-or-none process and that the difference between adults and children may be one of preference for rather than knowledge of particular category structures. Accordingly, models of the memory system and its development need to take into account the multiple criteria that are used to define concepts in semantic memory and developmental changes in the

---

[7]Denney and Ziobrowski (1972) reported a significant interaction between age and list type. However, the critical tests of age differences within the two lists (complementary versus similarity) were not reported. When these tests are carried out (using the presented means and standard deviations), there is no difference between the two age groups in terms of clustering with the complementary materials. The difference between the groups—in favor of the adults—with the similarity list was significant.

probability that particular criteria will dominate in the context of classification and recall tasks.

III. SUMMARY

The present chapter has been devoted to an overview of age-related improvements in recall performance and developmental changes in the utilization of mnemonic strategies. One set of strategies, organizational techniques, was explored in depth. Developmental changes in organizational attempts at stimulus input as well as the organization evident in subjects' recall, were viewed as critical to an understanding of children's memory. It was noted that both input and output organization follow a developmental course, but that these techniques were not always coordinated with each other. Age-related changes in recall were in general related to the use of organizational strategies, although the linkage between organization and recall seems stronger in the case of input organization. Further, children's spontaneous strategy utilization often lags behind their ability to execute such techniques. Indeed, it appears that young children frequently have knowledge available in permanent memory that could be used in the service of memorization, but, under typical recall conditions, this information is not strategically applied.

Age changes in memory performance were shown to vary considerably as a function of the task set for the subjects. Variations in instructions (e.g., to recall, to organize) have a profound influence on children's spontaneous deployment of strategies and subsequent recall performance. Similarly, the characteristics of the materials that are presented can significantly affect recall. These demonstrations of mnemonic situational specificity call attention to the critical relationship between a subject's underlying knowledge base and his performance in the context of a recall task. In some situations, information in the knowledge base influences memory performance by leading children to adopt mnemonic strategies that they might not otherwise use. Thus, for example, Corsale (1978) has shown that third graders engage in sophisticated input processing when given strongly salient category exemplars, whereas their performance with less structured materials seems nonstrategic. In other situations, information available in the knowledge base influences recall performance in a seemingly automatic fashion. Thus, for example, Lange (1978) has called attention to the fact that young children's category clustering may not represent the deployment of a mnemonic strategy, but rather may be a by-product of strong interitem associations.

The available data suggest that it is necessary to examine age changes in mnemonic processing in parallel with corresponding changes in the knowledge base. The structure of various aspects of children's knowledge (e.g., semantic knowledge, knowledge about specific topics, knowledge of strategies and their implementation) needs to be specified, and the linkages to mnemonic processing and performance must be articulated. Understanding the operation of organizational variables in children's memory depends heavily upon our ability to relate information that children have available in the knowledge base to their use of deliberate strategies.

ACKNOWLEDGEMENTS

Preparation of this chapter was supported in part by grant HD 08459 from the United States Public Health Service. Much appreciation is extended to David F. Bjorklund for his helpful comments on an earlier draft of this chapter.

REFERENCES

Anglin, J. M. *Word, object, and conceptual development.* New York: Norton, 1977.

Anglin, J. M. From reference to meaning. *Child Development,* 1978, *49,* 969–976.

Appel, L. F., Cooper, R. G., McCarrell, N., Sims-Knight, J., Yussen, S. R., & Flavell, J. H. The development of the distinction between perceiving and memorizing. *Child Development,* 1972, *43,* 1365–1381.

Atkinson, R. D., & Shiffrin, R. M. Human memory: A proposed system and its control processes. In K. W. Spence & J. T. Spence (Eds.), *The psychology of learning and motivation* (Vol 2). New York: Academic Press, 1968.

Bjorklund, D. F. Children's identification and encoding of category information for recall. Unpublished doctoral dissertation, University of North Carolina at Chapel Hill, 1976.

Bjorklund, D. F., & Ornstein, P. A. The development of taxonomic concepts: The effects of list saliency on recall. Unpublished manuscript, University of North Carolina at Chapel Hill, 1976.

Bjorklund, D. F., Ornstein, P. A., & Haig, J. R. Developmental differences in organization and recall: Training in the use of organizational techniques. *Developmental Psychology,* 1977, *13,* 175–183.

Bousfield, W. A. The occurrence of clustering in the recall of randomly arranged associates. *Journal of General Psychology,* 1953, *49,* 229–240.

Bousfield, A. K., & Bousfield, W. A. Measurement of clustering and of sequential constancies in repeated free recall. *Psychological Reports,* 1966, *19,* 935–942.

Bousfield, W. A., Esterson, J., & Whitmarsh, G. A. A study of developmental changes in conceptual and perceptual associative clustering. *Journal of Genetic Psychology,* 1958, *92,* 95–102.

Bower, G. H. Organizational factors in memory. *Cognitive Psychology,* 1970, *1,* 18–46.

Bowerman, M. Systematizing semantic knowledge: Changes over time in the child's organization of word meaning. *Child Development,* 1978, *49,* 977–987.

Bransford, J. D., Nitsch, K. E., & Franks, J. J. Schooling and the facilitation of knowing. In R. C. Anderson, R. J. Spiro, & W. E. Montague (Eds.), *Schooling and the acquisition of knowledge.* Hillsdale, N.J.: Lawrence Erlbaum Associates, 1977.

Brown, A. L. The development of memory: Knowing, knowing about knowing, knowing how to know. In H. W. Reese (Ed.), *Advances in child development and behavior* (Vol. 10). New York: Academic Press, 1975.

Brown, A. L. Theories of memory and the problems of development: Activity, growth, and knowledge. In F. I. M. Craik & L. Cermak (Eds.), *Levels of processing and memory.* Hillsdale, N.J.: Lawrence Erlbaum Associates, 1979.

Brown, R., & Berko, J. Word association and the acquisition of grammar. *Child Development,* 1960, *31,* 1–14.

Cann, L. F., Liberty, C., Shafto, M., & Ornstein, P. A. Release from proactive interference with young children. *Developmental Psychology*, 1973, *8*, 396.

Carroll, J. D., & Chang, J. J. Analysis of individual differences in multidimensional scaling via an *N*-way generalization of 'Eckart-Young' decomposition. *Psychometrika*, 1970, *35*, 238–319.

Chi, M. T. H. Short-term memory limitations in children: Capacity or processing deficits? *Memory and Cognition*, 1976, *4*, 559–572.

Chi, M. T. H. Age differences in memory span. *Journal of Experimental Child Psychology*, 1977, *23*, 266–281.

Chi, M. T. H. Knowledge structure and memory development. In R. Siegler (Ed.), *Children's thinking: What develops?* Hillsdale, N.J.: Lawrence Erlbaum Associates, 1978.

Chiesi, H. L., Spilich, G. J., & Voss, J. F. Acquisition of domain-related information in relation to high and low domain knowledge. *Journal of Verbal Learning and Verbal Behavior*, 1979, *18*, 257–273.

Clark, E. V. What's in a word? On the child's acquisition of semantics in his first language. In T. E. Moore (Ed.), *Cognitive development and the acquisition of language*. New York: Academic Press, 1973.

Cole, M., Frankel, F., & Sharp, D. Development of free recall in children. *Developmental Psychology*, 1971, *4*, 109–123.

Collins, A. M., & Quillian, M. R. Retrieval time from semantic memory. *Journal of Verbal Learning and Verbal Behavior*, 1969, *8*, 240–248.

Collins, A. M., & Quillian, M. R. How to make a language user. In E. Tulving & W. Donaldson (Eds.), *Organization of memory*. New York: Academic Press, 1972.

Corsale, K., & Ornstein, P. A. *Developmental changes in the use of semantic information for recall.* Paper presented at the meetings of the Psychonomic Society, Washington, D. C., November, 1977.

Corsale, K. Factors affecting children's use of organization in recall. Unpublished doctoral dissertation, University of North Carolina at Chapel Hill, 1978.

Craik, F. I. M., & Lockhart, R. S. Levels of processing: A framework for memory research. *Journal of Verbal Learning and Verbal Behavior*, 1972, *11*, 671–684.

Denney, N. W. A developmental study of free classification in children. *Child Development*, 1972, *43*, 221–232.

Denney, N. W., & Ziobrowski, M. Developmental changes in clustering critiera. *Journal of Experimental Child Psychology*, 1972, *13*, 275–282.

Douglas, J. D., & Corsale, K. The effects of mode and rate of presentation on evaluative encoding in children's memory. *Child Development*, 1977, *48*, 46–50.

Esrov, L. V., Hall, J. W., & LaFaver, D. K. Preschoolers' conceptual and acoustic encoding as evidenced by release from PI. *Bulletin of the Psychonomic Society*, 1974, *4*, 89–90.

Fillenbaum, S., & Rapoport, A. *Structures in the subjective lexicon*. New York: Academic Press, 1971.

Flavell, J. H. Developmental studies of mediated memory. In H. W. Reese & L. P. Lipsitt, (Eds.), *Advances in child development and behavior* (Vol. 5). New York: Academic Press, 1970.

Flavell, J. H., & Wellman, H. M. Metamemory. In R. V. Kail & J. W. Hagen (Eds.), *Perspectives on the development of memory and cognition*. Hillsdale, N.J.: Lawrence Erlbaum Associates, 1977.

Friendly, M. L., Ornstein, P. A., & Bjorklund, D. F. *Organizational structure in children's free recall.* Paper presented at the meetings of the Psychonomic Society, St. Louis, November, 1976.

Friendly, M. L. In search of the M-gram: The structure of organization in free recall. *Cognitive Psychology*, 1977, *9*, 188–249.

Furth, H. G., & Milgram, N. A. Labeling and grouping effects in the recall of pictures by children. *Child Development*, 1973, *44*, 511–518.

Hagen, J. W., & Hale, G. W. The development of attention in children. In A. D. Pick (Ed.), *Minnesota symposia on child psychology* (Vol. 7). Minneapolis: University of Minnesota Press, 1973.

Hagen, J. W., Jongeward, R. H., & Kail, R. V. Cognitive perspectives on the development of memory. In H. W. Reese (Ed.), *Advances in child development and behavior* (Vol. 10). New York: Academic Press, 1975.

Hall, J. W., & Halperin, M. S. The development of memory encoding processes in young children. *Developmental Psychology,* 1972, *6,* 181.

Haynes, C. R., & Kulhavy, R. M. Conservation level and category clustering. *Developmental Psychology,* 1976, *12,* 179–184.

Inhelder, B. & Piaget, J. *The early growth of logic in the child.* New York: Norton, 1964.

Istomina, Z. M. The development of voluntary memory in preschool-age children. *Soviet Psychology,* 1975, *13,* 5–64 (originally published, 1948).

Jacobowitz, D. The acquisition of semantic structures. Unpublished manuscript, University of North Carolina at Chapel Hill, 1974.

Johnson, S. C. Hierarchical clustering schemes. *Psychometrika,* 1967, *32,* 241–254.

Kail, R. V., & Hagen, J. W. (Eds.), *Perspectives on the development of memory and cognition.* Hillsdale, N.J.: Lawrence Erlbaum Associates, 1977.

Kobasigawa, A., & Middleton, D. B. Free recall of categorized items by children at three grade levels. *Child Development,* 1972, *43,* 1067–1072.

Kokobun, O. The subjective organization in free recall learning by school children. *Tohoku Psychological Folia,* 1973, *32,* 12–16.

Kreutzer, M. A., Leonard, C., & Flavell, J. H. An interview study of children's knowledge about memory. *Monographs of the Society for Research in Child Development,* 1975, *40,* Serial Number 159.

Lange, G. The development of conceptual and rote recall skills among school-age children. *Journal of Experimental Child Psychology,* 1973, *15,* 394–407.

Lange, G. Organization-related processes in children's recall. In P. A. Ornstein (Ed.), *Memory development in children.* Hillsdale, N.J.: Lawrence Erlbaum Associates, 1978.

Lange, G., & Griffith, S. B. The locus of organization failures in children's recall. *Child Development,* 1977, *48,* 1498–1502.

Laurence, M. W. Age differences in performance and subjective organization in the free-recall learning of pictorial material. *Canadian Journal of Psychology,* 1966, *20,* 388–399.

Liberty, C., & Ornstein, P. A. Age differences in organization and recall: The effects of training in categorization. *Journal of Experimental Child Psychology,* 1973, *15,* 169–186.

Mandler, G. Organization and memory. In K. W. Spence & J. T. Spence (Eds.), *The psychology of learning and motivation* (Vol. 1). New York: Academic Press, 1967.

McCauley, C., Weil, C. M., & Sperber, R. D. The development of memory structure as reflected by semantic-priming effects. *Journal of Experimental Child Psychology,* 1976, *22,* 511–518.

Miller, G. A. A psychological method to investigate verbal concepts. *Journal of Mathematical Psychology,* 1969, *6,* 169–191.

Moely, B. E. Organizational factors in the development of memory. In R. V. Kail & J. W. Hagen, (Eds.), *Perspectives on the development of memory and cognition.* Hillsdale, N.J.: Lawrence Erlbaum Associates, 1977.

Moely, B. E., Olson, F. A., Halwes, T. G., & Flavell, J. H. Production deficiency in young children's clustered recall. *Developmental Psychology,* 1969, *1,* 26–34.

Murphy, M. D., Campione, J. C., & Puff, C. R. *Measures of clustering in free recall.* Paper presented at the meetings of the Society for Research in Child Development, New Orleans, March, 1977.

Murphy, M. D., Sanders, R. E., & Puff, C. R. The measurement of subjective organization: A reply to Sternberg and Tulving. Unpublished manuscript, University of Akron, 1978.

Myers, N. A., & Perlmutter, M. Memory in the years from two to five. In P. A. Ornstein, (Ed.), *Memory development in children.* Hillsdale, N.J.: Lawrence Erlbaum Associates, 1978.

Naus, M. J., & Halasz, F. Developmental perspectives on cognitive processing and semantic memory structure. In F. I. M. Craik & L. Cermak (Eds.), *Levels of processing and memory.* Hillsdale, N.J.: Lawrence Erlbaum Associates, 1979.

Naus, M. J., Ornstein, P. A., & Hoving, K. L. Developmental implications of multi-store and depth of processing models of memory. In P. A. Ornstein (Ed.), *Memory development in children.* Hillsdale, N.J.: Lawrence Erlbaum Associates, 1978.

Nelson, K. The organization of free recall by young children. *Journal of Experimental Child Psychology,* 1969, *8,* 284–295.

Nelson, K. Concept, word, and sentence: Interrelations in acquisition and development. *Psychological Review*, 1974a, *81*, 267–285.

Nelson, K. Variation in children's concepts by age and category. *Child Development*, 1974b, *45*, 557–584.

Nelson, K., & Brown, A. L. The semantic-episodic distinction in memory development. In P. A. Ornstein (Ed.), *Memory development in children*. Hillsdale, N.J.: Lawrence Erlbaum Associates, 1978.

Nelson, K., Rescorla, L., Gruendel, J., & Benedict, H. Early lexicons: What do they mean? *Child Development*, 1978, *49*, 960–968.

Ornstein, P. A. (Ed.), *Memory development in children*. Hillsdale, N.J.: Lawrence Erlbaum Associates, 1978.

Ornstein, P. A., & Corsale, K. Process and structure in children's memory. In G. Whitehurst & B. Zimmerman (Eds.), *The functions of language and cognition*. New York: Academic Press, 1979.

Ornstein, P. A., Hale, G. A., & Morgan, J. S. Developmental differences in recall and output organization. *Bulletin of the Psychonomic Society*, 1977, *9*, 29–32.

Ornstein, P. A., & Naus, M. J. Rehearsal processes in children's memory. In P. A. Ornstein (Ed.), *Memory development in children*. Hillsdale, N.J.: Lawrence Erlbaum Associates, 1978.

Ornstein, P. A., Naus, M. J., & Liberty, C. Rehearsal and organization processes in children's memory. *Child Development*, 1975, *26*, 818–830.

Ornstein, P. A., Naus, M. J., & Stone, B. P. Rehearsal training and developmental differences in memory. *Developmental Psychology*, 1977, *13*, 15–24.

Ornstein, P. A., Trabasso, T., & Johnson-Laird, P. N. To organize is to remember: The effect of instructions to organize and to recall. *Journal of Experimental Psychology*, 1974, *103*, 1014–1018.

Pellegrino, J. W. A general measure of organization in free recall for variable unit size and internal sequential consistency. *Behavioral Research Methods and Instrumentation*, 1971, *3*, 241–246.

Perlmutter, M., & Lange, G. A developmental analysis of recall-recognition distinctions. In P. A. Ornstein (Ed.), *Memory development in children*. Hillsdale, N.J.: Lawrence Erlbaum Associates, 1978.

Piaget, J., & Inhelder, B. *Memory and intelligence*. New York: Basic Books, 1973.

Puff, C. R. Role of clustering in free recall. *Journal of Experimental Psychology*, 1970, *86*, 384–386.

Puff, C. R., Murphy, M. D., & Ferrara, R. A. Further evidence about the role of clustering in free recall. *Journal of Experimental Psychology: Human Learning and Memory*, 1977, *3*, 742–753.

Rosch, E. H. On the internal structure of perceptual and semantic categories. In T. E. Moore (Ed.), *Cognitive development and the acquisition of language*. New York: Academic Press, 1973.

Rosner, S. R. The effects of rehearsal and chunking instructions on children's multi-trial free recall. *Journal of Experimental Child Psychology*, 1971, *11*, 93–105.

Rossi, E. L., & Rossi, S. I. Concept utilization, serial order and recall in nursery school children. *Child Development*, 1965, *36*, 771–778.

Rossi, E. L., & Wittrock, M. C. Developmental shifts in verbal recall between mental ages two and five. *Child Development*, 1971, *42*, 333–338.

Rumelhart, D. E., Lindsay, P. H., & Norman, D. A. A process model for long-term memory. In E. Tulving & W. Donaldson (Eds.), *Organization of memory*. New York: Academic Press, 1972.

Salatas, H., & Flavell, J. H. Retrieval of recently learned information: Development of strategies and control skills. *Child Development*, 1976, *47*, 941–948.

Saltz, E., Soller, E., & Sigel, I. E. The development of natural language concepts. *Child Development*, 1972, *43*, 1191 - 1202.

Shapiro, S. I., & Moely, B. E. Free recall, subjective organization, and learning-to-learn at three age levels. *Psychonomic Science*, 1971, *23*, 189 - 191.

Smith, E. E. Theories of semantic memory. In W. K. Estes (Ed.), *Handbook of learning and cognitive processes* (Vol. 6). Hillsdale, N.J.: Lawrence Erlbaum Associates, 1978.

Smith, E. E., Shoben, E. J., & Rips, L. J. Structure and process in semantic memory: A featural model for semantic decisions. *Psychological Review*, 1974, *81*, 214–241.

Smith, M. D. The acquisition of word meaning: An introduction. *Child Development*, 1978, *49*, 950–952.

Spilich, G. J., Vesonder, G. T., Chiesi, H. L., & Voss, J. F. Text processing of domain-related information for individuals with high and low domain knowledge. *Journal of Verbal Learning and Verbal Behavior*, 1979, *18*, 275–290.

Sternberg, R. J., & Tulving, E. The measurement of subjective organization in free recall. *Psychological Bulletin*, 1977, *84*, 539–556.

Tenney, Y. J. The child's conception of organization and recall. *Journal of Experimental Child Psychology*, 1975, *19*, 100–114.

Tulving, E. Subjective organization in free recall of "unrelated" words. *Psychological Review*, 1962, *69*, 344–354.

Tulving, E. Episodic and semantic memory. In E. Tulving & W. Donaldson (Eds.), *Organization of memory*. New York: Academic Press, 1972.

Tulving, E., & Donaldson, W. (Eds.), *Organization of memory*. New York: Academic Press, 1972.

Tulving, E., & Thomson, D. M. Encoding specificity and retrieval processes in episodic memory. *Psychological Review*, 1973, *80*, 352–373.

Wellman, H. M., Ritter, K., & Flavell, J. H. Deliberate memory behavior in the delayed reactions of very young children. *Developmental Psychology*, 1975, *11*, 780–787.

Worden, P. E. Effects of sorting on subsequent recall of unrelated items: A developmental study. *Child Development*, 1975, *46*, 687–695.

Worden, P. E. The effects of classification structure on organized free recall in children. *Journal of Experimental Child Psychology*, 1976, *22*, 519–529.

Young, F. W. Scaling replicated conditional rank-order data. In D. R. Heise (Ed.), *Sociological methodology: 1975*. San Francisco: Jossey-Bass, 1974.

Yussen, S. R., & Levy, V. M. Developmental changes in predicting one's own span of short-term memory. *Journal of Experimental Child Psychology*, 1975, *19*, 502–508.

Categorical and Schematic
Organization in Memory

I. INTRODUCTION

A new approach to the study of comprehension and memory has appeared on the psychological scene. If one leafs through the pages of the current journals, scattered among the traditional studies of lists of words and paired associates, one finds new paradigms and new materials. Recent studies have attacked extraordinarily complex materials, from long passages of text to

ISBN 0-12-566750-7

pictures of intricately detailed scenes. Much of this research is rooted in concepts drawn from artificial intelligence and in a sense is more a part of the new discipline of cognitive science than of psychology classically conceived. With the advent of computer programs designed to simulate complex intellective processes have come new vocabulary, new emphases, and new theory. As often happens when new paradigms develop in a science, there is some danger of a gulf forming between old ideas and new, with potential loss of important concepts and acquired wisdom to workers on both sides. Such a division is not inevitable—indeed some researchers easily bridge the two worlds—but tends to be a practical fact for many of us, especially as the literature in both camps exponentially expands.

The present chapter is the result of an attempt to draw together two seemingly disparate sets of concepts and principles that I use in my own research. On the one hand, I maintain an unusually close association with a colleague who has long studied problems of memory for lists of words, and I have carried out similar work with children. This research inherits an old tradition growing out of verbal learning and calls frequently upon concepts of categorical or taxonomic organization. On the other hand, I also study how children and adults remember stories and complex pictures. The latter work makes use of different concepts of organization, in particular the schematic organization of event sequences and scenes. Different ways of organizing the knowledge domains seem to be involved in the two cases.

The notion of organization is central to both kinds of studies. Indeed, it could hardly be otherwise since both avenues of research seek to uncover the structure of memory. I use the two terms—organization and structure—synonymously. A cognitive structure is an organized set of concepts and procedures. Vice versa, a cognitive organization is a structured set of concepts and procedures. However, even though both research approaches investigate the structure of the mind, it may be that the different kinds of organizations under study have different implications for remembering.

At the outset we should note that repeated experience of similar events and situations generates mental structures that represent them. The mind creates order and structure out of the welter of stimulation, seeks for and finds regularities, and comes to expect them in the future. These repeated experiences and their internal representation lead to the phenomenon known as "familiarity." Because of the individual nature of experience, one person's "familiar" organization can be another's chaos (cf. Chi, 1978). For example, although my desk would undoubtedly appear chaotic to others, as far as I am concerned everything is in its expected place and the ensemble is a structured whole within which I move efficiently. The organization consists of a representation of a set of familiar items in designated locations and a set of visual–motor procedures for finding them. It does all the things for me that an organization is supposed to do. It helps me to encode items rapidly and to retrieve them from memory—in this case, since the structure has major spatial components, by means of a spatial search strategy.

Almost any spatial or temporal sequence, any collection of assorted objects, sounds, sights, or words can become organized and familiar. I stress this point because so much of the memory literature has involved categorical or taxonomic organization that we sometimes assume this kind of organization to be more natural and possibly superior to other kinds. This assumption has been especially common in the developmental literature. Hierarchical taxonomic organizations are relatively late accomplishments in mental development. This fact, along with their use in logical reasoning, has seemed to elevate them to some special status. However, categorical organization does not hold a unique status and is only one of several kinds of organizations that are used and useful for memory.

G. Mandler (1970) has suggested three major types of organizations: categorical, relational, and serial (see also Chapter 9). This is a broad classification and one that cuts across the two types of organizations discussed in this chapter: the schematic organization of events and scenes, and the categorical (taxonomic) organization of objects or words. The contrast is to some extent an artificial one, since it is possible to define categorical organization in terms of schemata and vice versa. Just as one can have a schema of an object such as a *table* (i.e., knowledge about its appearance, function, construction), so one can have a schema of a more general category such as **furniture,** which includes the concept of *table*. Looked at from the other point of view, the schemata organizing our knowledge of events and scenes can be given categorical, or taxonomic, organization. Our schematic knowledge of what kitchens look like is a subcategory of our broader knowledge of rooms in general. Similarly the variety of ways I use to get to work in the morning, although each one is a schematically organized set of procedures, may all be considered subcategories of methods of transportation.

It should be borne in mind in the following pages that both schematizing and categorizing activities are primitive, innate, human abilities and that we engage in both types of activities all the time, whether planning future actions or remembering old ones. Nevertheless, from the point of view of typical memory studies, a distinction between categorically and schematically organized stimuli can be made. Most memory experiments have been set up to study one or the other type of organization, not the interactions between the two that continually take place in daily life. Since our understanding of the workings of human memory come from such experiments, a comparison of the principles derived from each may be useful as long as we remember that the contrasts between the two are being deliberately highlighted.

II. CATEGORICAL ORGANIZATION

Many of our notions about memory—how it is organized, how retrieval is accomplished, why we forget—came from the study of lists of words, and so it behooves us to look closely at the kinds of organization that have been investigated in this type of research. My remarks are concentrated here on categorical organization, and since the most common type of categorical organization in memory experiments is taxonomically based, the two terms— taxonomic and categorical—unless some other type of categorization is specif- ically under discussion, are used interchangeably. Memory for paired associates is not considered. The formation of associations between pairs of arbitrarily chosen items involves subjective organization based on many other types of relationships than taxonomic ones. Only passing reference is made to the large body of research in which subjects are asked to categorize randomly chosen collections of words (cf. G. Mandler, 1967). The idiosyncratic categories thus formed clearly organize retrieval in ways similar to taxonomic categories, but the nature of their organization and the extent to which they vary from subject to subject are largely unknown.

In general, categorical, or taxonomic, organization refers to the cognitive structures, hierarchically arranged, that govern our understanding of the rela- tionships among superordinate, subordinate, and coordinate classes. In addi- tion to lists of items that belong to a given category, this kind of organization includes the more abstract knowledge of class inclusion relations, which enables both inductive and deductive thinking.

Categorical organization is highly flexible. Most sets of objects can be classified in a number of different ways by varying the principles of similarity and difference along which the classification is carried out. Form and function are two common principles, but many others are possible. If we consider the class of people, we can devise hierarchies based on kinship, geography, occupations, size, skin color, sex, and so on. Such flexibility of organizing principles is one basis of our problem-solving abilities (and sometimes lack thereof). It is a useful characteristic of categorical organization, but it also makes retrieval more ambiguous. For example, it allows different sets of retrieval cues to be available, some arising from classificatory schemes other than the one built into a list by an experimenter.

Insofar as categorical organizations have been studied in memory experi- ments, they are relatively unstructured. This need not be the case; a list of words can be constructed with a tightly knit, multileveled hierarchical organi- zation (e.g., Bower, Clark, Lesgold, & Winzenz, 1969). The more typical case, however, is to present a simple categorized list consisting of several unrelated categories and a small selection from the large number of available exemplars. Such lists have little within-category or between-category structure. Taxonomic frequency is usually invoked in the selection of categories and items within categories, but there are no principles governing the connections between categories and between items within categories. The only principled connec- tions are the "vertical" ones that occur in a hierarchy of superordinate and subordinate classes. There are many different kinds of "horizontal" associative connections among items, but these are usually unknown. Relationships can be based on similarity or prototypicality of exemplars, on common associations, or even on cross-classification among the categories. However, because there are many different kinds of such relationships and because order of occurrence of items is arbitrarily determined, these kinds of connections are unpredictable and subjects' discovery or use of them is uncertain.

The lack of a rule governing the relationships among items in a categorical organization is the characteristic that most distinguishes it from schematic organizations. As we shall see, the latter have important spatial or temporal components. Even in a multileveled categorical organization, however, there is no particular spatial or temporal order in which the items should occur or in which they are apt to be retrieved. There are other principles by which categorized lists could be given relational structure. For example, a category of animals might be ordered according to their size or ferocity, occupations according to their lucrativeness or prestige, and so forth, but to my knowledge these have not been studied in memory experiments.

To the extent that the structure of a list is increased by amplifying its hierarchical structure and by including principles of ordering of the items, it becomes more predictable. The more predictable, the more subjects can use an ordered set of expectations to guide their processing and later their retrieval. It is not always the case, however, that subjects will uncover these organizational principles unless they are thoroughly instructed about them beforehand. Depending somewhat on instructions and manner of presentation, a categorical organization may or may not be discovered or used. Subjects must typically engage in a good deal of "bottom-up," or data-driven, processing; that is, they must search for the overall structure of the list or impose one of their own. Even when informed in advance about a categorical organization, lists of categorized words do not appear to arouse expectations about what will be presented next to the degree that occurs for schematically organized event sequences.

III. SCHEMATIC ORGANIZATION

Like a categorical organization, a schema (also often termed "frame," Minsky, 1975) is a cognitive structure—an organized representation of a body of knowledge. Unlike a categorical organization, the structure is not based on class membership and similarity relationships among class members. Rather, it is a spatially and/or temporally organized structure in which the parts are connected on the basis of contiguities that have been experienced in space or time. A schema is formed on the basis of past experience with objects, scenes, or events and consists of a set of (usually unconscious) expectations about what things look like and/or the order in which they occur. The parts, or units, of a schema consist of a set of variables, or slots, which can be filled, or instantiated, in any given instance by values that have greater or lesser degrees of probability of occurrence attached to them. Schemata vary greatly in their degree of generality—the more general the schema, the less specified, or the less predictable, are the values that may satisfy any given slot.

One can have a schema for anything with which one is familiar, from the details of appearance of a Hepplewhite chair, to the procedure required to cook a soufflé, or the events that occur during a trip to the theater. In this chapter, I concentrate on two broad classes of schemata, those governing our expectations of familiar event sequences and familiar scenes. (For a more detailed discussion of schemata, see the excellent chapter by Rumelhart and Ortony, 1977.)

A. Scene Schemata

A scene schema is a cognitive representation of what one expects to see when viewing (or entering) a scene. Its variables consist of categories of furniture, buildings, plants, and so forth, and the spatial arrangement of these various items. Scene schemata, like all others, vary in their degree of generality. A "room schema," for example, is highly general. It has a small number of obligatory variables (often called defining features) that must be filled, but the range of values these may take is broad. For example, a room must have walls of some kind to be considered a room. Although their exact shape, number, and composition are not specified, some types of walls are much more proba-ble (expected) than others. A room schema also has a number of optional variables. It is expected to have furniture in it, although the range of values that can fill this slot is also large, and it is possible for a room to be completely empty. A "kitchen schema" is less general because the furniture variable has a narrower range of values—not any kind of furniture will do. As this schema in turn is made more concrete, moving from kitchen to French Provincial kitchen to my kitchen, the range of acceptable values becomes progressively narrower.

At this point it might appear that we have done little more than use another label for the more traditional term "concept." However, a schema is not the same as the use of that term to mean a set of defining features and perhaps a specification of class membership. A schema consists of sets of expectations that may have little to do with the defining attributes of a concept in the narrow sense. Most values of variables in a schema are only more or less probable and certain concatentations of them may remove the obligatory character of any single one. The stronger one's expectations for certain kinds of objects to be present, the more "defining" these values can be said to be, but this definingness is a continuum rooted in the strength of our expectations.

At the same time, a schema is not coterminous with the set of everything we know about a concept. It is a limited set of expectations that usually are centered around variables that have had functional significance in the past. The slots for objects in a kitchen schema, for example, are perceptual generaliza-tions deriving from our interactions with typical kitchen items.[1] The crucial aspect of a scene schema is that it consists of expectations about the normal

[1] I do not mean to imply that a schema cannot be developed on the basis of a single exposure; indeed, schemata probably are formed at least in a crude way on the first encounter with something new.

appearance of things and thus is only a subset of our knowledge about the concept in question.

Similar considerations apply to the spatial organization of a scene. Some of our knowledge about locations of objects in a scene might be considered part of the definition itself, primarily those aspects that have to do with the bounds of physical causality—furniture rests on floors and does not hang in midair. Other kinds of knowledge about locations are a looser generalization from past experience, and this too is typically of a functional nature. Furniture is usually arranged to accommodate people, and so chairs are not typically turned to the wall. Small objects, even if their function is unknown, are more apt to appear on tables or shelves than on the floor. Thus, many of our expectations about spatial relationships among objects come from past experience rather than from definitional knowledge of a particular concept.

Little theoretical work has been done on the specification of scene variables. The structure of a scene schema is probably hierarchically organized in that each of the variables has more detailed schemata embedded within it, but it is uncertain at what levels of the hierarchy, or at how many levels, we operate when encoding and storing information about a scene. For example, a brief glance at a room tells us that it contains tables and chairs, but do we also encode smaller details that are appropriate to the schemata for tables or chairs themselves? Some work from our laboratory has addressed this problem (e.g., Mandler & Johnson, 1976; Mandler & Parker, 1976), but it is fair to say that the hierarchical structure of scene schemata is still poorly understood.

Similar problems arise concerning the nature of the spatial organization. We have demonstrated that spatial organization is crucial to the activation of a scene schema but know less about which dimensions are the most important. Mandler and Parker (1976) found that most of our general spatial knowledge about pictures of scenes represents the vertical rather than the horizontal dimension. That is, furniture rests on floors, windows appear on walls that are above floors, and airplanes typically appear in the sky. Whether a desk is to the left or right of a chair does not seem to enter into our schematic knowledge of rooms to the same degree. However, this kind of work is only a beginning and tells us nothing about depth relationships and other potentially important spatial aspects of scenes.

B. Event Schemata

We turn now to event schemata, for some of which we do have better theoretical specification. A major shift in focus—and one probably important for memory—is from spatial to temporal organization. Another shift is that we are dealing with events rather than the physical objects that most often appear in scene schemata and, for that matter, in traditionally used categorical organizations. Although events can be categorized (e.g., types of baseball plays, vacations I have taken), this way of organizing events is rarely if ever used in memory experiments. Most memory research on recall of categorical organizations has concentrated on common nouns, rarely even on verbs, let alone the complex descriptions that characterize events.

Event schemata are temporally organized representations of common sequences of events. They may also be described as hierarchically arranged sets of expectations about what will occur in a given situation. As with scene schemata, each variable has embedded within it descriptions at a greater level of detail. Again, event schemata vary in degree of generality. Some concrete schemata have been labeled "scripts" by Schank and Abelson (1975/1977, 1977). An example is a restaurant script that describes the typical sequence of events one expects to occur when going to a restaurant for a meal. A script has a series of temporally ordered variables such as entering the restaurant, ordering, eating, and exiting. These variables in turn have subparts; for example, ordering consists of getting a menu, reading it, deciding what to eat, and telling the waitress. Such a schema can be made even more concrete by specifying further details of the type of restaurant—drive-in, diner, or supper club. Once again, as event schemata become more concrete, the acceptable range of values for the variables becomes narrower and thus more predictable.

Scripts are concrete to the point that they cannot account for the way we organize the many relatively novel event sequences we encounter every day. Schank and Abelson use the term "plans" to describe more general event schemata. These are broad sets of expectations organized around knowledge of the motivations and goals people have when engaging in various sequences of behavior. Plans are more tentative than scripts; the range of values of their variables is broader. To the extent that plans are general formulations, they have more of the status of "bottom-up," or data-driven, hypothesis formation, different from the "top-down," or conceptually driven, processing mehcanism provided by a script. Scripts control our expectations of the sequence of events rather precisely, whereas plans are more general hypotheses based on the incoming data. A plan organizes these data but is easily modifiable in the light of later information.

Although not a great deal is known about plans, there are some general event schemata for which we do have detailed theoretical specifications. A good example is that of a story schema (e.g., Mandler & Johnson, 1977; Rumelhart, 1975). This kind of schema specifies the general form and sequence of the events that occur in simple stories such as folktales and fables. Both the structure and sequence of the events are specified, but these variables are open as to content.[2] Stories whose content varies as widely as *The Three Little Pigs* and *Rumpelstiltskin* follow similar structural formats, and the listener is readily able to identify the units as they come.

To facilitate comparison of scripts and story schemata, an example of each is presented in Figure 8.1. The restaurant script is taken from Schank and

---

[2]It is also possible to include some content specifications and restrictions in a story schema, at least for stories from certain cultures (Colby, 1973).

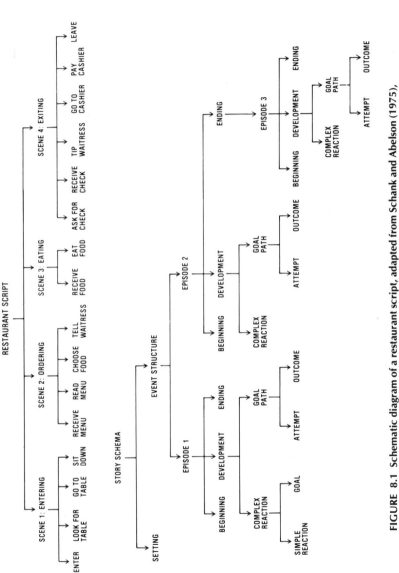

FIGURE 8.1 Schematic diagram of a restaurant script, adapted from Schank and Abelson (1975), and a simplified diagram of the structure of a typical three-episode story. For clarity, the division of Complex Reaction into its subparts has been omitted from the second and third episodes. For further details, see Mandler and Johnson (1977).

Abelson (1975/1977), although presented here in abbreviated and somewhat different format. I have followed Schank and Abelson's own structuring of this kind of script, although a case could be made for a greater degree of hierarchical structure than they have given it. For example, Ordering and Eating may be more closely related than the other two scenes and might better be represented as subcategories embedded under a larger category. Similarly, subcategories could be made of some of the events listed under each of the scenes.

The story schema is a representative example of a typical structure for a multiepisode story. It consists of three episodes: The first two are temporarily connected, and the third episode is causally connected to the second by means of an Ending-embedded relationship. Because the variables of the story schema are less obvious than those of the restaurant script, brief definitions of each unit, or basic node, in the structure are given in Table 8.1. The formal rewrite rules for each unit may be found in Mandler and Johnson (1977) and fuller descriptions, in J. M. Mandler (1978).

The difference in generality of the two types of schema shown in Figure 8.1 is obvious. The range of values that can fill each of the slots in the restaurant script is narrow, so narrow in fact that one could easily write an instantiation simply on the basis of the variable names. Clearly, that is not the

Table 8.1
An Informal Description of the Units in a Story[a]

Story	A Setting atemporally connected to an Event Structure
Setting	Introduction to a protagonist; optional statements about time, locale, etc.
Event structure	A series of causally or temporally connected Episodes
Episode	A Beginning that causes a Development that causes an Ending
Beginning	An event that causes a Simple or Complex Reaction; may be rewritten into a new Episode
Development	A Complex Reaction that causes a Goal Path or a Simple Reaction that causes an Action
Complex reaction	A Simple Reaction that causes a Goal
Simple reaction	The protagonist's internal reaction to the Beginning (thought, emotional response, etc.)
Goal	What the protagonist plans to do about the Beginning; caused by Simple Reaction
Action	A nonplanful action by the protagonist; caused by Simple Reaction
Goal path	An Attempt that causes an Outcome; may be recursive
Attempt	What the protagonist does to reach the Goal
Outcome	Success or failure of an Attempt; may be rewritten into a new Episode
Ending	A consequence caused by the Development; may be a reaction to the events of the Episode by protagonist or other character or an emphatic statement of long-term consequences. May be rewritten into a new Episode

[a]Adapted from Mandler and Johnson (1977).

case with the story structure, which is highly general indeed. It might also be noted that although the story schema is more general it has more redundancy. The exact number and ordering of episodes vary from story to story, but each episode within the story consists of the same basic nodes structured in the same way.

Both scripts and story schemata have a hierarchical structure with a limited number of units at each level. In their hierarchical structure they are much like categorical organizations, but in the sharp limitations on the number of units at a given level of the hierarchy and in their temporal constraints they are completely different. In both scripts and story schemata (and presumably in plans as well), the categories are singularly ordered. Although there are typically choice points in event schemata, once a particular path is begun its units run off in a relatively determined fashion. In some cases the temporal sequence is causally determined; one has to order food before one eats it. In others it is determined by custom and in fact may vary from script to script, although invariant for each; for example, paying before or after the meal depends on the type of restaurant. These differences in causally determined or custom-based expectations are similar to those described earlier for scene schemata.

In general, story schemata have more causal than custom-based connections, although the causal relations in stories are of a weaker sort than physical causality. Each of the units within an episode is causally as well as temporally connected with its neighbors. Connections between episodes are more variable and can be either causally or merely temporally determined. For both scripts and stories, however, the causal and temporal constraints, as well as the limited and determinate number of categories, make them more tightly organized hierarchical structures than categorical ones, at least as the latter have been used in memory research.

A final characteristic of schematic organizations that differs from the categorical case is the extent to which the former are automatically activated. It is uncertain whether this difference should be considered a difference in kind or only one of extent. A great deal of categorizing goes on as an automatic part of perception; nevertheless, unless advance information is provided by the experimenter, the overall categorical organization of a list has to be uncovered through bottom-up, or data-driven, processing during the course of presentation. On the whole, subjects have more advance knowledge about the structure of what is to come when they hear "Once upon a time, . . . " Our advance knowledge of and expectations about familiar scenes and common event sequences, even of stories, is used to guide the encoding process in a highly detailed way. Especially in the case of scripts, schemata serve as top-down, or conceptually driven, processing mechanisms, structuring and giving meaning to incoming information. A case can be made and *is* made by Rumelhart and Ortony (1977) that comprehension actually consists of selecting sets of schemata and binding their variables to the presented stimuli.

The more the comprehension process is directed in this top-down fashion, the more inferential it is. We often do not—in fact, cannot—attend to all of the details of familiar experiences; they are often filled in by the schema itself rather than by actual perception. This inferential aspect of perception is called "default processing," in which the most expected (default) value of a variable is assumed to have been instantiated. This aspect of schemata obviously has important implications for memory since we are typically unaware that we have engaged in such inferential processing. Like the automatic filling in of detail in the blind spot on our retina, a schema automatically fills in details that we did not actually see. Unfortunately for accurate memory, they sometimes did not occur! The implications for memory are discussed in Section IV. Here, attention is drawn to the difference between top-down and bottom-up processing as a difference between schematic and categorical organizations in terms of how they control what is encoded.

C. Some Comments on Episodic and Semantic Memory

Since scripts and stories and other event schemata are typically described in terms of episodes and in fact are called episodic memory by some investigators (e.g., Schank & Abelson, 1977), a few words of clarification may be needed about the relationship between the schematic organization of episodes and "episodic memory" as that term is used by Tulving (1972). Tulving uses "episodic memory" to refer to autobiographical, spatiotemporally dated experiences. An episodic memory is one that one personally remembers and that contains some information as to time and location (not necessarily veridical). Episodic memory in this sense is antithetical to the notion of event schemata. The latter are generalized representations of the types of events that occur in common kinds of episodes. Although they are formed out of personal experience, as is all knowledge, they do not carry spatiotemporal tags nor are they autobiographical. They are, as we have noted, spatially and/or temporally organized, but this has to do with the organization of the cognitive structure itself, not with a tag that says this or that happened to me last year in La Jolla.

Categorical organization is more readily identified with the term "semantic memory," although it is only a subset of our knowledge, much of which is schematically rather than categorically organized. My knowledge of what happens in a restaurant is just as basic as my categorization of a bird as a type of animal—perhaps even more basic. Some psychologists have used the term "semantic memory" to refer primarily to lexical knowledge. Although on the face of it, categorical organization would seem to play a larger role in lexical knowledge, a deeper analysis shows that much of our lexical knowledge is also schematically (and syntactically) based (cf. Miller & Johnson-Laird, 1976).

Thus, the two kinds of organizations discussed here cut across Tulving's distinction between episodic and semantic memory. The overlap in meaning of the terms "episode" and "episodic" is unfortunate. It would be clearer to use the term "autobiographical" for Tulving's "episodic" memory, but to avoid proliferation of terms I will attempt to work within current usage appending the phrase "in Tulving's sense" where clarity requires.

IV. IMPLICATIONS FOR MEMORY

In the preceding brief discussion, we have uncovered both similarities and differences in schematic and categorical organizations. On the one hand, both are hierarchically arranged cognitive structures that can be used for purposes of encoding and retrieval. At the most general level, then, we should expect the two kinds of organizations to influence memory in similar ways. On the other hand, at a more detailed level, we have found a number of differences, and so we should expect a number of secondary principles to differ markedly.

The chief difference has to do with the nature of the organization in the two cases. Schemata are temporally or spatially organized and categorical organizations are not. Each item in a schema is either spatially or temporally (and/or causally) connected to its neighbors. In a categorical organization, items are not directly related to each other by the nature of the particular categorization being used, but are only vertically related to their superordinates and subordinates. Furthermore, insofar as categorical organizations have usually been studied in memory experiments, they are less well integrated forms of organization with fewer specifications as to the particular units that will be included. Schematic organizations are not only more tightly integrated due to the connections between each unit, but the units themselves are limited in number and precisely specified. This characteristic is more obviously the case for event schemata than for scene schemata, but whether this is a genuine or important difference between the two kinds of schemata or merely a reflection of our ignorance about the structure of scenes, is uncertain at this time.

The other difference between schematic and categorical organizations is more problematical. However, because schemata consist of elaborate sets of expectations about what is currently being or about to be processed, they appear to be used more extensively as top-down processing mechanisms to guide and structure the encoding process in a relatively automatic way. Their use also involves more inferences and filling-in of details. Unless advance information about a list of words is provided, and thus substitutes for the advance knowledge that a schema automatically provides, the categorical organization of a list induces fewer explicit expectations about what is to be processed next; therefore, it probably requires more bottom-up analysis of the incoming data. In this sense a categorical organization is less automatically applied; it may also encourage less filling-in of information.

In this section, these differences are related to retrieval processes in some detail. The discussion deals with sequential ordering effects in memory, the question of amount remembered, and finally with the problem of accuracy of memory for material structured in the two different ways. Automatic activation and frequency of use of the two kinds of organization are discussed in Section V.

The focus is on the contrast between two common memory paradigms about which we have at least some comparative information—the recall of categorized lists of words and the recall of stories. The contrasts between these two kinds of verbal material seem most informative, although some occasional discussion of memory for scenes will be appended as appropriate. It is obvious that the comparison of data from the various paradigms is difficult because of many differences in experimental method, scoring procedures, and not least because of the paucity of data on memory for schematically organized materials.

A. Sequential Order Effects

Because of the temporal order built into schematic organizations (of the event variety) and the atemporal character of categorical organizations, we should expect to find profound differences in recall order effects. These are of two types: (a) the extent to which items in various positions of the input order are differentially recalled, and (b) the extent to which output order reflects input order. For all practical purposes, the only relevant comparisons available come from recall of stories and categorized lists of words. To make these comparisons, we must first make a decision as to which units of stories are considered comparable to categories and which to within-category items. Because of the intricate hierarchical nature of story structure, this decision may be somewhat arbitrary. However, the highest level categories within a story are episodes, and these often occur relatively independently, much as taxonomic categories within a list. Within episodes we can identify five basic nodes, or within-category "items," which are not themselves hierarchically ordered; that is, none is nested within another.[3] These units (Beginning, Complex Reaction, Attempt, Outcome, and Ending) were briefly defined in Table 8.1. These units are necessarily more abstract than words in a taxonomic category. Nevertheless, they are the lowest level units in a story schema that participate in the temporal strucure of the schema, and they may be considered subordinate members of the superordinate episode categories.

1. SERIAL POSITION CURVES

Serial position effects are ubiquitous in list learning. Subjects recall more words from the beginning and often from the end of the list, than from the middle. The phenomenon is especially strong in arbitrarily ordered material. It

[3]In fact, six basic nodes can be identified, since the Complex Reaction node is itself subdivided into a Simple Reaction and a Goal. However, most of the stories we have studied have not included both of these statements, more frequently including only one or the other and occasionally omitting both. Therefore, for expository purposes, I assume the basic "items" within an episode to be five in number.

even occurs when recalling categories from semantic memory that have an arbitrary ordering, such as the presidents of the United States (Roediger & Crowder, 1976). As list structure is increased, the phenomenon lessens. It is less prominent in categorized lists, especially with blocked presentation, but even in this case, if the categories are large, serial position effects occur within categories, in the sense that earlier presented exemplars are better remembered than later ones.

Since primacy and recency effects seem to be dependent on the amount of structure in the material, it is perhaps not surprising that they do not occur in memory for stories or for that matter in memory for sentences (Mandler & Mandler, 1964). Probability of recall of words from sentences is a function of grammatical structure, and probability of recall of stories is a function of story structure. In a series of experiments that varied widely in the stories used and populations studied (see Section V), the same pattern of recall of basic nodes was found (J. M. Mandler, 1978; Mandler & Johnson, 1977; Mandler, Scribner, Cole, & De Forest, 1978; Stein & Glenn, 1979). To illustrate the "serial position curve" for stories, Figure 8.2 shows the probability of recall of each basic node for stories consisting of two sequentially presented episodes. Presumably the pattern would continue to repeat if more episodes were added, although without data from longer stories we cannot tell if the slight flattening of the curve that appears in the second episode would increase.

This kind of serial position curve is different from that found in recall of lists of words. Its shape is due to the fact that story comprehension and recall are schematically based. Subjects have an organization that assigns differential

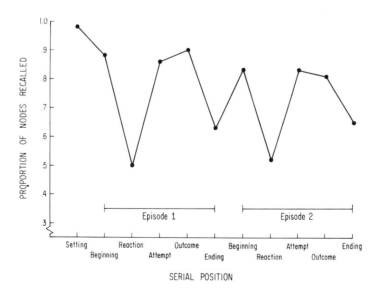

FIGURE 8.2 Proportion of propositions recalled by adults from each basic node for a sequentially presented two-episode story. [Data taken from J. M. Mandler (1978).]

weight to various types of propositions. This advance knowledge can be used to apportion processing time or depth of analysis in ways appropriate to the materials. As an example, the Setting node of a story, which has not been further subdivided in Figure 8.2, can be divided into the mandatory introduction of a protagonist and optional statements about time and locale. The former is always well recalled, and the latter, poorly.

It is important to note that this pattern of recall occurs whether stories are told in their normal fashion or are presented in at least a partially arbitrary ordering. Data from randomly presented stories have not been analyzed in this manner. However, the same stories used to obtain the curves shown in Figure 8.2 were also told in a somewhat irregular fashion (J. M. Mandler, 1978), and the same curves were obtained. Lists of words, whether categorical or not, do not have as much predictability of structure. At least one theory of the serial position curve found in lists suggests that without foreknowledge of what is to come, subjects will merely begin to organize the items as they are presented, producing the familiar primacy effect. In stories, patterns of recall are structurally determined from the beginning; this is only true of lists when they are categorically blocked or special foreknowledge about their structure is provided.

2. INPUT–OUTPUT CORRESPONDENCE

The second sequential order effect concerns the extent to which recall order reflects presentation order. At first glance, stories appear to be different from categorized lists in this regard. For lists, subjects cluster their output into the categories. For stories, output order strongly reflects input order, especially when the stories are well structured (Mandler & Johnson, 1977; Stein & Glenn, 1979). This difference might be thought explicable solely on the grounds of different instructions. Subjects are at least implicitly instructed to tell stories in the same order they heard them, whereas in free recall they are explicitly instructed to recall in any order they choose. The matter is, however, more complicated than that.

It is informative to compare output order for stories and categorized lists when both are randomly presented. If stories are told in completely random fashion, the underlying structure often cannot be recovered at all. Not only does amount recalled decrease (Thorndyke, 1977), but order of output no longer reflects the schematic order (Stein & Nezworski, 1978).[4] If, however, stories are presented in irregular but not completely random fashion, subjects tend not to follow the input order but to reorganize their output to follow the schematic order (J. M. Mandler, 1978; Stein & Nezworski, 1978). This aspect of control of output is similar for both schematic and categorical organizations. The difference is that the organization of event schemata *depends* on the

[4]If enough study time is given, subjects may be able to infer the correct sequence of the story (cf. Kintsch, Mandel, & Kominski, 1977).

temporal connections between items. The assignment of any particular event to an Attempt, for example, depends in large part on the fact that a Reaction precedes it and an Outcome follows it. Random presentation can therefore mask the organization to such an extent that activation of the relevant schema does not occur, and so output order does not reflect it.

Categorical organization depends solely on the connections between items and their superordinate categories, not on relationships between the items themselves; for example, whether the word "apple" is assigned to the category of **fruit** or **red objects** indeed depends on the other words in the list but not on whether they immediately precede or follow it. Therefore, although subjects recall slightly less from categorized lists when presentation is random rather than blocked (Cofer, Bruce, & Reicher, 1966), adults typically can uncover the categorical structure during the course of presentation and reorganize their recall accordingly.

Unless completely masked in the preceding fashion, the temporal connections in story schemata exert more powerful control over retrieval than does the categorical organization of lists. Mandler and Barsalou (1978) reported that subjects can order their recall of lists according to input order or categorical order upon request. Another study indicates that this is not the case for stories (Mandler & DeForest, in press). We used stories consisting of two sequentially presented episodes. Some subjects heard the stories in their natural order. Others heard the two episodes presented in interleaved fashion. That is, the Beginning of the first episode was followed by the Beginning of the second; next, the Reaction of the first episode was told, followed by the Reaction of the second, and so forth. These versions of the stories were perfectly sensible; no causal sequences were reversed and care was taken to maintain referential clarity. After listening to the stories, half of the subjects in the interleaved-story condition were asked to recall the stories in their ideal separate-episode order; the other half were asked to maintain the interleaved input order. Subjects had no difficulty rearranging the interleaved stories during output to conform to the ideal order. However, those subjects asked to maintain the interleaved input order were unable to do so; they tended to produce the schematic order instead.

It is of some interest that when subjects were constrained to recall the interleaved stories according to input order, the kind of serial position effect that typically is found in serial recall of word lists began to occur. Subjects were better at maintaining input order at the beginning and end of the "list" of propositions. They reverted to the schematic order more frequently in the middle of the list. Since there may have been structural reasons for this finding, it is only suggestive, but it does hint that the classic serial ordering curve not only occurs with atemporally structured materials but also with temporally structured materials that are arbitrarily presented and required to be so recalled.

Thus, the temporal structure of schematic organizations plays a prominent role in ordering retrieval. In stories, items are sequentially ordered and that order is almost always respected in recall. As far as free recall of categorized lists is concerned, apparently there has been little attempt to analyze the extent to which order of retrieval of either categories or items within categories is influenced by the input order of the list. Because categorical structures are atemporal, input order is unlikely to play much of a role.[5] One would expect instead that output order would reflect associations among items and categories in terms of overlaps of features, typicality of items, and so on. In fact, most models of category and item search that have been devised to account for recall of categorized lists (e.g., Patterson, Meltzer, & Mandler, 1971; Rundus, 1973) have relied either on random sampling of categories and items within categories or assumed that such sampling is a function of unknown strengths of items and categories in the list.

The two main components of models of category search have been random entry and sampling with replacement. Neither of these concepts is appropriate for temporally ordered schematic organizations. In the latter, not only is the point of entry into the category specified, but sampling with replacement does not occur. This point is discussed further in the next section.

B. Amount Recalled

A schematic organization such as a story has a more tightly integrated structure (i.e., it has more interconnectedness of its parts) than does a categorical organization. One predictable result is that people should be able to recall stories more completely than categorized lists of words. There are serious difficulties, of course, in comparing the two cases. We demand verbatim recall of lists, whereas for stories, synonymous expressions, or even gist expressions, are usually considered accurate reproduction. Nevertheless, it is generally true that we can recall more of a story than of a list of sentences (Thorndyke, 1977) and more words from a sentence than from a list. It is commonplace in the literature that subjects simply cannot recall *all* of the words on a list when it is first presented, whereas not infrequently they can recall all of the sentences of a story after a single presentation, often with a high degree of verbatim accuracy.

However, before we conclude that stories are always easier to recall than shopping lists, we must ask what happens when we increase the complexity of the taxonomic structure used in categorized lists. Bower et al. (1969) used a more complex hierarchical taxonomic structure than the two-level superordinate–subordinate organization of most categorized lists. They studied recall of a list consisting of four unrelated hierarchies, each hierarchy having four levels. The list was unusually long—112 words—yet recall was excellent even on the first trial (although not perfect) and completely correct by the third trial. Using a matrix form of organization, Broadbent, Cooper, and Broadbent

---

[5]This is not the case for lists that have been learned in a serial fashion, even when free recall is allowed (cf. Kellas, Ashcraft, Johnson, & Needham, 1973).

(1978) found results similar to those of Bower et al. (although with shorter lists). Items were cross-classified on two independent dimensions and two such lists were presented before recall was required. Again, performance was very good on the first trial and approached ceiling levels on the second. Thus, when lists of words are as intricately structured as stories, they may be equally memorable.

These two sets of results implicate increased structure as a major factor in increased recall. A multileveled hierarchical structure provides a series of nested retrieval cues, in which one cue automatically leads to several others under it (similar to stories). A matrix structure provides two (or more) independent retrieval cues for each item on the list. Broadbent et al. point out that this difference in structure should predict some differences in patterns of recall. In a four-level hierarchy, there are three cues provided for each terminal item, but they are not independent. If a higher node is forgotten, there are no other routes to the items nested under it. In a 2 × 2 matrix organization, there are only two higher order retrieval cues for each "terminal" item, but they are independent, so if one is lost the other may still be accessible. In line with this prediction, Broadbent et al. found equally good overall recall from the two kinds of organizations. However, in the case of hierarchically organized materials, whole branches were forgotten, whereas in the matrix-organized materials, forgetting was more evenly distributed across the categories. In passing, I add the informal observation that the hierarchical structure of stories produces patterns of recall similar to hierarchical lists: Whole episodes are sometimes lost, just as whole categories are sometimes forgotten in lists.

1. CATEGORY SIZE AND BLOCKED PRESENTATION

Although the Bower and the Broadbent results implicate increasing complexity of structure as a factor in increased recall, there are two other aspects of the organizations they used that are confounded with complexity. The first of these is category size, that is, the number of items associated with each higher level retrieval cue. For a constant number of items, as the levels of a hierarchy or number of dimensions in a matrix increase, the number of items associated with each cue becomes smaller. In both studies under discussion, no more than four items were included in a given category. As G. Mandler (1967) has pointed out, there is a good chance of retrieving all of the items in a category if their number is five or smaller. In the Broadbent et al. study, although no category ever included more than four items, in one experiment 12 categories were used and recall dropped markedly.

Story structure, as analyzed by Mandler and Johnson (1977), has the same advantageous characteristic of limited category size. The highest level category, the episode, consists of five or six subcategories or items. Thus, when an episode has been entered in memory, all of these units are potentially retrievable. Three of them can themselves be rewritten into episodes, resulting in an economical set of retrieval cues similar to the hierarchical organization used by

Bower *et al.* Unless a story has a great many episodes indeed, the structure seems well designed to recover most of the material it contains.

The other aspect of the Bower and the Broadbent studies that is confounded with complexity of structure was their use of spatially blocked presentation of the categories. The hierarchies were laid out in the form of trees and the matrices were presented in 2 × 2 tables. It is tempting to speculate that borrowing this aspect of schematic structure also played a role in producing such good recall. In any case, Bower *et al.* found that subjects who were not shown the hierarchies simultaneously but were presented the material in successive fashion performed more poorly. There could be other reasons, of course, for the advantages of successive over simultaneous presentation. One of these is discussed in Section IV, C.

It becomes apparent that there are many unanswered questions about the role that the hierarchical organization of structures plays in recall that have not been generally addressed by the literature on memory for lists of words. Some of the apparent advantages of schematic structure for recall may be due to secondary aspects of their hierarchical structure, such as limited numbers of items per category and blocked presentation. There are, however, other aspects of schematic organization not related to their hierarchical structure that should have predictably different effects on recall from categorical organization. These are discussed next, with the caveat that more relevant data are available from studies of words than from stories.

2. OUTPUT INTERFERENCE AND CATEGORY SEARCH RULES

It was mentioned earlier that subjects find it essentially impossible to recall all the items in a list of words. A related phenomenon is that of output interference (Slamecka, 1968, 1972). This extensively studied phenomenon refers to the fact that providing one or more words from a category inhibits recall of other words in the same category. The only time when providing category items is beneficial is when the items cue whole categories that otherwise would have been forgotten. The most important conclusion that has been drawn from this finding (Crowder, 1976; Roediger, 1974) is that items within a category are independent; that is, they are not connected directly to each other but only to the superordinate category within which they are nested. If this characterization of categorical structure is correct, it constitutes an important difference between schematic and categorical organizations. A story schema, for example, has strong temporal (and causal) ordering of its components. It seems highly likely that providing one of them would facilitate, not interfere with, the retrieval of the others. This assumption has not yet been tested for stories, although cueing with the first items of an episode often produces further material from within that category.[6] It has, however, been tested with sentences, and no output interference was found (Park, 1979).

---

[6] It is an interesting question (currently being tested) whether cueing with "late" items in an episode would facilitate recall of earlier items, i.e., whether the temporal sequencing of a schema can be used bidirectionally.

A related advantage for schematic organizations as exemplified by scripts and stories is that their categories are exhaustive. To the extent that people have internalized the form of a story schema, they know how many units to expect in any given episode. They also know approximately what those units are, even though their exact content is not known in the same way as the contents of exhaustive taxonomic categories (such as the directions of the compass). In general, we should expect retrieval to be improved by this characteristic of stories, just as it is when exhaustive categories are used in lists of words (Cohen, 1963).

It was also mentioned earlier that one of the advantages of a temporally ordered organization such as a story schema is that subjects do not enter a category randomly but know where to begin their retrieval search. It should now be added that since the items in a story category are exhaustive, subjects also know when to stop. Retrieval search in categorical organizations has a different character. Most models of category search have used a stop rule based on the ratio of items recovered to the items remaining. Since sampling with replacement is assumed, as this ratio becomes larger there is an increasing number of failures to find a previously unrecalled item (Rundus, 1973). Associated with this type of probabilistic process is a negatively accelerated curve in the rate of retrieval of new items.

A probabilistic model of retrieval search is not appropriate for retrieval of schematically based materials. Although there are as yet no data available for rate of retrieval of story units, there are some relevant data on different methods of retrieving items from semantic memory. Indow and Togano (1970) found the usual negatively accelerated curve when subjects were asked to recall all the cities in Japan they could think of. When subjects were told to retrieve cities by geographical location, however, the rate was constant. Subjects applied a spatial schema to their search, which gave them an ordered and "exhaustive" method.

We have discussed a number of characteristics of schematic organization in this section that affect not only the way in which retrieval proceeds but also the likelihood of retrieving all or most of the material to be remembered. We have noted that probabilistic models of retrieval search and associated concepts such as random entry or sampling with replacement are not appropriate to a cognitive structure that directs retrieval in clearly specified ways. Next, some aspects of schema-directed retrieval search that may be less "beneficial" are considered.

C. Accuracy of Recall

When schematically organized materials such as stories are presented, subjects know either beforehand or upon the opening words the formal structure of the material they are hearing (one of the virtues of "Once upon a time . . ."). A set of expectations is aroused not just about the next category to occur but about the overall form and meaning of the material. The activation of a story schema results in the encoding of each item within the context of a whole, even though most of that "whole" has not yet been presented. The advantages of such knowledge about how to structure incoming information were illustrated even for categorical organization in the Bower et al. (1969) experiment, in which the four hierarchies were presented simultaneously. Under such conditions, performance was better than when the material was presented successively, and the hierarchies had to be built up at the same time as the list was being learned.

Having a preexisting structure to guide comprehension has great advantages in terms of economy of processing and, as we have seen, advantages for retrieval as well. However, the other side of the coin of speed and economy is accuracy. We often see or hear what we expect, not necessarily what was actually presented. I offer a sad illustration. In a course I taught last year, I thought to engage in a bit of consciousness-raising by giving the terms "he" and "she" equal time. I deliberately tried to couch my references to subjects half the time as "he," half the time as "she." Toward the end of the course I made casual reference to this plan and was astonished to find that the overwhelming consensus in the class was that I *always* said "she" and *never* used "he." Since the students and I were equally positive about our memories, a student volunteered to do an independent count of my usage of the two words from the tape recordings of two of my lectures. Her report was that in fact I had said "he" about 80% of the time and "she" only 20%. I was chagrined by the feebleness of my efforts at equal time, but the students were even more upset at the extent of their misperceptions. Their expectations were such that they simply did not hear when I used the term "he," but every mention of "she" was a violation of those expectations and vividly remembered as such.

This example illustrates the way in which we give only limited processing to the details of material that fits our expectations. We usually get along very well merely by noting that a schema is being instantiated and assigning expected or default values to most of the variables. Bobrow and Norman (1975) concluded from the prevalence of this kind of default processing that memory for expected or "normal" events is poor; the normal will become normalized. Another way of putting it is to say that when a schema has been aroused the stimuli do not require very much deep processing, in the Craik and Lockhart (1972) sense, and therfore will not be well remembered.

1. GIST VERSUS DETAIL

We have arrived at somewhat of a dilemma. We know that something will not be well remembered if it cannot be fitted into a cognitive structure, and yet it has just been suggested that the better things *do* fit a cognitive structure the less well they will be remembered. Since there are data to support both horns of this dilemma, it is advisable that we be clear about how we define the two points. There are countless studies showing that organized material is remembered better than unorganized or unfamiliar or meaningless material. Truly meaningless material is essentially not memorable at all. However, because something is organized enough to be memorable does not imply that it will be accurately remembered in all its detail.

The aspects of schematic material that Bobrow and Norman (1975) refer to as being shallowly processed and poorly remembered are at a low level indeed. They use a ketchup stain on the page of the book as an example. The reader might not even notice it since it can be accounted for by low-level schemata for stains and shadows, unimportant to the brunt of the message the reader is trying to encode. Even if noticed, little processing will be expended; what was seen will be assimilated to a schema and take on a default value. This level of detail is indeed poorly processed; it is maintained in memory largely through assimilation to schemata and retrieved by the reconstructive processes that schemata engender. Countless other examples could be given of memory for gist or overall meaning rather than exact details (e.g., Bransford & Franks, 1971).

Can we assume, then that a schema guides attention to and memory for the overall meaning or import of the materials and at the same time interferes with accurate processing of detail? First, we must specify exactly what is to be considered detail and what overall gist. Second, we must consider possible differences in processing detail when a schema has been activated in contrast to a situation in which no schema has been found and a new organization of the material must be formed. This point can be illustrated by contrasting some data comparing memory for organized and unorganized scenes with other data comparing memory for expected and unexpected objects *within* organized scenes.

In a number of experiments, we compared recognition of pictures of scenes (pictures that are schematically organized) with unorganized pictures (nonschematically arranged collections of the same objects). Some of these experiments have focused on immediate recognition tests, providing an assessment of the kinds of information that were encoded in the first place (Mandler & Johnson. 1976). Others have focused on recognition after delays of up to four months and thus assessed the effects of a schema in maintaining information in memory (Mandler & Ritchey, 1977).

If a picture arouses a scene schema, some kinds of information are well attended and also well retained. In particular, relative locations (and to a lesser extent, orientation) of objects are better recognized in organized scenes, not only at immediate test but over time. The schema not only focuses attention on this kind of information but organizes it in such a fashion that it is well retained. Inventory information, on the other hand, is equally well recognized in both types of pictures at immediate test but is better recognized in organized scenes after four months. This seems to be a case in which activation of a schema is not essential to focus attention on the objects in a picture. At least with pictures of only a modest degree of complexity, such as we have studied, people are able to encode a listing of the objects they contain whether or not a scene schema is activated. However, a schema is necessary for maintaining this information in long-term memory.

Descriptive information about objects, such as the details of dress or the figurative detail of a piece of furniture, is not only less well recognized in general, it is also not differentially recognized in the two kinds of pictures at immediate test or over varying delays. This kind of "token" information can be considered a schema-irrelevant detail. It does not enter into schematic organization and is neither enhanced nor hindered by the use of a schema to guide encoding or to maintain information in memory.

A final kind of information we have studied is spatial composition. This kind of "detail" concerns areas of filled and empty space in a picture and is somewhat akin to figure–ground relationships. Although it is in general more poorly processed than the other types of information, it is nevertheless better recognized in *unorganized* pictures. Not only is this kind of information schema-irrelevant, but schematic processing seems to discourage its encoding. When the relative locations of objects are not informative, as in a haphazard collection of items, more attention is paid to the overall composition of a picture. Thus, the case of spatial composition information would be one in which activation of a schema hinders processing of a certain kind of detail. It might be called schema-opposing information.

Overall, these data suggest a three-way classification of details. If a detail is *schema-relevant,* it will be more accurately remembered if a schema has been activated. If a detail is *schema-irrelevant,* it will be unaffected by activation of a schema. Finally, if a detail is *schema-opposed,* it will be more poorly processed when a schema has been activated. Such a conclusion differs considerably from the prediction of Bobrow and Norman (1975) that there will be more cursory processing and poorer memory for schema-relevant (expected) information.

However, there are other recognition data that support the Bobrow and Norman notion. Friedman (in press) studied recognition of details *within* organized scenes. Based on subjects' rankings of the likelihood of occurrence of various objects in familiar places, such as a kitchen or a farm, she constructed complex pictures of familiar scenes in which the items ranged from high-probability (obligatory) objects to low-probability (unexpected but not unreasonable) objects. She found that even in an immediate test, recognition of *all* changes made on high-probability objects was poor indeed); low-probability objects were more accurately recognized. This finding supports the kind of processing Bobrow and Norman predicted: a cursory examination of expected objects followed by their rapid normalization to default value. Eye movement data indicated that examination of expected objects was indeed more cursory. Subjects looked longer at the unexpected objects, especially during the first fixation. Further analysis of the data indicated, however, that the probability of the objects was a more important factor in determining accurate recognition than looking time per se.

On the surface, these two sets of data seem to be in conflict. On the one hand, comparing accuracy of recognition *across* organized and unorganized pictures, schema-relevant information is more accurately processed. On the other hand, *within* organized scenes, schema-relevant objects are less accurately processed than schematically unpredicted ones. There are several possible resolutions of this dilemma. First, we are dealing with two somewhat different questions. One concerns whether or not a schema is activated in a given situation. If it is, we can expect the kinds of processing that occur, due to the top-down nature of schematically directed encoding, to differ from those that occur when no schema is found and a more bottom-up analysis of the incoming data is used to form some sort of new organization. The second question concerns what happens when a schema has been activated and the extent to which expected versus unexpected details (all of which may be relevant to the schema) are processed. In addition, the complexity of the stimulus materials should play a role. The more complex the situation, the more likely a schema is to be used in a highly selective fashion. For example, Friedman's scenes contained many objects; subjects may have had to use their schematic knowledge to skip over expected objects in order to concentrate on the more unusual ones. Obviously, a great deal more work is needed to clarify this issue.

2. ACCURACY OF RECOGNITION VERSUS ACCURACY OF RECALL

We have been discussing accuracy of memory without specifying whether recall or recognition tests are used. Not surprisingly, accuracy for detail differs in the two cases.

Mandler and Parker (1976) showed that subjects more accurately reconstruct (recall) the locations of objects in organized than in unorganized scenes and concluded that this effect was due to the operation of schematically based knowledge. Two findings were relevant to this conclusion. The unorganized versions of the pictures had been constructed from the organized scenes by turning the pictures upside down and then reinverting the objects to an upright position. This method of construction effectively removed any known spatial organization and left proximity relations among the objects the same. The method also resulted in objects from the top of organized pictures appearing at the bottom of unorganized ones and vice versa.

When tested immediately after seeing the pictures, subjects viewing the organized scenes were more accurate in reconstructing the locations of objects on *both* the horizontal and vertical dimensions. After a week's delay, they were more accurate only on the vertical dimension, with placement along the horizontal dimension approaching chance levels for both groups. The difference between the organized and unorganized pictures on the vertical dimension remained, not so much because of "accuracy" on the part of subjects in the organized condition, but because subjects in the unorganized condition began showing schematic distortion. They began placing objects they had seen at the bottom of the pictures at the top and vice versa. In short, they reconstructed their pictures to look like the organized versions, which of course they had not seen. Thus, these subjects were "accurate" with respect to their schemata rather than to what they had actually viewed.

That both groups after a week's delay were recalling on the basis of their schematic knowledge was further indicated by the fact that delayed performance in the organized picture condition was not significantly better than that of a control group who were asked to construct the pictures without previously seeing them. As mentioned earlier, most of our schematic knowledge about locations of objects in scenes lies along the vertical dimension. Since scene schemata for the most part have fewer values specified for the horizontal dimension, much of this information is fairly quickly lost, and responses, having no schema to guide them, become random with respect to the original placement. Information on the vertical dimension, whose values are specified by a scene schema, becomes normalized. These findings suggest that long-term recall of details is mediated by schematically relevant variables. It is indeed often accurate, but only because most of the time the details match the default values of the schema. Usually our cognitive structures fit the world so well that guessing is an excellent strategy for remembering.

It may have been noted that in the Mandler and Parker study, recall of spatial location had reached chance levels after a week's delay. This finding can be contrasted with above-chance levels of recognition of spatial location in organized pictures after four months. A recognition test provides a "copy cue" for the target information. The better recognition of organized scenes indicates that the activation of a schema allowed more elaboration of schema-relevant details in these pictures than occurred for unorganized scenes. However, just because this kind of information has been stored does not mean that it is readily accessible. When no copy cue is presented and subjects are left to their own retrieval devices, they use their schematic knowledge as a guide. A schema as a retrieval cue can lead us astray and find default values rather than the instantiated values that were actually presented. If this is the case, then schematic organization plays a complex role in memory indeed! It improves encoding and recognition of at least some kinds of detail; in contrast, it may impede their recall by the tendency to arouse default values when a retrieval search is carried out.

There are some commonalities between these findings and those reported for recall and recognition of high- and low-frequency words (e.g., Kinsbourne & George, 1974). High-frequency words are in some sense more expected and are also better recalled; low-frequency words are not as well recalled but are better recognized. The latter finding is comparable to the Friedman recognition data for pictures.[7] Despite there being some common ground between phenomena associated with the two types of organizations, it is obvious that we

---

[7]Goodman (1978) reported similar data: better recognition of schematically irrelevant details in pictures and better recall of schematically relevant details.

still understand little about the role that schematic organization plays in accurate memory for detail. What the data we have discussed do indicate is the active, reconstructive, even confabulative, nature of schematically determined memory. This role seems much more prominent than in categorically organized memory, or at least in the types of taxonomic organizations that we have studied.

3. INTRUSIONS AND FALSE ALARMS

It may be helpful to our comparison of accuracy of memory for schematically and categorically organized materials to turn from the study of scenes to that of stories and lists of words. A difficulty mentioned earlier remains: We apply a stricter criterion to lists of words. Recall of lists must be verbatim, whereas approximations or synonymous expression are usually accepted as accurate in recall of stories. The different criteria create different response biases, and in fact intrusions and distortions decrease in recall of stories when subjects are given a stricter criterion (Gauld & Stephenson, 1967). Nevertheless, the comparison of rates of intrusion may be informative, especially since similar phenomena appear when recognition tests are used and false-alarm rates measured.

Intrusions are rare in immediate recall of categorized lists. Failure of recall is almost always a question of omission rather than of distortion.[8] The intrusions that do occur are almost invariably from the presented categories but are otherwise unpredictable. Intrusions are both more frequent and more predictable in stories. A common type of intrusion is an attempt to fill a known missing story category (J. M. Mandler, 1978; Stein & Glenn, 1977). The determinate nature of the story schema not only indicates to the subject that something has not been retrieved, but provides an approximate form for the content. New material is thus constructed from the schema that is formally appropriate to the story but wrong with respect to the actual content. These intrusions often appear to be default values in the sense that they are the most likely thing to have happened.

The more concrete the schema, the more frequent and predictable intrusions become. For example, Bower, Black, and Turner (1979) studied recall of common scripts such as eating in a restaurant or visiting a doctor. Subjects read individual "stories," each of which contained some but not all of the expected slots in the script. In some cases, subjects read more than one story instantiating a similar script (visiting a doctor, a dentist, and a chiropractor). Subjects recalled more of the actually presented items but also produced a high rate of "script fillers," that is, default values, or expected instantiations of script slots that had not been presented. These intrusions ranged from 16% for

---

[8]It might be noted that the most common kind of omission in recall of stories is of schema-irrelevant details. Elaborative clauses that do not bear on the overall structure of the story are the least likely type of material to appear in recall (Mandler & Johnson, 1977).

stories that were the sole examples of a particular type of script to around 30% when more than one story of a given type had occurred.

The same type of finding occurred on recognition tests of the stories. Although Bower et al. present their recognition data in terms of confidence ratings, it is apparent that false-alarm rates to unpresented script fillers were high. Similar results occur in scene recognition. For example, in our laboratory we typically find false-alarm rates of around 40% for token distractors (the closest thing to a synonymous word in that only the physical appearance, not the meaning, of an object is changed). These data from schematically organized materials stand in marked contrast to the low rates of synonym confusion found in recognition tests of categorized lists of words (Mandler, Pearlstone, & Koopmans, 1969).

The difference in recognition rates of synonyms, paraphrases, script fillers, and the like points up one of the major reasons why we should expect difference in accuracy for the "surface detail" of scripts versus lists. When encoding a list of words one must pay attention to the meaning of each word as it is presented. Each word in our language carries a unique meaning—in fact it is difficult to find synonymous words. Even in a categorized list, few items could reasonably be substituted without changing the "content" of the list. Most of us would feel that our shopping list had been distorted if we were given zucchinis in place of cucumbers or marmalade instead of jam. The meaning of a script or story, however, resides not so much in the individual sentences as it does in the higher level categories of which they are a part. Stories are too complex for us to remember verbatim, nor is it usually reasonable to try to do so. Instead we use our schematic knowledge to direct our attention to the higher level categories, and there are many paraphrases that will satisfy their essential meaning.

The many comparisons that have been made in these pages suggest that there are a number of differences in the roles that schematic and categorical organizations play in memory. We have found many indications that a schema provides a more powerful set of retrieval cues than does a taxonomic organization, but also that it is a much more active and constructive type of retrieval mechanism. Its powerful assimilative character can be a hindrance to memory for the surface detail in which the general meaning of a scene or story is embedded. In short, it is a marvelous mechanism both for storage and retrieval as long as we care more about the message than the medium. Fortunately in daily living that is usually where our priorities lie.

V. DEVELOPMENTAL AND CROSS-CULTURAL CONSIDERATIONS

The final comparison of schematic and categorical organizations, namely, the extent to which they are automatically activated and used in a memory situation, can perhaps best be discussed in the context of developmental and cross-cultural studies. The reasons are twofold. First, the achievement of hier-archically arranged taxonomic organizations is a relatively late accomplishment in the course of development—long after children demonstrate a good bit of skill in remembering. Second, there is increasing evidence that organization by taxonomic categories is in large part a function of Western schooling, and many reported cross-cultural differences in memory may be due to that fact. Schematic organizations are automatically activated by familiar situations re-gardless of age, culture, or schooling. Whether or not a categorical organiza-tion will be activated seems to be more problematical.

A. Development of Schematic Organization

At the outset we should note again that in this chapter taxonomic catego-ries are under discussion. Categorization as a psychological process begins at birth. In its broad sense, it cannot be distinguished from forming a schema. The neonate engaged in learning the category of faces can just as well be described (and often is) as learning a "face schema." However, the kind of organization we are concerned with here has to do with hierarchical classification, with the nesting of subordinate classes within superordinate ones. It is this develop-ment, as amply documented by Piaget, that occurs relatively late.

It seems reasonable that the earliest categorizing activities take place within the framework of what I have called schematic organization. More specifically, the earliest knowledge acquired by the infant occurs within the framework of daily, repetitive episodes. Infants learn to organize their world spatially, leading to perceptual categorization and, temporally, leading to categories of events. From an early age, the representation of these commonly experienced events appears to have some of the characteristics ascribed here to scripts (Nelson, 1977; 1978; Schank & Abelson, 1977).

Although no one would dispute that our knowledge of the world is built up from episodic experience (using the term in Tulving's sense of the word as temporally tagged autobiographical experience), it is a much stronger assertion to state that knowledge is organized in the first instance around episodes (in the sense of familiar, temporally structured event sequences). Yet an interesting case can be made for this view. Nelson (1974) described the young child's earliest concept formation within such a framework. Schank and Abelson (1977) provided some informal examples of impressive knowledge of scripts from 2-year-old children and suggested that evidence for scriptlike knowledge may be found in infants under the age of 1 year. More formally, Nelson (1978) has studied 4–5-year-olds' descriptions of common event sequences, such as having lunch at a daycare center or eating at McDonald's. These verbalizations are all the more impressive when we consider that preschool children have difficulty in verbalizing hierarchical classificatory relations (Anglin, 1975; Macnamara, 1972).

In what sense can such descriptions be called scripts? The Nelson data indicate that these event sequences are temporally structured for the children and show a great deal of commonality from child to child as to the level of description. That is, the same sorts of events are singled out for mention so that we can say that there is a common set of categories or units. Furthermore, these units are ordered in the same way with similar beginnings and ends. There is even some suggestion in her data that these structures are hierarchically organized, in the sense that probe questions sometimes led to more detailed descriptions of the individual categories that had been spontaneously mentioned.

The greatest value of this type of schematic organization is in providing sets of expectations that bring order and predictability into the young child's world. However, the organization of cognitive life around schematic structures has important implications for memory as well. The process of comprehension itself is so interwoven with schematic understanding that we must posit automatic schematic activation when one is remembering. A schema provides a mechanism by which so-called natural or incidental remembering occurs, and it is, as we have seen, a highly effective mechanism. A schema is automatically aroused by a familiar situation; it orders recall and provides both a start and stop rule. In this sense, retrieval can run off by itself without requiring deliberate or planful search strategies.

A great deal of the recent literature in cognitive development has stressed the difficulty young children have in deliberate memorizing (e.g., Brown, 1975). Many of the studies have involved tasks in which the child is asked to remember arbitrarily selected sets of materials. Under these circumstances, children do poorly because they have few rehearsal and organizational strategies at their disposal (cf. Flavell & Wellman, 1977). However, if the material is not arbitrary but fits a familiar schema, it will be relatively easy for the child to recall it, whether it is a deliberate memory task or not. The schema is automatically activated at the time of comprehension and will be available at the time of retrieval.

Although during the elementary school years children gradually learn the value, indeed the necessity, of imposing organization on arbitrary or new material for purposes of remembering, they seem in the main to be dependent on their customary schematic organizations, at least until the end of this period. For example, Mandler and Day (1975) found that by the second grade, children recognized the left–right orientation of familiar figures almost as well as adults. Up to the sixth grade, however, recognition of left–right orientation of unfamiliar figures was much poorer than that of adults. Similarly, Mandler and Robinson (1978) found that recognition of complex pictures of scenes approached adult performance by the third grade, but recognition of unorganized pictures resulted in consistently poor performance at least up to the fifth grade.

Even more dramatic evidence of children's reliance on schematic organization for retrieval was shown by using the normal and interleaved stories discussed earlier (J. M. Mandler, 1978; Mandler & DeForest, in press). First, children recalled less of the interleaved stories, that is, stories told out of their customary format. These data are consistent with the picture-recognition studies just discussed. More importantly, up to the sixth grade the children were less able than adults to maintain the input order in their recall of the interleaved stories, even when specifically requested to do so. As mentioned in Section IV, A, adults had some difficulties with this task, but the children had even more. If asked to output interleaved stories in their canonical order, even second graders did so perfectly. However, when asked to produce interleaved storied in interleaved fashion, second and fourth graders still showed a strong tendency to recall in canonical order. Only sixth graders showed some modest ability to follow the unfamiliar input order. These data suggest that children have no choice as to how to search their memory if it has been schematically ordered in the first place. They seem to have only one retrieval mechanism, and that is schematic search according to the structure that was activated at the time of input.

In addition to the greater flexibility of retrieval search that is available to adults, we should expect to find some memory improvement due to development of schemata themselves. Both Schank and Ableson (1977) and Nelson (1978) provide some evidence for growth in complexity and completeness of scripts with increasing age and experience. One can see a similar process at the more general level of a story schema. Informal analysis of the corpus of stories children tell, collected by Pitcher and Prelinger (1963), suggests a gradual acquisition of a story schema such as we have described (see also Glenn & Stein, 1978; and Poulsen, Kintsch, Kintsch, & Premack, in press). Botvin and Sutton-Smith (1977) have shown that structural complexity in children's self-generated stories continues to grow at least up to age 10 or 11.

B. Development of Categorical Organization

Even young children categorize in simple ways, and as young as 2 years, they show some responsivity to taxonomic relatedness in memory tasks (Goldberg, Perlmutter, & Meyers, 1974). Two-year-old children also show habituation to new members of an old taxonomic category when looking at pictues (Faulkender, Wright, & Waldron, 1974), and at least by 3 years of age show release from proactive inhibition when a new category is introduced in a memory task (Esrov, Hall, & LaFaver, 1974). Thus, at least some rudimentary response to taxonomic similarity occurs from an early age.

Nevertheless, there is a dramatic difference between the use of schematic and categorical organizations in the remembering process. At least up to the third grade, children show little spontaneous clustering in their recall of categorized lists, even when informed of the organization (e.g., Kobasigawa & Middleton, 1972). Worden (1974) showed that this phenomenon is not due to ignorance of the taxonomic categories present in the materials. If asked to sort a list of categorized words into groups, first graders spontaneously choose the "correct" taxonomic categories. Therefore, they are familiar with this type of organization, but it is not activated by presentation of a list.

Once children have actually sorted items, their recall becomes clustered like that of adults. At this point, the chief difference between children and adults is a quantitative parameter of the search. Children stop their within-category search sooner than do adults (Worden & Ritchey, 1979). If a stop rule such as suggested by Rundus (1973) is correct, children's lesser recall may be due to smaller category sizes and thus to a more rapid growth in the ratio of successfully recalled items to those remaining.

What is involved in the sorting task that activates a categorical organization and allows its use as a retrieval mechanism? Worden, Mandler, and Chang (1978) found that if a taxonomic organization was familiar to second graders, it was equally effective in producing clustering and in elevating recall whether the children sorted the items themselves, merely told the experimenter how to group the items while he did the sorting, or simply watched the experimenter sort the items into groups. Thus, neither the sensorimotor activity of sorting itself nor the decision-making activity as to what items belonged together was essential to the activation of a familiar organization. Merely watching a model group the items was sufficient.

When the list consisted of unrelated items, however, the modeling condition was no longer effective. Only children who sorted the items themselves or told the experimenter how to sort the items showed category clustering and improved recall. Most of the children in the modeling condition did learn a good deal about the new organization. Following the recall task, they were able to resort most of the items into the originally seen groupings, but this learning was not sufficient to form a useful retrieval guide. For children to be able to use a *new* organization for retrieval, they must have engaged in active analysis and decision-making about "what goes with what." Presumably, a more stable and integrated structure is created by this analytic activity.

Because it is necessary to go to great lengths, such as sorting or blocking items, to activate categorical organizations in young children, one might speculate that categorizing is not a spontaneous way of organizing the world but comes about only as a deliberate memorizing strategy. On this view, categorical organization is effective for adults because they deliberately impose it on lists of words as a mnemonic strategy. Yet there is ample evidence that this is not the case. Even very young children show some responsivity to taxonomic categories. Furthermore, some studies of adults' recall of categorized lists have used "incidental" memory paradigms, in which recall tests are not necessarily expected; clustering according to taxonomic categories nevertheless occurs. For example, Ritchey (1978) found no categorical clustering in recall of items by second-graders in which they were trying to image each item. Sixth graders showed more clustering and adults a good deal, although not as much as is found in the typical deliberate memory task. Similar developmental differences were found by Bjorklund (1976), studying children from kindergarten to the sixth grade.

Nevertheless, adults do not always discover and use the categorical structure of a list, even in a deliberate memory situation (Puff, 1970; Puff, Murphy, & Ferrara, 1977). As mentioned in Section IV, A, they can use a categorical or serial organization upon request with equal efficiency. It is in this sense that the automatic activation of a categorical organization is more questionable than activation of a schematic one. It is typical for young children not to discover the overall categorical structure of a list; such failure is less common but still occurs in adults. However, it is almost impossible for either children or adults to ignore the schematic structure of a script or story or to avoid this organization during retrieval.

The fact remains, however, that categorical organizations are more likely to be activated in adults than in children. Why 6–8-year-old children, who are familiar with such organizations, do not spontaneously uncover and use them when remembering lists is still not well understood. It can be only partially due to their lesser tendency to search for ways of structuring superficially arbitrary collections, whether trying to memorize or not. More importantly, the Worden et al. (1978) study suggested that recently acquired organizations are not necessarily useful for retrieval. Although that finding concerned truly new organizations, it is still the case that taxonomic organizations are a more recent acquisition than schematic ones. In the early years there is little hierarchical categorical organization in the mental life of the child. Concepts are learned and organized (and thus the structure of semantic memory built up) within the framework of individual episodes and their generalized forms (scripts and higher level schemata). Only gradually are these concepts freed from the contexts in which they were learned and regrouped into hierarchical relationships on the basis of similarity, class membership, and logical definition (cf. Nelson, 1977). The work of Rosch fits this point of view (Rosch, 1973; Rosch, Mervis, Gray, Johnson, & Boyes-Braem, 1976), since she has shown that even as adults our conceptual knowledge tends to be organized around the prototypes developed in childhood rather than around logical classificatory systems.

We still know relatively little about the course of this development insofar as it affects the likelihood of automatic activation of a categorical organization. The 2-year-old who shows some sensitivity to categorical relatedness in a memory task does not yet have a hierarchically arranged organization of superordinate, subordinate, and coordinate classes, but something more like small collections of items whose principles of relatedness vary in unpredictable ways (Inhelder & Piaget, 1964; Lange, 1978). Bjorklund (1976) has suggested that young children, like adults, categorize individual items in a list, but then somehow fail to link them together. This is a complex notion, suggesting that we may have ignored the role of horizontal connections between categorically related items in our emphasis on the vertical connections between superordinates and subordinates.

In any case, taxonomic structures are slowly developing forms of organization. Children prefer to group items on a schematic rather than on a taxonomic basis (Denney & Moulton, 1976), and when they do form taxonomic classifications they make smaller groups and are more variable in their assignments than adults (see Ornstein & Corsale, Chapter 7, for a discussion of relevant data). Taxonomic structures seem to be added onto a knowledge base that is basically schematically organized and that probably remains so in adulthood. It also seems clear that we use schema-based organizations for most of our daily negotiations with the world and for much of our daily remembering.

Automatic activation of taxonomic organizations probably also depends a great deal upon the extent to which they are required in daily life. We may or may not become accustomed to use categorical organization, most likely as a function of schooling or lack thereof. Whether or not schematic and categorical organizations become equally prominent in the structuring and use of knowledge is a question that cannot be answered without considerably more development of theories of semantic memory. Not only the developmental data however, but cross-cultural data as well, suggest that we may have overemphasized the role of categorical organization when discussing the importance of organization in memory.

C. Cross-Cultural Studies

Since development and schooling are almost completely confounded in industrialized societies, studies of memory performance in nonliterate societies become of great importance in determining whether the adult use of taxonomic categories represents a maturational end point or whether it is the product of a specific kind of training. Many of the most relevant studies have been carried out by Cole and Scribner in a number of studies (summarized in Cole & Scribner, 1977) among the Vai and Kpelle of Liberia. In general, they found little effective use of categorical organization among either children or adults who had little or no formal schooling. The same factors that foster the use of categorical organization in American school children, namely, sorting, blocking, and constraining recall by cueing categories at the time of output, improved both clustering and recall in the Kpelle. However, their summary statement of the factor most likely to be associated with clustering and high levels of recall is more than four years of Western schooling. Furthermore, only students who had been in school for some time tended to sort materials on the basis of taxonomic categories. Uneducated adults tended to sort into functional or other categories (Scribner, 1974). Their personal groupings, however, were used to cluster their recall. Thus, the effects of organizations activated in the learning situation were evident; only the use of taxonomic organization was lacking.

Cole and Scribner (1977) also found that embedding materials to be learned in story context improved recall. They assumed that the relative ease of recalling story-like materials was due to the automatic activation of familiar "cultural" schemata, relieving the subjects from the bottom-up task of finding or imposing organization on the materials. They pointed out that this hypothesis was as yet untested because most attempts to vary cultural familiarity have been concerned with the context in which memorizing is carried out, not with the organization of the material itself.

If the assumption that schematic organization is the primary way of structuring memory is correct, however, then story formats should be universally memorable, regardless of cultural proclivities. Furthermore, our informal analysis of stories from many cultures has suggested that the particular structure of folktales, fables, and myths (that is, stories from oral traditions) is also universal, in part at least because oral stories must respect fundamental properties of and limitations on human memory (Mandler & Johnson, 1977).

Certain evidence (Mandler, Scribner, Cole, & DeForest, in press) indicates that this is the case. We presented the same stories used with American subjects in the Mandler and Johnson study to Vai subjects in Liberia. The stories were identical with the exception of translation of foreign concepts to locally meaningful ones. Subjects ranged in age from 6 years to approximately 50 and varied in education as well. Data were analyzed in terms of performance by younger and older children, schooled literate adults, nonschooled literate adults, and nonschooled nonliterate adults. Patterns of recall among these groups and data taken from American subjects are shown in Figure 8.3. It can be seen that approximately the same patterning of recall is found for everyone,

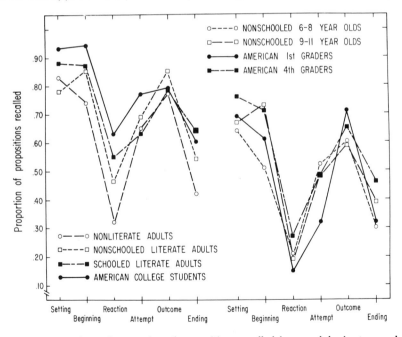

FIGURE 8.3 Comparison of proportion of propositions recalled from each basic story node by differing populations. The left panel shows data from Liberian nonliterate adults, nonschooled literate adults, schooled literate adults, and American college students. The right panel shows nonschooled younger and older Liberian children, and American first and fourth graders. The Liberian data are taken from Mandler, Scribner, Cole, and DeForest (in press) and the American data from Mandler and Johnson (1977).

across ages, literacy, and culture. There is improvement of recall in both the United States and Liberia as a function of age. There is also an improvement among Liberian adults as a function of literacy, although this increase is slight and barely significant.

Such data suggest that schematically based organizations such as stories provide a universally effective means of retrieval across cultures, schooling, and age. These data illustrate Nelson's (1977) and Brown's (1977) contention that there is a fundamental continuity in conceptual development. Knowledge is episodically based, but formal schooling adds context-free taxonomic systems of organization to a continuing and ongoing schematically based memory system. These new ways of organizing knowledge do not replace schema-based organization but are added to it. How this addition takes place and what its implications are for our understanding of the overall structure of semantic memory in both child and adult are questions that we have hardly begun to explore.

VI. CONCLUSIONS

The developmental and cross-cultural data are compelling. They remind us that by focusing so much of our memory research on lists of words—or even, as is more recently the case on lists of sentences—we have missed principles of organization that may be prevalent in our daily lives. To the extent that the principles used to organize lists vary from other commonly used organizations, we are apt to develop lopsided theories of memory, applicable only to limited phenomena.

The emphasis on categorical organization, especially of the taxonomic variety, led, I think, to the notion of a semantic memory system that is primarily hierarchically based (e.g., Collins & Quillian, 1969). There seems little doubt that our memory is to some extent organized in this fashion and that hierarchically arranged taxonomic organization can facilitate retrieval. However, most of our daily experience is not so arranged, and much of the remembering we do makes little use of such principles. Schank and Abelson (1977) made a powerful case for the view that because our experiences are episodically based and remembered, it is likely that our semantic memory (used here in the sense of knowledge about the world) is also episodic in its organization. Episodes are schematically, not taxonomically, organized, although they are undoubtedly grouped into larger sets in a categorized fashion. Our taxonomic knowledge appears to be a secondary kind of organization that has been built onto a basically schematically organized memory system.

To argue about the fundamental structure of human knowledge is clearly beyond the scope of this chapter. An attempt has been made to examine some of the available data from studies of categorically based and schematically based materials to see if the same principles of memory apply. At the most general level they clearly do. For example, recall is ordered not in terms of the way in which it was presented, but in terms of how the particular material has been cognitively structured. However, this kind of finding only indicates that cognitive organization—of whatever sort—plays a major role in what and how we remember.

At a more detailed level, we have seen some considerable differences. Schematic organizations provide different memory-search mechanisms; probabilistic or random-search models are not appropriate. More importantly, the linkage among items in a schematic organization is not based on similarity or class membership but on spatial or temporal sequences. Those studies of temporal and spatial organization that have been carried out have often used lists of items that are not themselves spatially or temporally ordered. Since we know that adults *can* organize arbitrary collections of items in almost any way we require, this may not be an ideal way to study how people remember events that are naturally spatially and/or temporally organized.

It has become fashionable to emphasize that most of our studies of memory, including studies of lists of words, concern episodic memory, in Tulving's sense of the word, rather than semantic memory (Craik, 1979; Crowder, 1976). If, as seems likely, our episodic memory is indeed episodically based, why not study memory for episodes themselves in addition to episodic memory for categorical collections? Different principles seem to be at work. We have emphasized accuracy of detail in our studies of lists, whereas the usual case of memory is not accuracy but a kind of reconstructive faithfulness to overall meaning or gist. Schematically determined memory is fundamentally reconstructive; yet we study situations in which reconstruction is not the rule and, when it does occur, is called an intrusion and treated as "error." Memory is fundamentally full of errors, and these are of as great or greater interest than cases of accurate recall. To the extent that we emphasize accuracy in our discussions of memory we emphasize omission or loss. We lose sight of the processes of normalization, the filling-in of gaps in things that were never well attended, the guessing at what must have been. Since it is along these lines that many of the most interesting phenomena of memory occur, perhaps we should study them more directly. We have an enormous body of data on recall of lists. We have hardly begun to explore recall of scripts, stories, scenes, and personally important events.

ACKNOWLEDGMENTS

Preparation of this chapter was supported in part by NIMH Grants MH-24492 and MH-15828. I am grateful to the Department of Experimental Psychology, Oxford University, where this chapter was written, and to Nancy Johnson, Endel Tulving, and George Mandler for many helpful discussions.

REFERENCES

Anglin, J. The child's first terms of reference. In S. Erlich & E. Tulving, (Eds.), *Bulletin de Psychologie, Special Issue, on Semantic Memory,* July 1975.

Bjorklund, D. F., *Children's identification and encoding of category information for recall.* Unpublished doctoral dissertation, University of North Carolina, Chapel Hill, 1976.

Bobrow, D. G., & Norman, D. A. Some principles of memory schemata. In D. G. Bobrow and A. Collins (Eds.), *Representation and understanding: Studies in cognitive science.* New York: Academic Press, 1975.

Botvin, G. J., & Sutton-Smith, B. The development of complexity in children's fantasy narratives. *Developmental Psychology,* 1977, *13,* 377–388.

Bower, G. H., Black, J. B., & Turner, T. J. Scripts in memory for text. *Cognitive Psychology,* 1979, *11,* 77–220.

Bower, G. H., Clark, M. C., Lesgold, A. M., & Wizenz, D. Hierarchical retrieval schemes in recall of categorized word lists. *Journal of Verbal Learning and Verbal Behavior,* 1969, *8,* 323–343.

Bransford, J. D., & Franks, J. J. The abstraction of linguistic ideas. *Cognitive Psychology,* 1971, *2,* 331–350.

Broadbent, D. E., Cooper, P. J., & Broadbent, M. H. P. A comparison of hierarchical and matrix retrieval schemes in recall. *Journal of Experimental Psychology: Human Learning and Memory,* 1978, *4,* 486–497.

Brown, A. L. The development of memory: Knowing, knowing about knowing, and knowing how to know. In H. W. Reese (Ed.), *Advances in child development* (Vol. 10). New York: Academic Press, 1975.

Brown, A. L. Development, schooling, and the acquisition of knowledge: Comments on Chapter 7 by Nelson. In R. C. Anderson, R. J. Spiro, & W. E. Montague (Eds.), *Schooling and the acquisition of knowledge.* Hillsdale, N.J.: Lawrence Erlbaum Associates, 1977.

Chi, M. T. H. Knowledge structure and memory development. In R. Siegler (Ed.), *Children's thinking: What develops?* Hillsdale, N.J.: Lawrence Erlbaum Associates, 1978.

Cofer, C. N., Bruce, D. R., & Reicher, G. M. Clustering in free recall as a function of certain methodological variations. *Journal of Experimental Psychology,* 1966, *71,* 858–866.

Cohen, B. H. Recall of categorized word lists. *Journal of Experimental Psychology,* 1963, *66,* 227–234.

Colby, B. N. A partial grammar of Eskimo folktales. *American Anthropologist,* 1973, *75,* 645–662.

Cole, M., & Scribner, S. Cross-cultural studies of memory and cognition. In R. V. Kail & J. W. Hagen, (Eds.), *Perspectives on the development of menory and cognition.* Hillsdale, N.J.: Lawrence Erlbaum Associates, 1977.

Collins, A. N., & Quillian, M. R. Retrieval time from semantic memory. *Journal of Verbal Learning and Verbal Behavior,* 1969, *8,* 240–247.

Craik, F. I. M. Human memory. In M. R. Rosenzweig & L. W. Porter (Eds.), *Annual Review of Psychology,* Vol. 30. Palo Alto, Cal.: Annual Reviews, Inc., 1979.

Craik, F. I. M., & Lockhart, R. S. Levels of processing: A framework for memory research. *Journal of Verbal Learning and Verbal Behavior,* 1972, *11,* 671–684.

Crowder, R. G. *Principles of learning and memory.* Hillsdale, N.J.: Lawrence Erlbaum Associates, 1976.

Denney, D. R., & Moulton, P. A. Conceptual preferences among preschool children. *Developmental Psychology,* 1976, *12,* 509–513.

Esrov, L. V., Hall, J. W., & LaFaver, D. K. Preschoolers' conceptual and acoustic encodings as evidenced by release from PI. *Bulletin of the Psychonomic Society,* 1974, *4,* 89–90.

Faulkender, P. J., Wright, J. C., & Waldron, A. Generalized habituation of concept stimuli in toddlers. *Child Development,* 1974, *45,* 1002–1010.

Flavell, J. H., & Wellman, H. M. Metamemory. In R. V. Kail & J. W. Hagen (Eds.), *Perspectives on the development of memory and cognition.* Hillsdale, N.J.: Lawrence Erlbaum Associates, 1977.

Friedman, A. Framing pictures: The role of default knowledge in automatized encoding and memory for gist. *Journal of Experimental Psychology: General,* in press.

Gauld, A., & Stephenson, G. M. Some experiments relating to Bartlett's theory of remembering. *British Journal of Psychology,* 1967, *58,* 39–49.

Glenn, C. G., & Stein, N. L. Syntactic structures and real world themes in stories generated by children. Unpublished manuscript, University of Illinois, 1978.

Goldberg, S., Perlmutter, M., & Meyers, N. Recall of related and unrelated lists by 2-year-olds. *Journal of Experimental Child Psychology,* 1974, *18,* 1–8.

Goodman, G. S. Memory for high- and low-relevant information in pictures. Paper presented at the meetings of the Psychonomic Society, San Antonio, 1978.

Indow, T., & Togano, K. On retrieving sequences from long-term memory. *Psychological Review,* 1970, *77,* 317–331.

Inhelder, B., & Piaget, J. *The early growth of logic in the child.* New York: Harper, 1964.

Kellas, G., Ashcraft, M. H., Johnson, N. S., & Needham, S. Temporal aspects of storage and retrieval in free recall of categorized lists. *Journal of Verbal Learning and Verbal Behavior,* 1973, *12,* 499–511.

Kinsbourne, M., & George, J. The mechanism of the word-frequency effect on recognition memory. *Journal of Verbal Learning and Verbal Behavior,* 1974, *13,* 63–69.

Kintsch, W., Mandel, T., & Kominsky, E. Summarizing scrambled stories. *Memory & Cognition,* 1977, *5,* 547–552.

Kobasigawa, A., & Middleton, D. B. Free recall of categorized items by children at three grade levels. *Child Development,* 1972, *43,* 1067–1072.

Lange, G. Organization-related processes in children's recall. In P. A. Ornstein (Ed.), *Memory development in children.* Hillsdale, N.J.: Lawrence Erlbaum Associates, 1978.

Macnamara, J. Cognitive basis of language learning in infants. *Psychological Review,* 1972, *79,* 1–13.

Mandler, G. Organization and memory. In K. W. Spence & J. T. Spence (Eds.), *The psychology of learning and motivation: Advances in research and theory.* New York: Academic Press, 1967.

Mandler, G. Words, lists, and categories: An experimental view of organized memory. In J. L. Cowan (Ed.), *Studies in thought and language.* Tucson: University of Arizona Press, 1970.

Mandler, G., & Barsalou, L. W. Steady state memory: What does the one-shot experiment assess? Technical Report Number 84, Center for Human Information Processing, University of California, San Diego, La Jolla, California, 1979.

Mandler, G., & Mandler, J. M. Serial position effects in sentences. *Journal of Verbal Learning and Verbal Behavior,* 1964, *3,* 195–202.

Mandler, G., Pearlstone, Z., & Koopmans, H. J. Effects of organization and semantic similarity on recall and recognition. *Journal of Verbal Learning and Verbal Behavior,* 1969, *8,* 410–423.

Mandler, J. M. A code in the node: The use of a story schema in retrieval. *Discourse Processes,* 1978, *1,* 14–35.

Mandler, J. M., & Day, J. Memory for orientation of forms as a function of their meaningfulness and complexity. *Journal of Experimental Child Psychology,* 1975, *20,* 430–443.

Mandler, J. M., & DeForest, M. Is there more than one way to recall a story? *Child Development,* in press.

Mandler, J. M., & Johnson, N. S. Some of the thousand words a picture is worth. *Journal of Experimental Psychology: Human Learning and Memory,* 1976, *2,* 529–540.

Mandler, J. M., & Johnson, N. S. Remembrance of things parsed: Story structure and recall. *Cognitive Psychology,* 1977, *9,* 111–151.

Mandler, J. M., & Parker, R. E. Memory for descriptive and spatial information in complex pictures. *Journal of Experimental Psychology: Human Learning and Memory,* 1976, *2,* 38–48.

Mandler, J. M., & Ritchey, G. H. Long-term memory for pictures. *Journal of Experimental Psychology: Human Learning and Memory,* 1977, *3,* 386–396.

Mandler, J. M., & Robinson, C. A. Developmental changes in picture recognition. *Journal of Experimental Child Psychology,* 1978, *26,* 122–136.

Mandler, J. M., Scribner, S., Cole, M., & DeForest, M. Cross-cultural invariance in story recall. *Child Development,* in press.

Miller, G. A., & Johnson-Laird, P. M. *Language and perception.* Cambridge, England: Cambridge University Press, 1976.

Minsky, M. A framework for representing knowledge. In P. Winston (Ed.), *The psychology of computer vision.* New York: McGraw-Hill, 1975.

Nelson, K. Concept, word, and sentence: Interrelations in acquisition and development. *Psychological Review,* 1974, *81,* 267–285.

Nelson, K. Cognitive development and the acquisition of concepts. In R. C. Anderson, R. J. Spiro, & W. E. Montague, (Eds.), *Schooling and the acquisition of knowledge.* Hillsdale, N.J.: Lawrence Erlbaum Associates, 1977.

Nelson, K. How young children represent knowledge of their world in and out of language: A preliminary report. In R. Siegler (Ed.), *Children's thinking–What develops?* Hillsdale, N.J.: Lawrence Erlbaum Associates, 1978.

Park, N. W. *Superadditivity of retrieval cues as a function of encoding conditions.* Unpublished doctoral dissertation, University of Toronto, 1979.

Patterson, K. E., Meltzer, R. H., & Mandler, G. Inter-response times in categorized free recall. *Journal of Verbal Learning and Verbal Behavior,* 1971, *10,* 417–426.

Pitcher, E. G., & Prelinger, E. *Children tell stories: An analysis of fantasy.* New York: International Universities Press, 1963.

Poulsen, D., Kintsch, E., Kintsch, W., & Premack, D. Children's comprehension and memory for stories. *Journal of Experimental Child Psychology,* in press.

Puff, C. R. Role of clustering in free recall. *Journal of Experimental Psychology,* 1970, *86,* 384–386.

Puff, C. R., Murphy, M. D., & Ferrara, R. A. Further evidence about the role of clustering in free recall. *Journal of Experimental Psychology: Human Learning and Memory,* 1977, *3,* 742–753.

Ritchey, G. H. *Elaborative processing in semantic memory: A developmental perspective.* Unpublished doctoral dissertation, University of California, San Diego, 1978.

Roediger, H. L., III. Inhibiting effects of recall. *Memory & Cognition,* 1974, *2,* 261–269.

Roediger, H. L., & Crowder, R. G. The serial position effect in recall of U.S. presidents. Unpublished manuscrppt, cited in Crowder, R. G., *Principles of learning and memory.* Hillsdale, N.J.: Lawrence Erlbaum Associates, 1976.

Rosch, E. H. On the internal structure of perceptual and semantic categories. In T. E. Moore (Ed.), *Cognitive development and the acquisition of language.* New York: Academic Press, 1973.

Rosch, E. H., Mervis, C. B., Gray, W., Johnson, D., & Boyes-Braem, P. Basic objects in natural categories. *Cognitive Psychology,* 1976, *8,* 382–439.

Rumelhart, D. E. Notes on a schema for stories. In D. G. Bobrow & A. M. Collins (Eds.), *Representation and understanding: Studies in cognitive science.* New York: Academic Press, 1975.

Rumelhart, D. E., & Ortony, A. The representation of knowledge in memory, In R. C. Anderson, R. J. Spiro, & W. E. Montague (Eds.), *Schooling and the acquisition of knowledge.* Hillsdale, N.J.: Lawrence Erlbaum Associates, 1977.

Rundus, D. Negative effects of using list items as recall cues. *Journal of Verbal Learning and Verbal Behavior,* 1973, *12,* 43–50.

Schank, R. C., & Abelson, R. P. Scripts, plans, and knowledge. *Proceedings of the fourth international joint conference on artificial intelligence.* Tbilisi, 1975. [Reprinted in P. N. Johnson-Laird & P. C. Wason (Eds.), *Thinking: Readings in cognitive science.* Cambridge, England: Cambridge University Press, 1977.]

Schank, R. C., & Abelson, R. P. *Scripts, plans, goals, and understanding*. Hillsdale, N.J.: Lawrence Erlbaum Associates, 1977.

Scribner, S. Developmental aspects of categorized recall in a West African society, *Cognitive Psychology*, 1974, *6*, 475–494.

Slamecka, N. J. An examination of trace storage in free recall. *Journal of Experimental Psychology*, 1968, *76*, 504–513.

Slamecka, N. J. The question of associative growth in the learning of categorized material. *Journal of Verbal Learning and Verbal Behavior*, 1972, *11*, 324–332.

Stein, N. S., & Glenn, C. G. The role of structural variation in children's recall of simple stories. Paper presented at the meeting of the Society for Research in Child Development, New Orleans, 1977.

Stein, N. S., & Glenn, C. G. An analysis of story comprehension in elementary school children. In R. Freedle (Ed.), *New directions in discourse processing*. Hillsdale, N.J.: Ablex, 1979.

Stein, N. S., & Nezworski, T. The effect of organization and instructional set on story memory. *Discourse Processes*, 1978, *1*, 177–194.

Thorndyke, P. W. Cognitive structures in comprehension and memory of narrative discourse. *Cognitive Psychology*, 1977, *9*, 77–110.

Tulving, E. Episodic and semantic memory. In E. Tulving & W. Donaldson (Eds.), *Organization of memory*. New York: Academic Press, 1972.

Worden, P. E. The development of the category-recall function under three retrieval conditions. *Child Development*, 1974, *45*, 1054–1059.

Worden, P. E., Mandler, J. M., & Chang, F. R. Children's free recall: An explanation of sorts. *Child Development*, 1978, *49*, 836–844.

Worden, P. E., & Ritchey, G. H. The development of the category-recall relationship in the sorting-recall task. *Journal of Experimental Child Psychology*, 1979, *27*, 384–394.

PART V

PERSPECTIVES ON THE SCOPE
OF ORGANIZATIONAL
CONCEPTS

CHAPTER 9

Organization, Memory, and Mental Structures

During the past 15 years, the concept of organization has become respectable to the point where it has become fashionable to relate one's research to "the organizational point of view," whatever the data of the experiment or the reason for doing it might be. One might argue that such a state of affairs is simply a deplorable symptom of fashion, of sheeplike devotion to a current fad, but I would rather classify it as the acceptance of a point of view. The acceptance of organizational points of view is a significant symptom of the break with the behaviorist S–R tradition. Organizational interpretations of human action, related as they were to the Gestalt tradition of decades earlier, took up the search for a construction of complex theoretical processes, of convenient fictions that were essentially proscribed during the functionalist –behaviorist interlude. Organizational points of view, by ascribing complex theoretical structures to the organism, made possible once again an experimental psychology of human "learning" that was willing to see its data, the

MEMORY ORGANIZATION
AND STRUCTURE

ISBN 0-12-566750-7

behavior of organisms, as starting points for the inference of theoretical structures. These structures, whether borrowed from Gestalt psychology, from the
neurosciences, or couched in computational metaphors, not only allowed for a
greater variety of inferred processes, but also made again possible—as the
Gestaltists, the French school of the turn of the century, Selz, and others had
done in another generation—a strong differentiation from associationist dogma.
Fundamentally, association theory had insisted on two principles: *(a)* the
establishment of associations by contiguity and *(b)* the monistic insistence that
associations varied only in strength or probability. Current organizational
approaches (and cognitive psychology in general) reject both of these principles. First, contiguity is seen as neither empirically necessary nor theoretically
sufficient for the state of affairs where a particular intra- or extrapsychic event
leads to the occurrence of some other event. Second, there has been a steady
decline in the use of strength and energy models; empirical associations
between two events are not viewed as varying in strength (and strength only)
but rather are seen as defined by relations that hold between them, as "labeled
associations." This trend not only has enveloped the investigation of human
memory but also has replaced related energy concepts in such areas as emotion
(Mandler, 1975b) and motivation (Gallistel, 1975, 1979).

In the following pages, the range of an organizational psychology of
memory is loosely defined and the current problems and trends of the field are
assessed in terms of structural approaches. My intent is to look only at traditional memory research, thus excluding more complex fields such as the
relation between memory and linguistics or the application of organizational
approaches to more complex events such as actions, visual structures, temporally
organized events such as scripts and stories, and other extensions. It is not my
intent to review the literature of the field; rather I illustrate frequently the
arguments to be made by the literature I know best—data from our laboratory.
In no sense is this intended to slight the frequently more important contributions made on similar subjects by others. One final caveat: Although I believe
that the development of organizational approaches and of the new cognitive
psychology has been coextensive, I do not believe that these developments
represent a paradigm shift in the Kuhnian sense. To the contrary, the cyclical
shifts between associationist and organizational approaches over the past 75
years, the eminent predecessors of current trends (cf. Katona, 1940), and a new
discernable current toward strength and associative concepts all suggest the
preparadigmatic nature of our field—the paradigmatic crown is still to be won.

I. ORGANIZATION AND STRUCTURE IN
MEMORY RESEARCH

Regardless of other preoccupations, the basic paradigm for memory researchers is the same. Some materials, events, or items are presented to an
individual, and some time after that presentation (with the interval varying from

seconds to weeks), the subject is asked either to reproduce that material or to identify a copy of it.

From the organizational point of view, the interesting theoretical and empirical events are:

1. The use of existing mental structures to operate on the input events. This step involves the organization of the input in terms of expectations on the one hand and in terms of structures built into the input events on the other. In the latter case, the subject needs to discover possible relations in the input.
2. Given that some coding is imposed on the structure in the initial step, then these codes must be organized into existing mental organizations, or new structures must be developed in order to accommodate the presented material.
3. Output instructions must be coded and identified and in turn related to existing mental structures. This may also involve certain relational, structural requirements in the conditions of retrieval (including the instructions) that need to be identified or discovered.
4. The codes and primed structures derived from the output conditions must be used to search for or retrieve events (or structures) that satisfy these codes.
5. The result of the retrieval processes involved in the previous step must be coordinated with some output system, be it verbal or otherwise.

The repeated use of the concept of structure here points to some differences in usage between structure and organization. We tend to speak of the representations of past experience as mental structures, whereas organization typically refers to the relationships within those structures. However, this difference in usage is not general, nor will I necessarily keep to it in these pages; organized processes are structured and structures are organized.

It follows from the preceding characterization that organizational processes are not something to be detected in the behavior of our subjects but rather that they are inferred events. Such inference, as always in the case of the erection of scientific theories, can arise out of the observation of human action or can be postulated a priori by the theorist, together with a specification of the behaviors that shall count as indices of these internal structures. More important, and in contrast to the positivistic predilections of previous decades, these theoretical structures are not seen as strongly anchored in antecedent and consequent variables. In fact, the antecedent variables that give rise to these structures are largely unknown, except for some instances of developmental work, and the organization theorist may remain neutral on the issue of whether these structures are the result of experience or are invariant structural features of the human mental apparatus. Similarly, the outcome of the operation of these structures is not tied to some specific dependent variable; rather, the theory specifies certain indices or symptoms that should occur if the structure is operative. Furthermore, the theory may not even specify a single relevant class of dependent variables. In some cases, the effect may be on the magnitude of output (the traditional learning variables), in other cases only on the structure of the output (the familiar output dependencies), and in still other cases on some combination of the two.

If a definition, in the general sense, of the nature of structure or organization is needed, it can only refer to classes of relations since, as we shall see, there are a number of different kinds of organizations that may operate within mental structures. I prefer as a starting point some combination of the definitions I provided in 1967, and Bower in 1970. I argued that sets of objects or events can be said to be organized when consistent relationships among the members of the set can be specified. I added that memberships of objects or events in subsets must in turn be stable and identifiable (Mandler, 1967b). The latter point was made more clearly by Bower when he advocated a formulation "in terms of the notions of groups (or classes) and relations (or relational rules) [Bower, 1970, p. 19]." It should be added that these grouping and relating processes operate on the representations of objects and events. Thus, what is organized or structured is always the mental representations of external or internal objects and events.

Organizational theory is more a point of view than a theory, a point that has become increasingly obvious during the past few years. Cognitive psychologists are willing to speculate about the kind of mental structures that might have been operating given that they observe some particular behavior or input–output correlation. As a belief, as a point of view, organizational approaches are not testable in any conventional sense of the term. The organization of mental contents is assumed to be axiomatic—it guides the kind of theoretical endeavor its adherents propound; it does not itself lead to any testable or falsifiable consequences. Thus any kind of observation about human memory is grist for the organization theorists' mill. Even the remaining strongholds of association theorists, pairwise and serial "associations," are viewed as nothing but challenges for the construction of appropriate structures that will generate the organization of relations among members of pairs and of spatiotemporal series.

One final general point needs to be stressed. In a peculiar sense, many organization theorists working on problems of memory are not primarily interested in the characteristics of human memory. Rather, the memory experiment is used as a convenient paradigm for probing the structure of the human mental apparatus. This is not to say that other paradigms are not equally or even more useful. Psycholinguistics, visual and auditory information processing, and others, all play their part in this expedition to the interior of the mind. In a sense, we have all become cognitive scientists, using whatever methods and theories that are at our disposal to specify the structure of human mental life. The more that is known about that structure, the better we can then answer questions about specific human tasks, including memory problems. The final outcome of this development is the tendency to look at the requirements of a particular task—to perform a task analysis—and then to draw on whatever known cognitive processes are available to provide the common goal—prediction, explanation, and understanding.

II. CLASSES OF STRUCTURES

Traditional memory research—the verbal learning field of old—has confined most of its effort to variations on just a few paradigms. Leaving aside short-term memory studies, most of the studies fall into three groups. First, and over the years the most ubiquitous, is the study of paired associates. Although the terminology has changed, from S–R to A–B to LC–TBR and, most recently, to context–target, the basic paradigm remains the same; individuals are given pairs of items and required to recall one or the other given the remaining item as a cue. Second is the serial learning task in which subjects are given a list of items and required to recall them in the order presented, where order can be defined either temporally or spatially, though usually these two parameters are confounded. Finally, and in terms of popularity the most recent addition to the armamentarium, there is free recall in which the task is to recall a list of items, typically with no special cues provided, although sometimes category names are provided in the recall of categorized lists. How can we account for the popularity of these few paradigms?

It is reasonable to suggest that these three classes of research paradigms have survived because they show a large degree of overlap with three popular organizational structures: relational structures, seriation, and categorical structures (Mandler, 1970). The term "popular" is used here to avoid a definite commitment to terms such as primary, fundamental, or basic. Whereas one could argue that these three classes of structures are indeed at the basis of more complex organizations, the enterprise in general is in too early a stage to make definite claims about structural taxonomies. However, more complex, and typically more useful, structures show specifiable relationships with the simpler ones. The general problem of imagery and the argument between propositional and analogical representations (cf. Pylyshyn, 1973) builds on the general question about the nature of the internal representations that relate two (or more) events one to the other. Similarly, the fundamental question of the serial structure of speech and action (cf. Lashley, 1951) expands on the simpler, and often more simplistic, question of the representation of spatially or temporally organized series of events. Hierarchical models of semantic networks and their descendants (e.g., Collins & Quillian, 1972) are clearly related to the notion of the hierarchical structure of categories.

A. Coordinate, Subordinate, and Proordinate Structures

I previously referred to the three simple structures as relational, categorical, and serial (Mandler, 1970). However, this particular terminology is unsatisfactory, because it tells little about the differences among the three classes, and furthermore all of them are, of course, relationships. I shall therefore switch to the more satisfactory description of coordinate, subordinate, and proordinate structures, terms that allude to the general relational ordering operations involved as well as to the specific character of the three classes. Spatial descriptions of the structures and relations among the structures are shown in Figure 9.1.

Coordinate (relational) structures involve typically two (or more) units, items, or events. The relations involved are strictly among the units. The structure is holistic in the sense that access to one part of the structure entails access to the whole structure. The multidirectional nature of these relations is shown in Figure 9.1. Relations among coordinate structures are shown as coordinate between holistic units. Whether there is a limit to the number of units that can be accommodated within such a structure has not been specifically investigated. However, given the limitation of a limited-capacity consciousness or executive process (Mandler, 1975a), it is highly likely that the limit is not much larger than three. In the case of four units, six coordinate relations need to be involved and may not be simultaneously accessible to the cognitive system.

Subordinate (categorical) structures are usually, but not necessarily always, hierarchically organized. The basic relation is between some superordinate node or concept and the subordinate members of the class. In the pure case, there are no relations among the units (cf. Slamecka, 1968, 1972); all relational operators function between the instances and the superordinate node (as shown in Figure 9.1). The number of units subordinate to a node is about five (cf. Graesser & Mandler, 1978).

Proordinate (serial) structures are temporally or spatially organized in a ballistic sense. Access to a target event is dependent on access to some number of serially preceding events. These serial structures are not a chain of pairwise coordinations, but rather the unit is some small set of proordinated units. Again the number is likely to be within the span of human apprehension (less than five), and longer serial structures are constructed out of hierarchically organized proordinate units.

Although Figure 9.1 shows the extension of a *particular* structural principle to two structures each, it should be understood that the organization of

COORDINATE   SUBORDINATE   PROORDINATE

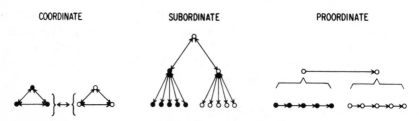

FIGURE 9.1 Spatial presentation of coordinate, subordinate, and proordinate structures. The figure also shows more extended relations between two such structures.

several structures may use any of the three principles. For example, two coordinate structures may be proordinately or subordinately organized.

Structures needed to explicate the apprehension and organization of complex events, at least those closer to the experience of real people in the real world, frequently go beyond the simpler structures discussed here (cf. J.M. Mandler, Chapter 8). They "go beyond" in the sense that it is doubtful whether these complex spatiotemporal heterarchies can be in any reasonable sense decomposed into simpler structures. The utility of dealing with relational, categorical, and serial structures in their simple forms is that they do represent a reasonable set of possible windows into the structure of the human mind.

Given the utility of these three classes of structures, what is their relationship to paired-associate, serial, and free-recall paradigms? I suggested that these two groups of three are correlated, and all I intend by that assertion is the observation that coordinate structures are an important strategy for paired-associate learning, proordination for serial learning, and subordination for the free recall of lists. In no sense do I wish to imply that task and structure are identical. On the contrary, it is now well know that the three different tasks frequently call on more than one structure for their effective organization.

For example, in the paired-associate paradigm, subjects also impose a categorical organization on the items, that is, items that appear on the "left" and "right" of the pairs are organized independently of the pairwise coordinate organization (Segal & Mandler, 1967). In addition, there is reason to believe that directional organizations (proordinate, in other words) also occur in paired associates (cf. Wolford, 1971; Rabinowitz, Mandler, & Barsalou, 1977). In serial organization, the hierarchical structuring of subsets or chunks of a series has been assumed by one of the most influential models of serial structure (Restle, 1970). In free recall, outputs within chunks or categories often have sequential (proordinate) characteristics (Patterson, Meltzer, & Mandler, 1971; Graesser & Mandler, 1978).

B. Intraitem Organization

There is one other class of structures that is of particular interest. It is in a sense orthogonal to the classes discussed before and refers to the organization of events or items as such, specifically to organization within items or events. I was led to a concern with processes that affect individual items rather than the relation among items and events, primarily by two sets of observations: (a) the discovery that sheer repetition, primary or maintenance rehearsal, of an item affected recognition but not recall (Woodward, Bjork, & Jongward, 1973; Craik & Watkins, 1973) and (b) the establishment of the fact that retrieval processes affect recognition performance (e.g., Mandler, 1972). It was in particular the latter development in our own laboratory that engendered a greater concern with intraitem organization.

In 1969 we had postulated a two-stage process for recognition, that is, a task in which a copy of an old item is presented and the subject must make an "old" or "new" judgment. The model assumed that an initial decision about prior occurrence is made on the basis of information derived directly from the item, what we then called occurrence information. For those items that fail to match some criterion of that information, a retrieval process is initiated that inquires (in the free-recall situation) whether the item is retrievable; if yes, then it is called old (Mandler, Pearlstone, & Koopmans, 1969). The same general formulation was presented by Juola, Fischler, Wood, and Atkinson (1971) and later elaborated (e.g., Atkinson & Juola, 1974). These theorists referred to the occurrence information as familiarity, and there have been other proposals for naming that particular dimension (e.g., list tags, presentation code).

The subsequent data on maintenance rehearsal suggested a single general dimension that generates phenomenal experiences of familiarity, prior presentation, or prior occurrence. I have referred to that dimension as the integration of the target item or event (Mandler, 1979). In any case, the general case of the 1969 formulation still stands: Recognition consists of the sum of two probabilities, first the probability that an item will be automatically considered "old" if the familiarity or occurrence information retrieved from its copy reaches some criterial value, plus the probability (for the remaining items) that some appropriate retrieval process can produce evidence that the items belonged to the target input.

It is not my purpose here to discuss the extensive evidence available in support of that formulation, but rather to distinguish between these two kinds of structures, intrastructural ones referred to as integration, and interstructural ones best labeled as elaboration (cf. also Craik & Tulving, 1975) and represented for our purposes primarily by the three classes of structures discussed earlier. Another topic left for speculation is whether intraitem processes are the same three classes of structures proposed for the interitem organizations.

I assume that integration, and the resultant familiarity and occurrence judgments, are a function of attention and processing capacity being directed to the structure of the target item, regardless of its relations with other events, items, contexts, etc. In a sense, this is a perceptual process (cf. also Atkinson & Wescourt, 1975) in which such structural nodes as letters, phonological components, spatial envelope, and physical context play the important role. The more attention is paid (time spent) to these features, the more compact, distinctive, invariant the structure of the target event becomes. Repetition effects and so-called rote-learning effects can be ascribed to this process (Mandler, 1979).

The importance of integrative structures for the organizational point of view is that questions of structure are being extended to issues that have not heretofore been addressed from this vantage point. In fact, even theorists of the organizational persuasion have been known to refer to some processes as "mere rote learning" or as the effects of overlearning without asking how organizational theory would deal with these phenomena. In a sense, they have been seen as belonging more to associationist concerns, and they have been left aside in the pursuit of the more powerful and interesting interitem phenomena. If I am correct in describing organizational theory not as a theory but as a general approach, then its proponents have the responsibility of at least trying to bring most phenomena of interest to a psychology of memory under that umbrella.

In the absence of any clean classification of tasks that maps into possible mental structures, the organizational theorist must approach each task, and its extended definition in terms of materials used and instructions given, as a novel puzzle. What organizational structures and processes are or might be relevant and at what stages in the coding and retrieval process might they be used? The problem of organizational theory and task analysis is discussed in the next section.

III. TASK ANALYSES AND THE USE OF ORGANIZATIONAL PRINCIPLES

No task or situation prescribes a priori the use of particular structures or organizations. Given a specific task, it is useful to analyze it in terms of the five events listed earlier as the loci of structural intervention. In general terms, the following kinds of considerations would enter into such analyses:

1. What is the nature of the material that either demands or easily accommodates to existing structures, that is, what particular aspects of the input will be attended to by the experimental subject, what kind of structures are primed by the nature of the instructions and the characteristics of the experimental subject?
2. Given the products of this initial phase, can they easily be assimilated within preexisting structures, or is it necessary to construct a somewhat novel (never entirely so, of course) structure to define the relations among input materials and instructions?
3. What is the nature of the output instructions? What information (cues) is made available to the subjects that will prime particular structures? In addition, what is the time interval since input and storage and what do we know or can we speculate about the fate of storage structures over time?
4. What does the analysis of the instructions and output conditions generate in terms of access to points and addresses of the structures within which the original input was coded?
5. Given some product of the search process, are there output systems that can accommodate to these products? In a more general sense, how and when can one observe the appropriate output; what data reductions are relevant to the expected output?

At no time do I wish to imply that these are five serial "stages" or even "boxes" in the processing of memorial information. On the contrary, these five loci of analysis interact, overlap, and are even sometimes indistinguishable. For example, we know that expectations of the output conditions significantly affect both input and storage strategies; the availability of particular search strategies probably determines or at least bounds the choice of storage strategies; the character of the input materials and particular instructions given at that time may constrain choices of storage, retrieval, and output structures, and so on.

I shall apply this kind of approach in a nonsystematic manner to a number of problems, contemporary and ancient, in memory research. I start with the free-recall paradigm because it was responsible, more than any other kind of research, for making the organizational approach respectable. It all started, in this corner of the field, with Miller's crucial breakthrough by advocating a structural limitation on human information processing—the magic number 7 ± 2 (Miller, 1956). The notion that the limitation could be overcome by chunking or unitization led directly to Tulving's seminal 1962 paper and the notion of subjective organization. Tulving's analysis of output protocols convinced psychologists that active processes organized unrelated lists. This kind of approach derived directly from a use of structural principles and a task analysis, by asking the question how, given the Millerian limitation, subjects ever remember more than seven items from a list. Given that they must impose some organization, like chunking, how would such internal structures then become observable in output protocols? The important step was to apply these principles to lists of items that contained no deliberate or decipherable structure, thus placing the locus of organization inside the mental apparatus. After all, it had been known for some time that categorized lists show organizational effects (e.g., in the work of Bousfield, 1953), but there the effect was directly ascribed to structures "contained" in the input material. Some years later we showed that the organizational processes imposed on "unrelated" material could be externalized by having subjects categorize unrelated sets of items— an approach that further established the importance of structural principles (Mandler, 1967b, 1977). Here again the initial step was to determine now people could assimilate new material to preexisting semantic structures and to use the Millerian principle as a starting point for the analysis of the task involved. We have all gone beyond those beginnings so that Postman's insightful analysis of the organizational position in 1972, which stressed chunking and unitizations, seems to address only a small part of relevant applications.

The general implications from Tulving's analyses were essentially neutral as to the nature of the organizational processes involved, particularly whether the output consistencies that he found were related to subordinated or coordinated structures. If coordinated, then breaking up pairs shown in subjects' output should prevent improvement in performance. We performed such an experiment (Mandler, Worden, & Graesser, 1974) in which the important manipulation was to remove every other item in output from the input of the subsequent trial. Compared with the appropriate control, this manipulation showed no effect on performance. One can conclude, therefore, that the output consistencies were not relational or coordinate in character.

Again the question of task analysis arises. If the structures used are categorical, how can such an effect be demonstrated? We used another method developed by Tulving (1967)—the triple recall method in which subjects produce three consecutive outputs after each presentation of a list. Items that occurred in all three outputs were called "common" items and were postulated to be the foci around which the list was organized. Again, an analysis of the structures used and relevant to the task suggested that if these common items were removed from the subsequent input list, performance should be seriously impaired, which in fact it was. This approach brought the organization of lists of unrelated words into line with the analysis of recall of categorized lists. In unrelated lists, subjects establish their own subjective categories around a small number of common items that define the semantic dimension for such organization, just as the explicit categories define the loci in the recall of categorized lists. In a subsequent paper (Mandler & Graesser, 1976), we further developed this notion and showed, for example, that the list length effect was due to the recruitment of items other than these common items; the number of common items is unrelated to list length and varies around eight, while the other (variable) items that occur in only one or two of the three outputs increase linearly with list length. The organization of lists around these common items was shown also to be relevant to the free emission of semantic categories, a nonexperimental example of the retrieval of hierarchically organized structures (Graesser & Mandler, 1978). All these studies confirmed the view that hierarchical subordinated structures predominate in the acquisition of categorized and unrelated lists, as well as in the structure of semantic memory.

The paired-associate paradigm has been less subject to organizational analyses than free recall, though some years ago there was an intensive argument concerning the holistic nature of paired associates when Asch (1968) insisted on the associate symmetry of pairwise associations. We became interested in a structural analysis of paired-associate units when we tried to apply to them the general recognition model mentioned earlier. In part, the search was motivated by Tulving's demonstration of the phenomenon of recognition failure. In the A–B pair, he demonstrated reliably and repeatedly that subjects were able to recall some B items (given A), which, however, they could not recognize. Given the counterintuitive and generally countertheoretical nature of this finding, it presents a challenge to any respectable and aspiring theory of recognition.

Our analysis started with the assumption that initial recognition decisions of these B items would be made on the basis of occurrence or familiarity information and that only those that failed to achieve an "old" judgment on this basis would undergo a retrieval test. However, what retrieval would be relevant to the recognition of a B item? Given the coordinated encoding that we assumed that the pair had undergone, we concluded that the retrieval phase must be of the nature of trying to find an A–B pair of which the target B item is a member. In other words, the recognition of B depended first on its familiarity (or integration) and second on the probability of the correct retrieval of the appropriate A item. We showed that recognition failure is in fact dependent on the failure to retrieve A, given B, in contrast to the "recall" test, which investigates the probability of retrieving B, given A (Rabinowitz, Mandler, & Barsalou, 1977).

Another test of the holistic relational encoding of item pairs involved a free-recall test following the presentation of A–B pairs. In contrast to cued recall, free recall (without explicit cues) of pairs would show a preponderance of pairs recalled, which it did. Even though subjects were encouraged to recall either whole pairs or single items, 72% of the correct recalls were intact, correct pairs. Given that an A item was recalled, the probability was .81 that it was part of an intact pair; for B items, the probability was .82. Thus, in contrast to categorically organized events, paired items depend primarily on the relation between the items. In categorical organizations, relations among instances are either irrelevant or negligibly effective; the structure depends primarily on the relation between the items and a superordinate node.

Relatively little work has been done on the retrieval of serially organized material, with Restle's contribution being an important exception, demonstrating the combination of serial and categorical structures. Another relevant attempt, though not directly related to strictly memorial concerns, is Martin's (1972) work.

Aristotle suggested in *De Anima* that serial orders are ballistically organized, so that retrieval of a particular item depends on the availability of some number of organized preceding events. Given that hypothesis, similar analyses of serial organization ought to be possible, both for recall and recognition. It is doubtful whether any of the past work on serial learning has achieved tasks that are purely or even predominantly dependent on serial structures. Apart from the chunking effect, that is, the subordinate organization of series, it is likely that much of the work with meaningful material also involves relational codes among two or more items, or, as Bower's work has shown (Bower, 1972; Bower & Winzenz, 1969), even more complex organizations that organize strings of words or digits.

The challenge of investigating serial organization also raises the traditional question of the role of contiguity. I want to argue briefly that the effects of contiguity as a determining variable are more apparent than real and that an organizational approach must look deeper than the appearance for a satisfactory explanation. In short, a correlation between input and output contiguities provides descriptive but not theoretical or explanatory satisfactions.

IV. ORGANIZATION, CONTIGUITY, AND OTHER ISSUES

Starting with the problem of spatiotemporal contiguity, I want to address a number of issues here that are directly relevant to an organizational point of view.

What is the reason for the appeal of contiguity as an explanatory principle? Why has the relation between spatiotemporal contiguities in input events and their appearance in output dominated speculations about human learning and memory literally for centuries?

The major, and obvious, source for this attraction resides in the spatiotemporal structure of the world about us. Organisms move in space and time; the important events in their environment are spatially and temporally marked. The first adaptive characteristic of organisms is that they must respond to the problem of what is where and what happened when. Given this spatiotemporal matrix of dealing with the world, however, does this necessarily imply that the mechanisms and processes whereby these spatiotemporal events are coded and stored are themselves merely a reflection of these external consistencies? Or should a theoretical psychology concentrate on the mechanisms that deal with these contiguities, abstract from them, and in important ways transcend them? Clearly I argue for the latter. If contiguity and nothing but contiguity determined storage, categorization, and classification, we would be dealing with a poorly adapted human being indeed. Since the organism does abstract and classify, that is, uses strategems and processes that go beyond mere environmental contiguities, it is proper to ask about the processes that code the regularities of contiguity as well as those that overcome them.

Among the three kinds of structures that we have discussed, clearly proordination responds directly to spatiotemporal contiguities in the environment. However, I have noted that the structures that underlie the seriation process are not simple reflections of the environmental relations, but rather organize these events such that the output from the mental apparatus is in itself serially structured. In other words, the associationist position is primarily descriptive and capitalizes on the frequent and predominant structure of the environment, that is, it describes the frequently strong correlation between input and output contiguities. It does not, however, provide the explanatory mechanism for the structure of the output. Such mechanisms cannot be mere mirrors of the input, if for no other reason than that we know that the mental apparatus does not physiologically or psychologically provide structures that are mere put-through devices.

As far as experimental evidence is concerned, there is not even evidence that people use the contiguities of unordered lists in preference to other modes of organization. Seriation is preferred whenever memorial and processing capacities are not overloaded (Mandler & Dean, 1969). However, even then, some subjects, given the choice between a categorical and a serial structure, choose the former (Mandler, 1969). Data from our laboratory indicate that experimental subjects can, regardless of personal preferences, equally well use serial or categorical organization when instructed to do so. In other words, organizational capacity is extremely pliable, and people often use whatever strategy they may prefer or are instructed to use.

Finally, contiguity is not only reflected in the use of serial structures, but may find a niche in a variety of different organizational strategies. Thus, relational mnemonics take advantage of the contiguity of sets of events, and the imposition of more complex schemas and syntaxes responds directly to the spatiotemporal structure of the surround.

If it is the case that individuals under some circumstances take advantage of the contiguous structure of input materials and under other circumstances do not do so—what determines such choices? The issue to be addressed concerns the identification or discovery of structures available in the input that correspond to some extent to mental structures. Just because the experimenter builds some structure into the input material does not imply that the individual subjects will either discover that structure or, if discovered, make use of it (Mandler, 1967a). The use of serial structures depends in part on the fact that contiguity in the input events is so easily (and probably automatically) discernable. However, we know that the use of such input structures depends to a large extent on the subject's expectations and on instructions for output, that is, on the mental structures that are primed for the organization of the input material. Whether or not an individual will discover, for example, the categorical structure of the input list depends on the nature of the prepared mind—is the structure sought for, will it be used if discovered? For the unprepared mind, structure in input by itself predicts nothing about the nature of the acquisition process—some people may discover it, others may not; some may use it, others not. As a result, organizational principles dictate that we should know as much as possible about the expectations, knowledge, and intentions of our experimental subjects—mere presentation of materials is inadquate.

A similar argument applies to the use of mere repetition as an experimental variable—one of the beloved manipulations of the associationist tradition. Again the question must be: What use is made of the repetition, what processes and structures are invoked, and on which repetitious occasions? The multitrial experiment has lost adherents because we cannot learn enough from descriptive acquisition functions; we need to know about the processes that operate at each encounter between the subject's prepared mind and the to-be-remembered material. As a further example, one can consider the distinction between integrative and elaborative processes discussed earlier. Only an extensive task analysis will provide some insights as to whether sheer repetition provides an occasion for integration, for elaboration, or both.

Similar kinds of considerations apply to many different currently popular or unpopular notions. The generation–recognition hypothesis of free recall, for example, can be shown to be an unlikely candidate for a theoretical explanation of free recall. At the same time, it can be an effective auxiliary strategy for free recall, though not for the acquisition of paired associates (cf. Rabinowitz, Mandler, & Patterson, 1977; Wiseman & Tulving, 1975). Again, the encoding specificity principle works fairly well for relationally or coordinately encoded material, but it is not useful for other paradigms, such as schematically encoded material (e.g., Anderson & Pichert, 1978).

One final comment: I have used process and structure concepts somewhat interchangeably in these pages. It is generally assumed that mental structures determine relevant processes. On the other hand, the establishment of mental structures—their erection—is a function of the operation of certain mental processes. At the present time, it may be premature to make strong distinctions between processes and structures. It may be preferable to let growing organizational theories specify what, within the confines of each appropriate model, is structure and what process. After all, it has been only a decade or two since we have been able to speak freely and constructively about mental structures and mental processes at all.

In a sense, the organizational approach has been neutral in terms of specific theories. Notwithstanding my own predilections and enchantment with three kinds of structures, the major impact has been that of cognitive theory in general. The importance of such theory has been the encouragement of useful fictions, of theoretical events and entities. To the extent that the investigation of human memory has followed this road it has, under the influence of organizational position, become theoretically enriched and a proper part of the fledgling amalgam of the cognitive sciences.

ACKNOWLEDGMENTS

Preparation of this chapter was supported in part by Grant BNS 76-15154 from the National Science Foundation. I am grateful for the hospitality of the Department of Experimental Psychology, Oxford University, where this chapter was written.

REFERENCES

Anderson, R. C., & Pichert, J. W. Recall of previously unrecallable information following a shift in perspective. *Journal of Verbal Learning and Verbal Behavior,* 1978, *17,* 1–12.

Asch, S. E. The doctrinal tyranny of associationism. In T. R. Dixon & D. L. Horton (Eds.), *Verbal behavior and general behavior theory.* Englewood Cliffs, N.J.: Prentice Hall, 1968.

Atkinson, R. C., & Juola, J. F. Search and decision processes, in recognition memory. In D. H. Krantz, R. C. Atkinson, R. D. Luce, & P. Suppes (Eds.), *Contemporary developments in mathematical psychology.* (Vol. 1). San Francisco: W. H. Freeman, 1974.

Atkinson, R.C., & Wescourt, K. T. Some remarks on a theory of memory. In P. M. A. Rabbitt & S. Dornic (Eds.), *Attention and performance V.* London: Academic Press, 1975.

Bousfield, W. A. The occurrence of clustering in the recall of randomly arranged associates. *Journal of General Psychology,* 1953, *49,* 229–240.

Bower, G. H. Organizational factors in human memory. *Cognitive Psychology,* 1970, *1,* 18–46.

Bower, G. H. Perceptual groups as coding units in immediate memory. *Psychonomic Science,* 1972, *27,* 217–219.

Bower, G. H., & Winzenz, D. Group structure, coding, and memory for digit series. *Journal of Experimental Psychology Monographs,* 1969, *80,* 1–17.

Collins, A. M., & Quillian, M. R. How to make a language user. In E. Tulving & W. Donaldson (Eds.), *Organization of memory.* New York: Academic Press, 1972.

Craik, F. I. M. & Watkins, M. J. The role of rehearsal in short-term memory. *Journal of Verbal. Learning and Verbal Behavior,* 1973, *12,* 599–607.

Craik, F. I. M., & Tulving, E. Depth of processing and the retention of words in episodic memory. *Journal of Experimental Psychology: General,* 1975, *104,* 268–294.

Gallistel, C. R. Motivation as central organizing process: The psychophysical approach to its functional and neurophysiological analysis. In J. K. Cole & T. B. Sonderegger (Eds.), *Nebraska Symposium on Motivation: 1974.* Lincoln: University of Nebraska Press, 1975.

Gallistel, C. R. The organization of action. Hillsdale, N.J.: Lawrence Erlbaum Associates, 1979.

Graesser, A. C. II, & Mandler, G. Limited processing capacity constrains the storage of unrelated sets of words and retrieval from natural categories. *Journal of Experimental Psychology: Human Learning and Memory,* 1978, *4,* 86–100.

Juola, J. F., Fischler, I., Wood, C. T., & Atkinson, R. C. Recognition time for information stored in long-term memory. *Perception & Psychophysics,* 1971, *10,* 8–14.

Katona, G. *Organizing and memorizing.* New York: Columbia University Press, 1940.

Lashley, K. S. The problem of serial order in behavior. In L. A. Jeffress (Ed.), *Cerebral mechanisms in behavior.* New York: Wiley and Sons, 1951.

Mandler, G. Verbal learning. In G. Mandler, P. Mussen, N. Kogan, & M. A. Wallach, *New directions in psychology: III.* New York: Holt, Rinehart and Winston, 1967(a).

Mandler, G. Organization and memory. In K. W. Spence & Janet T. Spence (eds.), *The psychology of learning and motivation: Advances in research and theory.* New York: Academic Press, 1967(b).

Mandler, G. Input variables and output strategies in the free recall of categorized lists. *American Journal of Psychology,* 1969, *82,* 531–539.

Mandler, G. Words, lists, and categories: An experimental view of organized memory. In J. L. Cowan (Ed.), *Studies in thought and language.* Tucson: University of Arizona Press, 1970.

Mandler, G. Organization and recognition. In E. Tulving & W. Donaldson (Eds.), *Organization of memory.* New York: Academic Press, 1972.

Mandler, G. Memory storage and retrieval: Some limits on the reach of attention and consciousness. In P. M. A. Rabbitt & S. Dornic (Eds.), *Attention and Performance V.* London: Academic Press, 1975(a).

Mandler, G. *Mind and emotion.* New York: Wiley and Sons, 1975(b).

Mandler, G. Commentary on "Organization and memory". In G. H. Bower (Ed.), *Human memory: Basic processes.* New York: Academic Press, 1977.

Mandler, G. Organization and repetition: Organizational principles with special reference to rote learning. In L.-G. Nilsson (Ed.), *Perspectives in memory research.* Hillsdale, N.J.: Lawrence Erlbaum Associates, 1979.

Mandler, G., & Dean, P. J. Seriation: The development of serial order in free recall. *Journal of Experimental Psychology,* 1969, *81,* 207–215.

Mandler, G., & Graesser, A. C. II. Analyse dimensionelle et le "locus" de l'organisation. In S. Ehrlich & E. Tulving (Eds.), *La memoire semantique.* Paris: Bulletin de Psychologie, 1976.

Mandler, G., Pearlstone, Z., & Koopmans, H. J. Effects of organization and semantic similarity on recall and recognition. *Journal of Verbal Learning and Verbal Behavior,* 1969, *8,* 410–423.

Mandler, G., Worden, P. E., & Graesser, A. C. II. Subjective disorganization: Search for the locus of list organization. *Journal of Verbal Learning and Verbal Behavior,* 1974, *13,* 220–235.

Martin, J. G. Rhythmic (hierarchical) versus serial structure in speech and other behavior. *Psychological Review,* 1972, *79,* 487–509.

Miller, G. A. The magical number seven, plus or minus two: Some limits on our capacity for processing information. *Psychological Review*, 1956, *63*, 81–97.

Patterson, K. E., Meltzer, R. H., & Mandler, G. Inter-response times in categorized free recall. *Journal of Verbal Learning and Verbal Behavior*, 1971, *10*, 417–426.

Postman, L. A pragmatic view of organization theory. In E. Tulving & W. Donaldson (Eds.), *Organization of memory*. New York: Academic Press, 1972.

Pylyshyn, Z. W. What the mind's eye tells the mind's brain: A critique of mental imagery. *Psychological Bulletin*, 1973, *80*, 1–24.

Rabinowitz, J. C., Mandler, G., & Barsalou, L. W. Recognition failure: Another case of retrieval failure. *Journal of Verbal Learning and Verbal Behavior*, 1977, *16*, 639–663.

Rabinowitz, J. C., Mandler, G., & Patterson, K. E. Determinants of recognition and recall: Accessibility and generation. *Journal of Experimental Psychology: General*, 1977, *106*, 302–329.

Restle, F. Theory of serial pattern learning: Structural trees. *Psychological Review*, 1970, *77*, 481–495.

Segal, M. A., & Mandler, G. Directionality and organizational processes in paired-associate learning. *Journal of Experimental Psychology*, 1967, *74*, 305–312.

Slamecka, N. J. An examination of trace storage in free recall. *Journal of Experimental Psychology*, 1968, *76*, 504–513.

Slamecka, N. J. The question of associative growth in the learning of categorized material. *Journal of Verbal Learning and Verbal Behavior*, 1972, *11*, 324–332.

Tulving, E. Subjective organization in free recall of "unrelated" words. *Psychological Review*, 1962, *69*, 344–354.

Tulving, E. The effects of presentation and recall of material in free recall learning. *Journal of Verbal Learning and Verbal Behavior*, 1967, *6*, 175–184.

Wiseman, S., & Tulving, E. A test of confusion theory of encoding specificity. *Journal of Verbal Learning and Verbal Behavior*, 1975, *14*, 343–351.

Wolford, G. Function of distinct associations for paired-associate performance. *Psychological Review*, 1971, *78*, 303–313.

Woodward, A. E. , Bjork, R. A., & Jongeward, R. H. Jr. Recall and recognition as a function of primary rehearsal. *Journal of Verbal Learning and Verbal Behavior*, 1973, *12*, 608–617.

Organization and Levels
of Processing

"The increasing recognition of the important role played by 'organization' of materials to be learned and remembered may well represent the most significant development of the past decade of intensive research in the general area of memory [Battig, 1973, p. 675]."

MEMORY ORGANIZATION
AND STRUCTURE

The foregoing is the first sentence from a review of *Organization of Memory* (Tulving & Donaldson, 1972), in which this book was evaluated as an important milestone that not only would generate increased research activity on organization in the free-recall paradigm that had spawned most of the empirical and methodological advances as described in *Organization of Memory*, but also promised to expand the study of organizational processes to encompass semantic memory and natural-language paradigms. Enhanced research effort and understanding seemed further assured because "there already have been significant advances in organizational measures in free recall (some, but not all, of which are discussed in the first part of *Organization of Memory*) [Battig, 1973, p. 677]."

As viewed 5–6 years later, this optimistic evaluation of the impact of the Tulving–Donaldson (1972) *Organization of Memory* book clearly has not been fulfilled. Most of those who had made major contributions to the research reviewed in the Tulving–Donaldson book have since shifted to other areas of research interest of little relevance to, if not incompatible with, the understanding of organization in memory. Consequently, there has been a significant decline in research directly concerned with organizational processes in memory. This is indicated by the presence of only one paper on the 1978 Psychonomic Society program even indirectly concerned with organization in free-recall memory, a percentage of total Psychonomic papers (.2%) only 8% as large as that found in the corresponding programs for 1971 and 1972 (both 2.7%) or 1973 (2.9%).

The reasons for this apparent decline in organizational research appear to reflect some general characteristics of psychological research, as well as factors specific to research on memory and/or organization. The present chapter begins with a brief description and analysis of some of these contributing factors. This is followed by an attempt to demonstrate the general importance of organizational factors for effective memory in list-learning or processing tasks, based primarily upon the results of some recent and as yet unpublished research from the Colorado and Ohio University laboratories of the present authors.

I. WHY THE DECLINE IN ORGANIZATIONAL RESEARCH?

The first author has on several occasions expressed concern over the strong preference among psychological researchers in general, and cognitively oriented memory researchers in particular, for problems, theories, or research paradigms that appear simple and easily studied, rather than the more basic and important problems that are invariably complex and difficult to resolve (e.g., Battig, 1962, 1977, 1979). For present purposes, this concern is most adequately expressed in the following excerpt from a presidential address (entitled "Parsimony or Psychology?") to the Rocky Mountain Psychological Association (April, 1978), which provides the following sketch of the typical sequence of events characterizing "progress" in any specific area of psychological research.

> First, somebody comes up with a new theory, research paradigm, or interesting and controversial empirical result, which appears quite simple, straightforward, and easy to investigate further. This catches on, creating a new "hot" research topic, which promises to be more productive than previous approaches, and therefore attracts the interest of a great many psychologists. But as more work gets done, the originally simple problem gets more complicated, because of failures to replicate the original findings, demonstrations that the original explanation is inadequate or at best incomplete, and increasing evidence that the problem is more complicated and less general than originally thought. So as this research develops, it becomes apparent that any further progress will require a great deal of painstaking detailed research activity directed toward limited aspects of the overall problem or phenomenon, as well as efforts to interrelate the topic appropriately with other previously distinct topics or phenomena. In other words, further research has reached a point of diminishing returns, because a threshold of too much complexity has been crossed, so the once hot topic now appears nonproductive or uninteresting, and soon dies out to be replaced by one or more different more simplistic types of research. So then the cycle starts all over again, often with almost total suppression of everything that was done or learned in the context of the previously "hot" research topic.

Certainly this general description coincides with the sequence of events involving research on organization in free-recall memory, although it probably has not yet reached the stage of final demise as demonstrated by the minority interest still evidenced in the present volume. Moreover, if we date its origin back to Bousfield's (1953) pioneering work on clustering, we have now surpassed a quarter century of research activity concerned with organization in memory, an unusually long life span as compared with most topics in human learning, memory, and/or cognition. Of course, organization in memory represents a broad, general topic, and its apparent durability reflects at least in part major changes in emphasis within the area, of which subjective organization (Tulving, 1962) and the combination of different bases of organization, or its surprising effects upon multiple-list transfer or long-term memory tests, are representative examples.

Nonetheless, the present scene contains disturbing implications that research directly concerned with organization in memory is declining to the point where both undergraduate textbooks in cognitive psychology (e.g., Reynolds & Flagg, 1977) and major conferences on human memory research (e.g., Cermak & Craik, 1979) have essentially nothing to say about it. We therefore attempt to identify and explicate what we see as major contributors to a weakening of concern with organization, especially in free-recall memory, with particular emphasis on its relationship (or lack of same) to some important approaches to memory research.

A. Multiplicity of Organizational Bases and Meausres

Much of the initial appeal of organizational research derived from its original limitation to clustering in free-recall output of items that were categorically or associatively related according to criteria established by natural-language relationships and controllable by the experimenter. The first major step toward the broadening of the conceptual scope of organization was Tulving's demonstration of its operation even within lists of unrelated words (Tulving, 1962). The inclusion of such "subjective organization" ultimately opened the gates to several other types of organizations, ranging from alphabetic or acoustic bases for grouping or ordering (e.g., Wood, 1972), to various types of seriations, including grouping together of items from the beginning and/or end of the list. The grudging acceptance of still another output-ordering phenomenon, the priority of recall of newly learned items (PRNI) (Battig, Allen, & Jensen, 1965), can also be viewed as a type of organization based upon previous recall and/or rehearsal status of subsets of items (e.g., Einstein, Pellegrino, Mondani, & Battig, 1974). In any event, recent evaluations of organization in free recall have included combinations of at least clustering, subjective organization, primacy, recency, and PRNI (e.g., Pellegrino & Battig, 1974). Coinciding with this increase in distinguishable types or bases of organization has been an excessive proliferation of closely related but allegedly different ways of obtaining measures for these various types of organizations. These have been compared and evaluated at length on several occasions (e.g., Colle, 1972; Hubert & Levin, 1976; Pellegrino, 1971; Sternberg & Tulving, 1977), but the researcher on organization in free recall still faces a puzzling myriad of alternative measures of organization, each with its own users and/or advocates. Comprehensive but excessively time-consuming computer programs are available to permit simultaneous calculation of any or all of these measures (e.g., Friendly, 1975), but there is little evidence of widespread or effective usage of such multiple-measure approaches.

Instead, this increased number of organizational types and measures appears to be negatively related to amount of organizational research, reflecting also the increasingly recognized limitations of output order as the primary data base for the assessment of such organization, and despite recent efforts of some (especially Buschke, 1976, 1977) to develop better techniques for obtaining evidence of organization from the data protocols of subjects. The central point of this discussion, however, is that increasing complexity and multiplicity of organizational types and measures appear as a major contributor to the current decline of interest in research on organization in memory, in line with the general characterization of what happens to active research areas as presented at the beginning of this section.

B. The Role of Theory

Another current limitation of research on organization in free recall, which derives at least in part from its increasing complexity and multifaceted nature, is the paucity of influential theoretical development since Anderson's (1971) FRAN model (see also Bower, 1972a). Paradoxically, the Tulving–Donaldson (1972) book appears to have had its major influence at the theoretical level, inasmuch as cognitive theorists subsequently shifted increasingly toward theoretical efforts in the area of semantic memory. The earlier work on the organization of semantic memory had concentrated on determining if semantic memory could best be described as a network model (Collins & Quillian, 1969), a set-theoretical model (Meyer, 1970), or a feature-comparison model (Smith, Shoben, & Rips, 1974). However, more recent theories, which deal with the comprehension and retention of linguistic material such as prose passages, are based upon hypothetical structures in semantic memory such as macrostructures (Kintsch, 1974), schemata (Rumelhart & Ortony, 1977), or scripts and plans (Schank & Abelson, 1977). Although such theories all seem to share at least implicit acknowledgement of the importance of organizational factors, they have yet to contribute anything substantial to the understanding of organization per se.

The present volume appears to continue this emphasis upon empirical and measurement concerns, with the notable exception of Friendly's (Chapter 4) attempt to specify general memory structure through his hierarchical clustering analysis. There is little empirical evidence, however, to indicate that subjects actually use multilevel hierarchies or organization unless instructed or forced to do so (e.g., Pellegrino, 1974). As we see it, the current state of knowledge and of research activity concerned with organization in memory is sufficiently complex and unstable that it would be both premature and nonproductive to focus our attention upon the development of detailed and comprehensive theoretical formulations. We also feel that a satisfactory theoretical account of organizational processes in memory must be far more complex, flexible, and nondeterministic than the typical information-processing "model" that still dominates most of the current research in cognitive psychology. Nonetheless, today's cognitively oriented research environment has little use for research topics or empirical efforts that are not subsidiary to some prior theoretical model(s), and the failure of most organizational researchers to conform to these theoretically oriented constraints is undoubtedly a contributing cause of the current reduction of research interest in this topic.

C. Levels of Processing

Probably more detrimental to organizational research than anything else has been the recent focus upon newer research topics or approaches that have little or no relevance to organizational processes and may even be incompatible with organization. The most significant case in point is "levels of processing" research, which probably represents the most influential approach stimulating much of the current research activity in human memory. The present authors can find nothing in the loosely described levels-of-processing formulation that is fundamentally inconsistent with organizational processes and would argue that levels-of-processing researchers must eventually incorporate organizational processes directly in order to develop a satisfactory account of human memory. Nonetheless, we see the current research emphases developing under the levels-of-processing banner as a major detriment to the study of organization. We also believe it to be instructive to examine how and why levels-of-processing researchers pay so little attention to organizational processes that the word "organization" is not even mentioned in Craik's concluding chapter nor does it get more than passing mention in any other chapter of the most recent detailed analysis of levels-of-processing research (Cermak & Craik, 1979). Moreover, Craik (1979) dismisses organization as "a concept that has not received much critical attention lately [p. 90]," and questions the generality of the results obtained by Bellezza and his associates discussed later in this chapter.

This apparent incompatibility can most readily be understood by looking at the specifics of the research paradigm employed in most levels-of-processing research. The emphasis is on the type(s) of processing at the level of each individual word or other unit in isolation. Thus the paradigm typically employs incidental-learning conditions where the subject is instructed only to perform a specific type of processing task for a single word, with different words often being processed in completely different ways. Moreover, each word is typically presented on only a single processing trial, and the words are selected so as to be maximally unrelated to one another.

In other words, the typical levels-of-processing experiment violates virtually all of the standard conditions that characterize experiments on organization in free recall and that are important for the occurrence and/or assessment of such organization. Incidental processing of individual words is used, instead of intentional learning conditions where the subject is free if not actively encouraged to group or organize the words. Only a single trial is used, precluding any assessment of the trial-to-trial output consistencies that represent subjective organization and severely restricting the extent to which this or other types of organizations can be observed, because free-recall organization both increases and changes dramatically over multiple trials (Pellegrino & Battig, 1974). Consequently, anyone interested in studying organization could hardly choose a less appropriate methodology than that employed by levels-of-processing researchers.

Thus it should come as no surprise that those few researchers who have evaluated organization within levels-of-processing experiments have typically found little evidence for such organization. For example, McDaniel and Masson (1977) reported little or no categorical clustering within 40-item lists consisting of four high-frequency instances from each of ten conceptual categories, under conditions where each item within a given category was processed using a different orienting task. For immediate recall, this absence of clustering was found for intentional as well as incidental learning conditions, and there was also reduced clustering 24 hours later. In a follow-up experiment, however, McDaniel and Masson (1977) reported a significant increase in clustering, especially under incidental-learning conditions, if subjects performed the same processing task on all items within the list. Since this latter experiment also rendered nonsignificant the delayed-recall superiority found in the first experiment for intentional over incidental instructional conditions (see rows 1 and 3 of Table 10.1), these combined results can be interpreted as evidence for the importance of organizational processes (and possibly also rehearsal) for effective long-term retention.

Further evidence suggesting the importance of organizational processes for optimal delayed retention within such levels-of-processing experiments comes from a series of follow-up experiments (McDaniel & Masson, 1978) comparing delayed retention following intentional and incidental learning instructions under varying conditions of list structure and number of orienting tasks. The results from four such comparisons are summarized in Table 10.1, along with those from McDaniel and Masson (1977). These include all possible combinations of categorized or unrelated-word lists with either the same orienting task on all items or different orienting tasks being required on different subsets of items. These results show a significant superiority for intentional over incidental recall only in the two experiments with categorized lists and multiple orienting tasks (McDaniel & Masson, 1977, 1978). If unrelated words and/or a single orienting task are used, however, this incidental–intentional difference is dramatically reduced or eliminated. Of particular interest is the last row of Table 10.1, which shows a marked increase in incidental delayed-recall performance if the same orienting task is used for all words within a single category, so that the congruence of orienting tasks with category membership presumably enables the incidental (as well as intentional) learners to organize their recall effectively by category. The apparent recall superiority

Table 10.1
Mean Percent 24-hr Delayed Recall following Intentional and Incidental Instructions for Six Experiments Varying in Category Structure and Number of Orienting Tasks.[a]

Structure	Orienting Tasks	Intentional	Incidental
Categorized	Four	24.7	10.0
Categorized	Three	28.0	15.7
Categorized	One	36.7	30.7
Unrelated	Three	15.7	13.7
Unrelated	One	17.7	20.0
Categorized [b]	Three	30.0	24.8

[a] McDaniel & Masson, 1977, 1978.
[b] All words of given category processed by same orienting task.

under these latter conditions for intentional over incidental learners, however, is reported as nonsignificant and is far smaller than that shown in the top two rows of Table 10.1 when different orienting tasks are used for each individual word in a given category. Although these results are interpreted on the basis of differences in usage of organization in recall, McDaniel and Masson (1978) regrettably do not report clustering comparisons like those of their previous (1977) experiments.

The point of the foregoing McDaniel–Masson (1977, 1978) evaluations within a typical levels-of-processing paradigm is that organizational differences may play an important role with respect to differences in delayed retention for intentional as compared with incidental learning conditions. The usual operation of organizational strategies or processes clearly can be suppressed through the use of incidental processing instructions, multiple encoding tasks, and/or unstructured word lists. However, to the extent that the experimental conditions encourage or even allow for some type of organization, subjects appear to use such organization in ways that benefit their subsequent delayed-recall performance.

Further evidence of the extent to which recall within a typical incidental-processing paradigm can be facilitated, by even a limited and indirect type of organization, comes from a recent experiment by the first author and Kathleen Weiss (see Battig, 1979). This employed a typical levels-of-processing paradigm and other experimental conditions that should reduce organization to an absolute minimum. More specifically, all subjects were required to process equal subsets of words by rating a given word once on one of three different semantic dimensions under incidental learning conditions and were subsequently tested for both recall and recognition of these words. Interpolated between the initial word-processing task and the recall and recognition test was a brief (2–3 min) reading of a 165-word "story" that contained exactly half of the previously processed words. Equal halves of the subjects read each of two different stories, which contained nonoverlapping halves of the processed words. To assure attention to and comprehension of the story, subjects were required to answer four true–false questions about the story content, but were told nothing about its inclusion of previously processed words.

Despite this limited and incidental opportunity to organize some of these words that was provided by the story, words included in the story showed 42.4% correct recall as compared with only 34.2% for words not contained in the story. This result has recently been replicated in a second experiment using different sets of words and stories, but with the story read before rather than after the words were processed and with 48-hr delayed recall, with recall over twice as high for story (9.8%) as for nonstory words (4.2%). Despite this marked facilitation of recall for words receiving limited organization in a story format, however, recognition was actually insignificantly worse for story than for nonstory words in both experiments. In other words, this particular type of organization has facilitative effects only upon recall and clearly does not facilitate recognition even when this was tested immediately following recall. For present purposes, the important point is that the separate and relatively weak opportunity to read a story containing a subset of the processed words nonetheless produced substantial improvements in recall performance on these words.

Before proceeding to more detailed evaluations of the significance of organizational processing for effective memory, it should be noted that levels of processing is not alone among currently popular memory research areas in its contribution to the decline of organizational research. We have emphasized it here primarily because in the remainder of this chapter we want to consider organization from a processing perspective that we see as entirely compatible with a levels-of-processing orientation. More specifically, we want to argue for the insufficiency of the original depth-of-processing formulation (Craik & Lockhart, 1972), and also of more recent extensions that focus upon breadth, elaboration, and/or distinctiveness as the keys to effective memory (Craik & Tulving, 1975; Cermak & Craik, 1979), because of their lack of attention to multiple-item organizational processes. In the following sections, organizational processes are considered as a necessary and key component of any levels-of-processing formulation providing a complete picture of the types of processing centrally involved in human memory.

D. Organizational Processing

Although organization is commonly labeled as a process or type(s) of processing, much of the research especially on organization in free recall appears more directly concerned with the operations by which organization is identified and measured, and/or the properties of the memory structures resulting from such organization. Although we see considerable value in such operational and structural views of organization, our desired rapprochement between organization and levels of processing can best be achived by focusing on organizational processing. In fact, the current lack of concern with organization by most levels-of-processing researchers may well reflect previous operational and structural rather than processing emphases by organizational researchers.

Our processing perspective on organization can be viewed as incorporating any and all types of processes during and following encoding that produce some kind of relationship between two or more items or events. There obviously are many different ways in which items can be organized together, a large proportion of which may be unique to a particular individual subject and/or set of materials. Thus, no effort is made here to identify even the principal types or bases of organizational processing in memory.

We do, however, want to broaden the scope of organizational processing to include not only the direct relationships between individual items that are emphasized in free-recall research, but also the use of previously developed organized structures in memory within which newly memorized units can be incorporated. To accomplish this, it will be helpful to return to a long-standing distinction in verbal-learning and memory research between direct and indirect mediated relationships or associations. Whether clustering in free recall consists of direct associative linkages or common associations with a mediating category label once was an important theoretical issue in free-recall research (e.g., Cofer, 1965). However, evidence for the importance of both associative and category clustering, combined with substantial complexities and inconsistencies emerging from research on this issue, soon led to the unresolved suppression typically encountered by such difficult theoretical issues in psychology (see quote from Battig, 1978, on p. 323), so this receives no direct mention in the 1972 Tulving–Donaldson book.

The important role in free-recall organization of both direct associative and indirect category relationships, however, can readily be expanded to constitute two separable general dimensions or levels according to which any specific instance of organization can be described. For present purposes, we shall label these as *horizontal* and *vertical* dimensions or types of organizational processing. More specifically, horizontal organizational processing refers to the formation or use of any kind of direct relationship between two or more words or other events, whereas vertical organizational processing involves the incorporation of individual words or events into some already existing higher level organizational structure available in memory. Thus the words *chair* and *table* could be organized horizontally as strong direct associates to one another or by forming an image or sentence that directly relates them together. Alternatively or in addition, *chair* and *table* could be organized vertically as exemplars of the conceptual category of furniture, as common household objects, as made from similar materials, or as parts of any of a variety of other organized structures in memory. It should further be emphasized that this horizontal–vertical distinction is far from absolute and that many instances of organization may represent combinations of both horizontal and vertical types of organizational processing.

This broadened horizontal–vertical processing framework not only provides a basis for bringing together organization in free-recall and semantic memory, but is also especially useful for the present purposes of relating organization to deeper and/or more elaborate processing of the kinds emphasized as critical for effective memory by recent levels-of-processing researchers (e.g., Craik & Lockhart, 1972; Craik & Tulving, 1975). A greater elaboration or spread of processing, where a given item is processed in two or more different ways or as part of a more complex phrase or sentence, would seem especially likely to involve some kind of vertical organization. Such organization is typically limited, however, because elaborated processing is unlikely to involve relationships with other to-be-remembered items. Moreover, the incidental processing instructions typically accompanying elaborated processing conditions in levels-of-processing experiments do not require nor even encourage the use of any type of organizational processing.

A fundamental difference between levels-of-processing and the typical free-recall organizational experiment is that the former typically requires subjects to perform one or more specific semantic or nonsemantic processing tasks on each individual item, thereby providing for greater specification and control over the subject's processing activities than is found in the typical experiment on organization in free recall. This suggests that the evaluation of organizational processing, especially as compared with nonorganizational semantic processing, can best be accomplished by giving subjects explicit instructions to use some specific type of interitem organization, analogous to the processing instructions for individual items that characterize the typical levels-of-processing experiment.

The use of mnemonic devices as the vehicle for producing controlled and specified organizational processing has been attempted with substantial success in a lengthy series of experiments by the second author (Bellezza, Cheesman, & Reddy, 1977; Bellezza & Reddy, 1978; Bellezza, Richards, & Geiselman, 1976). A summary of the resulting evidence for the importance of organizational processing for effective recall memory, along with five new experiments providing further clarification of the conditions under which organizational processing is particularly effective, is presented later in this chapter. Some preliminary discussion, however, appears appropriate concerning the relationships of mnemonic devices to organization, before describing the actual experiments.

E. Organizational Mnemonics

Mnemonic devices can be considered as organizational because they typically are based upon some type of linkage or relationship between two or more of the to-be-remembered words, which can involve both horizontal and vertical organizational processing. Several kinds of organizational mnemonics, differing considerably in their involvement of horizontal and vertical organizational processing, have been used in the several experiments by Bellezza et al. The initial experiments were based primarily upon a story mnemonic, where subjects were instructed to make up a sentence for each successive individual word so that all sentences could be combined into a continuing story (Bellezza et al., 1976, 1977), although some experiments have also used the method of loci (Bellezza & Reddy, 1978) or visual imagery linking words with their initial letters (Bellezza et al., 1977, Experiment 3). The new experiments to be described here, however, are based upon a modified peg-word mnemonic system in which the peg words have not previously been well learned or linked together. However, we shall illustrate the critical storage and retrieval characteristics of an organizational mnemonic using the mnemonic device known as the link system (Higbee, 1977, Chapter 6; Lorayne & Lucas, 1974, Chapter 3), which is somewhat closer to typical free-recall organization in its probable greater involvement of horizontal rather than vertical organizational processing.

The link procedure works especially well for words that represent concrete objects and consequently can be visually imaged. The organizing process consists of linking the first and second words in the list by forming a composite image of the referents of the two words. Similarly, an image is formed of the second and the third words, another image of the third and fourth words, and so on throughout the entire list. By using this strategy or mnemonic device, a person can encode into memory a string of linked or associated images that represent all of the presented words. Unless the memorizer actively engages in the particular storage processes required by the link procedure, however, the required type of organized-item representation in memory will not occur.

After an organized representation has been produced and stored via the link system, a related retrieval system is necessary in order to recall the words. This requires recall of the first word on the list, which acts as a cue for recall of the linked second word. The recalled second word then acts as a cue for the image linking the second and third words so that the third word can be recalled, and so on through the remainder of the list. Active usage of these imaginal links during retrieval, however, is critical to their use for successful recall. Although these storage and retrieval processes are related, they are not necessarily identical. For example, the link system makes it possible to start by retrieving the last word on the list and using visual imagery to recall the words in the order exactly opposite to that in which they were presented.

Such storage and retrieval mnemonic systems become organizational only if they are used in some predetermined way based on an organized system or strategy that controls their operation. Thus organizational processes alone can determine the structure of recall behavior with no corresponding structural representation of the items in memory. This latter possibility corresponds to Slamecka's (1968) suggestion that each list item is stored independently in memory and that an organized retrieval process is solely responsible for the organized characteristics of recall.

Another way of describing the role of organizational mnemonics during retrieval is in terms of their provision of a set of subjective retrieval cues that closely correspond to the cues used for encoding the presented information. Thus mnemonic devices provide a basis for self-cueing by the subject that is functionally equivalent to the presence during retrieval of the cues actually used in encoding.

Specific mnemonic devices can provide either for self-cueing during retrieval that is contingent upon the recall of other items (as in the story and link mnemonic systems) or for noncontingent self-cueing in which the cue words or images have been well memorized and repeatedly used in different learning situations (as in the method of loci and peg-word mnemonic systems). Thus the contingent story and link systems provide for recall only to the extent that each successive list word itself can be recalled. Consequently, the failure to recall a particular word in the organizational sequence is likely to diminish further effective use of the mnemonic system for retrieval. The use of previously well-learned cues in noncontingent self-cueing systems, however, should prevent such retrieval limitations due to failure of cued recall. Although little work has been done comparing the effectiveness of contingent and noncontingent self-cueing mnemonic systems, the latter may well be more effective especially for learning a single long list of items.

Mnemonic devices can also be thought of as schemata that serve to organize and retain in memory lists of words that have no obvious organization or as "plans" according to earlier (Miller, Galanter, & Pribram, 1960) although not more recent uses of this term (Schank & Abelson, 1977). In addition, the use of mnemonic devices such as the peg-word system or the method of loci can be considered as an instance of "top-down" analysis (Norman & Bobrow, 1975) in which the mnemonic schema is activated and used regardless of what particular verbal items are presented.

F. Previous Experiments Comparing Semantic and Organizational Processing

The initial attempts to produce separable experimental manipulations in semantic and organizational processes involved differential instructions to subjects presented with a lengthy list of unrelated words for 11–25 sec each across a series of six separate experiments (Bellezza et al., 1976, 1977). Subjects in semantic-processing conditions were given some combination of general learning instructions with additional semantic processing of each word individually that involved using it in a sentence, rating it for difficulty, defining the word, and/or forming a visual image of the word. In organizational-processing conditions, subjects who were inexperienced in previous use of these mnemonics were instructed to use an organizational mnemonic device, typically the combination of the sentences for each word into a continuing story. All six experiments showed at least a 30% increase in recall for the organizational as compared with the semantic processing group. In the single experiment using an alphabetic mnemonic, where subjects were instructed to associate a visual image of the referent of each word with a visual image of the word's first letter, subjects showed 75% correct recall, whereas semantic-processing subjects who gave a verbal definition for each presented word recalled only 42% of the words (Bellezza et al., 1977; Experiment 3).

This strong evidence for the importance of organizational mnemonics and insufficiency of semantic processing alone for optimal recall was found for between- as well as within-subjects comparisons and for 24-hr delayed as well as immediate recall. The amount forgotten over a 24-hr interval, however, was comparable for semantic and organizational processing. The superiority of the story mnemonic was found even when subjects were told to try to remember the semantically processed words, but only to make a story under organizational processing conditions. This superiority of organizational mnemonics, however, was limited to recall, and recognition performance was closely comparable for semantic and organizational processing conditions. Moreover, there was only limited evidence for greater organization of actual recall appropriate to the mnemonics used by the organizational processing groups, although the conditions of these experiments provided only limited measures of such organization of recall.

A particularly important contribution of these experiments was to show the relative ineffectiveness of added semantic elaboration in the processing of individual items alone, especially as compared with organizational processing. Thus neither greater elaboration in the form of longer sentences (Bellezza et al., 1977, Experiment 1) nor a verbal definition in addition to a visual image of the individual word (Experiment 3) produced any significant facilitation of recall.

Thus it appears that semantic processing of each individual list item may be necessary but not sufficient for optimal performance in free-recall learning. Additional organization of the list words themselves, through the use of an organizational mnemonic device, produces dramatic improvements in free recall over semantic processing alone. These experiments suggest that optimal recall is most likely to result from a combination of semantic processing of individual words followed by their further organizational processing through some mnemonic device. Questions remain, however, concerning what it is about these organizational mnemonics that facilitates free recall. More specifically, do the processes of organizing to-be-remembered material involve merely setting up a retrieval scheme based on self-cueing as is done with mnemonic devices, or are there other factors resulting from organization that facilitate recall? It is this latter question that led to the series of five new experiments, to be discussed in the following sections of this chapter.

II. NEW EXPERIMENTS ON CUEING, CHUNKING, AND MNEMONIC ORGANIZATION

If mnemonic devices provide for organizational aids beyond an improved retrieval scheme based on self-cueing, it is important to try to identify what these additional organizational factors might be and to evaluate experimentally their actual contribution. Described in this section is a series of five new experiments, conducted by the second author and B. Goverdhan Reddy, which focused upon three possible facilitative features of organization within mnemonic systems. One represents the chunking of individual items into a smaller number of multiple-item units (Miller, 1956). Another involves increased cumulative cueing and rehearsal such that initial cues of a series may serve as cues not only for the directly associated item, but also for one or more subsequent items. Third, the use of fewer cue words in an organizational system can serve to reduce the total number of words that have to be processed and stored with a consequent reduction in interitem interference in memory.

As for chunking, the limited available evidence indicates that the number and size of chunks have little effect upon recall performance. More specifically, Bower (1972b) reported little difference in recall across conditions ranging from 1 to 20 specified chunks (and peg-word cues) with 1 to 20 items per peg-word. Since chunks of about 5 items are claimed to be optimal for recall (Mandler, 1967), the absence of any superiority of 5-item chunks over either smaller or larger chunks appears inconsistent with any kind of chunking interpretation. To obtain additional evidence on the importance of number and size of chunks for recall, the first of the series of experiments to be described in this section was designed to evaluate recall performance following use of a peg-word mnemonic system in which both number of peg-word chunks and number of items per peg word were varied concomitantly over a wide range.

A. Experiment 1

In this experiment, each of 60 subjects was presented with a list of concrete words to be used as peg words in the learning of a list of 40 unrelated concrete nouns. Subjects were presented with a complete list of their peg words, which was available throughout the experiment so that the peg words did not have to be memorized. Three experimental groups differed only as to number of peg words (4, 10, or 40) and number of target words presented with each peg word (10, 4, or 1). With 40 peg words, each of these was presented individually along with its target word for 15 sec each. With 4 and 10 peg words, the 10 and 4 targets for each peg word were presented simultaneously for 150 and 60 sec, respectively. All subjects were instructed to form a composite image of each of the sets of presented words and to include in that composite image the peg word corresponding to that set. Thus the subjects with 40, 10, and 4 peg words were presented respectively with 40, 10, and 4 word sets containing 1, 4, and 10 target words along with each peg word. A 1-min distractor task followed the presentation of the last word set, after which subjects were instructed to use their peg words as cues to recall as many of the presented words as possible, with the peg words presented in the same order as that used during the study period.

Unlike Bower's (1972b) results, the present group with 40 peg words recalled a significantly ($p < .001$) smaller proportion of the 40 target words (.57) than either the 10-peg-word (.91) or 4-peg-word group (.89), which did not differ significantly. This recall inferiority of the 40-peg-word group, as compared with the groups using fewer and larger peg-word chunks, is consistent with the chunking hypothesis that fewer chunks lead to better memory. However, the equivalent recall by subjects associating 10 and 4 targets to each peg word in the 4- and 10-peg-word groups is inconsistent with Mandler's (1967) claim that 5-word chunks are optimal for recall memory.

B. Experiment 2

To determine more clearly whether the superiority of the groups with 10 or 4 larger chunks was due to greater organization of the to-be-remembered words, a second experiment included a condition with four peg words and 10 targets per peg-word chunk, but with minimal opportunity to organize or interrelate these 10 targets. This was done by presenting each peg word together with a set of 10 target words for 150 sec, but instructing subjects to use visual imagery only to associate each target individually with its peg word and not to associate or interrelate the target words with one another. This is designated as the 1–10 pairing condition. Also included were conditions with 40 peg-word–target pairs and with four peg words each for a set of 10 targets, identical to those of Experiment 1 and designated as the 1–1 pairing and 1–10 organizing conditions. An additional variable in Experiment 2 involved the use of abstract as well as concrete target words. Consequently, six groups of 16 subjects represented all possible combinations of concrete and abstract target words with the 1–10 pairing, 1–10 organizing, and 1–1 pairing conditions described previously.

Presented in Table 10.2 are the mean proportions of the 40 target words recalled correctly to their peg words for each group and condition. As in Experiment 1, the 1–10 organizing group was significantly superior to the 1–1 pairing group. The 1–10 pairing group, however, showed the poorest recall, although not significantly below the 1–1 pairing group. Moreover, these instructional differences were closely comparable for concrete and abstract target words, although performance on concrete targets was consistently and significantly ($p < .001$) superior to that on abstract target words.

The poorer recall by the 1–10 pairing than the 1–10 organizing group indicates that the superior recall by subjects in the latter group was the result of organizing together the words with a common peg word. However, the present 10-word chunks are well above the optimal chunk size of five (Mandler, 1967), so the organizational facilitation in the 1–10 organizing group probably reflects factors other than chunking per se. Three possible additional sources of organizational facilitation in the 1–10 organizing group are (a) the fact that fewer chunks are required to store the words in memory, making it easier to retrieve these chunks, (b) cumulative cueing, whereby previously processed target words along with the peg word combine to serve a cueing function, and (c) the fact that with fewer peg words, there are correspondingly fewer different words to be processed, resulting in less overload and interitem interference in memory.

Unfortunately, it is exceedingly difficult to disentangle these effects experi-

Table 10.2
Mean Proportion of Recalled Words for Each Group and Condition of Experiment 2

Word type	Instructional condition			Total
	1–10 pairing	1–10 organizing	1–1 pairing	
Concrete	.55	.92	.68	.72
Abstract	.30	.51	.37	.39
Total	.43	.71	.53	

mentally, because it is impossible to vary number of peg-word cues without covariations in number of target words per cue or total number of either target words or target plus cue words combined. The four factors of (a) number of peg-word cues, (b) number of target words per cue, (c) total number of target words, and (d) total number of targets plus cues, are mutually related in such a way that systematic variations in any one of these factors necessitate variations also in all but one of the other three factors. Thus the variations in number of peg words in the first two experiments involved concomitant variations both in number of targets per cue and in total number of words, with only total number of target words being held constant. One way that these four factors can be partially unconfounded is by holding different ones of the four factors constant while the other three are varied together. This was attempted in Experiment 3, where the total number of peg-word cues plus target words was held constant, across two groups that differed in number of peg words, number of targets, and number of targets per peg word.

C. Experiment 3

By equating the total number of words (including peg words plus target words) at 88, Experiment 3 attempted to determine whether the differences favoring the 1–10 organizing over 1–1 pairing conditions in the previous two experiments could have resulted from the greater total number of words processed by the latter (80) than the former groups (44). To accomplish this, the 16 subjects in the 1–1 pairing group received a list of 44 pairs of concrete nouns in succession for 15 sec each and were instructed to associate the 2 words in each pair through visual imagery. The 16 subjects in the present 1–10 organizing condition, however, were presented 80 word pairs for 15 sec each, with each of eight peg words being presented with 10 of the 80 target words. The 10 targets sharing the same peg word were always presented consecutively, so the peg word was changed after every tenth pair. These latter subjects were instructed to form a composite image including the peg word along with all 10 of the target words paired with it and to start to form a new image when the peg word changed. All subjects were subsequently tested for recall of the target words in the presence of the peg-word cues.

Despite the much larger number of target words for the 1–10 organizing group, this group still recalled a much larger proportion (.77) of its 80 target words than did the 1–1 pairing group of its 44 target words (.55). In an effort to evaluate the role of cumulative rehearsal and/or cueing in the 1–10 organizing group, the proportion of words recalled at each of the 10 serial positions was determined for each of the eight peg words. This showed a consistent linear decrease in recall from the first (.91) to the last word within a set (.63), with the linear component of the resulting "serial-position curve" accounting for 84% of the total serial-position variance. That subjects were in fact recalling words in an order corresponding to their presentation order was shown by a mean

Spearman rank correlation of .83 between the input and output position of each recalled word.

Clearly, the superiority of the 1 – 10 organizing over the 1 – 1 pairing group was not eliminated or even reduced by equating the two groups in total cue plus target words, so that the apparent organizing effects cannot be attributed to differences in numbers of words processed. The possible importance of cumulative rehearsal, however, is indicated by the marked superiority of recall for the initial over the late members of the 10-item sets, along with the slight and nonsignificant superiority for recall of the tenth word (.63) over recall by the 1 – 1 pairing group (.55).

These serial-position comparisons also suggest another possible reason for better recall by the 1 – 10 organizing than 1 – 1 pairing groups in Experiments 1 – 3. It may be that the study time of 15 sec per item is longer than the subjects in the pairing condition can use productively to form a composite image of the two words in a pair. Consequently, some of the 15-sec study time may be nonprocessing or "dead" time because the subjects are unlikely to retrieve and rehearse previously presented word pairs. For the organizing groups, however, the addition of each successive target word to a composite image strongly encourages retrieval and added rehearsal of some or all of the previously presented words from the set. Thus, in addition to extra processing and cumulative rehearsal of previously presented words, the 1 – 10 organizing and 1 – 1 pairing group differences may also reflect failure to use all the available study time under the latter condition.

Still another possible factor involved in the apparent organizational superiority, which has previously been mentioned but not directly evaluated, is that fewer chunks are required in the 1 – 10 organizing than 1 – 1 pairing conditions. This may lead to more efficient storage in memory and more effective retrieval of a smaller than of a larger number of chunks. Thus, Experiment 4 was designed to manipulate independently the number of words per chunk and number of chunks (of course with concomitant variations in total number of targets and of target plus cue words).

D. Experiment 4

In this experiment, each of four groups of 12 subjects each represented all possible combinations of 10 and 30 peg-word chunks with 1 and 5 concrete-noun target items per peg word. These are labeled as the 10–1, 30–1, 10–5, and 30–5 groups, which respectively received 10, 30, 50, and 150 target words, and 20, 60, 60, and 180 total words. As in Experiment 3, each peg-word–target pair was presented individually for 15 sec, with the peg word being changed after every fifth target word for the 10–5 and 30–5 conditions. All subjects were instructed to associate the presented words to the peg word using visual imagery.

Table 10.3
Mean Proportion of Recalled Words for Each Group and Condition of Experiment 3

	Words per chunk		
Chunks	1	5	Total
10	.86	.93	.89
30	.70	.87	.79
Total	.78	.90	

As shown in Table 10.3, recall was significantly (p < .01) and about equally improved by decreases in the number of chunks and by increases in number of words per chunk. Although recall is substantially worse in the 30–1 condition than in any of the other three conditions and this inferiority accounts for 90% of the total between-groups variance, the interaction of number of words per chunk and number of chunks did not approach significance (p > .10).

As in Experiment 3, recall by the 10–5 and 30–5 groups was higher for the first three than the last two serial positions within the five-item sets. Proportions of correct recall were .93 for each of the first three items, dropping to .85 and .82 for items four and five, respectively. Again, recall for the last item was only insignificantly superior to the pairing condition (.79). Also consistent with Experiment 3 was the mean Spearman rank correlation of .94 between input and output positions of the recalled words, which shows that recall order corresponded closely to the presentation order. Thus both Experiments 3 and 4 showed that subjects who had to associate multiple-list items to each cue tended to recall the items in each set in the same order as they were presented. It appears that these subjects were using a combination of the peg word and link mnemonics. Each peg word cued not a single word but a longer chain consisting of all target words with a common peg-word cue.

Also, the result that the final item in each set was recalled no better than a corresponding item in the pairing condition indicates that cumulative cueing was not occurring; that is, the previously recalled items were not combining in their cueing effects to facilitate the recall of the final word in each set.

These results provide further evidence for the importance of cumulative rehearsal and more effective use of study time under the organizing than under pairing conditions and indicate that both reductions in number of chunks and increases in number of words per chunk can contribute significantly to the superior recall under organizing conditions. Total number of target words, however, appears to have little effect upon recall, because the 30–5 condition was only insignificantly below the 10–5 group and was superior to both pairing groups.

The results thus far indicate both reprocessing of previous items while new words are being presented and easier recall of a smaller number of chunks, to be important contributors to the superior recall under oganized as compared with semantic processing conditions. Experiment 5 was designed to eliminate the advantage that the organizing groups have in continually reviewing previously presented items, by presenting all materials simultaneously and allowing subjects under both organizing and pairing conditions to study the materials in any order and to divide their study time among items in any way they wished.

E. Experiment 5

Three groups of 24–25 subjects each were all given 12 min to study a list of 48 unrelated concrete words. In the 1–1 pairing group, subjects were given a sheet of paper containing 48 different pairs of words and instructed to associate each target word with its corresponding peg word using visual imagery. The 1–8 organizing group received a study sheet with six peg words each followed by eight target words in two columns of 4 words each, with instructions to form a composite image containing all eight target words and the peg words for each of the six peg-word sets. The third 1–8 pairing group was given a study sheet containing 48 peg-word–target pairs, but with each of 6 peg words used eight times in randomly nonadjacent serial positions on the study sheet. These 1–8 pairing subjects were instructed to form a visual image associating each target with its corresponding peg word and were further instructed not to combine any of the pairs into a larger visual image even though the peg words occurred more than once on their study sheets. Subjects in all groups were also instructed to place a check mark next to each target word when they had successfully formed a visual image for that word and also to place additional check marks next to any target items that they restudied and reimaged if they had time to go back and study any items more than once. This provided a rough measure of number of rehearsals for each word. After the 12-min study period was completed, all subjects spent 10 min on an anagram-solving distractor task. Finally, subjects were given their 6 or 48 peg words in an order different from that on their study sheets and asked to write down the target word(s) associated with each peg word.

Presented in Table 10.4 are the mean proportions of target words recalled correctly by each of the three groups and also the mean numbers of reported rehearsals for each group. In contrast with the previous experiments, the 1–1 pairing group actually shows insignificantly higher recall than the 1–8 organizing group, and both are significantly superior to the 1–8 pairing group.

Table 10.4
Mean Proportion Correct Recall and Number of Rehearsals for Each Group of Experiment 5

	Condition		
	1–8 organizing	1–1 pairing	1–8 pairing
Recall	.66	.75	.42
Rehearsals	.93	1.85	.91

The 1–1 pairing group, however, reported an average of two rehearsals per word, while the 1–8 organizing and pairing groups rehearsed each word no more than once. These latter results suggest that it takes only about half as long to form a visual image of a pair of peg-word and target items as it does to integrate a target word into a composite image including other target words. In addition, interference from previous images of peg words with other target words apparently increased the amount of time required to form a pairwise image in the 1–8 pairing group.

These results indicate that when effective processing time was equated for the 1–1 pairing and 1–8 organizing groups, any differences between them in recall were eliminated. Contrary to the results of the previous experiments, a reduction in number of chunks from 48 to 6 produced no facilitation of recall. One difference from Experiment 4 that may help account for these discrepant results is that in Experiment 4 it took three times as long to present 30 chunks as 10 chunks, so that the inferior 30-chunk conditions had substantially longer retention intervals especially for the early-presented target words. When both total study time and retention interval were equated for the 1–1 pairing and 1–8 organizing groups in Experiment 5, however, there was no effect of number of chunks and consequently no evidence that recall is facilitated by a reduced number of chunks.

F. General Discussion

The best way of summarizing these results is to emphasize that neither reduced number of chunks nor increased number of words per chunk or total words, appears to be sufficient to account for the facilitation of recall produced by organizational mnemonics, either alone or in combination. Although the present results do not rule out the possible importance of any or all of these factors under certain conditions, they do indicate that the effectiveness of organizational mnemonics for subsequent recall is more directy related to the system of self-cueing created by such mnemonics, so that the items stored in memory can more easily be recalled. Especially when subjects in the organizing conditions must organize a supraspan number of target words in association with each peg word, successful recall may depend heavily upon their success in creating a retrieval scheme involving self-cueing contingent on the recall of other words.

The present results also indicate the importance with long study times of distinguishing actual presentation time from effective study time. Thus an organizing strategy is likely to produce added rehearsal and overlearning especially of the initially presented targets within a chunk, by forcing subjects to make more use of the presentation time as effective study time. More specifically, in the process of forming composite images under the present organizing conditions, subjects must continually rehearse, review, and re-image items presented prior to the target item being studied. Thus, when effective study time was equated for organizing and pairing groups in Experiment 5, there were no differences in recall between their self-cueing systems that respectively were and were not contingent upon the recall of other target words.

It seems that the self-cueing that occurs using mnemonic devices operates in accordance with the principle of encoding specificity (Tulving & Thomson, 1973), although it is unclear whether self-cueing falls within the domain of encoding specificity as it was originally formulated. For a subject-generated cue to be effective at recall, it must have been present at the time the target item was encoded. The thrust of this research on organization and self-cueing seems to indicate not only that organization of material during presentation is necessary for optimal recall, but that the retrieval system created involves some system of self-cueing.

The present results and conclusions concerning the principal source(s) of organizational facilitation in cued recall, of course, are limited to the particular peg-word mnemonic system and other conditions specific to these individual experiments. Although there is every reason to expect that more effective self-cueing and/or usage of study time are likely to be important facilitative consequences of organization in other situations as well, it may well be that one or more of the other possible factors underlying organization (such as reduced number of chunks, cumulative cueing, or hierarchical organization) may play more important roles with other types of organizational mnemonic systems or memory tasks.

In addition to their intended purpose of shedding some light on the processes by which memory is facilitated by a particular type of organizational mnemonic system, the experiments described in this section also support the more general demonstrations by Bellezza et al. (1976, 1977) that some type of interitem organization must be added to semantic processing to provide for optimal memory performance. When effective mnemonic systems are employed, recall levels can be demonstrated that are well beyond anything shown with semantic processing of individual items. Thus in the present Experiment 4, subjects using a peg-word mnemonic system showed 87% correct recall even under conditions where each of 150 words was presented once for 15 sec.

One final suggestion from these experiments is that the traditional verbal-learning and memory paradigms may not be adequate for studying organizational processes in memory, because such experiments use presentation times and other materials or procedural conditions that prevent subjects from making full usage of their organizational capabilities. Even the present experiments have been limited to single-trial recall situations using unstructured word lists. As noted previously (e.g., Pellegrino & Battig, 1974), the role of organization in general and organizational mnemonics in particular may be completely different with multitrial recall and/or with structured word lists. The evidence to date, however, clearly indicates that organization represents an important factor across a wide variety of memory tasks and conditions.

G. Further Evidence for the Importance of Organization

Before concluding, we want to describe briefly two additional demonstrations from the Colorado laboratories of the important role played by organization in recall memory. Both experiments were done primarily for other reasons, but nonetheless extend significantly the range of evidence for organizational factors.

One of these is a levels-of-processing experiment carried out by V. C. Keenan in the first author's laboratory. Keenan's experiment included processing tasks in which the subject was required to rank order each of 40 words from highest to lowest on a specified processing dimension, as compared with the more typical rating task where each word was rated individually for a specific property or dimension. Included in Keenan's design were two groups that respectively ranked and rated words for pleasantness. Subsequent recall performance was markedly superior for the pleasantness ranking (41.4%) over the pleasantness rating group (29.9%), showing again that the added opportunity to organize and interrelate the words within the ranking task produced a significant improvement even in comparison with the type of semantic rating task that is generally found to be optimal for recall memory (Packman & Battig, 1978).

A second type of evidence for the central role played by organization in free recall comes from a totally unsuccessful attempt to assess the usage of different kinds of encoding processes across different individual words and thus to extend the evaluation of within-individual differences to the free-recall task (Battig, 1975). To minimize the involvement of grouping or organizational processes, subjects were given a large number (60) of maximally unrelated words and instructed to group together those words for which they would use the same type of encoding (such as forming an image, a verbal encoding, or any other type they might find useful). Moreover, they were given detailed examples of these and various other types of encodings commonly reported by subjects in other experiments.

Despite this heavy emphasis on using different types of encodings for different individual items, most subjects insisted on grouping items according to semantic, syntactic, or acoustic relationships between them and paid no attention to our instructions. Furthermore, these relational strategies employed by subjects led to unusually high immediate recall of the words, making it impossible to evaluate the effects of the other variable manipulations incorporated into this experiment.

Thus our efforts to assess encoding strategies at the level of individual words demonstrated only the insistence of our subjects upon grouping or organizing these words together, which further suggests that levels-of-processing experiments that force subjects to process each word individually may be unusual and atypical of the techniques customarily employed in trying to learn and remember a list of words.

III. SUMMARY AND CONCLUSIONS

The main point that we have tried to make in this chapter is that the concept of organization and in particular the notion of organizational processing continue to have a vital role to play in memory research. Some current experimental frameworks, such as levels of processing, pay little attention to organization and generally limit the extent to which organizational processing can occur. However, the experimental results discussed in this chapter indicate that organizational processes must be considered as a necessary and key component of any levels-of-processing formulation.

Organizational processes have an effect on recall performance by interrelating items and thereby improving the retrieval process. Consequently, most experiments show large effects of organization on recall performance with relatively small effects on recognition. One way of ensuring that organization will occur in a list-learning experiment is by having the learner use some type of mnemonic device. Such mnemonic devices typically create a system of self-cueing by which each recalled item acts as a cue for some other item (contingent self-cueing) or by which components of the mnemonic process itself such as peg words or loci act as cues (noncontingent self-cueing).

There may be other manifestations of the organizing process in addition to self-cueing that operate in one-trial recall experiments of the kind discussed here. The number of chunks formed to store the word list in memory may affect recall performance as well as the number of words used in each chunk. However, when the effects of these two factors were tested using an experimental procedure in which a cue for each chunk was presented at recall, the number of chunks formed and the number of items per chunk had relatively small effects on recall performance.

In future research, we hope that the present broadened focus upon organizational processing may be extended across the artifactual boundaries that presently separate researchers concerned with organization in free recall from those psychologists who are interested primarily in linguistic and semantic-memory structures and schematic representations. Our consideration of vertical as well as of horizontal dimensions of organizational processing not only serves to enhance the relationships of free-recall to semantic-memory organization, but also permits the incorporation of organizational processing into research directly concerned with mnemonic devices and levels-of-processing in memory, as has been emphasized throughout the present chapter.

REFERENCES

Anderson, J. R. FRAN: A simulation model of free recall. In G. H. Bower (Ed), *The psychology of learning and motivation* (Vol. 5). New York: Academic Press, 1971.
Battig, W. F. Parsimony in psychology. *Psychological Reports*, 1962, *11*, 555–572.

Battig, W. F. Review of "Organization of Memory" by Tulving and Donaldson (Eds.), *American Journal of Psychology*, 1973, *86*, 675–677.

Battig, W. F. Within-individual differences in 'cognitive' processes. In R. L. Solso (Ed.), *Information processing and cognition: The Loyola symposium*. Potomac, Md.: Lawrence Erlbaum Associates, 1975.

Battig, W. F. Review of "Recall and Recognition" by J. Brown (Ed.), *American Journal of Psychology*, 1977, *90*, 165–168.

Battig, W. F. The flexibility of human memory. In L. S. Cermak & F. I. M. Craik (Eds.), *Levels of processing and human memory*. Hillsdale, N. J.: Lawrence Erlbaum Associates, 1979.

Battig, W. F., Allen, M., & Jensen, A. R. Priority of free recall of newly-learned items. *Journal of Verbal Learning and Verbal Behavior*, 1965, *4*, 175–179.

Bellezza, F. S., Cheesman, F. L., & Reddy, B. G. Organization and semantic elaboration in free recall. *Journal of Experimental Psychology: Human Learning and Memory*, 1977, *3*, 539–550.

Bellezza, F. S., & Reddy, B. G. Mnemonic devices and natural memory. *Bulletin of the Psychonomic Society*, 1978, *11*, 277–280.

Bellezza, F. S., Richards, D. L., & Geiselman, R. E. Semantic processing and organization in free recall. *Memory and Cognition*, 1976, *4*, 415–421.

Bousfield, W. A. The occurrence of clustering in recall of randomly arranged associates. *Journal of General Psychology*, 1953, *49*, 229–240.

Bower, G. H. Organizational factors in memory. In E. Tulving & W. Donaldson (Eds.), *Organization of memory*. New York: Academic Press, 1972a.

Bower, G. H. Mental imagery and associative learning. In L. W. Gregg (Ed.), *Cognition in learning and memory*. New York: Wiley and Sons, 1972b.

Buschke, H. Learning is organized by chunking. *Journal of Verbal Learning and Verbal Behavior*, 1976, *15*, 313–324.

Buschke, H. Two-dimensional recall: Immediate identification of clusters in episodic and semantic memory. *Journal of Verbal Learning and Verbal Behavior*, 1977, *16*, 201–215.

Cermak, L. S., & Craik, F. I. M. (Eds.). *Levels of processing in human memory*. Hillsdale, N.J.: Lawrence Erlbaum Associates, 1979.

Cofer, C. N. On some factors in the organizational characteristics of free recall. *American Psychologist*, 1965, *20*, 261–272.

Colle, H. A. The reification of clustering. *Journal of Verbal Learning and Verbal Behavior*, 1972, *11*, 624–633.

Collins, A. M., & Quillian, M. R. Retrieval time from semantic memory. *Journal of Verbal Learning and Verbal Behavior*, 1969, *8*, 240–247.

Craik, F. I.M. Human memory. *Annual Review of Psychology*, 1979, *30*, 63–102.

Craik, F. I. M., & Lockhart, R. S. Levels of processing: A framework for memory research. *Journal of Verbal Learning and Verbal Behavior*, 1972, *11*, 671–684.

Craik, F. I. M., & Tulving, E. Depth of processing and the retention of words in episodic memory. *Journal of Experimental Psychology: General*, 1975, *104*, 268–294.

Einstein, G. O., Pellegrino, J. W., Mondani, M. S., & Battig, W. F. Free-recall performance as a function of overt rehearsal frequency. *Journal of Experimental Psychology*, 1974, *103*, 440–449.

Friendly, M. L. Computer processing of free recall data: Program RECALL. *Behavior Research Methods and Instrumentation*, 1975, *7*, 47–50.

Higbee, K. L. *Your memory: How it works and how to improve it*. Englewood Cliffs, N.J.: Prentice-Hall, 1977.

Hubert, L. J., & Levin, J. R. A general statistical framework for assessing categorical clustering in free recall. *Psychological Bulletin*, 1976, *83*, 1072–1080.

Kintsch, W. *The representation of meaning in memory*. Hillsdale, N.J.: Lawrence Erlbaum Associates, 1974.

Lorayne, H., & Lucas, J. *The memory book*. New York: Ballantine, 1974.

Mandler, G. Organization and memory. In K. W. Spence & J. T. Spence (Eds.), *The psychology of learning and motivation* (Vol. 1). New York: Academic Press, 1967.

McDaniel, M. A., & Masson, M. E. Long-term retention: When incidental semantic processing fails. *Journal of Experimental Psychology: Human Learning and Memory,* 1977, *3,* 270–281.

McDaniel, M. A., & Masson, M. E. J. Organizational factors in delayed recall and recognition. Technical Report No. 78, Program on Cognitive Factors in Human Learning and Memory, Institute for the Study of Intellectual Behavior, University of Colorado, 1978.

Meyer, D. E. On the representation and retrieval of stored semantic information. *Cognitive Psychology,* 1970, *1,* 242–300.

Miller, G. A. The magical number seven plus or minus two: Some limits on our capacity for processing information. *Psychological Review,* 1956, *63,* 81–97.

Miller, G. A., Galanter, E., & Pribram, K. H. *Plans and the structure of behavior.* New York: Holt, Rinehart and Winston, 1960.

Norman, D. A., & Bobrow, D. G. On data limited and resource limited processes. *Cognitive Psychology,* 1975, *7,* 44–64.

Packman, J. L., & Battig, W. F. Effects of different kinds of semantic processing on memory for words. *Memory and Cognition,* 1978, *6,* 502–508.

Pellegrino, J. W. A general measure of organization in free recall for variable unit size and internal sequential consistency. *Behavior Research Methods and Instrumentation,* 1971, *3,* 241–246.

Pellegrino, J. W. Organizational attributes in list acquisition and retention. *Journal of Experimental Psychology,* 1974, *103,* 230–239.

Pellegrino, J. W., & Battig, W. F. Relationships among higher order organizational measures and free recall. *Journal of Experimental Psychology,* 1974, *102,* 463–472.

Reynolds, A. G., & Flagg, P. W. *Cognitive Psychology.* Cambridge, Mass: Winthrop, 1977.

Rumelhart, D. E., & Ortony, A. The representation of knowledge in memory. In R. C. Anderson, R. J. Spiro, and W. E. Montague (Eds.), *Schooling and the acquisition of knowledge.* Hillsdale, N.J.: Lawrence Erlbaum Associates, 1977.

Schank, R., & Abelson, R. *Scripts, plans, goals, and understanding: An inquiry in human knowledge and structures.* Hillsdale, N.J.: Lawrence Erlbaum Associates, 1977.

Slamecka, N. J. An examination of trace storage in free recall. *Journal of Experimental Psychology,* 1968, *76,* 504–513.

Smith, E. E., Shoben, E. J., & Rips, L. J. Structure and process in semantic memory. *Psychological Review,* 1974, *81,* 214–241.

Sternberg, R. J. & Tulving, E. The measurement of organization in free recall. *Psychological Bulletin,* 1977, *84,* 539–556.

Tulving, E. Subjective organization in free recall of "unrelated" words. *Psychological Review,* 1962, *69,* 344–354.

Tulving, E., & Donaldson, W. (Eds.) *Organization of Memory.* New York: Academic Press, 1972.

Tulving, E., & Thomson, D. M. Encoding specificity and retreival processes in episodic memory. *Psychological Review,* 1973, *80,* 352–373.

Wood, G. Organizational processes in free recall. In E. Tulving & W. Donaldson (Eds.), *Organization of memory.* New York: Academic Press, 1972.

Engrams As Cuegrams and Forgetting as Cue Overload: A Cueing Approach to the Structure of Memory[1]

This chapter considers how the structure of memory might be conceptualized in terms of the effectiveness of various memory cues. It begins with a discussion of the nature of memory cues and of the distinction between nominal and functional cues. The suggestion is made that all recall can be

[1]Preparation of this chapter was aided by the National Institute of Mental Health Grant No. 1-R01-MH31674.

thought of as mediated by cues, and this suggestion is discussed for the free-recall and recognition procedures. The idea of describing memory structure with respect to cue effectiveness is then considered. In particular, it is shown that by means of the *reduction method* it is possible to determine the relation between cues and that by means of the *cuegram* it is possible to depict this relation in an adequate and straightforward way. We turn next to the principle of cue overload and to the view that the organization or management of memory involves minimizing the load on memory cues. The chapter is concluded with a brief sketch of some of the advantages that a cueing approach to memory brings.

I. NOMINAL MEMORY CUES AND FUNCTIONAL MEMORY CUES

Recall always occurs within a physical environment, and at any given instant the prevailing physical environment is an important determinant of what, if anything, is recalled. It follows that there is a need to take the physical environment into account when documenting memory performance. But there is a problem here. The physical environment can never be fully described, for it is ever changing and never exactly the same as any other; any description can be made more complete. It seems, then, that we must content ourselves with a description of the physical environment that is less than complete. We must settle for characterizing it, for noting its salient features. These features we call memory cues or, more particularly, nominal memory cues.

But we can also speak of functional memory cues, which refer to the cognitive environment. By cognitive environment is meant something akin to William James' stream of consciousness, and as such it is a somewhat slippery concept. The functional memory cue is even more difficult to define, for just as the nominal memory cue is an abstraction of the physical environment so the functional memory cue is an abstraction of the cognitive environment. It should be thought of, at least for the present purposes, as a purely hypothetical entity serving to make theoretical speculation a little less abstruse. The functional memory cue used on any given occasion will, like the cognitive environment, reflect both the remember's history and the prevailing physical environment.

The four entities under discussion all differ in their theoretical status. Thus, the physical environment is usually thought of as "real," the nominal memory cue is a somewhat arbitrary abstraction of this reality, the cognitive environment is strictly subjective, and the functional memory cue is best regarded as a hypothetical construct. Whether emphasis is given to the physical environment and nominal memory cues or to the cognitive environment and functional memory cues is a matter of choice. This is an important point, for it means that adopting a cueing framework for memory does not constrain the abstractness of theoretical treatment. One can restrict consideration to nominal cues and remain relatively operational, or one can propose functional memory cues and be more hypothetical. Although this chapter does not pursue this distinction, the flexibility in style of theorizing offered by a cueing approach to memory structure could prove a valuable asset in its future development.

II. MEMORY CUES IN FREE RECALL AND RECOGNITION

Memory cueing might be taken as referring to a trendy, somewhat esoteric procedure having questionable relevance to the main business of memory research. However, the contention that recall is a function of the prevailing environment suggests that it should prove fruitful to think quite otherwise, to think that *all* procedures in memory research involve cueing, that recall is *always* in response to a cue, and that to understand the principles of memory it is necessary to understand the principles of cued recall. Certain traditional experimental procedures can be cast very readily within a memory-cueing framework. With the paired-associate procedure, for example, the response terms can be designated as target items and the stimulus terms as memory cues. It is, however, less obvious how a cueing terminology can be applied to certain other familiar procedures. The difficulty is perhaps most acute with two particularly well-used procedures, free recall and recognition. We now consider the case for a memory-cueing orientation for each of these procedures in turn.

A. The Free-Recall Cue

The term *free recall* is used to describe a procedure in which the subject is instructed to recall as many items as possible from a specified set without regard to order. Specification of the set may be given directly by the experimenter at the time that recall is required, in which case it will form part of the subject's physical environment. On other occasions, especially those in which several lists are studied and tested in succession, there are no explicit instructions. The subject "understands" his task and performs appropriately without instructions. In these cases instructions can be thought of as having been given implicitly; the subject may know, for instance, that he or she is required to recall after each list presentation "the members of the list just studied."

The free-recall procedure can be cast in memory-cueing terms simply by identifying the recall instructions—whether explicit or implicit—as a memory cue. Two obvious respects in which the free-recall instruction differs from conventional cues concern (a) its specification of the entire set of target items, and (b) its relative ineffectiveness. To understand the difficulty in thinking of the free-recall procedure as one of cued recall, it is necessary to consider these particular characteristics.

The free-recall situation entails only one nominal cue whereas the conventional cued-recall situation entails more than one. It does not follow, however, that this purely procedural distinction has any basic psychological significance. The point is perhaps most readily appreciated by conceiving of experimental arrangements that bridge the procedures of free recall and conventional cued recall, for such arrangements bring out a certain arbitrariness in the distinction.

Consider a procedure in which the target items have been randomly selected from some specified population and in which at test the recall of each target item is cued with a fresh stimulus word of which the target is a high associate: a clear case of cued recall. Suppose now that we change this procedure somewhat, so that the target items conform to several distinct categories and the names of these categories are presented as cues at test: another clear case of cued recall. But suppose that the number of categories is reduced from several to say four, or three, or two. Consider in particular a cued-recall procedure with just two categories (and thus two cues), and imagine further that at presentation the items are blocked. For instance, the subject may receive a 20-item list in which the first 10 items are names of four-legged animals and the second 10 are names of musical instruments. Suppose that the two cues are given in random order, and consider a particular case in which the second category (musical instruments) is tested first.

Now consider a free-recall procedure in which the subject is presented with a series of 10-item lists. Suppose that the items within each list are drawn from the same conceptual category, with the category changing from list to list. Consider a particular case in which the list items are names of musical instruments, and compare this free-recall procedure with the previous cued-recall procedure. More specifically, compare the procedures during the interval between the presentation of the first musical instrument and the end of the recall period for this category. If the presentation rate and recall time are the same, then the only point of difference in the procedure lies in the recall signal: "musical instruments" in the one case, "last list" in the other. This game could, of course, be played further, with residual differences in task demands and the like being chipped away. But perhaps it has been played far enough at least to call into question any assumption that the nominal free-recall instruction differs in a fundamental way from conventional memory cues.

The second source of difficulty in thinking of the free-recall instruction as a memory cue is that as such it would be comparatively weak. I suggest later that this difficulty may be related io the previous one in that the sharing of a nominal cue among many target items reduces its effectiveness with respect to any one item. For the present I suggest that, though the free-recall instruction is less effective than many conventional cues, it does not follow that its "mode of action" differs from that of any other cue, conventional or unconventional.

As it happens, recall in the standard free-recall procedure is not in fact lower than that in all conventional cued-recall procedures. It is not, for instance, lower than in Slamecka's (1968) part-set cueing procedure. In this procedure, a random subset of the words from the study list are supplied at test as cues for the remaining items of the list. Recall of the latter is at a lower level under these conditions than under standard free-recall instructions. This finding clearly weakens the case for a basic distinction between free and cued recall on the grounds of cue effectiveness.

Of more importance is the confusion that may arise from the very term *memory cue*. That the free-recall instruction is typically less effective than most conventional cues merely reflects the fact that the experimenter is, for obvious reasons, interested in those classes of environmental stimuli that will effect recall with some nontrivial probability. For this reason, he is justified in characterizing these stimuli as "memory cues," but in doing so he is using the term only in a descriptive sense. The stimuli that occur in a laboratory experiment could range from the presentation of a recognition test item through an instruction for free recall to a frantically delivered instruction to vacate the room because of fire. Although such varied environmental events would give rise to vastly different *levels* of recall, it does not follow that we would need to posit fundamentally different *accounts* of recall for those target items that are in fact remembered.

We may conclude that, although in some circumstances it may be reasonable to characterize some but not other events as memory cues in an arbitrary and descriptive way, any persuasive case for a more fundamental basis for this distinction has yet to be made. More particularly, that the free-recall instruction subsumes the entire set of target items and that it is typically rather ineffective are not convincing arguments against conceiving of the instruction as a memory cue.

B. The Recognition or Identity Cue

The recognition procedure can be cast within a memory-cueing framework simply by characterizing the recognition test item as a memory cue. Thus, as for the free-recall instruction, it is assumed that the effect of a recognition test item is not qualitatively different from that of a more traditional memory cue.

To some extent, the case against assigning the recognition cue special status gains support from the difficulties in defining the term. At first blush, the definition appears straightforward: A memory cue is a recognition cue if its relation to the target item is one of identity. But identity is itself a concept that is difficult to define. This issue has been discussed ever since Parmenedes and Heraclitus, and presumably it will not be resolved in the foreseeable future. With respect to the present concern, the target item is not a word but an event or episode in which a word is presented, and no two events are ever quite the same. Even if we restrict consideration to the actual word presentation and ignore contemporaneous factors, it is not obvious how similar the target and cue presentations need be before we can claim a relation of identity and define the procedure as one of recognition. The question is not merely academic, for level of recognition has been shown to vary according to whether the type-script or voice of presentation is changed from study to test (Craik & Kirsner, 1974; Hintzman & Summers, 1973). It would seem that, as with other cues, the concept of recognition cue is fuzzy, and that the change from a recognition to a nonrecognition cue may be gradual. This state of affairs clearly undermines the case for conceiving of recognition as a qualitatively distinct form of recollection.

The alternative hypothesis, that of no qualitative difference between recall and recognition, was given graphic, if somewhat lighthearted, support in an experiment described by Tulving and Watkins (1973). Subjects were presented with a list of five-letter words and then asked to write down as many of them as they could remember. The independent variable was the assistance provided at test. In some cases no assistance other than the free-recall cue was given. That is, the subjects were told that credit would be gained for each word from the preceding study list that they reported. In other cases, additional assistance was given. Specifically, for each target word the first two, three, or four letters were provided, and in some cases all five letters were provided. Thus, in conventional terminology, test conditions included free recall (no letters), cued recall (two, three, or four letters), and recognition (all five letters), with procedural differences other than the nature of the cues being kept to a minimum. Table 11.1 shows probability of recall as a function of the number of letters provided. It was concluded that, at least over the range of two- to five-letter cues, there was no obvious discontinuity in level of performance.

It is obvious that the Tulving and Watkins (1973) experiment does not disprove the notion that recall and recognition are qualitatively distinct; it merely calls for the reasons for making the distinction. The strongest reasons are theoretical, and they stem from the spatial conception of memory, to which just about all contemporary memory theorists subscribe. Foremost among these reasons is the idea that recognition provides a valid test of what is "in store" or "available." That is, whereas recall of available items is fallible, recognition is infallible and so provides an operational definition of availability. This assumption is discussed at length elsewhere (Watkins & Tulving, 1975; Watkins & Gardiner, in press); for the present it must suffice to note some of its major shortcomings.

Despite a certain heuristic value, the idea of infallible recognition is contrary to a great deal of evidence. In particular, the probability of recogniz-

Table 11.1
Probability of Recall as a Function of the Number of Letters Provided.[a]

Number of letters provided				
0	2	3	4	5
.24	.28	.56	.70	.85

[a]From Tulving and Watkins, 1973.

ing a target item has been shown to depend on the extent to which its study context is reinstated at test. For instance, if the target word JAM is studied in the context of the word *strawberry*, it is subsequently more likely to be recognized if tested in the context of the word *raspberry* than in the context of the word *traffic* (Light & Carter-Sobell, 1970). Such effects on recognition performance clearly demonstrate that the recognition test does not provide an infallible test of item "availability," for the availability of the target item is statistically equivalent for the two conditions. Of course, this demonstration is relevant only to the nominal cue; it does not rule out recognition infallibility at the functional level. Indeed, it seems entirely reasonable to suppose that JAM in the sense of fruity food is functionally distinct from JAM in the sense of crowded mass, so that the fallibility of recognition implied by the adverse effects of switching context could be merely a consequence of activating the "wrong" functional unit.

This functional version of the infallible-recognition theory is more difficult to test than the nominal version, since there appear to be no clear rules for identifying the functional units. To the extent that it has been tested, however, the functional version of the theory seems, like the nominal version, to be of no more than heuristic value. In the first place, recognition fallibility has been demonstrated for words that are not obviously homographic (e.g., Thomson, 1972; Tulving & Thomson, 1973). These findings have been reconciled with the theory by assuming that not only transparent homographs but indeed most common words are represented by more than one functional unit (e.g., Anderson & Bower, 1974; Martin, 1975; Reder, Anderson, & Bjork, 1974). This assumption reduces the predictive power of the theory and makes it even harder to test. Again, however, where it has been possible to put the theory to test, the theory has not fared well (see Tulving & O. C. Watkins, 1977; Watkins, Ho, & Tulving, 1976; Watkins & Park, 1976). Thus, for instance, Watkins and Park failed to find any evidence for the prediction that recognition failure should be alleviated by providing the subject with some assistance in gaining access to the various functional units subsumed by a given, nominal, target item. Specifically, subjects made their recognition responses for each target word both immediately before and immediately after reading its dictionary entry. Being reminded of the various senses of a target word (or the subset thereof given in the dictionary) did not lead to better performance even for target items that were subsequently shown to be recallable. In another study, Watkins et al. (1976) demonstrated recognition context effects and hence recognition fallibility when the target items were unfamiliar faces. Since it is unreasonable to suppose a multiple representation in memory of items that were entirely unknown to the subjects before their occurrence in the study sequence, the functional–nominal distinction does not apply in this case. This demonstration is therefore difficult to reconcile with the hypothesis of recognition infallibility at the functional, as well as at the nominal, level. In short, it seems that there is much to support the contention that the recognition test item is just another memory cue.

III. MEMORY TRACE AND CUE VALENCES

According to the cueing approach to memory being considered here, memory is specified by the probability of recall associated with each of various classes of memory cues. Indeed, such recall probabilities are considered to *define* memory. This viewpoint contrasts with conventional theory, which conceptualizes memory in terms of the *memory trace* or *engram*. Before developing the memory-cueing approach further, let us note some of the principal shortcomings of conventional trace theory.

The essential problem with traces is that there appears to be no way to get an unadulterated look at them. To study them we need to measure memory performance, and memory performance necessarily reflects the measurement procedure. A free-recall test might suggest that only 30% of the traces of a set of target events survive, whereas a recognition test might suggest that 60% survive. And other tests might suggest still other values. How can a given set of traces be manifest to such different extents?

This difficulty has been met with the constructs of trace strength and activation threshold. Trace strength is a unidimensional attribute that varies with such factors as the nature of the encoding and the time or the mental activity since encoding. The failure of a cue to elicit recall need not imply that the trace has completely faded away; it may merely have faded to a level below some critical activation threshold. And this threshold is assumed to vary with the nature of the cue. For instance, the activation threshold may be lower for recognition than for free recall, so that even relatively weak traces will be activated in response to the identity cue of the recognition test whereas only the stronger traces will be activated in response to a free-recall instruction.

It is clear that describing memory in terms of trace strength is simpler than describing it in terms of the efficiencies of various memory cues. On the other hand, the simplicity is bought at the cost of assuming that a unidimensional variable can adequately characterize recall potential. An implication of this assumption is that if one particular set of events is recalled to a greater extent than another in response to cue X, then the same should be true in response to cue Y. Conversely, if one particular type of cue is more effective than another for target set A, then the same should be true for target set B. However much evidence there may be in support of these predictions, there are well-documented exceptions, and these exceptions are fatal for trace-strength theory. For instance, study encounters with comparatively rare words are remembered with a greater probability than encounters with common words in response to the identity cues of a recognition situation (Gorman, 1961), whereas it is the encounters with common words that have the greater probability of being remembered in response to a free-recall cue (Sumby, 1963): Which have the greater strengths, encounters with the rare words or encounters with the common words? Similarly, Fisher and Craik (1977) have shown that for target words encoded under one set of conditions, "rhyme" cues are more effective than "associative" cues, whereas for target words encoded under other condi-tions the associative cues are more effective than the rhyme cues. Study–test interactions of this sort are, of course, at the heart of Tulving and Thomson's (1973) encoding specificity principle. They demonstrate a complexity that cannot be captured by a unidimensional variable such as trace strength.

It appears, then, that memory for a given population of target events is more adequately specified as a set of memory-cue efficiencies, or *valences,* than as some level of trace strength as indexed by the effectiveness of just one type of cue. On the other hand, a set of cue valences hardly constitutes an adequate description of memory "structure." To describe memory structure in terms of memory cues, we must call upon a construct proposed by Tulving and Watkins (1975). This construct we may refer to as the *cuegram.*

IV. THE CUEGRAM

The cuegram is nothing more than a summary of cue valences and of the relation between cue valences. It does *not* imply a physical entity bridging the temporal interval between an event and its recall, and consequently it avoids some of the difficulties of the trace metaphor. On the other hand, the systematic description that constitutes the cuegram is sufficiently concrete to capture certain of the advantages of the trace metaphor. These points can best be appreciated by means of an example.

Suppose that in a laboratory experiment the word HAT is presented as one of a list of target events, and that the cue *rhymes with bat* is given to one group of subjects after a short delay and to a second group after a long delay. Suppose that the cue effects recall for 70% of the subjects in the first group and for 50% of those in the second. In terms of the trace metaphor it is concluded that, on average, the trace has diminished during the interval between the two tests. But as soon as we try to specify just how much the trace has diminished we run into difficulties. Thus, whereas the rhyme cue data suggest a diminution of 20%, data corresponding to other cues may suggest other values. The recall rates for the short and long delays with, say, the identity cue (HAT) could be 90% and 80% respectively, suggesting a diminution of only 10%. And clearly other cues could yield yet other estimates. Indeed, it is logically possible that the efficiency of some cues would remain constant or even increase over the interval. In any case, it is clear that there is a fundamen-tal difficulty in stating in any simple way just how much the trace has diminished.

The difficulty can be resolved by focusing not on the "diminution" of memory over time, but merely on the changes with respect to various cues. This idea is expressed in the cuegram, the novel feature of which is the null element. The results of our imaginary experiment are summarized as cuegrams in Table 11.2. The cuegrams here are two-element cuegrams, the simplest kind. Each comprises two discrete elements, one corresponding to the proba-

Table 11.2
Two-element Cuegrams

	Short delay		Long delay	
	R	$\bar{R}$	R	$\bar{R}$
Rhyme cues	70	30	50	50
	I	$\bar{I}$	I	I
Identity cues	90	10	80	20

bility of the particular cue being effective, the other to the probability of its being ineffective. In some sense, each cuegram represents the structure of memory for a particular event after a particular delay and for a particular population of subjects.

It should be noted, parenthetically, that the cuegram is always a statement of probabilities. Its referent is always a population of subject-events, never a single event as experienced by a single subject. Our example involved a single item and could have involved—had it been witnessed by all of the subjects simultaneously—a single event. Alternatively, a cuegram could be derived from many events and a single subject. Most of the cuegram research to date, however, has involved both many events and many subjects. Notice that a single cuegram can refer to different events by virtue of the fact that any cue is a summary or abstraction of the environment and therefore subsumes a variety of instances.

We have seen that the two-element cuegram represents the structure of memory for a given population of subject-events and that different cuegrams can be obtained for the same population simply by measuring recall of a separate, random sample of subject-events in response to each of several types of cues. As was stressed in discussing the concept of trace strength, the effectiveness of one cue cannot be determined from that of another, and consequently the effectiveness of several cues tells more about a population of subject-events than does the effectiveness of one cue. Thus, an array of two-element cuegrams provides a more complete picture of the state of memory than does a single two-element cuegram.

Yet, even a vast array of two-element cuegrams might not tell us all we would like to know. In fact, it would provide no evidence at all on a crucial aspect of memory-cue efficiency, namely, the relation between cues. Knowing that cue A is more efficient (i.e., has a higher probability of effecting recall) than cue B tells us something about the relation between these two cues, but not very much. It tells us that some proportion of events is recallable in response to cue A but not to cue B, but it does not tell us, for example, whether there is some proportion for which the reverse is true. What is needed is a complete specification of the relation between recallability with respect to cue A and recallability with respect to cue B, as given by four proportions: the proportion of items recallable to both A and B (pAB), to A but not B (pA$\bar{B}$), to B but not A $(p\bar{A}B)$, and to neither A nor B $(p\bar{A}\bar{B})$. These proportions can be neatly expressed in the form of a contingency table.

Although the need for such a contingency table seems clear, it is less clear how it should be obtained. The obvious strategy is to cue each target item twice, once with each cue. The four entries of the table can then be determined directly. Unfortunately, the matter is not this simple. Although the strategy of cueing the target events with two successive cues may be appropriate in principle, in practice it requires considerable caution. In particular, care must be taken to prevent the subject from combining the information given by the respective cues, for such combinations could have emergent properties, which would preclude any deductions about the effectiveness of the individual cues. A simple way to avoid this state of affairs is to arrange the testing procedure in such a way that subjects cannot work out how the cues are paired. For instance, the cues can be arranged on two or more response sheets with each target event cued no more than once on any one sheet, and in an order separately randomized for each sheet.

A more subtle problem with the double-cueing strategy concerns the fact that memory, like temperature, may change as a result of being measured. Thus, performance on the second of two tests may be affected by the first test, and indeed such testing effects have long been known (Ballard, 1913; Cooper & Monk, 1976). Consequently, we can expect a bias in the four-element cuegram obtained from a simple double-cueing procedure.

A variant of the double-cueing procedure designed to avoid this problem has been proposed by Tulving and Watkins (1975). We refer to it as the *reduction method*. It begins with what may be referred to as the recall-or-nothing assumption, which says that any effects of the first set of cues on the second set will be mediated by only those events actually recalled in the first test. In other words, if a first-test cue does not produce recall of its target event, then it will not affect the probability of that event being recalled in response to its second-test cue.

Once this assumption is made, it is a relatively simple matter to construct an unbiased four-element cuegram. Suppose we cue a target set of events first with cue A and then with cue B, and then arrange the data directly into a contingency table. Suppose further that the data obtained are as in Table 11.3. The

Table 11.3
Contingency Table Obtained by Cueing First with Cue A and then with Cue B

		Cue B		
		+	−	
Cue A	+	.40	.20	.60
	−	.10	.30	.40
		.50	50	1.00

first thing to note about this table is that the marginal total of .60 for the overall effectiveness, or *gross valence,* of cue A is free of any possible contamination from the effects of cue B, for here cue A is the first cue presented. On the other hand, the breakdown of this value according to whether recall occurred in response to cue B could be contaminated. Specifically, the effectiveness of cue B for items recalled in response to cue A may be less than the value (.40) given in Table 11.3. Similarly, there may be an influence of the first test on the gross valence of cue B, such that the observed value of .50 is somewhat greater than it would have been if cue A had not previously been presented. There is, however, an entry in Table 11.3 in addition to the .60 gross valence of cue A free from any effects of prior cueing: the .10 of the $\overline{A}B$ cell. We refer to this cell as the *reduced valence* of cue B, since it refers to the effectiveness of cue B reduced by that of cue A. That this value is free from any influence of the first cue follows from the recall-or-nothing assumption. Because the second row of entries refers to items not recalled in response to cue A, they are assumed to be unaltered by cue A. We therefore have two values from Table 11.3 that can be used in the construction of an unbiased cuegram: the gross valence of cue A and the reduced valence of cue B. From these two values we can obtain by subtraction the marginal probability $\overline{A}$, and then in turn the "null element" $\overline{A}\overline{B}$. Thus, from Table 11.3 we are able to construct that part of the unbiased cuegram shown in Table 11.4.

It is clear from Table 11.4 that if we can obtain an unbiased estimate of any one of the remaining four proportions, we could derive by simple subtraction a complete unbiased cuegram. It turns out that this is a straightforward matter, since the gross valence of cue B can be determined simply by cueing fresh target events. Thus, the entries shown in Table 11.3 can be estimated by applying cue A and then cue B for only a proportion of the target events, and just cue B for the remaining events. Suppose, for instance, that the events tested first with cue A and then with cue B gave the results in Table 11.3 and that events tested with just cue B indicated a gross valence for B of .45. The complete cuegram would then be as shown in Table 11.5. This table also serves to illustrate the terminology.

In this way, an unbiased cuegram depicting the relation between cues A and B with respect to a specified set of events can be obtained with two testing conditions: an *A,B* condition in which cue A is applied first and cue B second,

Table 11.4
Part of a Cuegram Obtained from Data Shown in Table 11.3

		Cue B		
		+	−	
Cue A	+			.60
	−	.10	.30	.40
				1.00

Table 11.5
Complete Cuegram

		Cue B		
		+	−	
Cue A	+	.35	.25	.60
	−	.10	.30	.40
		.45	.55	1.00

Gross valence of cue A	=	.60
Gross valence of cue B	=	.45
Common valence	=	.35
Valence of cue A reduced by cue B		
(or, more simply, reduced valence of cue A)	=	.25
Valence of cue B reduced by cue A	=	.10
Null element	=	.30

and a B condition in which only cue B is applied. These two testing conditions could be applied as either a between-subject or a within-subject variable and, if the latter, as a between-list or a within-list variable. Note that in practice there is no need to construct the contingency table for the A,B condition. All that is needed from this condition is the gross valence of cue A and the reduced valence of cue B. These probabilities, together with the gross valence of cue B obtained from the B condition, can be used to derive the cuegram directly.

Although the A,B and B testing conditions are in principle adequate to allow derivation of an unbiased cuegram, it is more efficient to test all events twice, half in an A,B order and half in a B,A order. The resulting data can be used to derive two separate, unbiased versions of the cuegram. Given the assumptions underlying the reduction method, the only difference between the two versions will be that due to sampling variability. The best estimate of the population cuegram, therefore, is obtained by somehow averaging the two cuegrams. Just how this averaging is done follows from the recall-or-nothing assumption, for this implies that the probability of an item being recalled to at least one of two successively applied cues will be independent of the order in which the two cues are applied. Thus, to combine the two versions of the cuegram, the two critical proportions (the gross valence of the first cue and the reduced valence of the second) corresponding to each testing order are summed to give two independent estimates of the total number of events recallable to at least one cue. Then, for each testing order, the critical proportions are each multiplied by the ratio of the mean of the total-recall proportions for the two orders to the total-recall proportion of the order for which adjustment is being made. With these adjustments to the critical proportions, the two versions of the cuegram (derived as before by subtraction) will be identical and will represent the best estimate of the population cuegram.

An example should make this procedure clear. Suppose that in our previous example all items had in fact been tested with both cue A and cue B, half in an *A,B* order and half in a *B,A* order. Assume that the gross valence of each cue and the reduced valence of cue B were all as before and that the reduced valence of cue A was .21. These values are shown in the upper part of Table 11.6. The middle part of the table shows first the derivation of the best estimate of the probability of an event being recalled to at least one cue, and then how this estimate is used to adjust the observed valence to obtain the best population estimates. In the lower part of the table, the latter estimates are assembled to form the best estimate of the population cuegram.

We turn now from the mechanics of the reduction method to a brief consideration of its validity. We have seen that the method is a development of the assumption that cueing recall of an event will change the effectiveness of a second cue for that event only if the first cue does in fact effect recall. Although at present this assumption is not easy to evaluate, there are reasons why we might go along with it. First among these is the fact that what little relevant evidence is available is at least consistent with the assumption. In particular, a testable corollary is, as we have seen, that the probability of an event being recalled to at least one of two consecutively applied cues is independent of the order in which the cues are applied, and in general our own findings have been in good accord with this corollary (see, e.g., Tulving & Watkins, 1975, Table 4).

Table 11.6
Derivation of Best Estimate of Population Cuegram When All Items Are Tested with Both Cues

	Test Order	
Observed Probabilities	A,B	B,A
Gross valence of first cue	.60	.45
Reduced valence of second cue	.10	.21
Probability of recall to at least one cue	.70	.66

Best Estimates of Population Probabilities			
Probability of recall to at least one cue	$(.70 + .66)/2$	=	.680
Gross valence of cue A	$.60 \times .68/.70$	=	.583
Reduced valence of cue B	$.10 \times .68/.70$	=	.097
Gross valence of cue B	$.45 \times .68/.66$	=	.464
Reduced valence of cue A	$.21 \times .68/.66$	=	.216

Best Estimate of Population Cuegram

		Cue B		
		+	−	
Cue A	+	.367	.216	.583
	−	.097	.320	.417
		.464	.536	1.000

In studying the literature, we have found one experiment that appears to provide evidence inconsistent with the assumption. This experiment, reported by McLeod, Williams, and Broadbent (1971), involved presenting a list of to-be-remembered words (e.g., HEAD, SMOOTH, MUSIC) followed by first a free-recall test and then two successive cued tests. The first cued test was given for only those words not produced in the free-recall test, and it entailed presenting for each unrecalled word a specific semantic cue (e.g., *hair, rough, song*). The second cued test was for only those words recalled in neither of the previous tests, and it entailed adding for each unrecalled item a second semantic cue to the one given in the first cued test (e.g., *hair shoulder, rough silk, song sound*); the allocation of cues to the two tests was counterbalanced across subjects. McLeod *et al.* found that the probability of recall was higher in the second cued test than in the first, and this despite possible depression of recall in the second cued test through item selection effects. One interpretation of this finding, and indeed the one that the authors appear to adopt, is that during the first cued test even those cues that did not effect recall somehow influenced (in this case enhanced) the subsequent effectiveness of the new cues presented in the second cued test. There is, however, an alternative explanation. The greater probability of recall in the second cued test could result, not from the prior presentation of the first set of cues, but rather from the re-presentation of these cues along with the new cues. Although McLeod *et al.* took care to use cues that were not, according to normative data, related to one another, it is an empirical question whether the second set of cues would be more effective than the first when, as in the reduction method, the second set is presented alone. Recent experiments in our own laboratory (Watkins & Tulving, 1978) using the McLeod *et al.* materials have shown that this is not, in fact, the case. Consistent with the recall-or-nothing assumption, the second set of cues presented alone was substantially *less* effective than the first set.

Another reason for going along with the recall-or-nothing assumption is that its violation may not, in fact, be damning. There are two issues here. First, if cueing an event without success does affect the efficiency of a subsequent cue for that event, then it could well be that the effect is only transitory—in much the same way that nominally unattended information may have only transitory availability and transitory influence on that which is being attended (Glucksberg & Cowen, 1970; Lewis, 1970). In this case, with the procedures of the reduction method the effects should dissipate well before the presentation of the second cue, so that the method would be entirely valid. Second, even if there were relatively durable effects of cueing without recall, it does not follow that the reduction method should be discarded. Given the importance of determining the relation between cues, the reduction method should be discarded only if it can be replaced by a better method. At present, there are no obvious good alternatives to the double-cueing approach; and to the extent that cueing without recall influences the effectiveness of a subsequent cue to a lesser extent than does cueing with recall, the reduction method provides a more satisfactory solution than that given by contingency data obtained from a simple double-cueing procedure.

The recall-or-nothing assumption aside, it should be clear that in the final analysis the reduction method is in principle less than perfect. Inevitably, there is imperfection in a measurement procedure that takes finite time to determine a state that, presumably, is continuously changing. In fact, it can be shown that, as a general rule, the obtained cuegram would not reflect the "true" state of memory at any particular instant, even if it were free of sampling error. The situation is analogous to one in which the density of, say, a cube is to be determined when its weight and length are continuously changing and cannot be measured simultaneously. But in both cases, the problem may in practice be of little consequence. The error incurred will vary directly with the rate of change and with the lag between successive measures. Thus, to the extent that the inter-cue lag is small relative to the rate of change in the state of memory, the obtained cuegram will approximate the state of memory (with respect to those cues) throughout that interval.

The validity of the reduction method is perhaps most readily illustrated with cuegrams obtained for cues whose relation can be specified with some confidence on intuitive grounds. Endel Tulving and I have conducted two (unpublished) experiments that illustrate the point. In both experiments, the target events were the occurrences of unrelated words in a list at a rate of one every 2 seconds, and the two types of cues were chosen such that the information given by one could be assumed to be more or less completely included in that given by the other. In the first of these experiments, the two cues were, respectively, the first two and the first four letters of the target words. There were 30 targets and 40 subjects for a total of 1200 subject-events and 2400 subject-cue observations. Subjects responded on two successive test sheets, each of which included 15 two-letter cues and 15 four-letter cues selected such that each target word was cued with its first two letters on one sheet and with its first four letters on the other. On each test sheet the type of cue alternated, but otherwise the ordering of the cues was random with respect to both the order of the word-events in the study list and the cueing order on the other sheet. To allow an estimate of the extent to which target items were produced for reasons other than their occurrence in the study list, each target word had been randomly selected from a pair of words having the same initial four letters, and the extent to which the nonstudied members of the pairs were given at test was observed. Such "guessing" occurred in less than one case in a hundred. By subjecting the data to the reduction method, we obtained the cuegram shown in the left-hand panel of Table 11.7.

In the second validating experiment, the cues were both semantic category names, but as before, one was inclusive of the other. For instance, for the target word HAWK, one cue was *bird of prey* and the other was *bird*; for the target word CHAPEL, one cue was *religious building,* the other was *building.* There were 32 critical words and 40 subjects, so that the total number of cue–subject observations was 2560. The other procedural details were much the same as in the letter-cueing experiment. The resulting cuegram is presented in the right-hand panel of Table 11.7. As with the letter-cueing experiment, the cuegram for this experiment shows a substantial reduced valence for the specific cue but a reduced valence of the general cue that does not differ significantly from zero. The cuegrams for both experiments thus reveal the inclusive cue relation predicted from intuition.

Given, then, that a reasonable case can be made for the validity of the reduction method, brief mention should be made of some of the issues to which it has been applied. One recent application has been to the question of how remembering under conditions of recall is related to that under conditions of recognition (Watkins & Todres, 1978). In each of a series of experiments, the set of words from a study list that could be remembered in response to the identity cues of the recognition situation was found to subsume the set that could be remembered in response to a recall cue, whether the latter cue was one of free recall or involved word-specific association. In a somewhat different vein, Eich (1978) investigated the relation between fragrances and verbal descriptions as cues for recall of certain to-be-remembered words that depicted things having characteristic smells (e.g., PINE, CHOCOLATE). He found that the subset that could be recalled to the descriptive cues *(coniferous tree, cocoa)* subsumed the subset that could be recalled to appropriate fragrances, even when the normative associative strengths of the two types of cues were equated. An experiment by Tulving and Watkins (1975) revealed a very different relation, one of appreciable independence, between associative and rhyme cues, again with respect to the presentation of a list of to-be-remembered words.

Such experiments demonstrate in a compelling way that there is much more to memory than can be discovered from a single test. The results of interest in these experiments are to be found not in the gross valences or even in the relative values of the gross valences of the respective types of cues, but rather in the relation between the cues as depicted in cuegrams, and in the relations between cuegrams. Such results are often unexpected, as with, to take

Table 11.7
Cuegrams from Two Validating Experiments

		Experiment 1: Letter cues					*Experiment 2: Semantic cues*		
		First four letters					Specific cue		
		+	−				+	−	
First two letters	+	.21	.02	.23	General cue	+	.18	.02	.20
	−	.26	.51	.77		−	.13	.67	.80
		.47	.53	1.00			.31	.69	1.00

just one example, Tulving and Watkins' (1975) finding that as retention interval increases the association between rhyme and associative cues is reduced. The picture of memory given by the reduction method and summarized in cuegrams is a rich one and it highlights a challenge: Either we ignore the complexities of recall and continue to restrict observations of memory performance to a single measure, or we come up with new and different conceptions and theories. In my view, it may be worthwhile to at least consider the latter option.

But there is, of course, a limit to what even the cuegram might do for us. In particular, it is a purely descriptive device; it is devoid of explanatory power. It goes no way toward explaining even such a basic phenomenon as forgetting. This brings us to the question, How should we interpret remembering and forgetting from a memory-cueing perspective? One possible first step is given in what we refer to as cue-overload theory.

V. CUE-OVERLOAD THEORY

Cue-overload theory is the simple idea that recall is mediated by cues and that these cues are subject to overload. In other words, as a memory cue comes to subsume more and more events, its probability of effecting recall of any particular event declines.

This general theoretical notion is by no means new; it appears in various guises throughout the memory literature. If there is anything new in cue-overload theory, it is in the generality with which the essential idea is formulated. It does not specify the relation between cue effectiveness and the number of events subsumed beyond saying that it is inverse and monotonic. Neither does it offer any mechanism for the relation; its explanatory power is through the interpretation of specific phenomena in terms of a general principle. It integrates results from a wide variety of experimental paradigms, and so brings within a common framework seemingly diverse memory phenomena. The following examples illustrate the point.

A. List-Length Effect

Perhaps the experimental finding most readily interpreted in terms of cue-overload theory is the inverse relation between the probability of recall and list length. More precisely, the probability of recall of the presentation of a given member of a list declines monotonically as the list length increases (e.g., Murdock, 1960). Recall probability is virtually perfect for lists of up to three or four items, but as list length is further extended the probability of recall declines rapidly. Cue-overload theory predicts this inverse relation simply by adopting the assumption proposed earlier that recall of list items is, to some extent at least, mediated by a cue corresponding to "list" or, if a series of lists is being presented, "last list."

B. Recall of Categorized Lists

Although the list-length effect is often dramatic, it is not always so. The effects of list length can be countered by adding structure to the list. For instance, a high level of recall can be obtained if the list items are selected from several discrete categories. The bulk of the research involving categorized lists has used taxonomic categories, though it is likely that other forms of categorization would also effectively enhance recall relative to an uncategorized list.

These beneficial effects of list structure are neatly interpreted by cue-overload theory simply by assuming that the individual categories serve as effective memory cues and so reduce the overload that would occur with just a single "list" cue. Thus recall would in effect represent the sum of several sublists, each sublist corresponding to a category. This interpretation is, of course, merely a version of organizational theory as worked out by Miller (1956), Tulving (1962, 1964), Mandler (1967), and Bower (1970), and as such it is supported by a wealth of evidence. First, recall protocols reveal a marked clustering by category (e.g., Tulving & Pearlstone, 1966). Second, except where the number of categories is very small, whole categories are often unrecalled, whereas the recall of just one member of a category is relatively rare. Taken together these two facts suggest a difficulty in recalling individual categories, and little difficulty in recalling at least a few category members once a category has been recalled. Third, a high degree of recall occurs with a hierarchical list structure having several levels of nesting. Thus, Bower, Clark, Lesgold, and Winzenz (1969) found that, with lists structured hierarchically such that no more than 4 items were nested under the same category, subjects recalled, after a single presentation, an average of 74 out of 112 items, whereas subjects given the same items in an unstructured list averaged only 20 items. Presumably, with hierarchical structures cue overloading is minimal. Fourth, items from categories completely omitted in a free-recall test are subsequently well recalled when the category names are supplied as cues (Tulving & Pearlstone, 1966). A similar effect is obtained when the cue takes the form of a category member rather than the category name (Hudson & Austin, 1970; Slamecka, 1972).

Clearly, then, there is considerable evidence to support the idea that the recall of a categorized list is mediated by cues corresponding to the category names. There is also evidence that the individual category cues can be overloaded. Thus, the probability of recalling a given category member has been shown to vary inversely with the number of category instances presented (Patterson, 1972; Tulving & Pearlstone, 1966; Watkins, 1975).

C. Subjective Organization

Structuring of a list can occur even when the items are randomly sampled from a homogeneous population. That is, a subject facing a free-recall task can effectively impose his own organization. Mandler (1967) has demonstrated an impressive level of recall when subjects are allowed to literally sort the items of a list into various sets on whatever basis they choose. In terms of cue-overload theory, the subjective categories each provide a memory cue and thus avoid an overloading of a single "list" cue.

Even more spectacular than the recall that was demonstrated with Mandler's sorting technique is that achieved with more orthodox mnemonic techniques. These techniques minimize overloading effects by, for instance, linking each item to a separate locus of a well-learned structure. Thus, in the one-bun technique (Miller, Galanter, & Pribram, 1960), each memory cue is linked to just one item, and no overloading can occur.

D. Extralist Cueing

If memory is limited because cues are overloaded, then it should be possible to improve memory by providing at test fresh cues that are specific to individual items and therefore not overloaded by associations to other items. And indeed, it has been found that providing cues at test can increase the probability of recall well above that achieved under free-recall conditions (e.g., Bahrick, 1969; Bilodeau, 1967).

E. Inhibitory Effects of Part-Set Cueing

We have already noted Slamecka's (1968) finding that when in a free-recall situation some of the study words are re-presented at test, recall of the remaining words is lower than in a control condition involving standard free-recall instructions. This inhibitory effect can be interpreted in terms of cue-overload theory with the assumption that the "list" memory cue is over-loaded as a result of re-presenting study words. This assumption is perhaps more reasonable than it at first appears, for although the number of different words is the same for the two conditions, it is not really words that are being remembered, but rather word-presentations, and there are more of these in the "cueing" condition.

There is a fair amount of evidence consistent with the cue-overload account of the part-set cueing effect. First, category-specific inhibitory effects have been observed in the recall of categorized lists (see Roediger, 1974). Specifically, if at test the experimenter cues some of the categories of a list with their category names and others with both their category names and some of the category instances that appeared in the study list, then the proportion of to-be-remembered items recalled from the latter categories will be less than that for the former. This effect has been shown not only with taxonomic categories, but also with rhyme categories and subjective categories (Mueller & Watkins, 1977). Given that, in accounting for the high level of recall of categorized lists, cue-overload theory assumes category names to be effective memory cues, this inhibitory effect is precisely what we should expect. Second, cue-overload theory predicts that the extent of the inhibition will vary directly with the number of items re-presented, and indeed such a relation has been shown (Roediger, 1973; Rundus, 1973). Finally, it should be possible to obtain part-set cueing inhibition by providing at the time of test not only category instances that were part of the presentation list, but also category instances that did not occur in the list. This prediction of inhibition by category-specific, extralist cueing has also been confirmed (Watkins, 1975).

F. Paired-Associate Phenomena

Cue-overload theory is consistent with some of the major findings of paired-associate research. In particular, it is consistent with the finding that, when the same nominal stimulus term serves for more than one response (A–B, A–C), its effectiveness with respect to either response term is diminished. It should, however, be noted that the presumption is being made here that subjects cannot make full use of the fact that the target word is from one particular and clearly specified list; although subjects fully "understand" that they are to recall the response term from, say, the second list, it appears that "second list" does not constitute an entirely effective cue.

Further support for the cue-overload interpretation of interference effects in the paired-associate paradigm derives from a study by Postman, Stark, and Fraser (1968). This study entailed the A–B, A–C procedure plus a final test in which the A terms were presented either alone or along with the C terms. The presence of the C terms inhibited recall of the B terms. In terms of cue-overload theory, the A terms define arbitrary sets and the inhibition in recall is simply another instance of the part-set cueing effect. Postman et al., however, offered a different interpretation, one involving a response-set inhibition mechanism. The essential idea was that re-presenting the C terms served to maintain an inert selector mechanism on the A–C list.

An experiment by Mueller and Watkins (1977, Experiment 4) sought to distinguish between these two explanations. Subjects were presented with a string of six lists corresponding to an A–B, A–C, . . . A–G paradigm. They were then given a final test in which the A terms were presented either alone or with three of the responses; for each subject half of the A terms were presented alone, a quarter were presented along with B, D, and F, and a quarter along with C, E, and G. Consistent with cue-overload theory—but contrary to response-set inhibition theory—re-presenting some of the response terms was found to inhibit recall of the remainder.

G. Buildup and Release from Proactive Inhibition

In what has come to be known as the Brown–Peterson task, the subject briefly studies a subspan list of items, engages for some seconds in a distractor activity, and then tries to recall the items. On a single trial of this task, performance is characteristically high, but when several trials are given in immediate succession performance declines rapidly across the first few trials (Keppel & Underwood, 1962). This phenomenon is referred to as the buildup of proactive inhibition. If, after this inhibition has built up, the type of material is changed (e.g., from digits to letters or from one taxonomic category to another), performance is typically elevated (Wickens, Born, & Allen, 1963). This elevation is known as release from proactive inhibition.

The theoretical interpretation of the buildup and release effects has received a great deal of discussion. This discussion is not reviewed here; it is sufficient to note that one possible interpretation is provided by cue-overload theory. Specifically, the buildup effect can be attributed to the use of a category cue that becomes increasingly overloaded, and the release effect, to the use of a new and therefore unloaded category cue. This interpretation once again makes the assumption that the subjects do not rely solely on the nominal, temporal list cue corresponding to "last list." Thus, although the subjects know that they are always tested only for the last set of items studied, they will, at least to some extent, use the category cue that will still tend to be loaded by the events of the preceding trials. When the type of material is changed, the category cue will no longer be loaded with events of the preceding trials, and hence the "release from proactive inhibition."

In this way cue-overload theory relates the buildup-and-release-from-proactive-inhibition phenomena in the Brown–Peterson paradigm to the effects of categorization in, say, the free-recall procedure. An experiment by Craik and Birtwistle (1971) gives strong support for such a relation. A series of word lists was presented for immediate free recall, with the words of each list all conforming to a distinct taxonomic category. With successive lists comprising items from the same conceptual category, recall declined steadily; but when the category was shifted there was a marked recovery. Thus the pattern of data closely paralleled that found with the Brown–Peterson procedure.

Predictions of the cue-overload account of the buildup-and-release-from-proactive-inhibition phenomena have been confirmed in two experiments from our own laboratory (Watkins & Watkins, 1975). Each of these experiments involved a "continuous-release" variant of the procedure, in which a long sequence of word-triads was presented, with several shifts in categories being made during the sequence. There then followed a final recall test in which the category names were presented as cues. In the first experiment, there were six categories of three triads per category, plus a buffer category at each end. It was predicted that, although the initial tests would show the familiar decline across the successive triads within a category, in the final cued test the load on the category cue would be constant across triad positions, and hence recall should be independent of triad position. Unfortunately, this prediction is not quite so straightforward, since the final recall test could reflect the different levels of recall associated with the initial tests. To avoid this potential confound, some of the categories were not tested initially. The subject was persuaded that we were interested in the effects of probability of being tested and that he or she was in the "low probability" condition. Each distractor task was followed either by a recall cue for the last word-triad, or by the next triad, and it was not until this point that the subject knew whether recall was required. Apart from the buffer triads, subjects were in fact tested for only three triads, the first triad of one category, the second of another, and the third of yet another; there were therefore three categories that were completely untested until the final recall test. The initial tests showed the familiar decline in performance across the within-category triad positions. The important results were those from the final test of categories that were initially untested. As was predicted from cue-overload theory, recall of items from these categories was independent of triad position.

The second prediction we tested was that the probability of recall for an item in the final test would be inversely related to the number of triads (and hence number of items) in its category. Thus, in the second experiment the number of triads per category was varied, but otherwise the procedure paralleled closely that of the first experiment. As before, initial testing revealed the same decline in recall across within-category position, and in the final test, recall of the initially untested items was independent of within-category position. In addition, the final recall data also revealed that, as predicted from cue-overload theory, recall of an item (from an initially untested category) varied inversely with the number of triads in that category.

By way of summary, it seems that cue-overload theory can be readily applied to findings from a wide range of experimental procedures. True, the concept of cue overload can, of itself, take us only so far along the road to an adequate account of forgetting in all its aspects. It is, however, adequate to illustrate an approach, that of organizing data under simple principles. The nature of this approach is sometimes misunderstood. Although it invokes neither mechanisms nor processes, it is nonetheless both explanatory and predictive. Indeed, some of the applications of cue-overload theory described here take the form of explanations that are at once both plausible and powerful. Moreover, when its predictions have been pitted against those of other theories, cue-overload theory has fared remarkably well. Certainly, there have been successes enough to suggest that it may be worthwhile extending the general strategy of explaining findings by attributing them to a few, well-chosen general principles. It will be interesting to see whether, in such an extension, we can retain an overall memory-cueing framework.

VI. CONCLUDING COMMENTS

The cueing approach to the study of memory, as sketched here, is relatively atheoretical. One important way in which it differs from other approaches is that it does not assume the spatial model. Just about all extant theories of memory make the assumption that "information" is put *into* (acquired, encoded, registered), preserved *in* (stored, retained), and taken *out of* (retrieved, activated, utilized) some hypothetical "system" called memory. This spatial metaphor is a rich source of explanation: Memory can fail because of inadequate registration, loss of information during retention, or a failure of retrieval. In fact, there is a danger of an overabundance of explanatory devices. As I have tried to argue elsewhere (Watkins, 1978), there is often in principle no way of distinguishing between some of the alternative interpretations that the spatial metaphor offers for findings, and for this reason many a longstanding theoretical dispute remains unresolved. It is sobering to reflect, amidst the impressive array of paradigms and paraphernalia we now have before us, that still we can only observe what happens to our subject at time t_1 and how this affects his or her behavior at time t_2. The fact that there is more than one way that the spatial model can relate these two observations leads to all kinds of confusion. This state of affairs suggests that it may prove useful to develop an alternative, and especially a simpler, way of looking at memory. A functional, cueing approach of the sort outlined here could serve just that need.

Finally, it should be noted that although we have confined this entire discussion of the cueing approach to memory to what Tulving (1972) has called the episodic realm, this has been done merely for clarity of exposition. There is no reason why the approach cannot be applied to memory in a more generic sense.

REFERENCES

Anderson, J. R., & Bower, G. H. A propositional theory of recognition memory. *Memory & Cognition*, 1974, *2*, 406–412.

Bahrick, H. P. Measurement of memory by prompted recall. *Journal of Experimental Psychology*, 1969, *79*, 213–219.

Ballard, P. B. Obliviscence and reminiscence. *British Journal of Psychology Monographs*, 1931, *1*, (No. 2).

Bilodeau, E. A. Experimental interference with primary associates and their subsequent recovery with rest. *Journal of Experimental Psychology*, 1967, *73*, 328–332.

Bower, G. H. Organizational factors in memory. *Cognitive Psychology*, 1970, *1*, 18–46.

Bower, G. H., Clark, M. C., Lesgold, A. M., & Winzenz, D. Hierarchical retrieval schemes in recall of categorized word lists. *Journal of Verbal Learning and Verbal Behavior*, 1969, *8*, 323–343.

Cooper, A. J. R., & Monk, A. Learning for recall and learning for recognition. In J. Brown (Ed.), *Recall and recognition*. London: Wiley, 1976.

Craik, F. I. M., & Birtwistle, J. Proactive inhibition in free recall. *Journal of Experimental Psychology*, 1971, *91*, 120–123.

Craik, F. I. M., & Kirsner, K. The effect of speaker's voice on word recognition. *Quarterly Journal of Experimental Psychology*, 1974, *26*, 274–284.

Eich, J. E. Fragrances as cues for remembering words. *Journal of Verbal Learning and Verbal Behavior*, 1978, *17*, 103–111.

Fisher, R. P., & Craik, F. I. M. The interaction between encoding and retrieval operations in cued recall. *Journal of Experimental Psychology: Human Learning and Memory*, 1977, *3*, 701–711.

Glucksberg, S., & Cowen, G. N. Memory for nonattended auditory material. *Cognitive Psychology,* 1970, *1,* 149–156.

Gorman, A. M. Recognition memory for nouns as a function of abstractness and frequency. *Journal of Experimental Psychology,* 1961, *61,* 23–29.

Hintzman, D. L., & Summers, J. J. Long-term visual traces of visually presented words. *Bulletin of the Psychonomic Society,* 1973, *1,* 325–327.

Hudson, R. L., & Austin, J. B. Effect of context and category name on the recall of categorized word lists. *Journal of Experimental Psychology,* 1970, *86,* 43–47.

Keppel, G., & Underwood, B. J. Proactive inhibition in short-term retention of single items. *Journal of Verbal Learning and Verbal Behavior,* 1962, *1,* 153–161.

Lewis, J. L. Semantic processing of unattended messages using dichotic listening. *Journal of Experimental Psychology,* 1970, *85,* 225–228.

Light, L. L., & Carter-Sobell, L. Effects of changed semantic context on recognition memory. *Journal of Verbal Learning and Verbal Behvior,* 1970, *9,* 1–11.

Mandler, G. Organization and memory. In K. W. Spence and J. T. Spence (Eds.), *The psychology of learning and motivation: Advances in research and theory* (Vol. 1). New York: Academic Press, 1967.

Martin, E. Generation-recognition theory and the encoding specificity principle. *Psychological Review,* 1975, *82,* 150–153.

McLeod, P. D., Williams, C. E., & Broadbent, D. E. Free recall with assistance from one and from two retrieval cues. *British Journal of Psychology,* 1971, *62,* 59–65.

Miller, G. A. The magical number seven plus or minus two: Some limits on our capacity for processing information. *Psychological Review,* 1956, *63,* 81–96.

Miller, G. A., Galanter, E., & Pribram, K. H. *Plans and the structure of behavior.* New York: Holt, Rinehart, and Winston, 1960.

Mueller, C. W., & Watkins, M. J. Inhibition from part-set cueing: A cue-overload interpretation. *Journal of Verbal Learning and Verbal Behavior,* 1977, *16,* 699–709.

Murdock, B. B. The immediate retention of unrelated words. *Journal of Experimental Psychology,* 1960, *60,* 222–234.

Patterson, K. E. Some characteristics of retrieval limitation in human memory. *Journal of Verbal Learning and Verbal Behavior,* 1972, *11,* 685–691.

Postman, L., Stark, K., & Fraser, J. Temporal changes in interference. *Journal of Verbal Learning and Verbal Behavior,* 1968, *7,* 672–694.

Reder, L. M., Anderson, J. R., & Bjork, R. A. A semantic interpretation of encoding specificity. *Journal of Experimental Psychology,* 1974, *102,* 648–656.

Roediger, H. L. Inhibition in recall from cueing with recall targets. *Journal of Verbal Learning and Verbal Behavior,* 1973, *12,* 644–657.

Roediger, H. L. Inhibiting effects of recall. *Memory & Cognition,* 1973, *2,* 261–269.

Rundus, D. Negative effects of using list items as recall cues. *Journal of Verbal Learning and Verbal Behavior,* 1973, *12,* 43–50.

Slamecka, N. J. An examination of trace storage in free recall. *Journal of Experimental Psychology,* 1968, *76,* 504–513.

Slamecka, N. J. The question of associative growth in the learning of categorized material. *Journal of Verbal Learning and Verbal Behavior,* 1972, *11,* 324–332.

Sumby, W. H. Word frequency and serial position effects. *Journal of Verbal Learning and Verbal Behavior,* 1963, *1,* 443–450.

Thomson, D. M. Context effects in recognition memory. *Journal of Verbal Learning and Verbal Behavior,* 1972, *11,* 497–511.

Tulving, E. Subjective organization in free recall of "unrelated" words. *Psychological Review,* 1962, *69,* 344–354.

Tulving, E. Intratrial and intertrial retention: Notes towards a theory of free recall verbal learning. *Psychological Review,* 1964, *71,* 219–237.

Tulving, E. Episodic and semantic memory. In E. Tulving & W. Donaldson (Eds.), *Organization of memory*. New York: Academic Press, 1972.

Tulving, E., & Pearlstone, Z. Availability versus accessibility of information in memory for words. *Journal of Verbal Learning and Verbal Behavior, 1966, 5,* 381–391.

Tulving, E., & Thomson, D. M. Encoding specificity and retrieval processes in episodic memory. *Psychological Review, 1973, 80,* 1–52.

Tulving, E., & Watkins, M. J. Continuity between recall and recognition. *American Journal of Psychology, 1973, 86,* 739–748.

Tulving, E., & Watkins, M. J. Structure of memory traces. *Psychological Review,* 1975, *82,* 261–275.

Tulving, E., & Watkins, O. C. Recognition failure of words with a single meaning. *Memory & Cognition, 1977, 5,* 513–522.

Watkins, M. J. Inhibition in recall with extralist "cues." *Journal of Verbal Learning and Verbal Behavior, 1975, 14,* 294–303.

Watkins, M. J. Theoretical issues. In M. M. Gruneberg & P. E. Morris (Eds.), *Aspects of memory*. London: Methuen, 1978.

Watkins, M. J., & Gardiner, J. M. An appreciation of generate-recognize theory of recall. *Journal of Verbal Learning and Verbal Behavior,* in press.

Watkins, M. J., Ho, E., & Tulving, E. (1976) Context effects in recognition memory for faces. *Journal of Verbal Learning and Verbal Behavior, 1976, 15,* 505–517.

Watkins, M. J., & Park, N. W. Cueing with word senses: A test of generation–recognition theory. *Bulletin of the Psychonomic Society, 1976, 9,* 25–28.

Watkins, M. J., & Todres, A. K. On the relation between recall and recognition. *Journal of Verbal Learning and Verbal Behavior, 1978, 17,* 621–633.

Watkins, M. J., & Tulving, E. Episodic memory: When recognition fails. *Journal of Experimental Psychology: General, 1975, 104,* 5–29.

Watkins, M. J., & Tulving, E. When retrieval cueing fails. *British Journal of Psychology, 1978, 69,* 443–450.

Watkins, O. C., & Watkins, M. J. Buildup of proactive inhibition as a cue-overload effect. *Journal of Experimental Psychology: Human Learning and Memory, 1975, 1,* 442–452.

Wickens, D. D., Born, D. G., & Allen, C. K. Proactive inhibition and item similarity in short-term memory. *Journal of Verbal Learning and Verbal Behavior, 1963, 2,* 440–445.

PART V

CONCLUSION

Organization, Structure, and Memory: Three Perspectives

The contents of the present volume, taken as a whole, are concerned with the multifaceted problem of how organization and structure affect how we learn and how we remember. The present chapter follows this theme, and the problem is viewed from three perspectives. The first perspective is concerned with how human learning and memory theory, dominated by associationism at the midpoint of the present century, was question by organizational concepts. The second perspective suggests ways in which organizational concepts are important to some particular issues of contemporary memory theory. Finally, the third perspective presents some speculative ideas pertaining to how organizational and structural concepts will be important to future theoretical developments. In a general sense, the three perspectives may be regarded as an

MEMORY ORGANIZATION
AND STRUCTURE

ISBN 0-12-566750-7

"overview" of the significance of organizational concepts as found in the past when organizational concepts had a strong impact upon the existing theory, in the present when they are essentially assumed by many aspects of memory theory, and in the future when they will (according to the speculation) become absorbed into a more general view. Finally, it is the general thesis of this chapter that the study of organizational processes is in transition. The earlier work, the first perspective, was characterized by the manipulation of task and materials variables in order to demonstrate organizational processing on the part of the individual. It is argued that the current work, that is, the second perspective, places much greater emphasis on the organization of the structure of knowledge within the individual and how such knowledge is used to learn and remember. It is further suggested that future developments in the study of organization and structure, that is, the third perspective, will place such concepts in a problem-solving context that will emphasize the interaction of the individual and his/her environment. This approach thus views structure as a component feature of adaptive systems.

I. PERSPECTIVE I: ORGANIZATION, STRUCTURE, AND ASSOCIATIONISM

The dominant theory in human learning and memory, at least until the past two decades, was associationism, and there is little doubt that early free-recall studies involving categorical organization (e.g., Bousfield, 1953) generated data that produced questions pointing to potential weaknesses and limitations of associationistic theory. Furthermore, it was argued that organizational concepts had explanatory power not found in associationistic principles. Mandler, for example, has maintained this position both in his chapter in this volume (Chapter 9) and elsewhere (1962, 1967, and 1968). In the present section, the impact on associationism of the early research on organization is considered.

A. Associationism, circa 1950

Much has been written about associationism and its weaknesses, and I do not want to retrace a well-worn path. I do, however, want to discuss the relation of organizational theory to four assumptions of associationism, as defined in approximately 1950. These four assumptions are: (a) The Element Assumption; (b) The Associative Laws Assumption; (c) The Building-Block Assumption; (d) The Passivity Assumption. Briefly, these assumptions state that (a) there exists some type of basic element that during the course of learning becomes associated, although the proposed nature of the elements changed during the history of associationism; (b) the elements become associated via the operation of laws, the foremost of which is the law of contiguity, that is, two elements become associated if they are contiguous in time and/or space. Associations become stronger the more often they occur (frequency). *(c)* Associationism also assumed that more complex phenomena are composed of simple associations that are combined, probably in an additive manner. Finally, *(d)* associationism tended to maintain that what is learned and remembered is essentially a copy of the environment, and in such learning the individual is a passive recipient of information rather than an active processor.

In the 1950s, the theory of associationism was both a theory, in the sense of explaining a given phenomenon or set of phenomena, and a general framework in which research in human learning and memory was conducted (Laudan, 1977). As such, the four preceding assumptions were implicit in much of the human learning research, and the assumptions were not usually submitted to empirical test. Indeed, the two major experimental paradigms of verbal learning, paired-associate and serial learning, essentially assumed the laws of contiguity and frequency (Voss, 1972); that is, contiguous presentation of items over a number of trials was intrinsic to the methods. A second aspect of the research was that a considerable amount of empirical data was generated on the influence of task variables and materials variables. Theories explaining these efforts were then developed, but such theory was within the broader context of associationistic principles. Examples of such theories or models include the response learning—associative learning model (Underwood, Runquist, & Schulz, 1959), and Noble's (1952) theory of meaningfulness. Furthermore, associationistic models in areas such as problem solving (Maltzman, 1955) were also developed within the associationistic framework. The reader is referred to a handbook chapter by Hovland (1951) and the standard reference of verbal learning research, McGeoch and Irion's *The Psychology of Human Learning* (1952) for accounts of the research conducted within the framework.

Not only was associationism the dominant theory of information acquisition, but another associative offspring, interference theory, was the most widely held theory of forgetting. With its two prongs of retroactive inhibition and proactive inhibition, interference among associations was seen as the basis of forgetting, even though work within the associative context had shown the theory might be limited (cf. Melton & Irwin, 1940). Finally, we note that even in the area of transfer, the associationistic framework was dominant, although theoretical development within this area was not extensive.

B. Problems with Associationism

The associationistic framework came under attack both from internal and external sources. Although extensive discussion of the attacks is beyond the scope of this chapter, some of the major issues are mentioned briefly.

One of the major problems that emerged from within the associationistic framework involved the nature of the stimulus. Results indicated that what the experimenter presented to the subject as the stimulus was not always what the subject processed as the stimulus. This conclusion is illustrated by the phenomenon of stimulus selection (Underwood, Ham, & Ekstrand, 1962), which indicated that individuals sometimes selected part of the stimulus and associated that part with the response rather than associating the entire stimulus with the response. Similarly, it also was found that individuals often elaborated the stimulus by the use of natural language (Montague, Adams, & Kiess, 1966) or imagery (Bower, 1970; Bugelski, Kidd, & Segmen, 1968) and associated the complex (presented item + elaboration) with the response. Furthermore, different types of elaborations were classified, and it was shown that the level of recall was related to the type of mediation or elaboration (Martin, Boersma, & Cox, 1965; Martin, Cox, & Boersma, 1965). The fact that the presented stimulus often did not function as the "real" stimulus led Underwood (1963) to denote a difference between the nominal, that is, what is presented, and functional stimulus, that is, what operates as the stimulus. Another attack occurring within the associationistic position involved the issue termed "one-trial learning" (Estes, 1960; Rock, 1957; Underwood, 1969). The question under study was whether associations were formed on one trial or whether there was a gradual increment in associative strength until the strength was greater than a given threshold value (see Postman, 1963).

Serious theoretical problems also were posed within the serial-learning paradigm. The Lepley-Hull hypothesis (Hull, 1935; Lepley, 1934), which treated serial learning as the acquisition of a series of adjacent pairs by conditioning-based processes, was questioned. A dormant study by Primoff (1938) was discovered, repeated, and elaborated on, with the result that one prediction of an associative model of serial learning was shown to be difficult to demonstrate: When individuals acquire a serial list, there is little if any transfer to a paired-associate list consisting of pairs derived from adjacent items of the serial list (cf. Young, 1968). A large amount of research followed on the question of what constitutes the "functional stimulus" in serial learning, and a number of candidates were suggested (see Harcum, 1975). Interestingly, organizational ideas were advanced in emphasizing that grouping of the items of a serial list may occur (Jensen, 1962), whereas another view posited that serial learning involved placing items along a spatial dimension (Asch, Hay, & Diamond, 1960; Ebenholtz, 1963; Slamecka, 1967).

The attack from within also struck interference theory. Within the retroactive inhibition paradigm results pointed to the importance of a factor other than specific item intereference, a factor termed "unlearning" (Barnes & Underwood, 1959; Melton & Irwin, 1940). (See Petrich, 1975; Postman & Underwood, 1973.) Similarly, the associative interference explanation of proactive inhibition, as well as the associationistic view of transfer, was also questioned (see Greeno, James, DaPolito, & Polson, 1978).

The attacks from outside the associationistic framework also began to take their toll. One of the most important lines of research in raising questions about the associationistic notions involved the free recall of categorized lists (e.g.,

Bousfield, 1953). It was demonstrated that when items from different categories were randomly presented at input, output order did not usually reflect input order. Instead, individuals tended to cluster the items according to category membership. This result was important for at least two reasons: First, it showed that contiguous presentation of items was less important than category membership. Second, this finding contributed to the establishment of an "information processing" view, even though the earlier free-recall work did not emphasize this point. There were attempts of course to incorporate free-recall results such as those mentioned previously under the umbrella of associationism (e.g., Wallace, 1969), but such attempts have not been influential.

Another well-known attack from without involved the thesis that, despite a few efforts of theorists to consider language (e.g., Mowrer, 1954, 1960; Osgood, 1952), associationistic notions could not handle language comprehension and production (Chomsky, 1965; Bever, Fodor, & Garrett, 1968). The importance of syntactic rules was emphasized, and it was argued that sentences simply do not constitute a chain of associations.

Finally, one more attack from without will be noted, namely, the attack from Gestalt psychologists. The major point made was that the law of contiguity is not a reasonable basis for a theory. It is not contiguity per se that is important in developing an association, but it is the relation that is established between the items or events (cf. Asch, 1968, 1969; Asch, Ceraso, & Heimer, 1960; Rock & Ceraso, 1964). Interestingly, the S–R "connectionist," Thorndike, also asserted that contiguity per se was not a critical aspect of learning, but instead of stating his findings in terms of relations, he spoke of "belongingness" (Thorndike, 1931).

C. The Four Assumptions Reconsidered

1. THE ELEMENT ASSUMPTION

The existence of some type of basic psychological unit has never really been documented. Within the associationistic framework, the delineation of the unit was essentially arbitrary; in the paired-associate task, for example, the unit was the list item, whether a stimulus or a response and whether a word or a nonsense syllable. That this was a less than satisfactory state of affairs is shown by the fact that the importance of integrating a nonsense term into a unit was recognized (G. Mandler, 1954) and the previously mentioned research on stimulus selection and stimulus elaboration demonstrated that the unit that functioned as an element to be associated was not easily defined and was to a large degree strategy-dependent.

The notion of psychological elements also seemed inappropriate when considered in relation to language. Certainly, words do not seem to be basic units when recall of a sentence may involve the substitution of a synonym for one of the original words, that is, the gist of a sentence or passage may be recalled even though there is some change in the specific words stated.

Finally, whereas the free-recall research on organization had little to say about the element question, the work did raise an interesting point. When items from a given category are found within a list, the grouping of the items in recall suggests that the "unit" of importance may be category name rather than category instances. Indeed, the Tulving and Pearlstone (1966) finding, indicating that recall failure with categorized lists is often due to failure to recall categories rather than items from within a category, supports this view.

2. THE ASSUMPTION OF ASSOCIATIVE LAWS

The question of the status of the law of contiguity is somewhat nebulous because its status depends on how strongly the law is stated. If one argues that contiguity is a necessary and sufficient condition for learning to occur, there is trouble, for it certainly does not seem to be sufficient (Robinson, 1932; Thorndike, 1914; Warren, 1921). The question of whether it is necessary is a bit more complex.

If one assumes that learning does take place by establishing relationships, a number of questions then immediately occur. First, to establish a relation, there must be two things, items, events, etc. that become related. The interesting question from the point of view of contiguity theory is whether these two things occur together to establish a relationship. The answer is uncertain, but intuition and some data suggest that the answer may be negative. Specifically, assume an individual knows the names of a large number of sports, and one day learns the name of a new sport. According to a strict contiguity position, the association "Sport-X" or "X-Sport" should be established, but "X-football" or "X-badminton" should not be established, unless perhaps the individual perceived relations between "X" and the second sport when learning about "X." However, for most sports, a relation between "X" and the respective sports should not be established. Yet, there is evidence to suggest that there is a relationship established between "X" and other sports (Henry & Voss, 1970). Phrased generally, an acquired category member becomes associated with other members of the same category, even though not presented with particular members. Furthermore, some of the work on category membership (e.g., Rosch, 1973) would suggest that "X" would become most closely related, in a clustering sense, to the sports that are most similar to "X."

The contiguity theorist, to accommodate the preceding assertions, would need to argue that when "X" is acquired, not only the superordinate **Sport** is activated, but virtually all members of the category are activated, that is, activated by a process of implicit contiguity (Voss, 1972). Whereas implicit contiguity may indeed occur, the view clearly goes beyond a strict, traditional contiguity interpretation. Specifically, the traditional view states that the association develops between two items occurring together in the environment, not between two items that are activated implicitly. Needless to say, the implicit contiguity position is extremely difficult, if not impossible, to test empirically.

The preceding considerations raise another question that, as far as this writer is aware, has not been answered. The question is whether the acquisition of new items, that is, new items to be incorporated into a category, such as learning the name of a new color, is related to the structure of items already within the category. One might expect that the better defined the relations or dimensions of the category are, the more readily are new items distinguished and incorporated into the structure. Moreover, such incorporation may be especially important for learning by children who may have a poorer idea of category boundaries than adults. In any event, it would seem that the role of organization in establishing category membership requires study.

Still assuming that learning takes place via establishing relations, another question raised is whether the type of relation is important. Intuitively one would expect it should be. Indeed, the suggestion has been made elsewhere (Voss, 1972) that there may exist a hierarchy of relations that are related to learning, and contiguity per se may be at the lower end of this hierarchy. Thus, whereas humans may use semantics to relate events, conditioning is possible in single-cell organisms and the conditioning may be based upon the contiguous occurrence of events. This suggestion thus may be phrased for human learning— if two events cannot be related by a semantic representation, visual representation, or by some other type of relation, then they may be related by the individual simply because they occurred in close temporal relation to each other. It is interesting to note, however, that it is difficult to think of anything that has been learned in that manner. Generally, somehow, the individual establishes a relationship of some type between two events other than that they occurred in close temporal proximity. Indeed, even if two events do occur via contiguity, it is likely that most individuals would seek to find a relation or causal link (cf. G. Mandler, Chapter 9).

Turning now to the law of frequency, the "one-trial learning" issue raised a question concerning the role of frequency in establishing associations. Although an incremental position may be advocated, it would seem that results of the stimulus elaboration research previously mentioned strongly suggest that indeed the learning of an association may take place on one trial, namely, the trial on which a mediator is established. The law of frequency is thus called into question, at least with respect to establishing associations, because individuals are able to acquire an association if a relation can be established.

There seems to be another problem with the law of frequency that pertains to the concept of associative strength (cf. Asch & Lindner, 1963). First, it seems that the concept of associative strength cannot be used to compare the strength of two associations that have different stimuli. For example, is *table–chair* stronger than *king–queen*? Two measures traditionally used as indicators of strength are associative norms and reaction time. However, neither of these measures can really tell us which association is stronger. With norms, the "strength" of *table–chair* is clearly a function of other responses to *table,* as is the case with responses to *king.* With respect to reaction time, if the stimulus item is presented and the reaction time is measured (and the data are those in which the "appropriate" responses have been given—*chair* and *queen* in the present case), it must be assumed that the processing time of the two stimuli is equivalent, and a "good" associationist must also assume that response competition effects are the same in both cases.

The notion of response competition raises a second point, namely, that even for one association, strength may differ as a function of the number and strength of competing associations; for example, Erdelyi, Watts, and Voss (1964) found that anticipation of a response that had a probability of .70 of occurring with a particular stimulus item was a function of the probability and number of other responses related to the particular stimulus. Fewer anticipations of the .70 item occurred when one other item occurred the remaining 30% of the time than when more items occurred with lower frequencies, for example, two items, each with .15 probability. Similar results were obtained by Anderson in "fanning" studies (Anderson, 1976). Thus, we find that the "strength" of a pair is not independent of other associations to the stimulus.

Finally, we note that "associative strength" tends to be context-dependent, a finding that is related to the early twentieth century research on "determining tendencies" (see Humphrey, 1951). Under one set of conditions A–B may be "strong," but under another set of conditions, A–C may be "strong." In other words, "strength" is context-dependent. An example of an effect of context was provided by Clifton (1966) by using a priming technique. Also, the reader is referred to work described by Nisbett and Wilson (1977), which includes the report of a study in which, when a detergent was requested as a response, subjects gave the response *Tide* more often when a previous list of pairs included *ocean–moon* than when the prior list did not contain this pair.

Given the preceding considerations, the concept of "associative strength," which may yet be useful in some contexts, certainly may not be regarded as being a simple monotonic function of frequency of occurrence of a particular association.

3. THE BUILDING-BLOCK ASSUMPTION

This assumption has been of importance to associationism because it gave the theory explanatory power in dealing with complex phenomena. Specifically, it essentially indicated that relatively complex processes could be understood by knowing how the "basic" elements were connected to each other. Gestalt psychologists criticized the view because, they asserted, the position fails to take into account field or organizational factors and such phenomena as sudden reorganization in problem solving or insight. The associationistic counterargument was that such reorganization only occurred after the associations were well formed (Pavlov, 1927). Association-oriented theorists also argued that activities such as problem solving could be handled theoretically by use of the concept of habit–family–hierachy (Maltzman, 1955).

Although the free-recall work raised a question about the building-block assumption, at least with respect to how categories develop, the assumption was put to a greater test by results indicating that rules, strategies, and plans were important in producing complex behavior (e.g., Bourne & Haygood, 1959; Bruner, Goodnow, & Austin, 1956; Miller, Galanter, & Pribram, 1960). Moreover, although associative models of relatively complex behavior were developed, such models seemed inadequate because some additional factors were needed beyond associative principles to explain the phenomenon, for example, the reversal–nonreversal shift effects in discrimination learning (Kendler, 1963). We note also that Piaget's empirical and theoretical efforts have not emphasized the acquisition of basic associations but instead have stressed highly organized rule development. Research on early language learning also is centered on the acquisition of syntactic rules and meaning rather than on the operation of associative laws in producing complex behavior. Phrased simply, there is doubt whether the building-block assumption is workable.

4. THE PASSIVITY ASSUMPTION

Possibly the greatest challenge to the associationistic position involved this assumption. It is trivial today to state that the organism is not a "passive" recipient of information but an "active" processor of input. Indeed, this statement is a major tenet of the currently popular and loosely defined position termed "information processing." It seems clear that research on free recall helped to establish the importance of active processing; the results of Bousfield, for example, strongly suggested that input information was being operated upon because the output order was not a copy of the input order. The chapters by Pellegrino and Ingram (Chapter 2), Friendly (Chapter 4), and G. Mandler (Chapter 9) are germane to this point.

There is a point, however, that should be made with respect to the active–passive distinction and associationism. It is worth noting that during the nineteenth century, associations were classified as "voluntary" and "involuntary," or in general there was an active component to the associative process. An interesting argument that could be put forth is that the "active" component of processing diminished in importance with the rise in the theoretical significance of the reflexology tradition of Sechenov (1965) and Pavlov (1927) and later developed by Watson (1919).

5. SUMMARY

One of the major influences of early research on organizational processes was that it raised serious questions about the dominant theoretical viewpoint of the time, associationism. Associationism, in this chapter, was considered in terms of four assumptions, and how research on organizational processes influenced the acceptance of these assumptions was discussed. Organization was viewed broadly in reference to categorized lists, labeled connections, semantic networks, rules, and strategies. Before leaving this section, however, there are two important points that must be made. First, although it is clear that a number of the more traditional aspects of associationism are not at all in theoretical favor today, it nevertheless is clear that a number of the concepts of associationism are being found useful in today's cognitive environment. The area of semantic memory (see Lachman & Lachman, Chapter 5) is, in a sense, the study of associative networks, and work on knowledge representation has also included associationistic concepts (Anderson, 1976). Second, theoretically, perhaps the most significant departure from the more traditional view of associationism has not been getting rid of "associations"; indeed, associations are still with us even though there is little concern about "basic" elements. Instead, the most significant departure has involved the use of labeled links to describe associations (Selz, 1922). The use of such links provides recognition of two factors, namely, that associations are not bonds or connections, but relations, and that the associations are developed by the acquisition of relations. There is the question of whether the relations are limited in number, but nevertheless, given the two just mentioned, the notion of associative networks has provided at least a beginning in the problems of mental representation (e.g., Norman & Rumelhart, 1975).

II. PERSPECTIVE II: ORGANIZATION AND STRUCTURE IN DISCOURSE PROCESSING

A. Organization and Structure in Text Processing

The role of organization in text processing, demonstrated by Henderson (1903), and placed in a theoretical context by Bartlett (1932), has been a topic of considerable interest in recent years (cf. J. M. Mandler, Chapter 8).

Bartlett's (1932) theoretical position involved the concept of a schema, an "active organization . . . of past experiences [p. 201]." Although a review of this concept is beyond the scope of this paper (evaluations may be found by Northway, 1940 a,b; Oldfield & Zangwill, 1942; and Zangwill, 1972), the aspect of Bartlett's theory of particular importance to the present chapter was that input information is processed in terms of existing structural components of memory and is also stored in these terms. Although Bartlett's work had relatively little immediate impact, the view that information is processed in terms of existing knowledge structures has had considerable influence, and a thesis of the second and third sections of this chapter is that work on this general problem is only beginning.

The concept that organized structures or schemata exist in memory and that input information is processed in terms of such structures has taken on a variety of forms. The possible properties of schemata are considered by Rumelhart and Ortony (1977). One approach to the study of this problem has included showing that individuals with different interests and training interpret an ambiguous passage according to their interests (Anderson, Reynolds, Schallert, & Goetz, 1977). The schemata of the two groups were of course assumed to differ. Also, there is the story grammar approach (Rumelhart, 1975), which assumes that for particular classes of stories, for example, fables, individuals acquire a general structure that consists of the rules of composition of the particular class of story. Similarly, higher level structures, termed macrostructures, are assumed to aid in the interpretation of the text information (Kintsch & van Dijk, 1978; van Dijk, 1977). Macrostructures are taken to be a product of one's culture (Kintsch & Greene, 1978) and can also refer to particular text structures, such as experimental reports (Kintsch & van Dijk, 1978). Finally, organized structures of knowledge have been assumed to exist as sequences of familiar events, termed scripts (Schank, 1975; Schank & Abelson, 1977).

From the perspective of the present chapter, the significance of these various views is the common theme that the processing of information, as found at least in text, is strongly influenced by the knowledge structures of the individual. The contrast with a "passive" view of processing can hardly be more striking; when one reads a passage, what is stored is influenced by the person's interests (and background), and in specific domains of knowledge, text processing is influenced by such knowledge. For example, if high-knowledge and low-knowledge individuals (within the domain) read the same text, qualitative as well as quantitative differences in recall are obtained (Spilich, Vesonder, Chiesi, & Voss, 1979). The work of J. M. Mandler also points to the notion that children develop a knowledge of the rules of text structures, and she has presented results in agreement with this thesis (J. M. Mandler, 1978). Incidentally, similarity of findings with respect to the role of knowledge in text processing and the relation of development to text processing raises the interesting question of the extent to which knowledge differences and developmental differences reflect parallel or equivalent underlying processes.

Because of what is to follow, some aspects of the research of Spilich et al. (1979) are presented. Of particular importance is the idea that when one reads a given passage, the input is processed such that the passage contents map onto the individual's memory structure. When the memory structure is relatively undeveloped, that is, in the case of a low-knowledge individual, only a relatively small amount of input information may be mapped onto the existing structure, and thus the amount stored is relatively small. To store additional information would require the construction of a representation of the information not mapped onto the memory structure, and this process is apparently difficult. High-knowledge individuals, on the other hand, do not generally face this difficulty, for they have a more highly developed knowledge structure.

Results such as those of Spilich et al. (1979), J. M. Mandler (1978), Kintsch and van Dijk (1978), and Thorndyke (1977) all point to a critical conclusion about organization and structure: To understand processes such as learning, memory, and transfer, one needs to know how existing knowledge is represented and how that representation is utilized in the acquisition of new information. (See Anderson, 1976, to see how one person wrestled with this issue.) In prototypical terms, this viewpoint indicates that all learning should be viewed as not the learning of A but as the operation B–A, where A is what is to be learned and B represents the knowledge and skills of the individual. Furthermore, when two individuals are involved, learning consists of B–A as compared to C–A, where C represents a different set of knowledge and skills. The analogous design also holds at the group level, where, for example, in the research mentioned, the performances of high-knowledge, B, and low-knowledge, C, groups were compared. In such a study, it is of course assumed that the knowledge of individuals within a group is reasonably homogeneous. What is important about this issue is that it must be acknowledged that virtually *all* learning is in fact transfer.

The position that all learning essentially involves the study of transfer raises a number of questions. First, one may ask how existing knowledge is to be assessed. One possible way is to use some type of an aptitude measure in which the aptitude refers to a skill or specific set of skills or to an ability to acquire information and/or perform within a given domain (cf. Pellegrino & Glaser, 1979). This method may be useful in a general way, but unless the test is highly specific, it would seem that such a test would not be sensitive to processes underlying the development of particular structure relations (cf. Egan & Greeno, 1973).

Another related approach is to assess in detail the individual's knowledge within a given domain by a specific testing procedure in which achievement-type tests are used to ascertain knowledge differences, as was done in a general way by Spilich et al. Finally, still another approach is to use an external criterion of expertise, as was done in chess research (Chase & Simon, 1973).

A problem with these methods is that they do not go far enough, that is, knowledge differences may be obtained and these differences may be related to performance differences, but it would be surprising if such differences did not occur. The problem is that such differences may be obtained without a substantive rationale indicating when such differences may occur and when such differences may not occur.

The desirable procedure is to be able to assess the knowledge, aptitude, skill, etc., in such a manner that, with some theoretical assumptions, hypotheses may be generated about how known information is utilized to acquire new information and how the new information may become incorporated into the existing knowledge structure. Hopefully, such hypotheses could then be tested empirically. Essentially then, what is needed is to understand the nature of knowledge representation well enough so that hypotheses could be generated regarding how further knowledge could be acquired. However, it is clear that there is a long way to go in this area. As previously stated, though, it is a thesis of this chapter that it is not only important to gain insight into the question of how knowledge is represented and utilized, but it is necessary and imperative to do so if psychologists are to provide a reasonable theory of learning.

Assuming the importance of taking existing knowledge into account in the manner just outlined, we shall return to the topic of organization and structure. Within research in discourse processing, it is clear that there is increasing concern for the problems of what the individual brings into the situation and how this information and skill are utilized. In other words, there is increasing concern for how organization and structure influence acquisition. However, organization and structure in this context seem to mean something different from or more than the work on categorized free recall and sorting, and this point requires special consideration.

In the first section of this chapter, the study of organization basically involved the manipulation of task and materials from which the investigator could conclude whether the performance of the individuals showed that organizational processes were operative. However, within the present context of discourse processing, what is being referred to as organization and structure are basically properties of the mental characteristics of the individual. Thus, one may conclude that there has been a shift in the study of organization, a shift that has changed from an emphasis on task and material manipulation to an emphasis on the organization of knowledge. Interestingly, this shift appears as a special case of a more general shift in orientation from what is the more traditional behavioral and operational emphasis to the more cognitive emphasis.

Before leaving the topic of discourse processing, I want to make reference to an area of research that has been of considerable interest in human learning and memory, namely, "depth of processing" (Craik & Lockhart, 1972). A somewhat related view is described as "contextualism" (Jenkins, 1974). The reader is referred to the volume by Cermak and Craik (1979) for an extensive discussion of depth-of-processing issues. Although at first glance the depth-of-processing issue may seem to be somewhat remote from discourse processing, I would argue that there is a closer relation, although it is not empirically apparent at the present time. In Chapter 10, Battig and Bellezza make the point that depth-of-processing research is virtually opposed to the study of organizational processes, an argument that on the surface appears contradictory to the prior statement, although I do not believe it is.

To consider the issue in more detail, we turn to the previously mentioned research conducted in our laboratory (Spilich et al., 1979). Individuals of high knowledge and low knowledge in a given knowledge domain (baseball) were delineated. Both groups read a text consisting of one-half inning of a baseball game, and subsequently both groups were asked to recall the contents of the text. A completion test followed text recall. Following the work of Kintsch (1974) and Kintsch and Vipond (1977), the text was analyzed in terms of component propositions. The recall protocols were scored in terms of the propositional structure, and the protocols of the high-knowledge and low-knowledge individuals were compared. In addition to these anlayses, the text propositions were classified according to the goal structure of the particular domain. The goal structure was hierarchical, and goal-related propositions were classified according to their level in the hierarchy. Propositions not related to the goal structure were classified into categories such as setting, relevant (to the account) information, and irrelevant information. As one would expect, the high-knowledge individuals recalled more propositions than the low-knowledge individuals, and this difference was particularly striking for goal-related information. Furthermore, the high-knowledge individuals were more likely to provide an accurate account of the sequence of important events in the text.

The data were examined in relation to Kintsch and van Dijk's (1978) model of text processing. This model distinguishes between micropropositions and macropropositions, with the latter being propositions that are indicative of the "macrostructure" or general structure of the particular type of text. A variation of the Kintsch and van Dijk (1978) theory was applied, with the finding that the best-fitting model was one that postulated the existence of a short-term memory buffer for micropropositional information and the existence of a second memory structure that holds macroproposition information, often over reading relatively long portions of the text. This second buffer could be viewed as a working buffer or as an "active" list of propositions held in long-term memory. Interestingly, both the high-knowledge and low-knowledge data were best fit by this model. The primary difference found for the high-knowledge and low-knowledge individuals within the framework of the model was that the former recalled more macropropositions as well as more micropropositions and that they were more successful at carrying over the macroproposition information.

Put in general terms, one of the most striking results was that the high-knowledge individuals were better able to keep track of the sequences of goal-related events and to recall such events. The low-knowledge individuals, in most cases, apparently understood many individual events but could not relate these events to subsequent events and follow the significant "flow" of events.

Some of the other experiments of this series (Chiesi, Spilich, & Voss, 1979) demonstrated superior recognition performance by high-knowledge individuals of passages that contained domain-related information. In one study in which individuals listened to 16 passages and then were tested with those 16 as well as with 16 distractor passages, it was found that high-knowledge individuals required less information to recognize a passage than low-knowledge individuals. Moreover, other data supported the idea that high-knowledge individuals were more able than low-knowledge individuals to relate sequentially presented information and to unitize it. High-knowledge individuals were thus able to use context to a greater degree than low-knowledge individuals in assimilating new information.

Why should the high-knowledge individuals be more adept in such tasks? One interpretation is that they have a representation of the possible "flow" of events of a baseball game. Moreover, when the game is in any particular state, the high-knowledge individual has a better idea of what may come next. Thus, one may say that the high-knowledge individual has an organized representation of a baseball game that permits the individual to process input information in terms of a knowledge structure. Moreover, when an event occurs, it essentially reduces the uncertainty of what else is likely to occur. On the other hand, the low-knowledge individual, with a less developed knowledge structure, a knowledge structure that does not include the various sequences of events that are related to goal-related activity, is less able to relate input information to the goal structure, even though the low-knowledge person has little trouble with single events. (The similarity of these findings to Mandler and Johnson's [1977] findings involving differences in story grammar development by children and adults may be noted.)

The foregoing results are now considered in depth-of-processing terms. Craik (1979) discussed how the various depth-of-processing findings have been interpreted in terms of concepts such as elaboration, differentiation, and storage–retrieval compatibility. We would offer the following argument in this regard. Given the performance differences obtained the high- and low-knowledge groups, it could be argued that indeed there was a difference in the processing done by the groups but that the processing differences were basically at the semantic level. Although instructions were not manipulated, as is typical in the depth-of-processing paradigm, the results suggested that even with identical instructions, high-knowledge individuals process the input more "deeply" than low-knowledge individuals. However, by "deep" we do not mean a series of processing stages, but instead we mean that something within the knowledge structure differences of the individuals produces differential processing or at least differential effects. Such effects are probably attributable at least in part to greater differentiation of input on the part of high-knowledge individuals as well as to greater integration of input information.

Looking more broadly at the preceding issues, we may speculate about the nature of structure and organization and its relation to the acquisition of information. The knowledge we have provides a structure that we are able to use to provide meaning to input information. This organization may vary in form. However, the organization is taken to provide a context that simultaneously gives the individual a setting in which to process information and at the same time enables differentiation to occur. Without the existing knowledge structure, the individual must construct a structure from the input—an exceedingly difficult task.

We thus are suggesting that organizational processes and depth-of-processing are interwoven. The failure to emphasize this interaction is in part related to the tendency of investigators in the "depth" work to use lists of individual words. However, as Jacoby and Craik (1979) pointed out, the differentiation of any item occurs in the context of other items, and the same should hold true for more complex structures of information. The present analysis pushes this view further by emphasizing that the context may be considered in terms of what the individual knows rather than in terms of the context of a list.

B. Summary

Reviewing this section as a whole, the following argument is advanced. Organizational and structural factors, that is, macrostructures, knowledge, etc., have been shown to be of primary importance to the understanding of written or spoken discourse. This is especially important because it leads to the need to emphasize how the individual's knowledge relates to and is utilized in the acquisition of input information. The depth-of-processing line of research is mentioned briefly, and it is suggested there is a relation between ideas of organization and structure and concepts employed to interpret findings in the depth-of-processing literature. This relation is observed when processing differences among individuals is considered at the semantic level.

III. PERSPECTIVE III: ORGANIZATION, STRUCTURE, AND ORGANIZED SYSTEMS

Although some colleagues may disagree with this statement, it seems to this writer that there is an uneasiness in the area of human cognitive psychology. A number of factors may be contributing to this hypothesized uncertainty, including the lack of a cognitive theory of learning, the question of where the Artificial Intelligence movement is going and what impact it will have upon more traditional approaches to the study of memory, and finally, the lack of an integrated model of memory that provides a general orientation for work in the field. This comment is not meant to minimize the importance of the theoretical and empirical contributions in the field, for example, semantic memory, depth-of-processing and encoding specificity, organizational aspects of memory, the study of memory components in problem-solving behavior. However, there does not seem to be a general theoretical orientation that incorporates the work in areas such as these.

What direction cognitive research will take and how some of these uncertainties will be resolved is of course anyone's guess. However, this writer believes that there will be major changes in cognitive theory, both in the models and theory for empirical phenomena as well as in the general framework of world views (Laudan, 1977). Moreover, the concepts of organization and structure may well be central to these changes. Although not willing to place any money on predicting what changes may occur, this section presents some notions regarding possible directions, interests, and theoretical developments. It may be noted parenthetically that the contents of the forerunner of the present volume (see Puff, Chapter 1), the Tulving and Donaldson (1972) volume, not only provided a reasonable statement of the existing state of the field with respect to organization and memory, but also pointed to some of the problems that would be studied over the next decade. Similarly, I think the present volume has similar "pointers."

There are three potential movements in cognitive theory that I shall consider. The first is an elaboration on some of the comments made in the previous section. It seems not only important but necessary that cognitive theory view learning as essentially a transfer phenomenon in which initial learning, typically described as the first stage in the standard transfer paradigm, consists of the knowledge and skills the individual brings into the learning situation.

A number of investigators have also expressed the idea that memory should be regarded as transfer. Although such an assertion is essentially trivial in a method sense, that is, recall or recognition constitutes a transfer task relative to the acquisition phase, the concerns expressed have been more theoretical. Morris, Bransford, and Franks (1977), and subsequently Bransford, Franks, Morris, & Stein (1977), working within the area of depth-of-processing, have argued for adopting the concept of "transfer appropriate processing." Their argument is that the type of processing that occurs during acquisition is related to the goals the individual has in performing the task, and the nature of the subsequent recall or recognition test may or may not be consonant with the goals of processing employed at input. The operations taking place at input as well as the contents of the input are thus important, and the extent to which the memory task is related to the operations is important.

The point that individuals retain what operations are used in relation to contents has also been made strongly by Kolers (Kolers & Ostry, 1974; Kolers, 1975), and an emphasis on the similarity of the task at input and output has been stressed by Tulving (1979). Finally, older research by Bunch and Rogers (1936) and Bunch (1944) raises a similar point. A maze was learned, and different groups were tested after various intervals of time. The groups were tested either by a retention test or a transfer test in which they acquired a new maze. The interesting result is that whereas retention decreased over time, the ability to acquire the second maze remained at a relatively high level over time. In other words, although the organisms showed a loss in the retention of the "contents," they showed little loss in transfer to second maze acquisition. Nonspecific transfer effects have really never been adequately handled theoretically, but they do suggest the acquisition of operations that may be transferred.

The research described in the previous paragraph indicates that when we speak of the knowledge that individuals bring into a learning situation, such knowledge includes not only "what" the individual knows, or declarative knowledge, but also includes the skills the individual has developed in learning "how" to learn, the procedural knowledge (Ryle, 1949). The problem of assessing the knowledge brought into the learning situation and determining how it is utilized in acquisition thus becomes especially formidable because both declarative and procedural knowledge must be taken into account.

The emphasis that has been stated in this paper with respect to prior knowledge suggests a number of directions that future research could take. One is that work on knowledge representation, work that has already begun (Anderson, 1976; Rumelhart & Norman, 1975), will be continued and may become increasingly domain-specific. Furthermore, the work will need to deal with issues of representation and how represented knowledge is utilized. A line of related work that could develop is research on the operation of what may be termed "cognitive skills." Research on skills has usually involved study of motor skills, especially those pertaining to the execution of movements, and there has not been extensive work on the skills that are developed in the execution of cognitive operations. For example, searching long-term memory is important to a number of theories, and we may ask, "Is this a skill?" "Can this skill be acquired?" "Trained?" "How task-specific are cognitive skills?" The initial work on the general problem of cognitive skills may well have begun with Newell and Simon's (1972) delineation of "elementary information processing" activities that constitute an integral part of their problem-solving analysis.

The second predicted direction that memory research will take involves the study of problem solving. This statement, of course, requires classification. First, I would point out that a by-product of the research that has been conducted over the past few decades has in fact changed our concept of learning. McGeoch and Irion (1952) stated that "Learning, as we measure it, is a change in performance which occurs under the conditions of practice [p. 4]," and it should be noted that the authors discuss operational definitions and acknowledge that there have been other definitions advanced. However, prior to the movement in the cognitive direction, much of the study and measurement of learning involved the comparison of learning curves under different experimental conditions (the Trial X Condition interaction, when initial performance among groups was equivalent). However, with a decline in the study of list learning via multiple-trial procedures and with single-trial free recall and the research on sentence recall, the line between learning and memory became somewhat obliterated, or at least the use of the two terms became less precise. However, the effects have been greater than paradigmatic. The concept of learning now may require inclusion of the acquisition of rules and/or strategies, the assimilation of information into knowledge structures, and so forth. In short, what currently is entailed by the concept of learning is less than clear.

If this description of the concept of learning is somewhere near accurate, the question is, How will learning be handled in the future? The answer suggested is that the concept of learning will be redefined in terms of problem-solving activity.

It may be argued that one of the neglected factors in verbal learning research has been the role that the goal or purpose plays in acquiring information. When a subject came into an experiment and learned a list of paired associates, the goal was to learn the list. (It was hoped that all subjects had this goal and all were equally motivated to accomplish it.) Interestingly, many years ago it was argued that the paired-associate task should be viewed as one of the problem solving (Reed, 1931), but there was little follow-up of the work. Of more than passing interest is the fact that the problem-solving approach taken by Reed led him to consider the importance of the mediators the individual uses to learn the associations in a list of paired associates. The general importance of the problem to thinking was also of course an issue stressed by Dewey (1971). The fact that the movement toward a problem-solving interpretation has already started is suggested by research on text processing that may be approached in a problem-solving manner—the problem being how the individual extracts information from text. Indeed, J. M. Mandler (1978) has incorporated such an approach in her work on comprehension. Also, when Bransford et al. referred to the "transfer appropriate processing," they emphasized the importance of goals or purposes in relation to the processing.

The speculative prediction is therefore that if a general cognitive orientation is developed pertaining to learning and memory, the orientation will be one of problem solving. As noted, the "prediction" is not surprising because in some respects research with this orientation has begun. Fortunately, problem-solving research has increased in the past decades, spurred especially by computer-simulation work and by the increasing concern with studying complex human behavior (Newell & Simon, 1972; Reitman, 1970), and one would expect the developments in this area to be important to theoretical development in learning and memory.

The problem-solving approach is of course related to issues of organization and structure (Greeno, 1977). In solving a problem, the individual may be constructing a structure, a structure that later will provide solutions to additional problems. Thus, to understand problem solution, it is important to have an idea of the knowledge structure that relates to the individual's construction of the so-called problem space. Once again then, the concepts of organization and structure are present, but in a broader frame of reference than the early concepts of organization as they related to list learning.

The possibility of adopting a general problem-solving approach leads to some interesting issues about memory. First, it suggests that what is stored is a by-product of problem-solving activity. Second, what is stored should become assimilated with information already stored that is related to the general problem-solving activity. Third, it suggests that what is stored should be of particular importance to subsequent problem-solving activity. These considerations lead to the general idea that the problem-solving approach will involve a study of the problem-solving activity in relation to the environment, and this leads us to the next prediction.

The third guess involving the potential direction that memory research may take is that such research will view the individual in a broader biological-cultural context, with man's adaptive nature playing a central role in this movement. The similarity of this view to that espoused by Lachman and Lachman (Chapter 5) is apparent, as is the relation of the present view to that expressed by Simon (1969) regarding the adaptive nature of problem solving.

We shall begin with the assumption that man continually interacts with the environment. Such interaction involves feedback loops (Powers, 1978) that develop the individual's expectations about the events that transpire in the environment, events that are interpreted (given meaning and significance) in terms of what the organism already knows. The position taken by Lachman and Lachman emphasized that the history of centuries can play a role in what particular structures and functions are available to the organism. The present emphasis is not on the early predispositions, but on the notion of the adaptive function of the individual.

Within the preceding context, we may question what functions learning, memory, etc., have for the individual, a question echoing previous concerns of "functionalism." Clearly, the individual is able to acquire information about the environment and one's adaptation to it, information that often is reasonably permanent. However, a potentially important question involves how such adaptation takes place. Specifically, to what extent does experience leave reasonably permanent changes in the system and, if such changes take place, what happens to the related existing structures of the system.

The reader may view this question as trivial, but we shall look at an implication of the statement. If we take the notions of storage and retrieval in the sense of placing information into memory and later retrieving the information, we are left with the idea that the mind is a coded warehouse and that we are able to code incoming information and later retrieve it, if we know the code. Indeed, this concept seems to be a residual of faculty psychology. However, this position, although perhaps advocating that some change must occur in the organism when learning takes place, nevertheless seems to disregard this change by suggesting that the input and output are virtually independent of, or at least unrelated to, what is existing in the system. In a sense it seems that the emphasis is on information being "conveyed" in the system rather than on how the system itself is changed. What is assumed here is that experience literally changes the organism; the organism is not the same after an experience as before, in a literal sense. The basis of this assumption is the idea that the individual has flexibility or plasticity in adapting to the environment and that what is learned provides a basis for more "educated" and adaptive behavior in the future.

We now come to the main point of this matter. The individual functions on a daily basis by being faced with situations, problems, and circumstances. When a given problem arises, the system responds in a way to try to resolve and eliminate the problem. This responding may be complex, and more importantly, the problem-solving activity involved generally produces changes in the organism. When, at some future time, another problem situation is encountered that is similar to the first, the organism will again react to resolve and eliminate the problem and will change in the process. However, when the second encounter is compared to the first, what is the difference? The difference is that the activity that occurred in relation to the second encounter includes the changes that occurred during the problem-solving activity that took place in relation to the first encounter. We may then ask—What is the role of memory? Basically, we would argue that there is no need for the concept of memory when the organism is viewed as a problem-solving, adapting organism that is responding to given situations, circumstances, etc.

The immediate reaction to this assertion may readily be that it is absurd, stupid, or both, and the following questions may indeed be asked: "Is it not true that experience produces lasting effects in the organism?" The answer is, "Yes, of course." Then the next question may be, "Where is the information that is stored when it is not being used to solve a given problem?" The answer is that it does not exist. As counterintuitive as this notion may seem, it is not really unreasonable. The functioning, adapting organism is responding to situations as part of an environmental–organism interaction. By no means is this responding meant to be simple; it involves the knowledge structures of the individuals, the rules, the procedural knowledge, or whatever the organism is able to utilize effectively as a part of the functional system. There are also assumed to be expectancies that are related to what effect the reaction will have on the environment, and these are assumed to be matched with what does occur. If we view the individual in terms of its adaptation function, then the germane information will come into play when the situation calls for it (as interpreted by the individual). To assert that it does exist in an independent manner is to return to the warehouse notion, and the search of the elusive engram proceeds.

To use an analogy, one can consider a robot that reacts to environmental change and circumstances in the following way. When a given situation occurs, a given pattern of wires sets up activity on the part of the robot to respond to the situation. When a different situation occurs, a different pattern probably occurs and produces a reaction. Yet, some of the same wires may be used in the different patterns. Also, the patterns may have subsystems; nevertheless, the reactions are typically differential to various inputs. In this robot model, is there "storage?" No, not in the sense of spatially located, relatively permanent information. What does exist is the potential to react to a wide range of situations, and, indeed, the issue of pattern matching becomes extremely important. However, one may then ask what it is that we are remembering in a memory experiment. The answer is that we surely are not remembering the past in a literal sense, but we are responding with information that is tagged as past information but that is activated in the present in response to the memory test.

One may certainly ask, "Even if the preceding approach is granted, what does it buy us?" Well, at present, probably not much. However, it at least buys a chance to look at memory in a different and perhaps somewhat refreshing perspective. However, it may also require that we reconsider the study of learning or of memory and relate such study to the adaptive nature and function of human organisms and to the importance of problem solving in the adapting.

The problem of learning within this view becomes one of changes that occur as the individual solves problems. To understand learning then requires that we develop our understanding of problems and of problem solving. Interestingly, such an orientation may be expected to increase the interest in the study of problem solving in the "real world." In addition, to understand the man–environment system also requires a better understanding of an individual's knowledge and its utilization, a topic previously discussed. Finally, the concepts of organization and structure are assumed to be integral parts of the orientation considered here. The human individual is capable of developing complex structures that aid in the efforts to understand and adapt to the environment. Whether such structures are the product of simple processes and a complex environment, as advocated by Simon (1969), or whether the processes are more complex (Weizenbaum, 1976) is not clear, but the structures provide the individual with a tremendous adaptive capacity.

ACKNOWLEDGMENTS

The research described in this chapter was supported by the Learning Research and Development Center, supported in part as a research and development center by funds from the National Institute of Education (NIE), United States Department of Health, Education, and Welfare. The opinions expressed do not necessarily reflect the position or policy of NIE, and no official endorsement should be inferred. The author wishes to thank Jim Pellegrino, Richard Puff, Gregg Vesonder, and George Spilich for their helpful comments made on the contents of an earlier draft of this chapter.

REFERENCES

Anderson, J. R. *Language, memory, and thought.* Hillsdale, N.J.: Lawrence Erlbaum Associates, 1976.

Anderson, R. C., Reynolds, R. E., Schallert, D. L., & Goetz, E. T. Frameworks for comprehending discourse. *American Educational Research Journal, 1977, 14,* 367–381.

Asch, S. E. The doctrinal tyranny of associationism: or what is wrong with rote learning. In T. R. Dixon & D. L. Horton (Eds.), *Verbal behavior and general behavior theory.* Englewood Cliffs, N.J.: Prentice-Hall, 1968.

Asch, S. E. A reformulation of the problems of associations. *American Psychologist,* 1969, *24,* 92–102.

Asch, S. E., Ceraso, J., & Heimer, W. Perceptual conditions of association. *Psychological Monographs,* 1960, *74,* (Whole No. 490).

Asch, S. E., Hay, J., & Diamond, R. M. Perceptual organization in serial rote-learning. *American Journal of Psychology,* 1960, *73,* 177–198.

Asch, S. E., & Lindner, M. A note on the "strength of association." *Journal of Psychology,* 1963, *55,* 199–209.

Barnes, J. M., & Underwood, B. J. "Fate" of first-list associations in transfer theory. *Journal of Experimental Psychology,* 1959, *58,* 97–105.

Bartlett, F. C. *Remembering.* London: Cambridge University Press, 1932.

Bever, T. G., Fodor, J. A., & Garrett, M. A formal limitation of associationism. In T. R. Dixon & D. L. Horton (Eds.), *Verbal behavior and general behavior theory.* Englewood Cliffs, N.J.: Prentice-Hall, 1968.

Bourne, L. E., Jr., & Haygood, R. C. The role of stimulus redundancy in the identification of concepts. *Journal of Experimental Psychology,* 1959, *58,* 232–238.

Bousfield, W. A. The occurrence of clustering the recall of randomly arranged associates. *Journal of General Psychology,* 1953, *49,* 229–240.

Bower, G. H. Imagery as a relational organizer in associative learning. *Journal of Verbal Learning and Verbal Behavior,* 1970, *9,* 529–533.

Bransford, J. D., Franks, J. J., Morris, C. D., & Stein, B. S. An analysis of memory theories from the perspective of problems of learning. Paper for the Workshop on Levels of Processing and Memory, June, 1977.

Bruner, J. S., Goodnow, J. J., & Austin, G. A. *A study of thinking.* New York: Wiley and Sons, 1956.

Bugelski, B. R., Kidd, E., & Segman, J. Image as a mediator in one-trial paired-associate learning. *Journal of Experimental Psychology,* 1968, *76,* 69–73.

Bunch, M. E. Cumulative transfer of training under different temporal conditions. *Journal of Comparative Psychology,* 1944, *37,* 265–272.

Bunch, M. E., & Rogers, M. The relationship between transfer and the length of interval separating the mastery of two problems. *Journal of Comparative Psychology,* 1936, *21,* 37–52.

Cermak, L. S., & Craik, F. I. M. (Eds.), *Levels of processing and human memory.* Hillsdale, N.J.: Lawrence Erlbaum Associates, 1979.

Chase, W. G., & Simon, H. A. Perception in chess. *Cognitive Psychology,* 1973, *4,* 55–81.

Chiesi, H., Spilich, G., & Voss, J. F. Acquisition of domain-related information in relation to high and low domain knowledge. *Journal of Verbal Learning and Verbal Behavior,* 1979, in press.

Chomsky, N. *Aspects of the theory of syntax.* Cambridge, Mass.: M.I.T. Press, 1965.

Clifton, C., Jr. Some determinants of the effectiveness of priming word associates. *Journal of Verbal Learning and Verbal Behavior,* 1966, *5,* 167–171.

Craik, F. I. M. In L. S. Cermak & F. I. M. Craik (Eds.), *Levels of processing and human memory.* Hilisdale, N.J.: Lawrence Erlbaum Associates, 1979.

Craik, F. I. M., & Lockhart, R. S. Levels of processing: A framework for memory research. *Journal of Verbal Learning and Verbal Behavior,* 1972, *11,* 671–684.

Dewey, J. *How we think.* Chicago: Henry Regnery Co., 1971.

Ebenholtz, S. M. Position mediated transfer between serial learning and a spatial discrimination task. *Journal of Experimental Psychology,* 1963, *65,* 603–608.

Egan, D. E., & Greeno, J. G. Acquiring cognitive structure by discovery and rule learning. *Journal of Educational Psychology,* 1973, *64,* 85–97.

Erdelyi, M., Watts, B., & Voss, J. F. Effect of probability of competing responses in probabilistic verbal acquisition. *Journal of Experimental Psychology,* 1964, *68,* 323–329.

Estes, W. K. Learning theory and the new "mental chemistry." *Psychological Review,* 1960, *67,* 207–223.

Greeno, J. G. Process of understanding in problem solving. In N.J. Castellan, D. B. Pisoni, & G. R. Potts (Eds.), *Cognitive Theory,* (Vol. 2). Hillsdale, N.J.: Lawrence Erlbaum Associates, 1977.

Greeno, J. G., James, C. T., DaPolito, F. J., & Polson, P. G. *Associative learning: A cognitive analysis.* Englewood Cliffs, N.J.: Prentice-Hall, 1978.

Harcum, E. R. *Serial learning and para-learning: Control processes in serial acquisition.* New York: Wiley and Sons, 1975.

Henderson, E. N. A study of memory for connected trains of thought. *Psychological Monographs,* 1903, *5,* 1–92.

Henry, N., & Voss, J. F. Associative strength growth produced via category membership. *Journal of Experimental Psychology, 1970, 83,* 136–140.

Hovland, C. I. Human learning and retention. In S. S. Stevens (Ed.), *Handbook of experimental psychology.* New York: Wiley and Sons, 1951.

Hull, C. L. The conflicting psychologies of learning—a way out. *Psychological Review,* 1935, *42,* 491–576.

Humphrey, G. *Thinking: An introduction to its experimental psychology.* London: Methuen & Co. Ltd., 1951.

Jacoby, L. L., & Craik, F. I. M. Effects of elaboration of processing at encoding and retrieval: Trace distinctiveness and recovery of initial context. In L. S. Cermak & F. I. M. Craik (Eds.), *Levels of processing and human memory.* Hillsdale, N.J.: Lawrence Erlbaum Associates, 1979.

Jenkins, J. J. Remember that old theory of memory? Well, forget it! *American Psychologist,* 1974, *29,* 785–795.

Jensen, A. R. An empirical theory of the serial-position effect. *Journal of Psychology,* 1962, *53,* 127–142.

Kendler, T. S. Development of mediating responses in children. In J. C. Wright & J. Kagan (Eds.), *Basic cognitive processes in children. Monographs of the Society for Research in Child Development,* 1963, *28,* (2), 33–51.

Kintsch, W. *The representation of meaning in memory.* Hillsdale, N.J.: Lawrence Erlbaum Associates, 1974.

Kintsch, W., & Greene, E. The role of culture-specific schemata in the comprehension and recall of stories. *Discourse Processes,* 1978, *1,* 1–13.

Kintsch, W., & van Dijk, T. A. Toward a model of text comprehension and production. *Psychological Review,* 1978, *85,* 363–394.

Kintsch, W., & Vipond, D. Reading comprehension and readability in educational practice and psychological theory. Paper presented at the Conference on Memory, University of Uppsala, June, 1977.

Kolers, P. A. Specificity of operations in sentence recognition. *Cognitive Psychology,* 1975, *7,* 289–306.

Kolers, P. A., & Ostry, D. J. Time course of loss of information regarding pattern analyzing operations. *Journal of Verbal Learning and Verbal Behavior,* 1974, *13,* 599–612.

Laudan, L. *Progress and its problems: Towards a theory of scientific growth.* Berkeley, Calif.: University of California Press, 1977.

Lepley, W. M. Serial reactions considered as conditioned reactions. *Psychological Monographs,* 1934, *46,* (Whole No. 25).

Maltzman, I. Thinking: From a behavioristic point of view. *Psychological Review,* 1955, *62,* 275–286.

Mandler, G. Association and organization: Facts, fancies and theories. In T. R. Dixon & D. L. Horton (Eds.), *Verbal behavior and general behavior theory.* Englewood Cliffs, N.J.: Prentice-Hall, 1968.

Mandler, G. From association to structure. *Psychological Review,* 1962, *69,* 415–427.

Mandler, G. Organization and memory. In K. W. Spence & J. T. Spence (Eds.), *The psychology of learning and motivation: Advances in research and theory.* New York: Academic Press, 1967.

Mandler, G. Response factors in human learning. *Psychological Review,* 1954, *61,* 235–244.

Mandler, J. M. A code in the node: The use of a story schema in retrieval. *Discourse Processes,* 1978, *1,* 14–35.

Mandler, J. M., & Johnson, N. S. Remembrance of things parsed: Story structure and recall. *Cognitive Psychology,* 1977, *9,* 111–151.

Martin, C. J., Boersma, F. J., & Cox, D. L. A classification of associative strategies in paired-associate learning. *Psychonomic Science,* 1965, *3,* 455–456.

Martin, C. J., Cox, D. L., & Boersma, F. J. The role of associative strategies in the acquisition of P-A material: An alternate approach to meaningfulness. *Psychonomic Science,* 1965, *3,* 463–464.

McGeoch, J. A., & Irion, A. L. *The psychology of human learning.* New York: Longmans, 1952.

Melton, A. W., & Irwin, J. M. The influence of degree of interpolated learning on retroactive inhibition and the overt transfer of specific responses. *American Journal of Psychology,* 1940, *53,* 173–203.

Miller, G. A., Galanter, E., & Pribram, K. *Plans and the structure of behavior.* New York: Holt, Rinehart, & Winston, 1960.

Montague, W. E., Adams, J. A., & Kiess, H. O. Forgetting and natural language mediation. *Journal of Experimental Psychology,* 1966, *72,* 829–833.

Morris, C. D., Bransford, J. D., & Franks, J. J. Levels of processing versus transfer appropriate processing. *Journal of Verbal Learning and Verbal Behavior,* 1977, *16,* 519–533.

Mowrer, O. H. *Learning theory and the symbolic processes.* New York: Wiley and Sons, 1960.

Mowrer, O. H. The psychologist looks at language. *American Psychologist,* 1954, *9,* 660–694.

Newell, A., & Simon, H. *Human problem solving.* Englewood Cliffs, N.J.: Prentice-Hall, 1972.

Nisbett, R. E., & Wilson, T. D. Telling more than we can know: Verbal reports on mental processes. *Psychological Review,* 1977, *84,* 231–259.

Noble, C. E. An anlaysis of meaning. *Psychological Review,* 1952, *59,* 421–430.

Norman, D. A., & Rumelhart, D. E. *Explorations in cognition.* San Francisco: W. H. Freeman and Co., 1975.

Northway, M. L. The concept of the "schema." *British Journal of Psychology,* 1940a, *30,* 316–325.

Northway, M. L. The concept of the "schema." *British Journal of Psychology,* 1940b, *31,* 22–36.

Oldfield, R. C., & Zangwill, O. L. Head's concept of the schema and its application in contemporary British Psychology. Part III. Bartlett's theory of memory. *British Journal of Psychology,* 1942, *33,* 113–129.

Osgood, C. E. The nature and measurement of meaning. *Psychological Bulletin,* 1952, *49,* 197–237.

Pavlov, I. P. [*Conditioned reflexes*] (G. V. Anrep, Ed. and trans.) Oxford: Oxford University Press, 1927.

Pellegrino, J. W., & Glaser, R. Components of inductive reasoning. In R. Snow, P-A. Federico, & W. Montague (Eds.), *Aptitude, learning and instruction: Cognitive process analysis.* Hillsdale, N.J.: Lawrence Erlbaum Associates, 1979.

Petrich, J. A. Storage and retrieval processes in unlearning. *Memory and Cognition,* 1975, *3,* 63–74.

Postman, L. One-trial learning. In C. N. Cofer & B. S. Musgrave (Eds.), *Verbal behavior and learning: Problems and processes.* New York: McGraw-Hill, 1963.

Postman, L., & Underwood, B. J. Critical issues in interference theory. *Memory and Cognition,* 1973, *1,* 19–40.

Powers, W. T. Quantitative analysis of purposive systems: Some spadework at the foundations of scientific psychology. *Psychological Review,* 1978, *85,* 417–435.

Primoff, E. Backward and forward association as an organizing act in serial and in paired-associate learning. *Journal of Psychology,* 1938, *5,* 375–395.

Reed, H. J. The influence of change of conditions upon the amount of recall. *Journal of Experimental Psychology,* 1931, *14,* 641.

Reitman, W. What does it take to remember? In D. Norman (Ed.), *Models of human memory.* New York: Academic Press, 1970.

Robinson, E. S. *Association theory today.* New York: Century, 1932.

Rock, I. The role of repetition in associative learning. *American Journal of Psychology,* 1957, *70,* 186–193.

Rock, I., & Ceraso, J. Toward a cognitive theory of associative learning. In C. Scheerer (Ed.), *Cognition: Theory, research, promise.* New York: Harper & Row, 1964.

Rosch, E. On the internal structure of perceptual and semantic categories. In T. E. Moore (Ed.), *Cognitive development and acquisition of language.* New York: Academic Press, 1973.

Rumelhart, D. E. Notes on a schema for stories. In D. Bobrow & A. Collins (Eds.), *Representations and understanding: Studies in cognitive science.* New York: Academic Press, 1975.

Rumelhart, D. E., & Norman, D. A. The active structural network. In D. A. Norman & D. E. Rumelhart (Eds.), *Explorations in cognition*. San Francisco: W. H. Freeman and Co., 1975.

Rumelhart, D. E., & Ortony, A. The representation of knowledge in memory. In R. C. Anderson, R. J. Spiro, & W. E. Montague (Eds.), *Schooling and the acquisition of knowledge*. Hillsdale, N.J.: Lawrence Erlbaum Associates, 1977.

Ryle G. *The concept of mind*. London: Hutchinson, 1949.

Schank, R. C. The structure of episodes in memory. In D. G. Bobrow & A. Collins (Eds.), *Representations and understanding: Studies in cognitive science*. New York: Academic Press, 1975.

Schank, R., & Abelson, R. *Scripts, plans, goals, and understanding*. Hillsdale, N.J.: Lawrence Erlbaum Associates, 1977.

Sechenov, I. M. *Reflexes of the brain*. Cambridge, Mass.: M.I.T. Press, 1965.

Selz, O. *Zur Psychologie des Produktiven Denkens*. Bonn: Cohen, 1922.

Simon, H. A. *The sciences of the artificial*. Cambridge, Mass.: M.I.T. Press, 1969.

Slamecka, N. J. Serial learning and order information. *Journal of Experimental Psychology*, 1967, *74*, 62–66.

Spilich, G. J., Vesonder, G. T., Chiesi, H. L., & Voss, J. F. Text processing of domain-related information for individuals with high and low domain knowledge. *Journal of Verbal Learning and Verbal Behavior*, 1979, in press.

Thorndike, E. L. *Human learning*. New York: Century, 1931.

Thorndike, E. L. *The psychology of learning*. New York: Teachers College, 1914.

Thorndyke, P. W. Cognitive structures in comprehension and memory of narrative discourse. *Cognitive Psychology*, 1977, *9*, 77–110.

Tulving, E. In L. S. Cermak & F. I. M. Craik (Eds.), *Levels of processing and human memory*. Hillsdale, N.J.: Lawrence Erlbaum Associates, 1979.

Tulving, E., & Donaldson, W. (Eds.), *Organization of memory*. New York: Academic Press, 1972.

Tulving, E., & Pearlstone, Z. Availability versus accessibility of information in memory for words. *Journal of Verbal Learning and Verbal Behavior*, 1966, *5*, 381–391.

Underwood, B. J. Some correlates of item repetition in free-recall learning. *Journal of Verbal Learning and Verbal Behavior*, 1969, *8*, 83–94.

Underwood, B. J. Stimulus selection in verbal learning. In C. N. Cofer & B. S. Musgrave (Eds.), *Verbal behavior and learning: Problems and processes*. New York: McGraw-Hill, 1963.

Underwood, B. J., Ham, M., & Ekstrand, B. Cue selection in paired-associate learning. *Journal of Experimental Psychology*, 1962, *64*, 405–409.

Underwood, B. J., Runquist, W. N., & Schulz, R. W. Response learning in paired-associate lists as a function of intralist similarity. *Journal of Experimental Psychology*, 1959, *58*, 70–78.

van Dijk, T. A. Semantic macro-structures and knowledge frames in discourse comprehension. In M. A. Just & P. A. Carpenter (Eds.), *Cognitive processes in comprehension*. Hillsdale, N.J.: Lawrence Erlbaum Associates, 1977.

Voss, J. F. On the relationship of associative and organizational processes. In E. Tulving and W. Donaldson (Eds.), *Organization of memory*. New York: Academic Press, 1972.

Wallace, W. P. Consistency of emission order in free recall. *Journal of Verbal Learning and Verbal Behavior*, 1969, *9*, 58–68.

Warren, H. C. *A history of the association psychology*. New York: Scribner, 1921.

Watson, J. B. *Psychology from the standpoint of a behaviorist*. Philadelphia: Lippincott, 1919.

Weizenbaum, J. *Comptuer power and human reason*. San Francisco: W. H. Freeman and Co., 1976.

Young, R. K. Serial learning. In T. R. Dixon and D. L. Horton (Eds.), *Verbal behavior and general behavior theory*. Englewood Cliffs, N.J.: Prentice-Hall, 1968.

Zangwill, O. L. Remembering revisited. *Quarterly Journal of Experimental Psychology*, 1972, *24*, 123–138.

Subject Index